Skip·Beat!

Shojo Beat

Skip·Beat!

Kyoko made
her flowers into
resin jewelry.

44
Story & Art by Yoshiki Nakamura

Skip·Beat!

Volume 44

CONTENTS

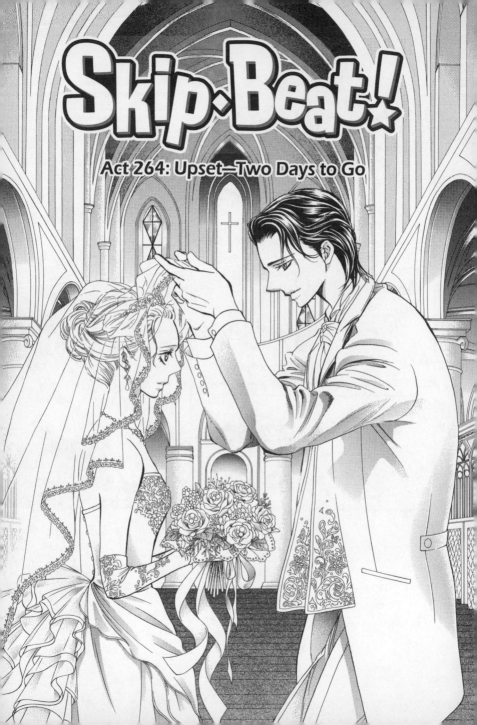

Skip·Beat!

Act 264: Upset—Two Days to Go

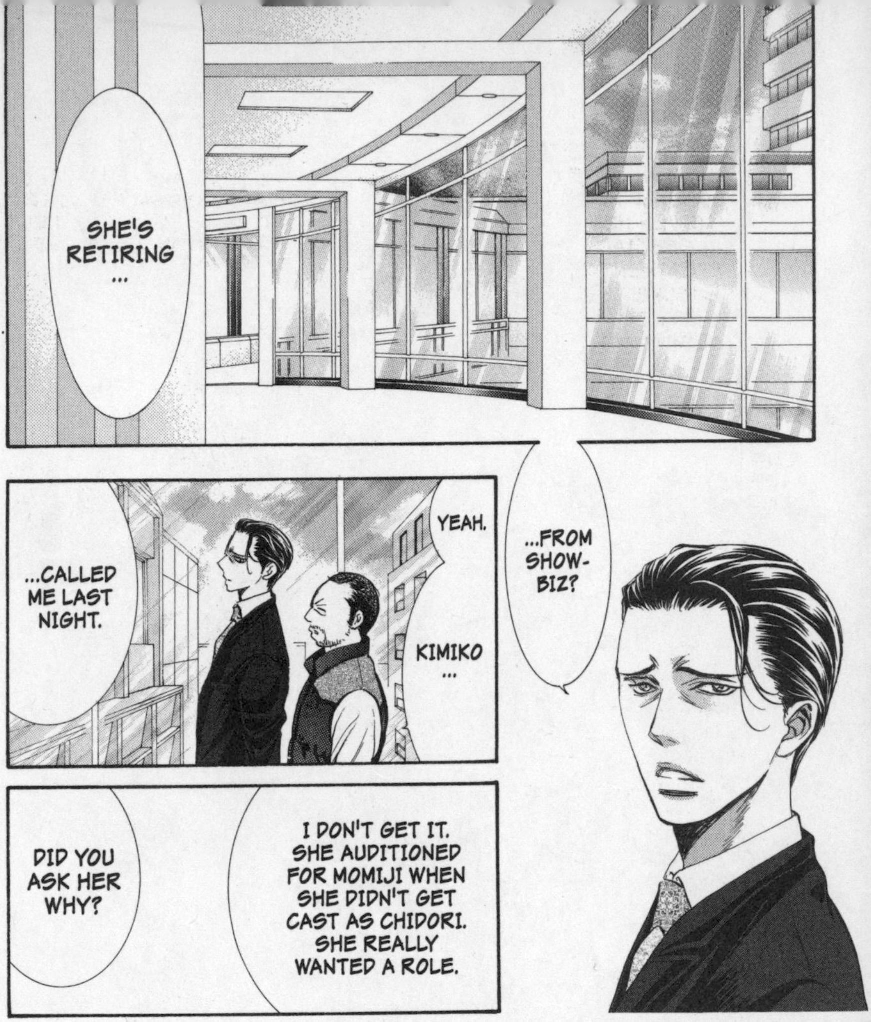
SHE'S RETIRING ...
...FROM SHOW-BIZ?
YEAH.
KIMIKO ...
...CALLED ME LAST NIGHT.
I DON'T GET IT. SHE AUDITIONED FOR MOMIJI WHEN SHE DIDN'T GET CAST AS CHIDORI. SHE REALLY WANTED A ROLE.
DID YOU ASK HER WHY?

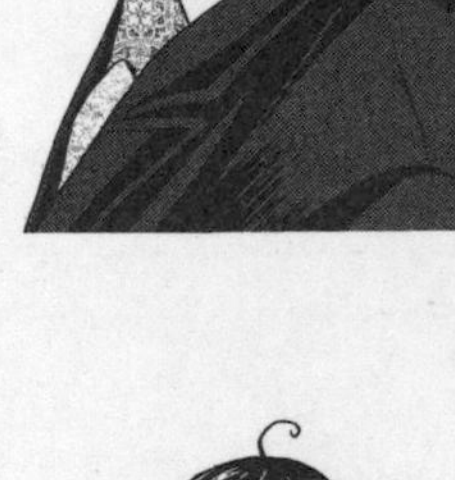

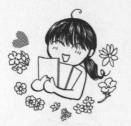

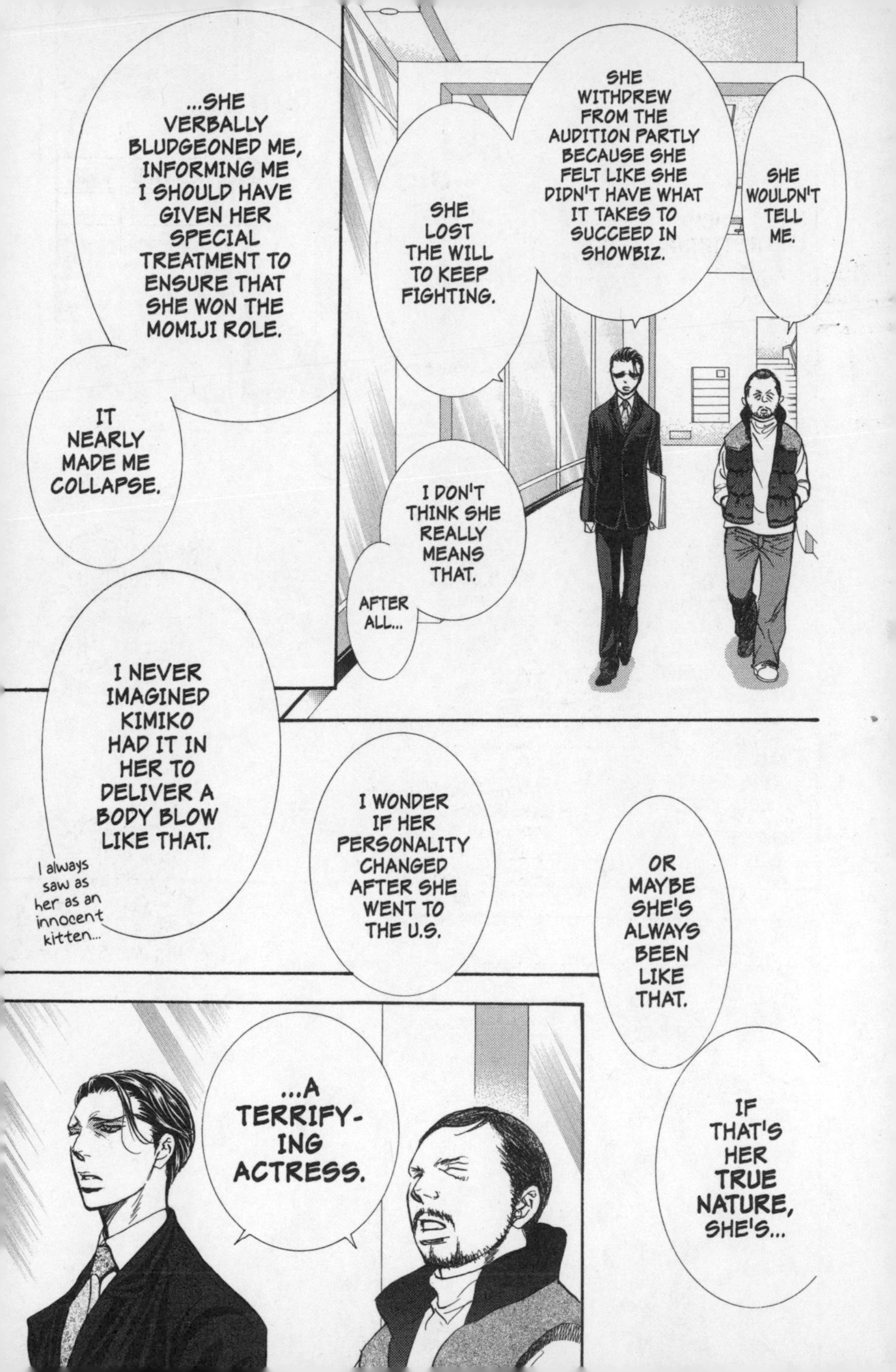
SHE WOULDN'T TELL ME.
SHE WITHDREW FROM THE AUDITION PARTLY BECAUSE SHE FELT LIKE SHE DIDN'T HAVE WHAT IT TAKES TO SUCCEED IN SHOWBIZ.
SHE LOST THE WILL TO KEEP FIGHTING.
I DON'T THINK SHE REALLY MEANS THAT.
AFTER ALL...
...SHE VERBALLY BLUDGEONED ME, INFORMING ME I SHOULD HAVE GIVEN HER SPECIAL TREATMENT TO ENSURE THAT SHE WON THE MOMIJI ROLE.
IT NEARLY MADE ME COLLAPSE.
I NEVER IMAGINED KIMIKO HAD IT IN HER TO DELIVER A BODY BLOW LIKE THAT.
I always saw as her as an innocent kitten...
I WONDER IF HER PERSONALITY CHANGED AFTER SHE WENT TO THE U.S.
OR MAYBE SHE'S ALWAYS BEEN LIKE THAT.
IF THAT'S HER TRUE NATURE, SHE'S...
...A TERRIFY-ING ACTRESS.

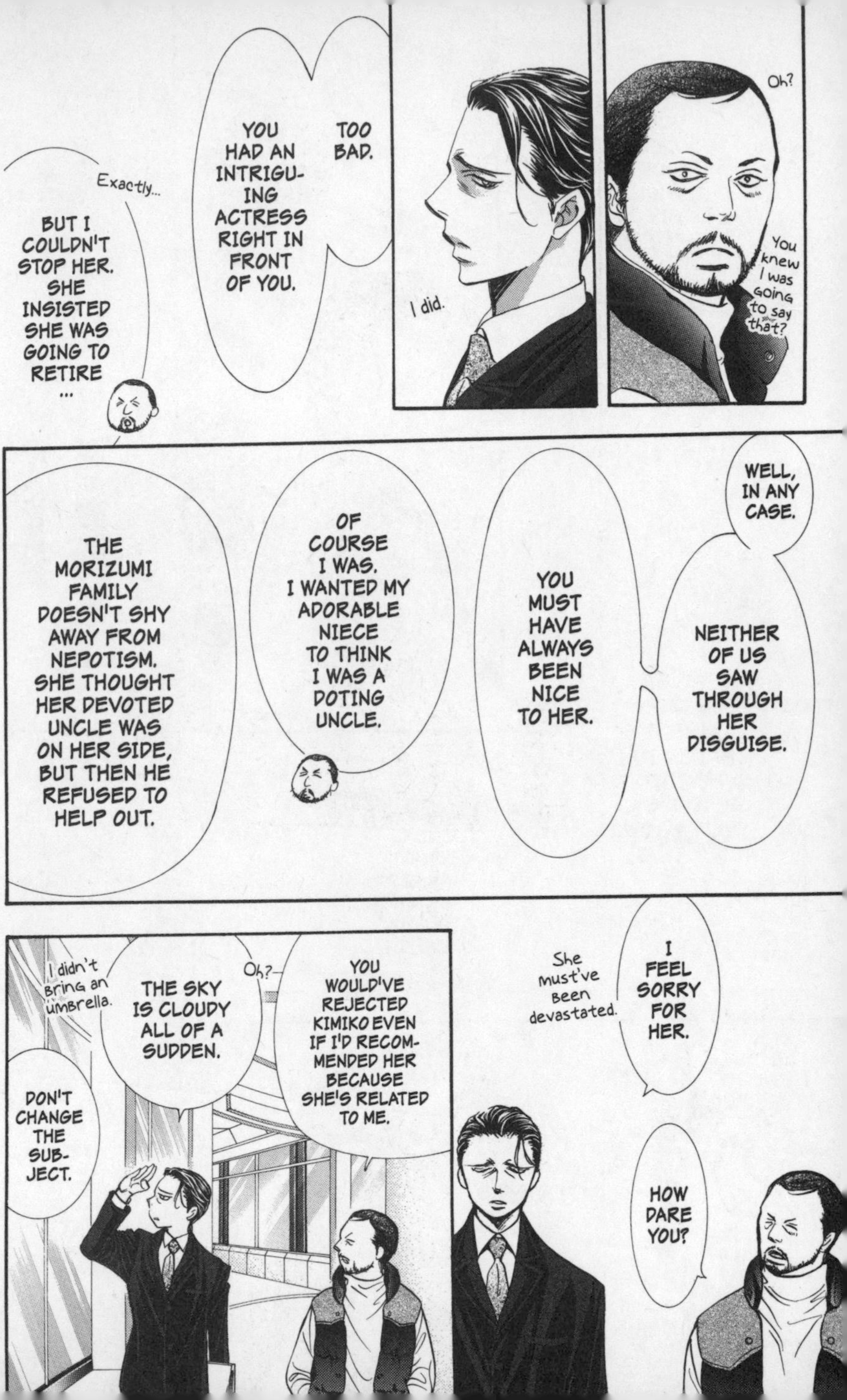
Oh?
You knew I was going to say that?
I did.
TOO BAD.
YOU HAD AN INTRIGUING ACTRESS RIGHT IN FRONT OF YOU.
Exactly...
BUT I COULDN'T STOP HER. SHE INSISTED SHE WAS GOING TO RETIRE ...
WELL, IN ANY CASE.
NEITHER OF US SAW THROUGH HER DISGUISE.
YOU MUST HAVE ALWAYS BEEN NICE TO HER.
OF COURSE I WAS. I WANTED MY ADORABLE NIECE TO THINK I WAS A DOTING UNCLE.
THE MORIZUMI FAMILY DOESN'T SHY AWAY FROM NEPOTISM. SHE THOUGHT HER DEVOTED UNCLE WAS ON HER SIDE, BUT THEN HE REFUSED TO HELP OUT.
I FEEL SORRY FOR HER.
She must've been devastated.
HOW DARE YOU?
YOU WOULD'VE REJECTED KIMIKO EVEN IF I'D RECOMMENDED HER BECAUSE SHE'S RELATED TO ME.
Oh?—
THE SKY IS CLOUDY ALL OF A SUDDEN.
I didn't bring an umbrella.
DON'T CHANGE THE SUBJECT.

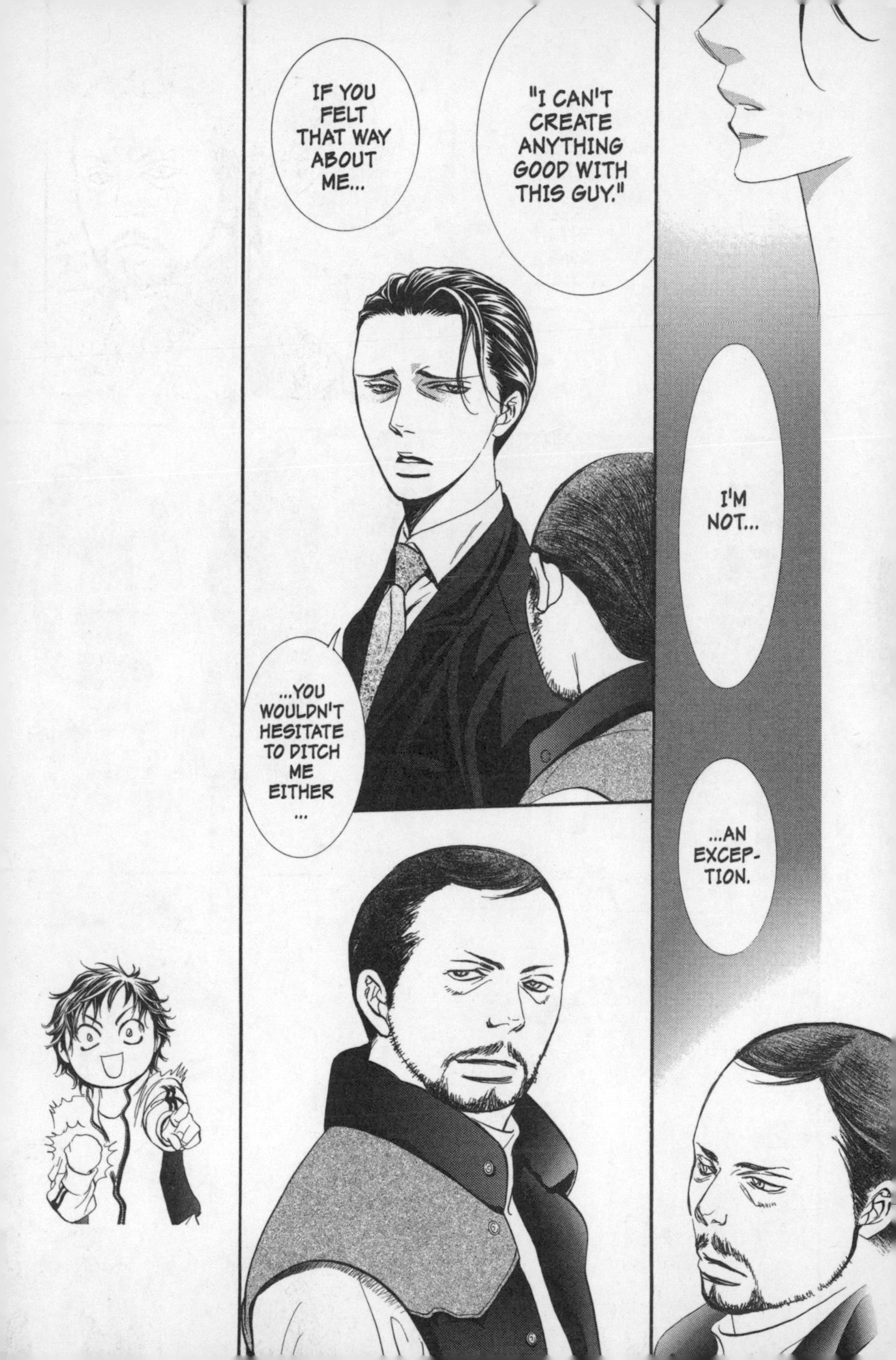

I'M NOT...
...AN EXCEPTION.
"I CAN'T CREATE ANYTHING GOOD WITH THIS GUY."
IF YOU FELT THAT WAY ABOUT ME...
...YOU WOULDN'T HESITATE TO DITCH ME EITHER ...

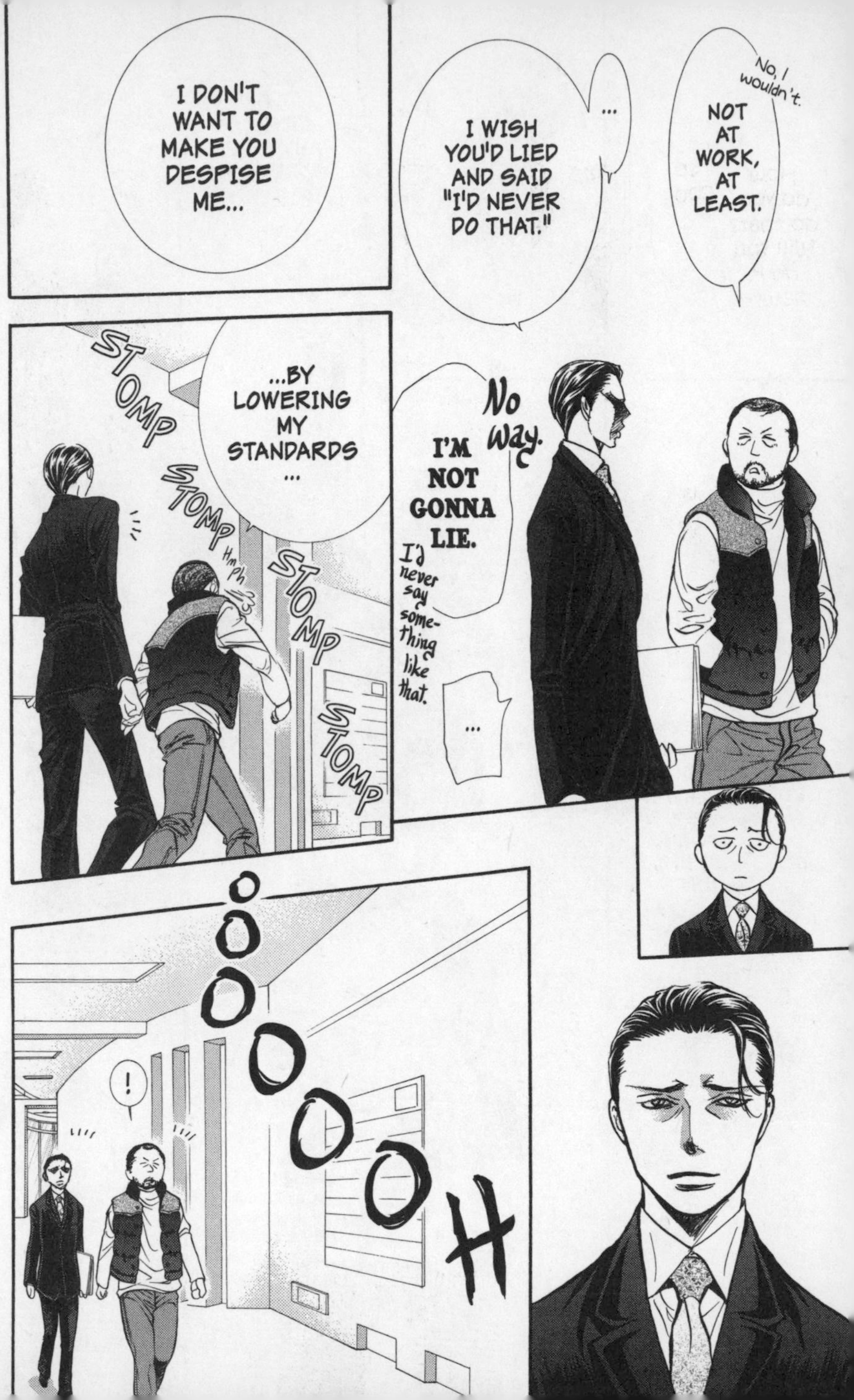
No, I wouldn't.
NOT AT WORK, AT LEAST.
...
I WISH YOU'D LIED AND SAID "I'D NEVER DO THAT."
I DON'T WANT TO MAKE YOU DESPISE ME...
No way.
I'M NOT GONNA LIE.
I'd never say something like that.
...
...BY LOWERING MY STANDARDS ...
STOMP STOMP
STOMP
Hmph
STOMP
STOMP
!
OOOOOOOH

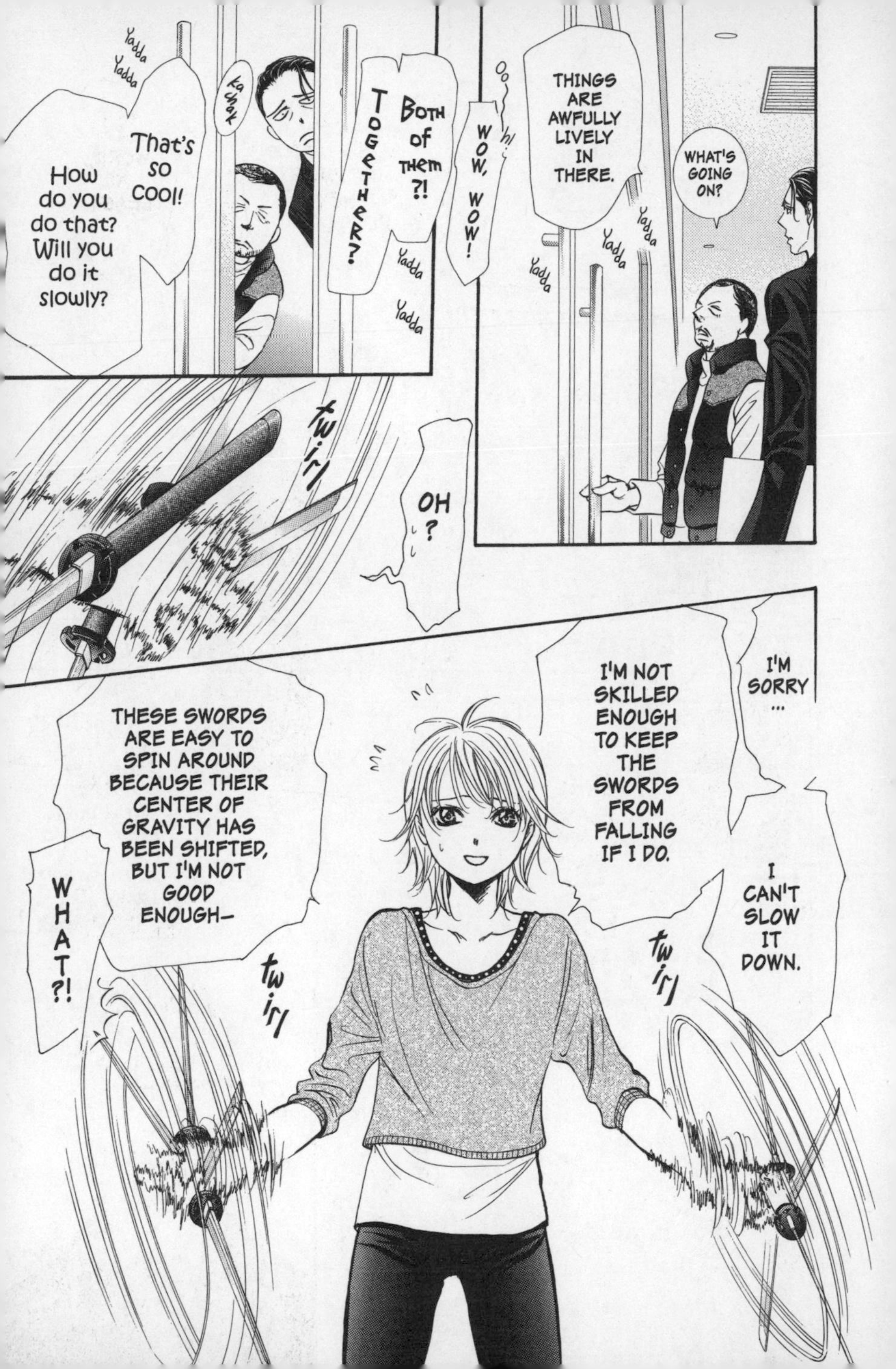
WHAT'S GOING ON?
THINGS ARE AWFULLY LIVELY IN THERE.
Yadda Yadda Yadda
WOW, WOW, WOW!
Both of them?!
TOGETHER?
Yadda Yadda
ka shak
That's so cool!
How do you do that? Will you do it slowly?
Yadda Yadda
OH?
twirl
I'M SORRY...
I CAN'T SLOW IT DOWN.
I'M NOT SKILLED ENOUGH TO KEEP THE SWORDS FROM FALLING IF I DO.
twirl
THESE SWORDS ARE EASY TO SPIN AROUND BECAUSE THEIR CENTER OF GRAVITY HAS BEEN SHIFTED, BUT I'M NOT GOOD ENOUGH—
WHAT?!
twirl

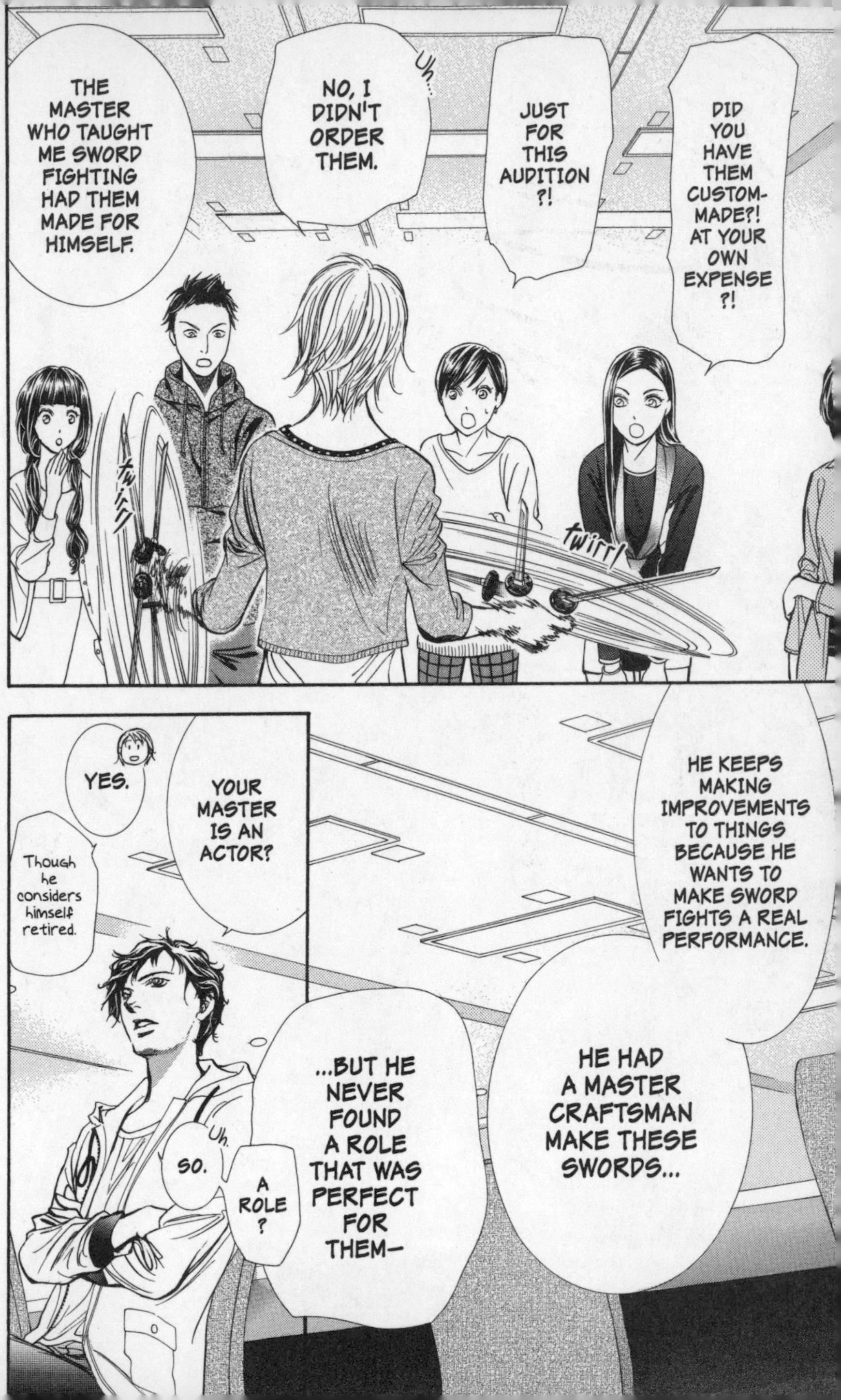
DID YOU HAVE THEM CUSTOM-MADE?! AT YOUR OWN EXPENSE?!
JUST FOR THIS AUDITION?!
Uh...
NO, I DIDN'T ORDER THEM.
THE MASTER WHO TAUGHT ME SWORD FIGHTING HAD THEM MADE FOR HIMSELF.
twirl
twirl
HE KEEPS MAKING IMPROVEMENTS TO THINGS BECAUSE HE WANTS TO MAKE SWORD FIGHTS A REAL PERFORMANCE.
HE HAD A MASTER CRAFTSMAN MAKE THESE SWORDS...
...BUT HE NEVER FOUND A ROLE THAT WAS PERFECT FOR THEM—
A ROLE?
Uh.
SO.
YOUR MASTER IS AN ACTOR?
YES.
Though he considers himself retired.

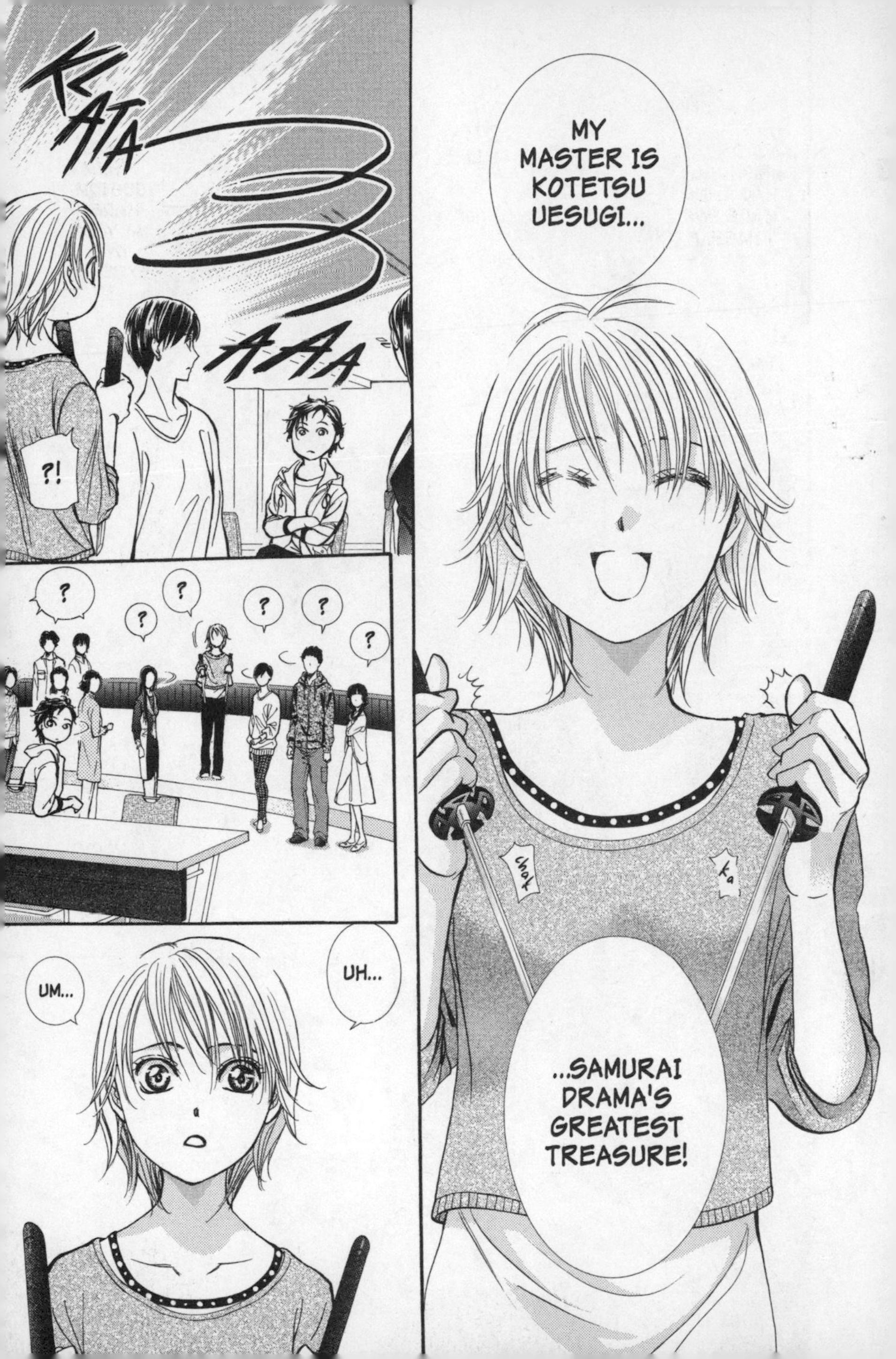

MY MASTER IS KOTETSU UESUGI...
chok
ka
...SAMURAI DRAMA'S GREATEST TREASURE!
KATA
AAA
?!
?
?
?
?
?
?
UH...
UM...

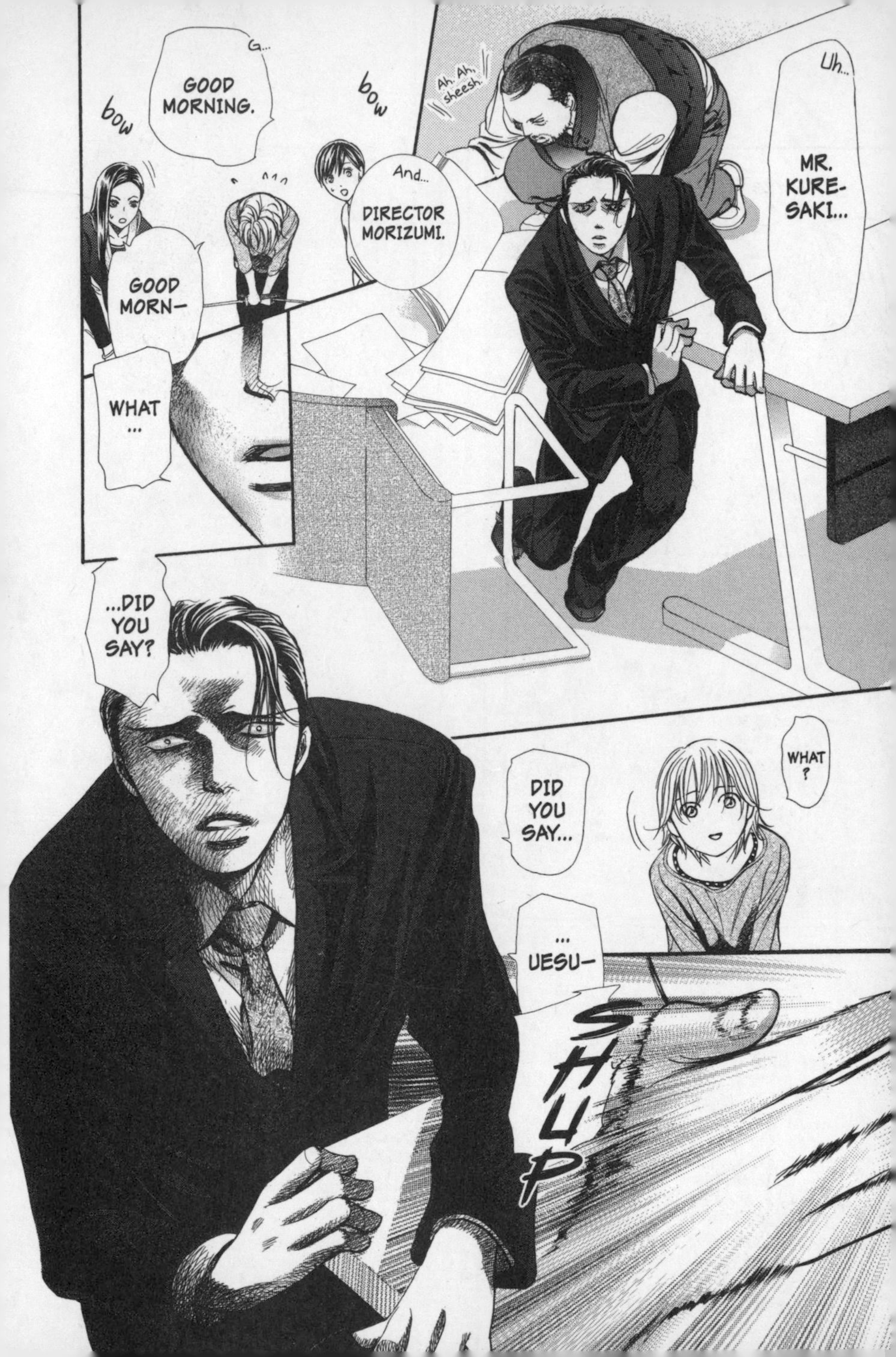
Uh...
MR. KURE-SAKI...
Ah. Ah, sheesh.
And...
DIRECTOR MORIZUMI.
bow
G...
GOOD MORNING.
bow
GOOD MORN—
WHAT ...
...DID YOU SAY?
WHAT ?
DID YOU SAY...
... UESU—
SHUP

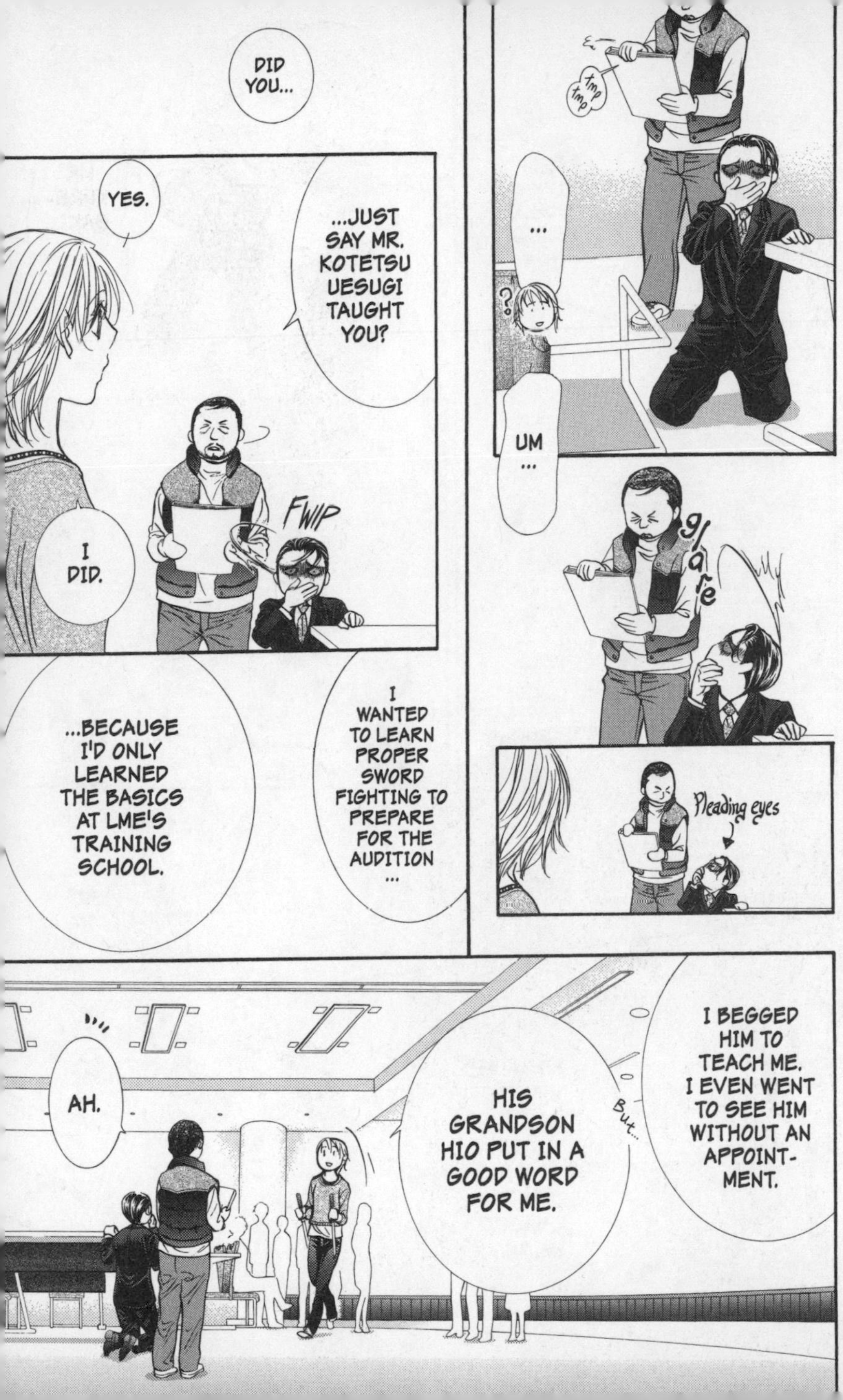
tmp tmp
...
?
UM ...
glare
Pleading eyes
DID YOU...
...JUST SAY MR. KOTETSU UESUGI TAUGHT YOU?
YES.
FWIP
I DID.
I WANTED TO LEARN PROPER SWORD FIGHTING TO PREPARE FOR THE AUDITION ...
...BECAUSE I'D ONLY LEARNED THE BASICS AT LME'S TRAINING SCHOOL.
I BEGGED HIM TO TEACH ME. I EVEN WENT TO SEE HIM WITHOUT AN APPOINT-MENT.
But...
HIS GRANDSON HIO PUT IN A GOOD WORD FOR ME.
AH.

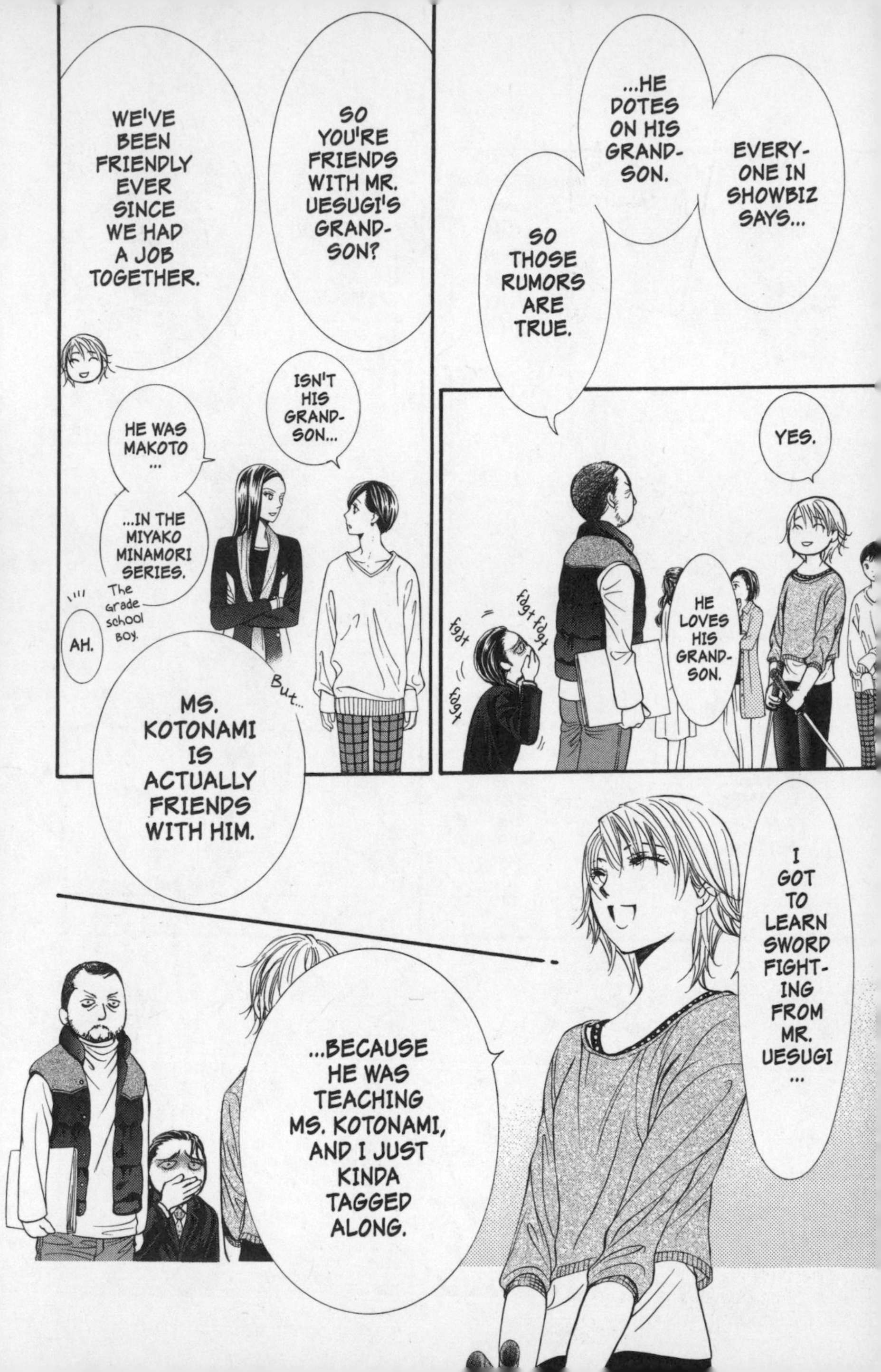
EVERY-ONE IN SHOWBIZ SAYS...
...HE DOTES ON HIS GRAND-SON.
SO THOSE RUMORS ARE TRUE.
YES.
HE LOVES HIS GRAND-SON.
fdgt fdgt fdgt fdgt
SO YOU'RE FRIENDS WITH MR. UESUGI'S GRAND-SON?
WE'VE BEEN FRIENDLY EVER SINCE WE HAD A JOB TOGETHER.
ISN'T HIS GRAND-SON...
HE WAS MAKOTO...
...IN THE MIYAKO MINAMORI SERIES.
The grade school boy.
AH.
But...
MS. KOTONAMI IS ACTUALLY FRIENDS WITH HIM.
I GOT TO LEARN SWORD FIGHT-ING FROM MR. UESUGI...
...BECAUSE HE WAS TEACHING MS. KOTONAMI, AND I JUST KINDA TAGGED ALONG.

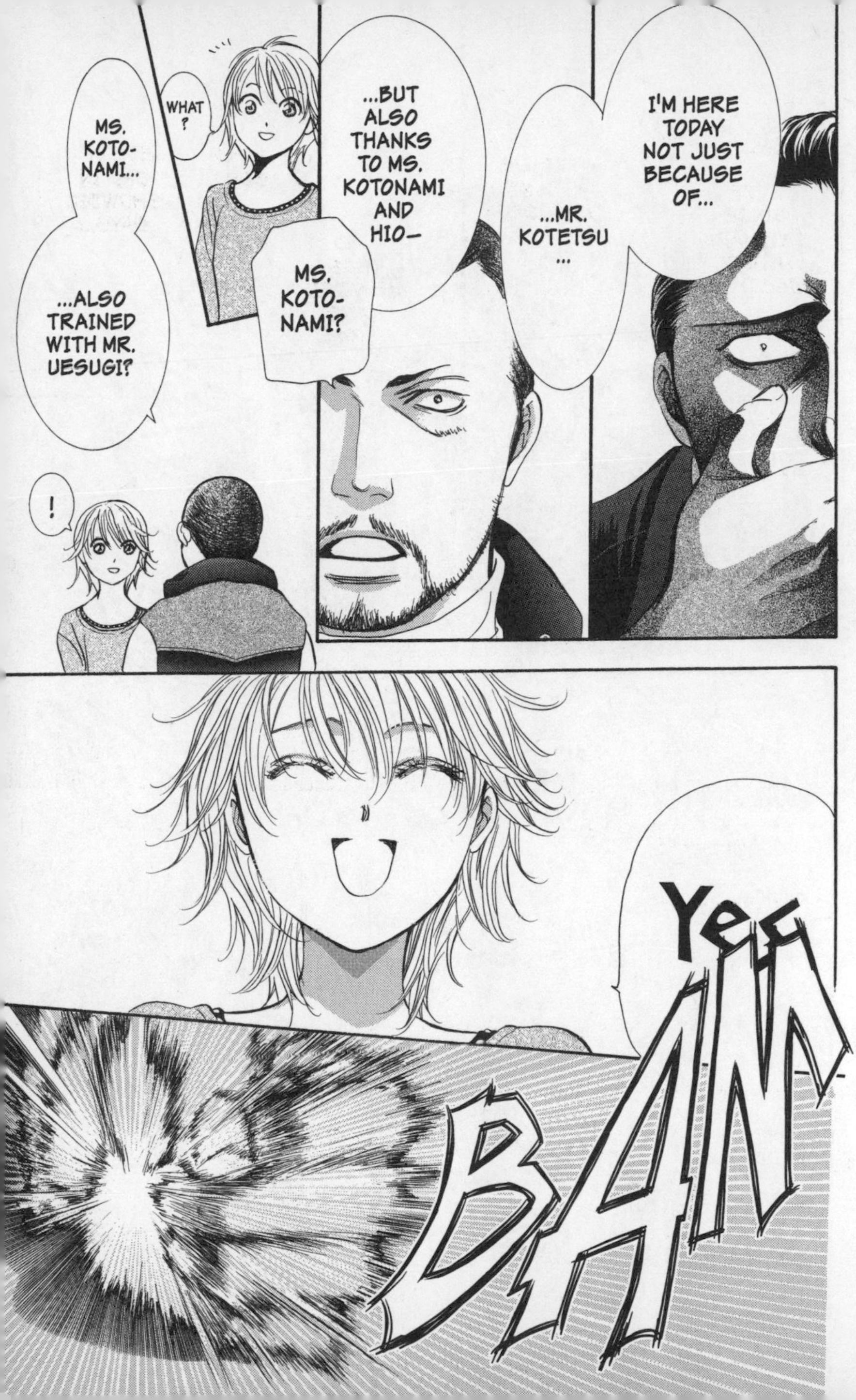
I'M HERE TODAY NOT JUST BECAUSE OF...
...MR. KOTETSU ...
...BUT ALSO THANKS TO MS. KOTONAMI AND HIO—
MS. KOTO-NAMI?
WHAT ?
MS. KOTO-NAMI...
...ALSO TRAINED WITH MR. UESUGI?
!
Yes
BAM

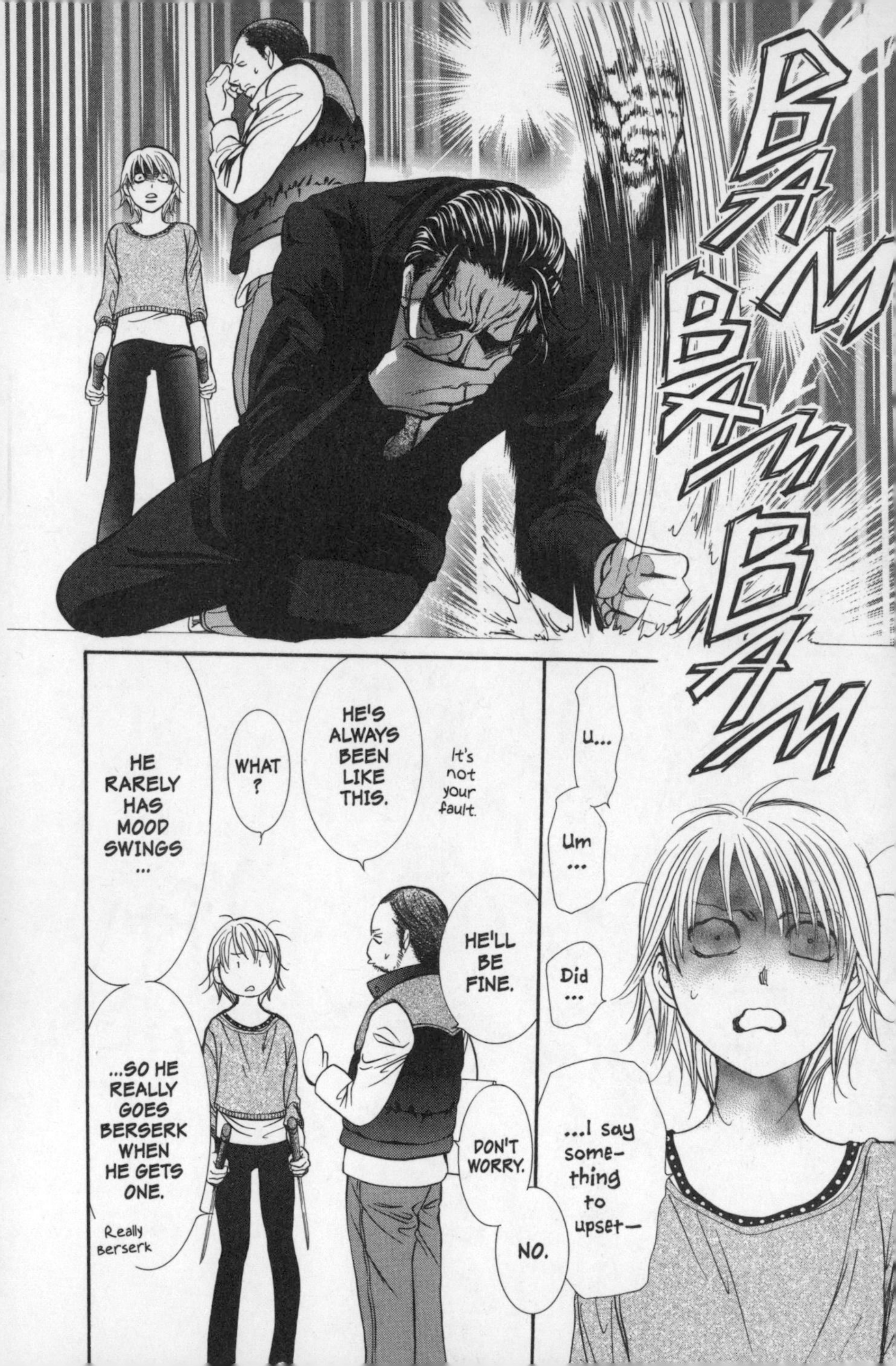
BAM BAM BAM
U...
Um...
Did...
...I say something to upset—
NO.
DON'T WORRY.
HE'LL BE FINE.
HE'S ALWAYS BEEN LIKE THIS.
It's not your fault.
WHAT?
HE RARELY HAS MOOD SWINGS...
...SO HE REALLY GOES BERSERK WHEN HE GETS ONE.
Really Berserk

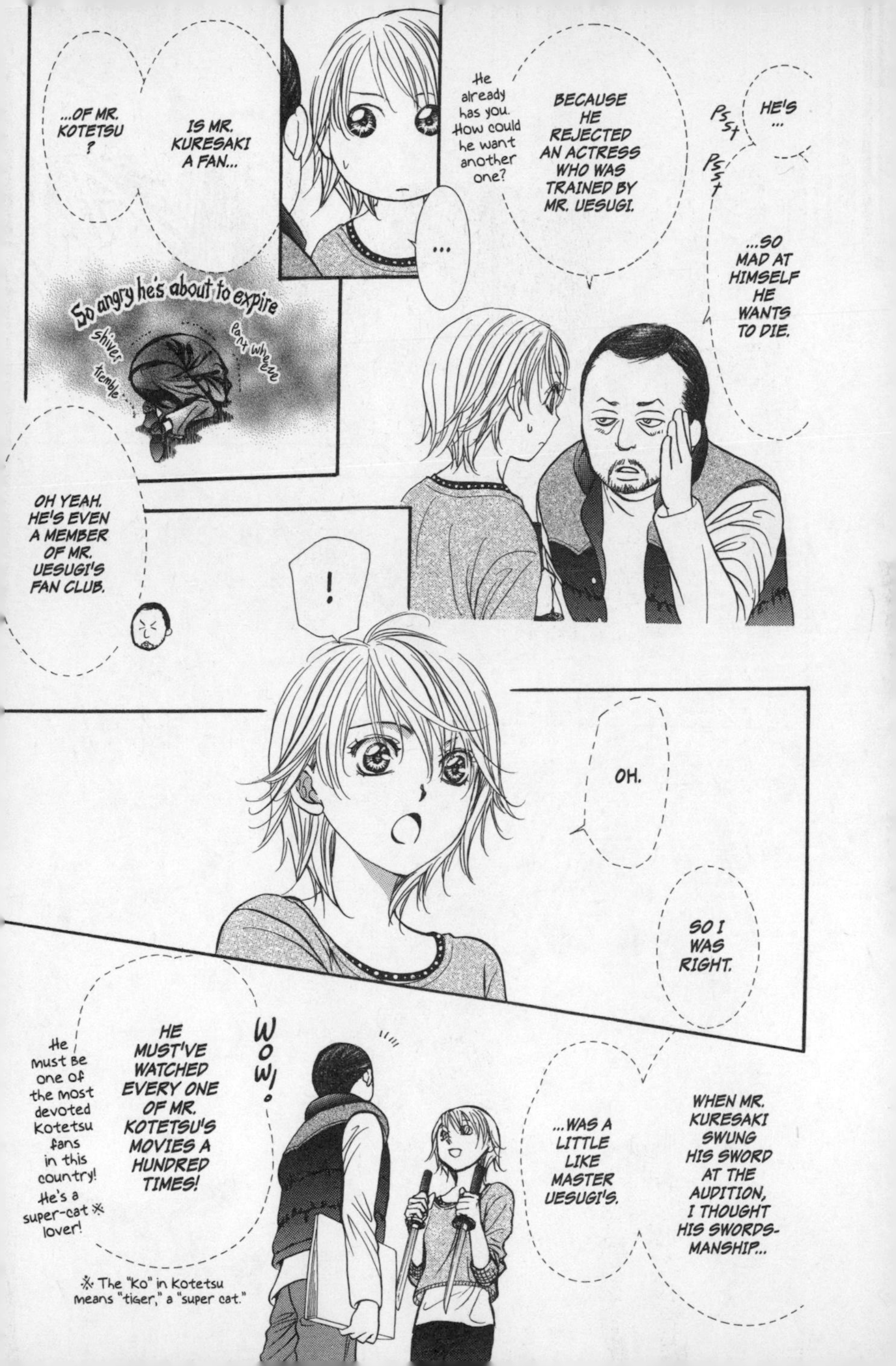
Psst
HE'S...
Psst
BECAUSE HE REJECTED AN ACTRESS WHO WAS TRAINED BY MR. UESUGI.
He already has you. How could he want another one?
...
...SO MAD AT HIMSELF HE WANTS TO DIE.
IS MR. KURESAKI A FAN...
...OF MR. KOTETSU?
So angry he's about to expire
Pant wheeze
shiver
tremble
OH YEAH. HE'S EVEN A MEMBER OF MR. UESUGI'S FAN CLUB.
!
OH.
SO I WAS RIGHT.
WHEN MR. KURESAKI SWUNG HIS SWORD AT THE AUDITION, I THOUGHT HIS SWORDSMANSHIP...
...WAS A LITTLE LIKE MASTER UESUGI'S.
WOW!
HE MUST'VE WATCHED EVERY ONE OF MR. KOTETSU'S MOVIES A HUNDRED TIMES!
He must be one of the most devoted Kotetsu fans in this country! He's a super-cat※ lover!

※ The "Ko" in Kotetsu means "tiger," a "super cat."

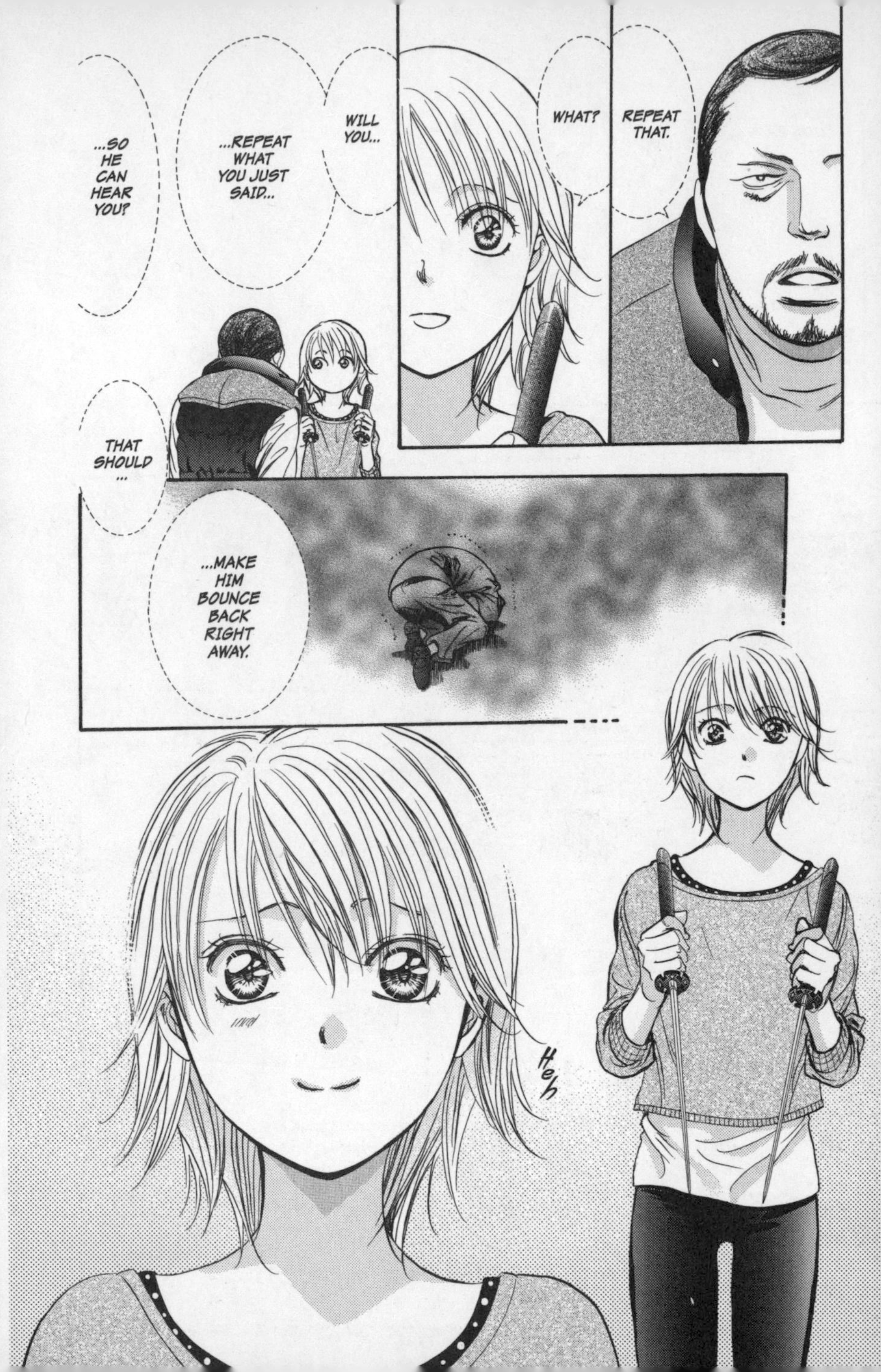
REPEAT THAT.
WHAT?
WILL YOU...
...REPEAT WHAT YOU JUST SAID...
...SO HE CAN HEAR YOU?
THAT SHOULD ...
...MAKE HIM BOUNCE BACK RIGHT AWAY.
Heh

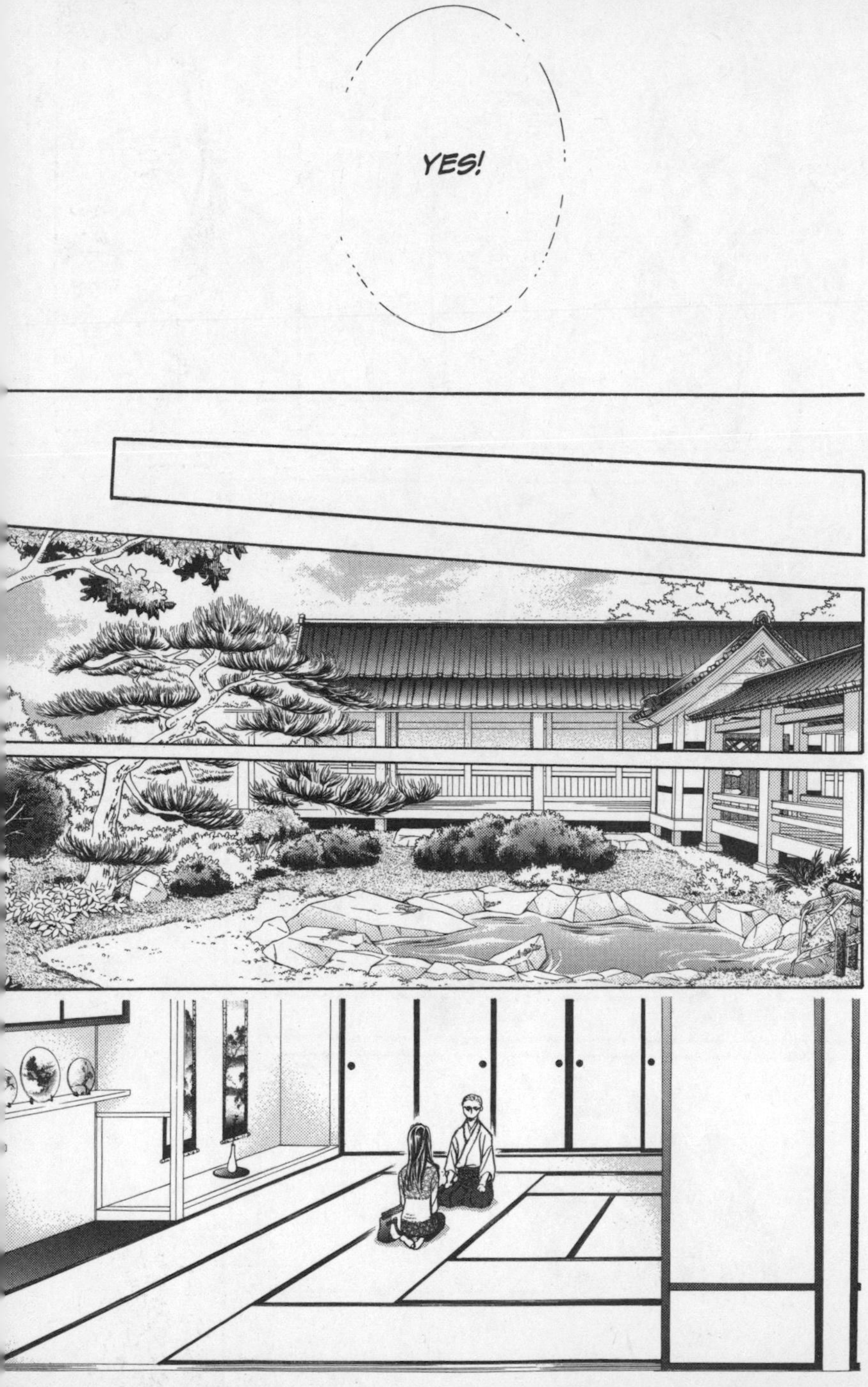
YES!

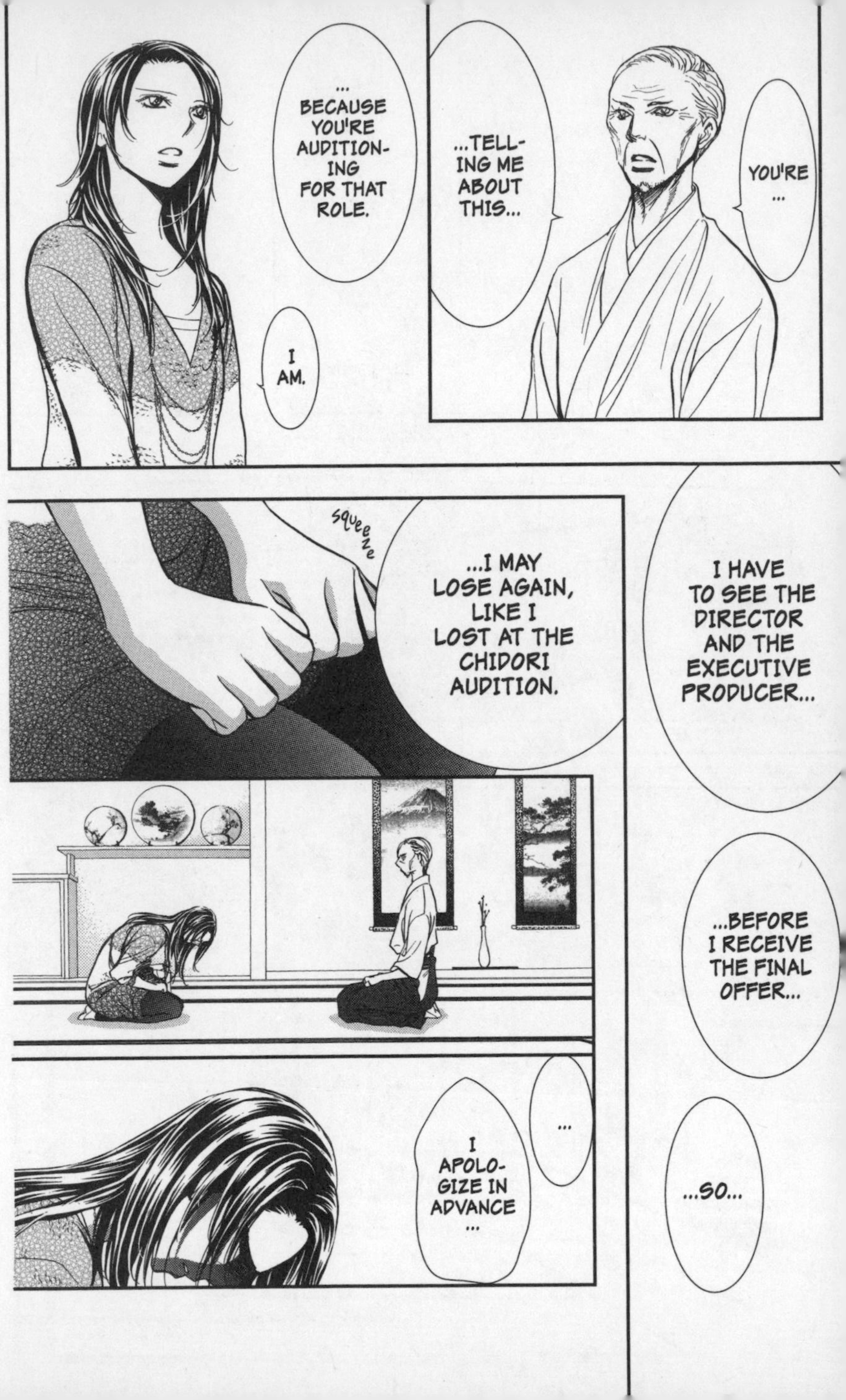
YOU'RE ...
...TELLING ME ABOUT THIS...
... BECAUSE YOU'RE AUDITIONING FOR THAT ROLE.
I AM.
I HAVE TO SEE THE DIRECTOR AND THE EXECUTIVE PRODUCER...
...BEFORE I RECEIVE THE FINAL OFFER...
...SO...
SQUEEZE
...I MAY LOSE AGAIN, LIKE I LOST AT THE CHIDORI AUDITION.
...
I APOLOGIZE IN ADVANCE ...

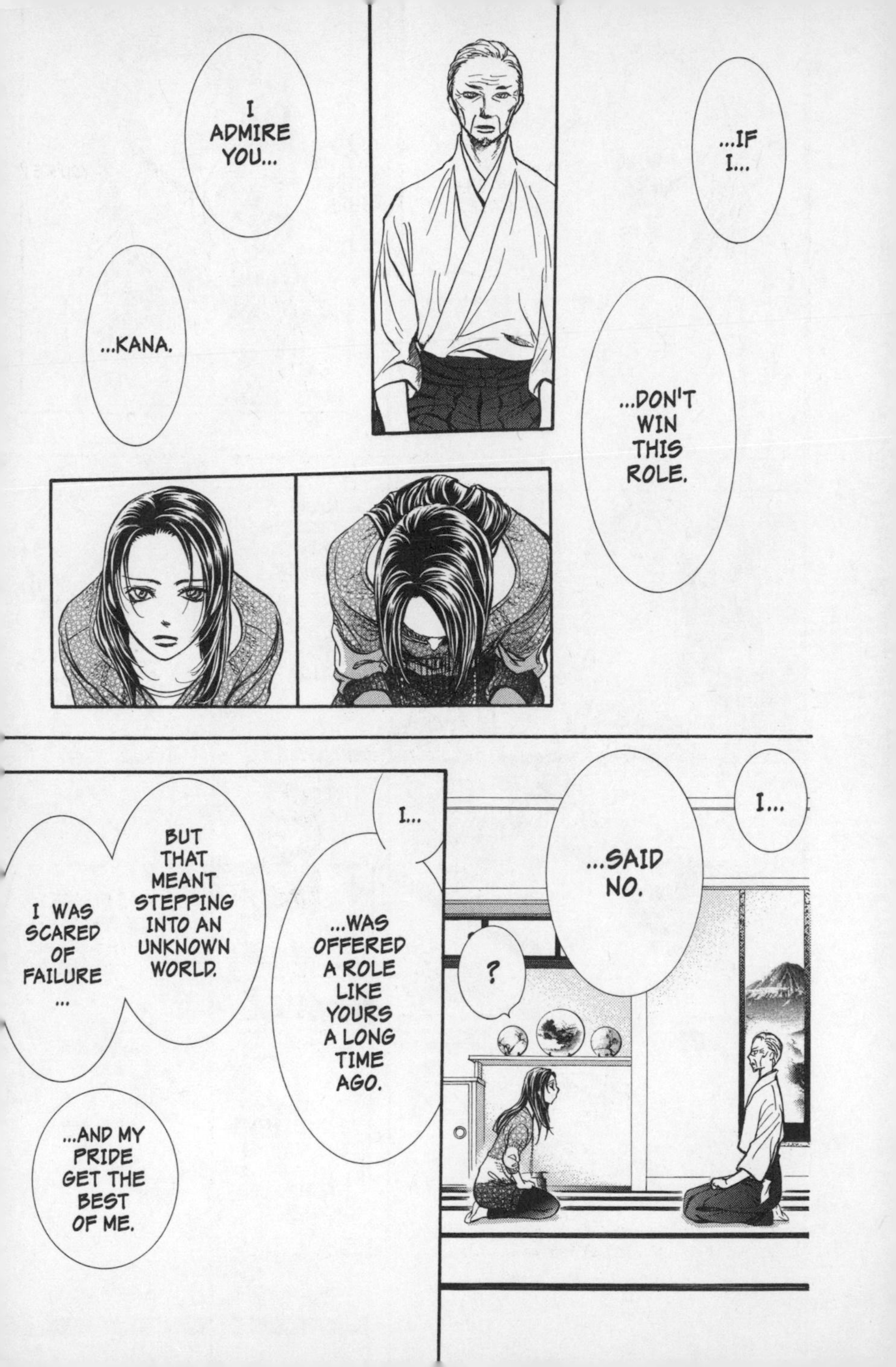
...IF I...
...DON'T WIN THIS ROLE.
I ADMIRE YOU...
...KANA.
I...
...SAID NO.
?
I...
...WAS OFFERED A ROLE LIKE YOURS A LONG TIME AGO.
BUT THAT MEANT STEPPING INTO AN UNKNOWN WORLD.
I WAS SCARED OF FAILURE ...
...AND MY PRIDE GET THE BEST OF ME.

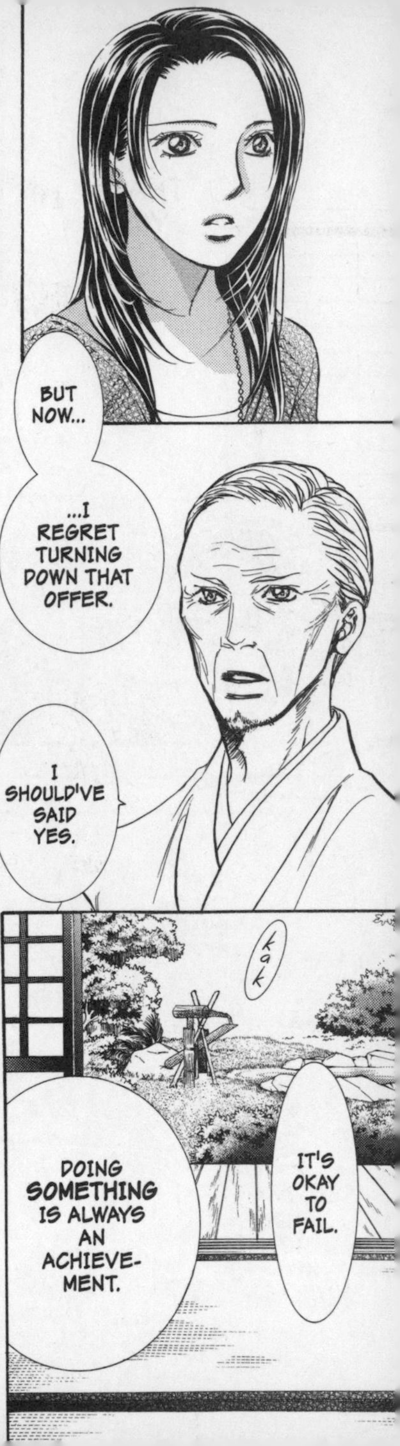
BUT NOW...
...I REGRET TURNING DOWN THAT OFFER.
I SHOULD'VE SAID YES.
kak
IT'S OKAY TO FAIL.
DOING SOMETHING IS ALWAYS AN ACHIEVEMENT.
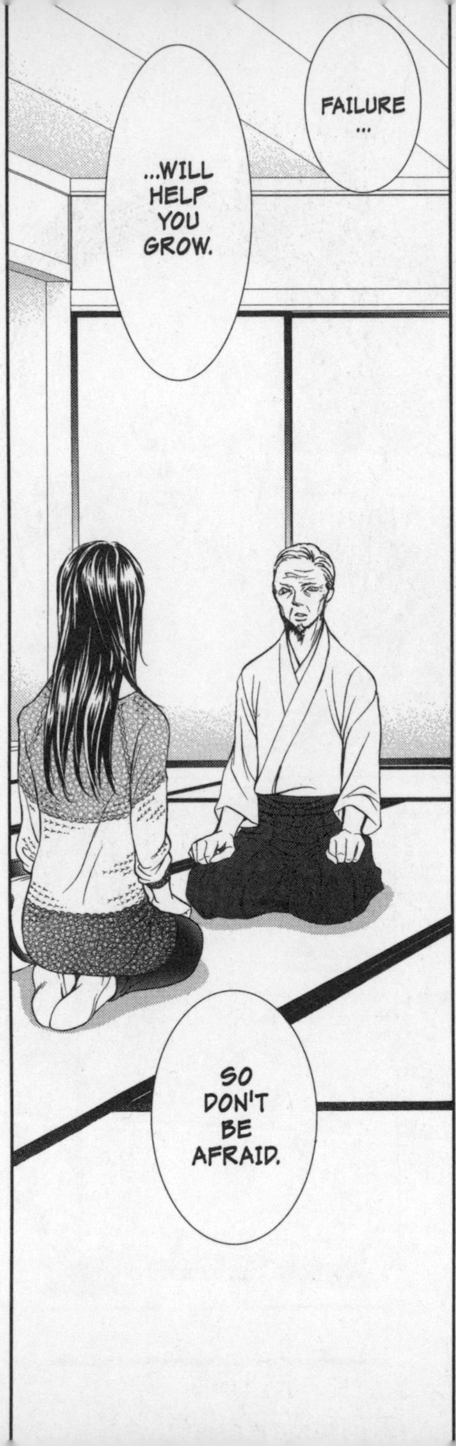
FAILURE...
...WILL HELP YOU GROW.
SO DON'T BE AFRAID.

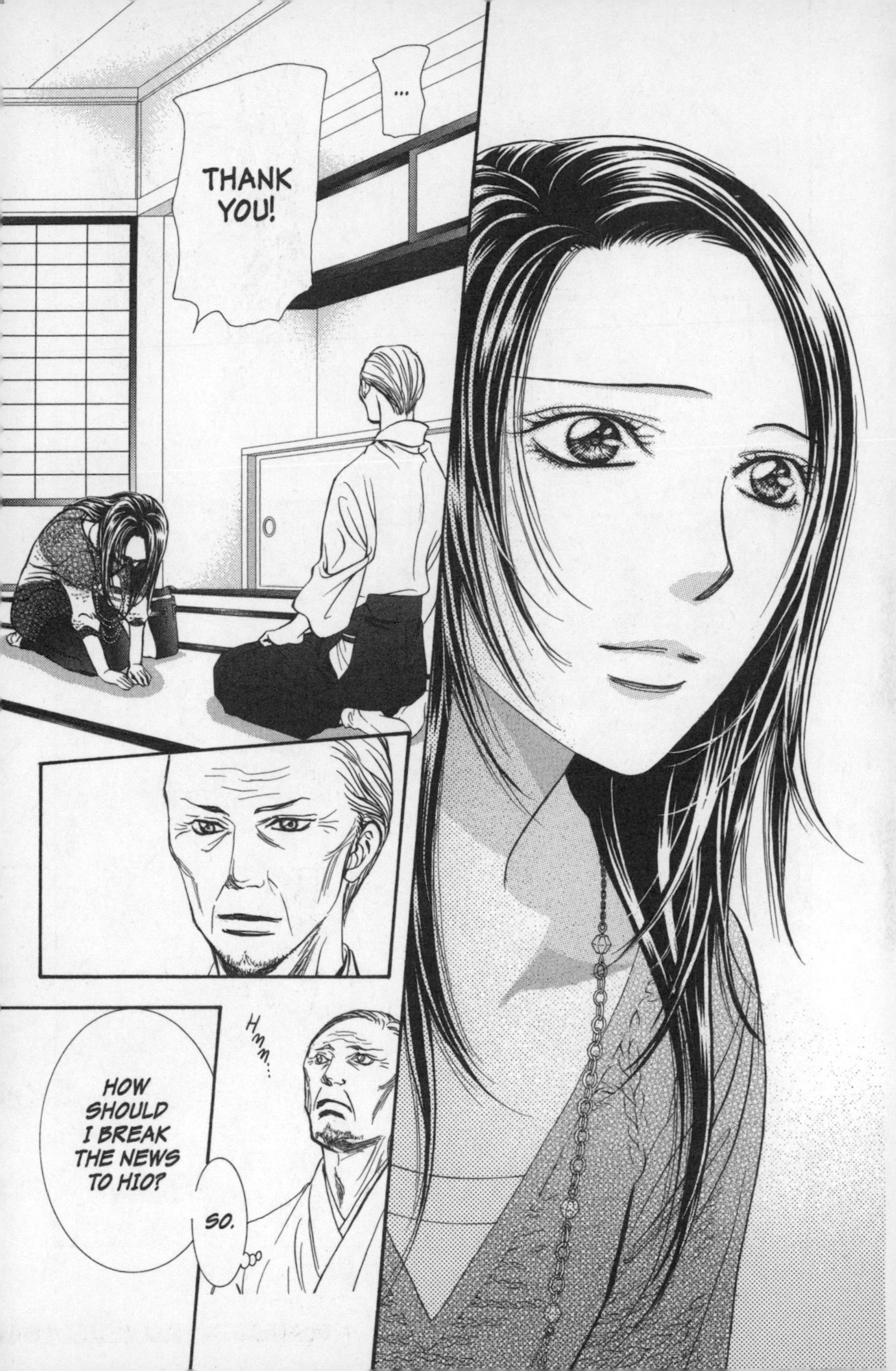
...
THANK YOU!
Hmm...
SO.
HOW SHOULD I BREAK THE NEWS TO HIO?

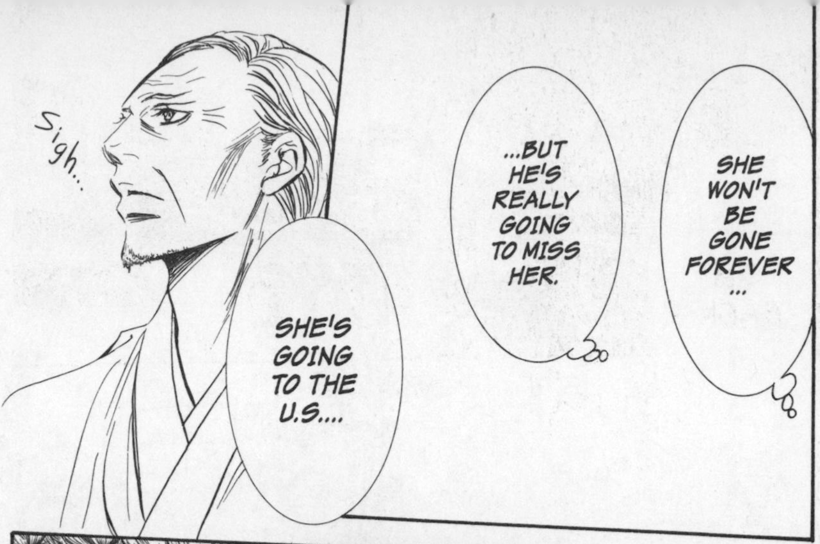
SHE WON'T BE GONE FOREVER ...
...BUT HE'S REALLY GOING TO MISS HER.
Sigh...
SHE'S GOING TO THE U.S....

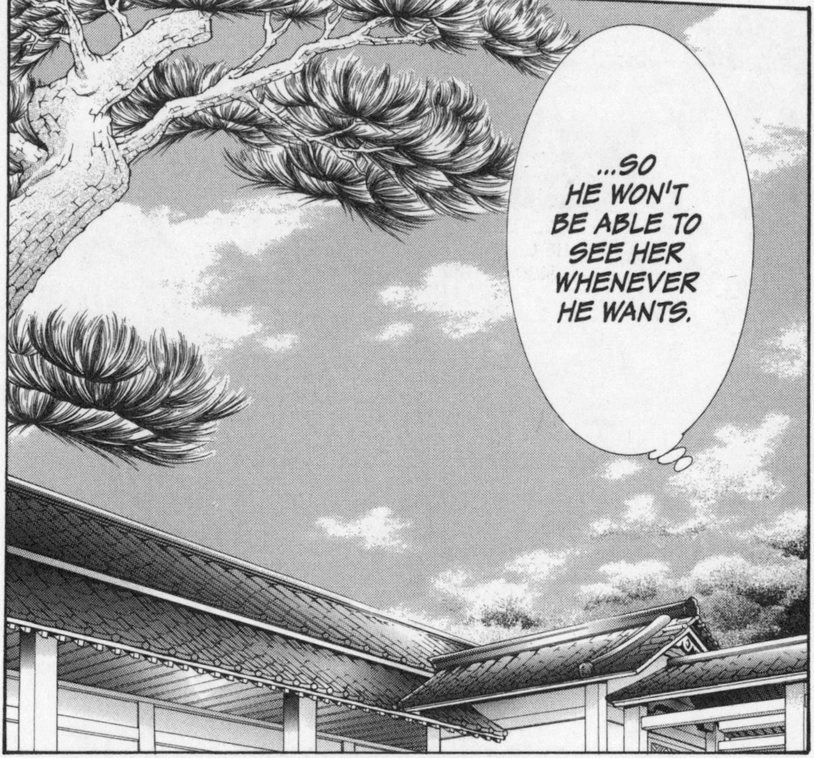
...SO HE WON'T BE ABLE TO SEE HER WHENEVER HE WANTS.

End of Act 264

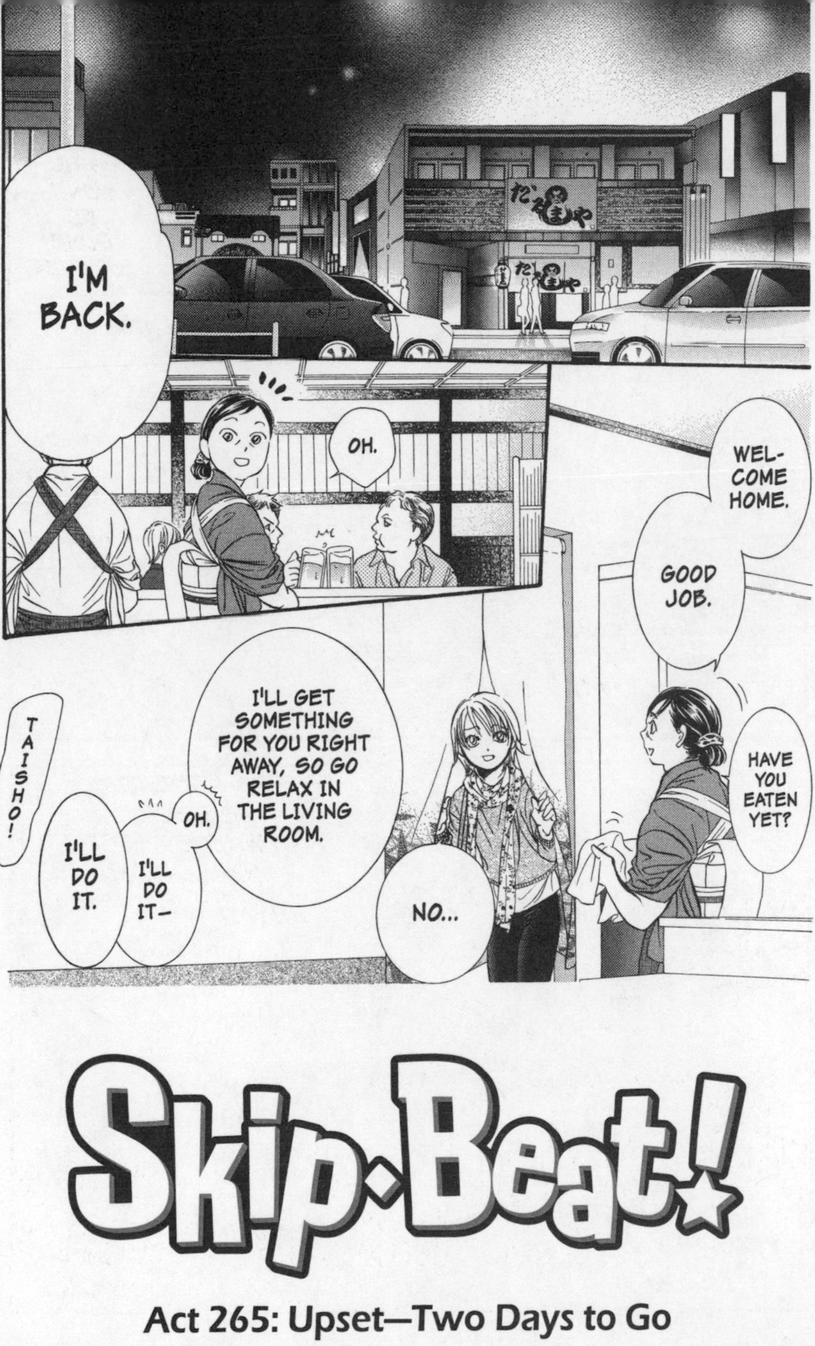
I'M BACK.
OH.
WEL-COME HOME.
GOOD JOB.
HAVE YOU EATEN YET?
NO...
I'LL GET SOMETHING FOR YOU RIGHT AWAY, SO GO RELAX IN THE LIVING ROOM.
OH.
I'LL DO IT—
I'LL DO IT.
TAISHO!

Skip·Beat!

Act 265: Upset—Two Days to Go

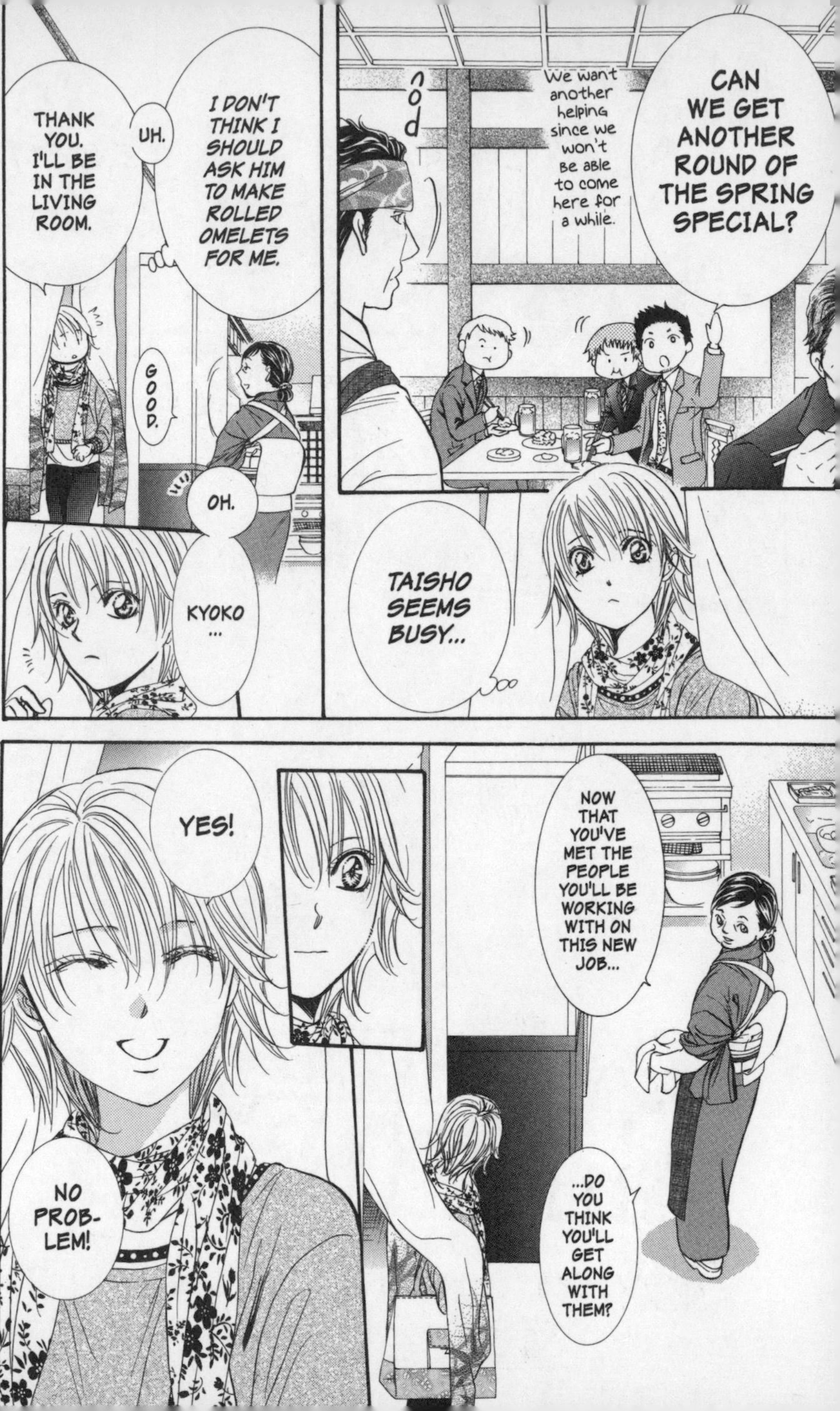
CAN WE GET ANOTHER ROUND OF THE SPRING SPECIAL?
We want another helping since we won't be able to come here for a while.
I DON'T THINK I SHOULD ASK HIM TO MAKE ROLLED OMELETS FOR ME.
UH.
THANK YOU. I'LL BE IN THE LIVING ROOM.
GOOD.
TAISHO SEEMS BUSY...
OH.
KYOKO...
NOW THAT YOU'VE MET THE PEOPLE YOU'LL BE WORKING WITH ON THIS NEW JOB...
...DO YOU THINK YOU'LL GET ALONG WITH THEM?
YES!
NO PROBLEM!

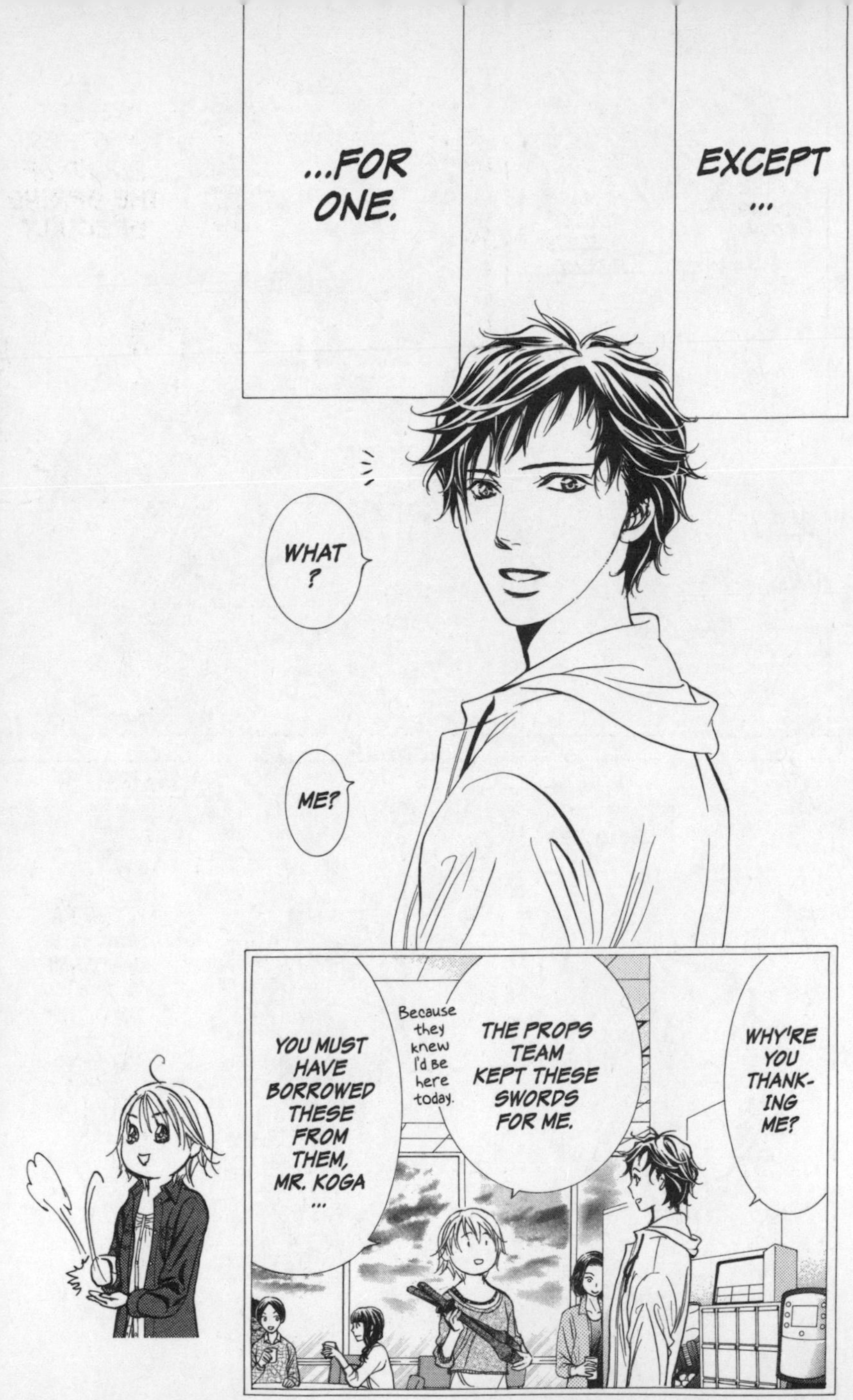
EXCEPT ...
...FOR ONE.
WHAT?
ME?
WHY'RE YOU THANKING ME?
THE PROPS TEAM KEPT THESE SWORDS FOR ME.
Because they knew I'd be here today.
YOU MUST HAVE BORROWED THESE FROM THEM, MR. KOGA ...

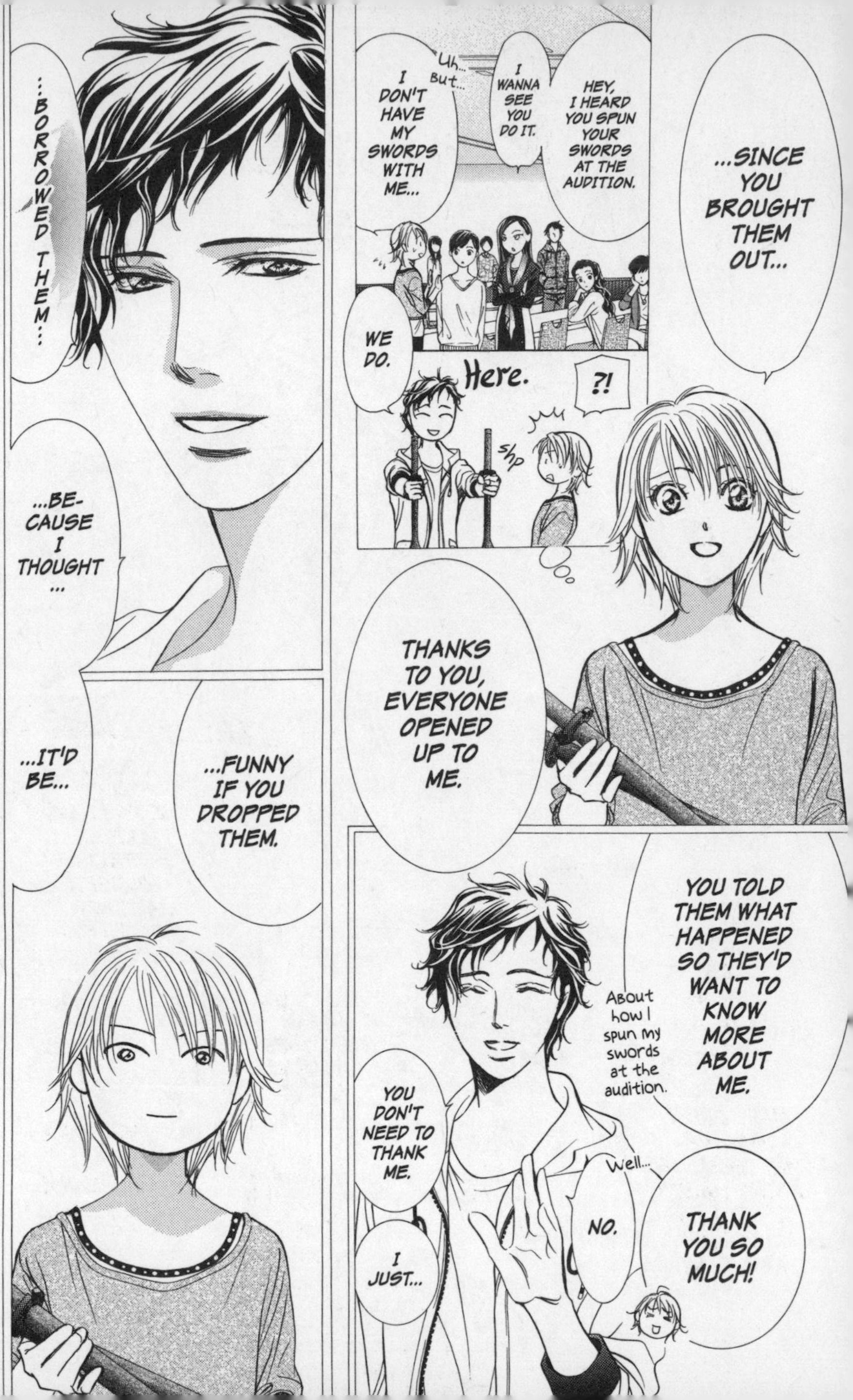
...SINCE YOU BROUGHT THEM OUT...
HEY, I HEARD YOU SPUN YOUR SWORDS AT THE AUDITION.
I WANNA SEE YOU DO IT.
Uh... But...
I DON'T HAVE MY SWORDS WITH ME...
?!
Here.
WE DO.
shp
THANKS TO YOU, EVERYONE OPENED UP TO ME.
YOU TOLD THEM WHAT HAPPENED SO THEY'D WANT TO KNOW MORE ABOUT ME.
About how I spun my swords at the audition.
THANK YOU SO MUCH!
Well...
NO.
YOU DON'T NEED TO THANK ME.
I JUST...
...BORROWED THEM...
...BE-CAUSE I THOUGHT...
...IT'D BE...
...FUNNY IF YOU DROPPED THEM.

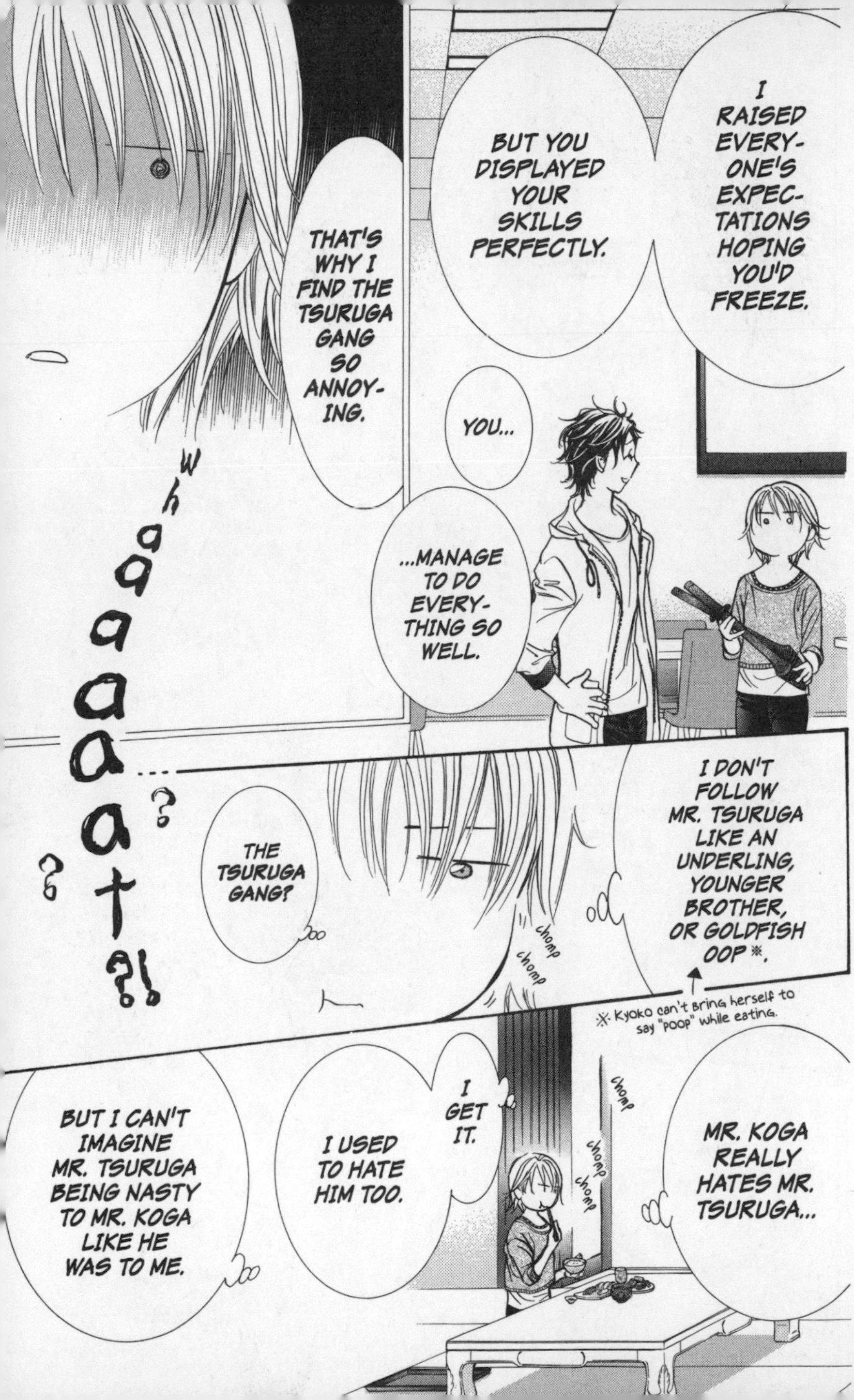
I RAISED EVERYONE'S EXPECTATIONS HOPING YOU'D FREEZE.
BUT YOU DISPLAYED YOUR SKILLS PERFECTLY.
YOU...
...MANAGE TO DO EVERYTHING SO WELL.
THAT'S WHY I FIND THE TSURUGA GANG SO ANNOYING.
I DON'T FOLLOW MR. TSURUGA LIKE AN UNDERLING, YOUNGER BROTHER, OR GOLDFISH OOP※.
※ Kyoko can't bring herself to say "poop" while eating.
chomp chomp
THE TSURUGA GANG?
...??
Whaaaaaaat?!
MR. KOGA REALLY HATES MR. TSURUGA...
chomp chomp chomp
I GET IT.
I USED TO HATE HIM TOO.
BUT I CAN'T IMAGINE MR. TSURUGA BEING NASTY TO MR. KOGA LIKE HE WAS TO ME.

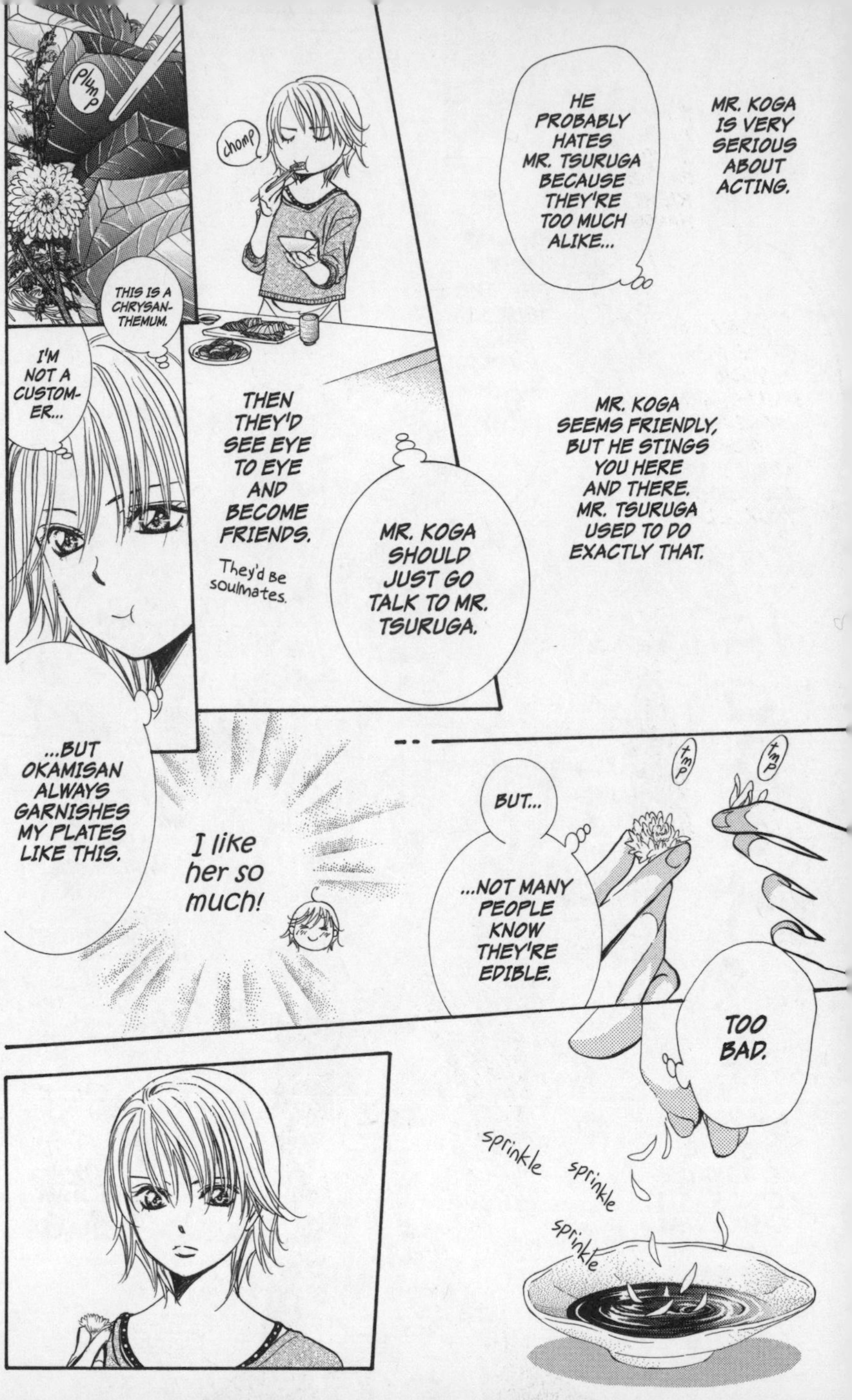
MR. KOGA IS VERY SERIOUS ABOUT ACTING.
HE PROBABLY HATES MR. TSURUGA BECAUSE THEY'RE TOO MUCH ALIKE...
plump
chomp
THIS IS A CHRYSANTHEMUM.
MR. KOGA SEEMS FRIENDLY, BUT HE STINGS YOU HERE AND THERE. MR. TSURUGA USED TO DO EXACTLY THAT.
MR. KOGA SHOULD JUST GO TALK TO MR. TSURUGA.
THEN THEY'D SEE EYE TO EYE AND BECOME FRIENDS.
They'd be soulmates.
I'M NOT A CUSTOMER...
...BUT OKAMISAN ALWAYS GARNISHES MY PLATES LIKE THIS.
I like her so much!
tmp
tmp
BUT...
...NOT MANY PEOPLE KNOW THEY'RE EDIBLE.
TOO BAD.
sprinkle
sprinkle
sprinkle

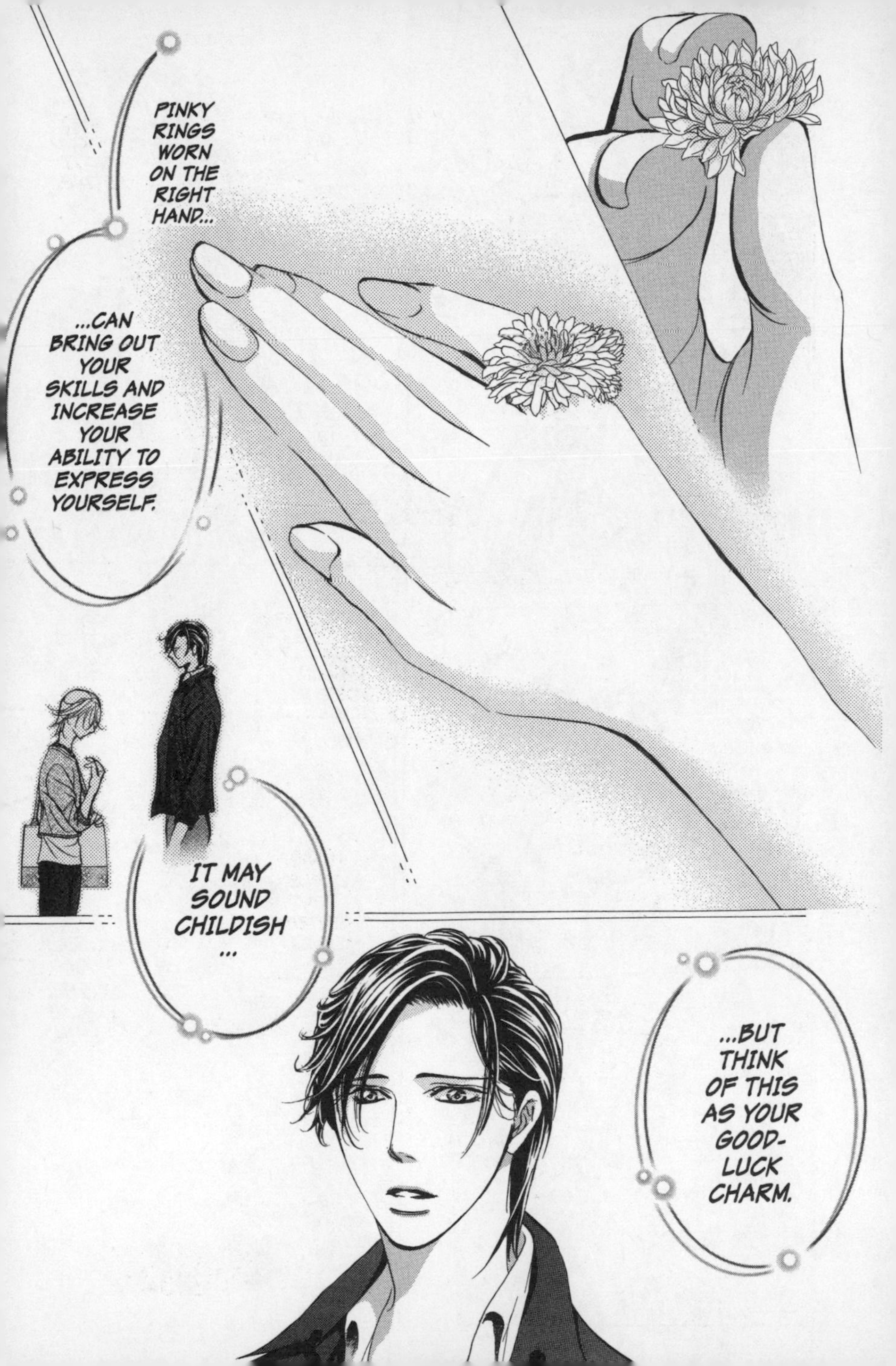
PINKY RINGS WORN ON THE RIGHT HAND...
...CAN BRING OUT YOUR SKILLS AND INCREASE YOUR ABILITY TO EXPRESS YOURSELF.
IT MAY SOUND CHILDISH...
...BUT THINK OF THIS AS YOUR GOOD-LUCK CHARM.

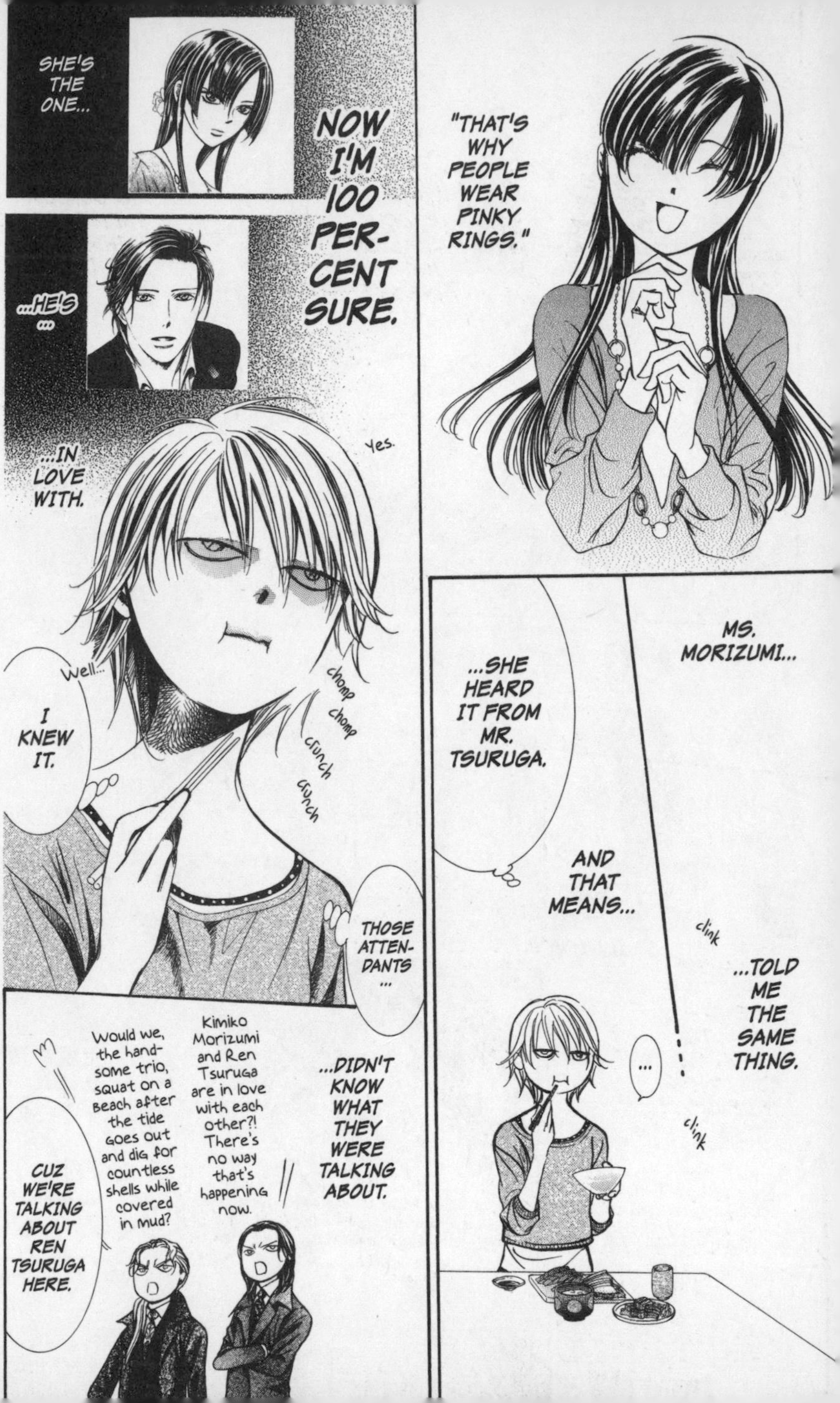
"THAT'S WHY PEOPLE WEAR PINKY RINGS."
MS. MORIZUMI...
...TOLD ME THE SAME THING.
clink
...
clink
AND THAT MEANS...
...SHE HEARD IT FROM MR. TSURUGA.
NOW I'M 100 PER-CENT SURE.
SHE'S THE ONE...
...HE'S...
...IN LOVE WITH.
Yes.
chomp chomp
crunch crunch
Well...
I KNEW IT.
THOSE ATTEN-DANTS...
...DIDN'T KNOW WHAT THEY WERE TALKING ABOUT.
Kimiko Morizumi and Ren Tsuruga are in love with each other?! There's no way that's happening now.
Would we, the hand-some trio, squat on a beach after the tide goes out and dig for countless shells while covered in mud?
CUZ WE'RE TALKING ABOUT REN TSURUGA HERE.

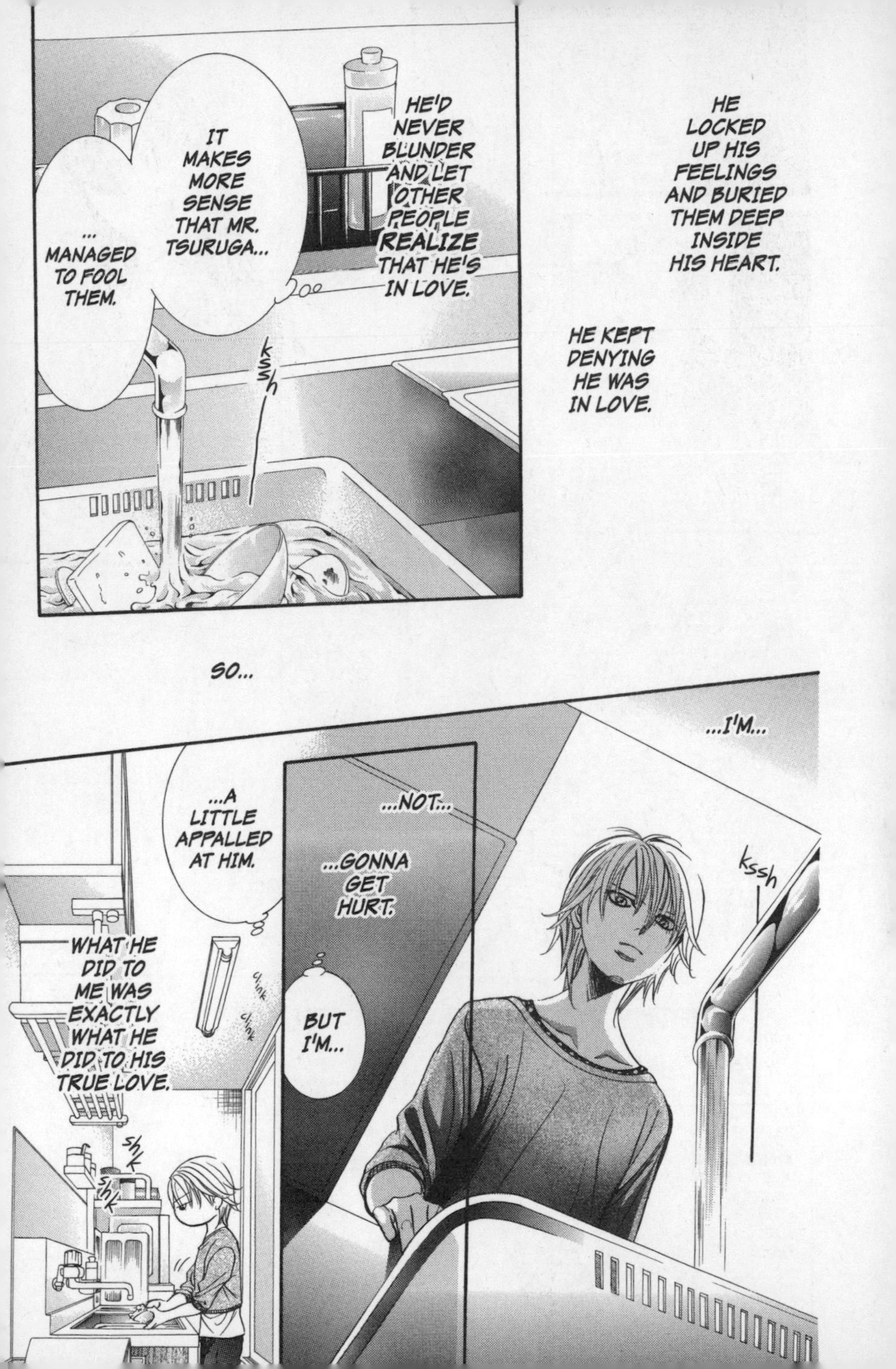
HE LOCKED UP HIS FEELINGS AND BURIED THEM DEEP INSIDE HIS HEART.
HE KEPT DENYING HE WAS IN LOVE.
HE'D NEVER BLUNDER AND LET OTHER PEOPLE REALIZE THAT HE'S IN LOVE.
IT MAKES MORE SENSE THAT MR. TSURUGA...
...MANAGED TO FOOL THEM.
kssh
SO...
...I'M...
...NOT...
...GONNA GET HURT.
kssh
WHAT HE DID TO ME WAS EXACTLY WHAT HE DID TO HIS TRUE LOVE.
BUT I'M...
...A LITTLE APPALLED AT HIM.
clink
clink
shk
shk

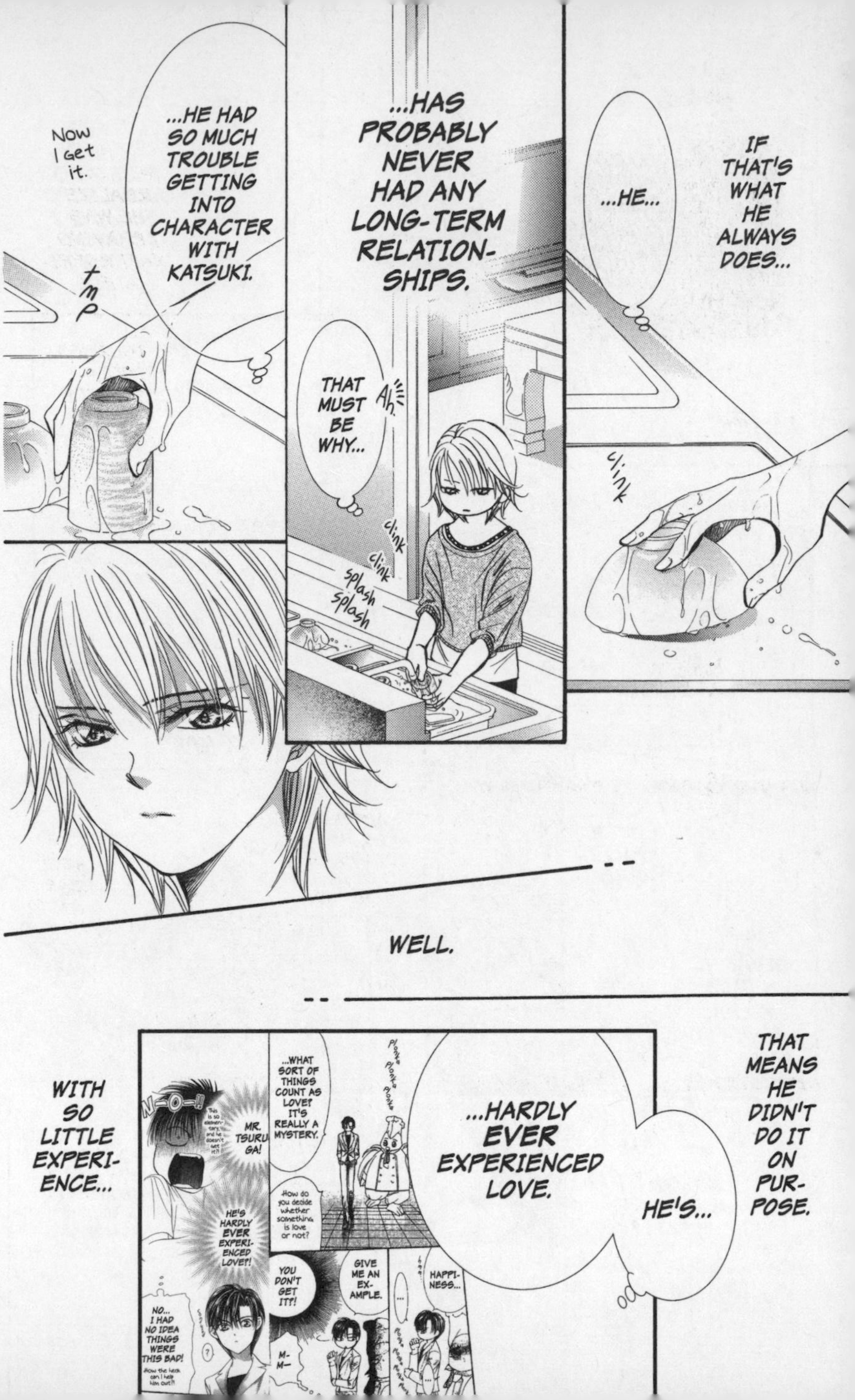

IF THAT'S WHAT HE ALWAYS DOES...
...HE...
clink
...HAS PROBABLY NEVER HAD ANY LONG-TERM RELATION-SHIPS.
THAT MUST BE WHY...
Ah.
clink
clink
splash
splash
...HE HAD SO MUCH TROUBLE GETTING INTO CHARACTER WITH KATSUKI.
Now I get it.
tmp
WELL.
THAT MEANS HE DIDN'T DO IT ON PUR-POSE.
HE'S...
...HARDLY EVER EXPERIENCED LOVE.
...WHAT SORT OF THINGS COUNT AS LOVE? IT'S REALLY A MYSTERY.
How do you decide whether something is love or not?
Plonka Plonka Plonka
N-O-!!
MR. TSURUGA!
This is so elementary, and he doesn't get it?!
HE'S HARDLY EVER EXPERIENCED LOVE?!
HAPPI-NESS...
...
GIVE ME AN EX-AMPLE.
YOU DON'T GET IT?!
M-M—
NO... I HAD NO IDEA THINGS WERE THIS BAD!
How the heck can I help him out?!
WITH SO LITTLE EXPERI-ENCE...

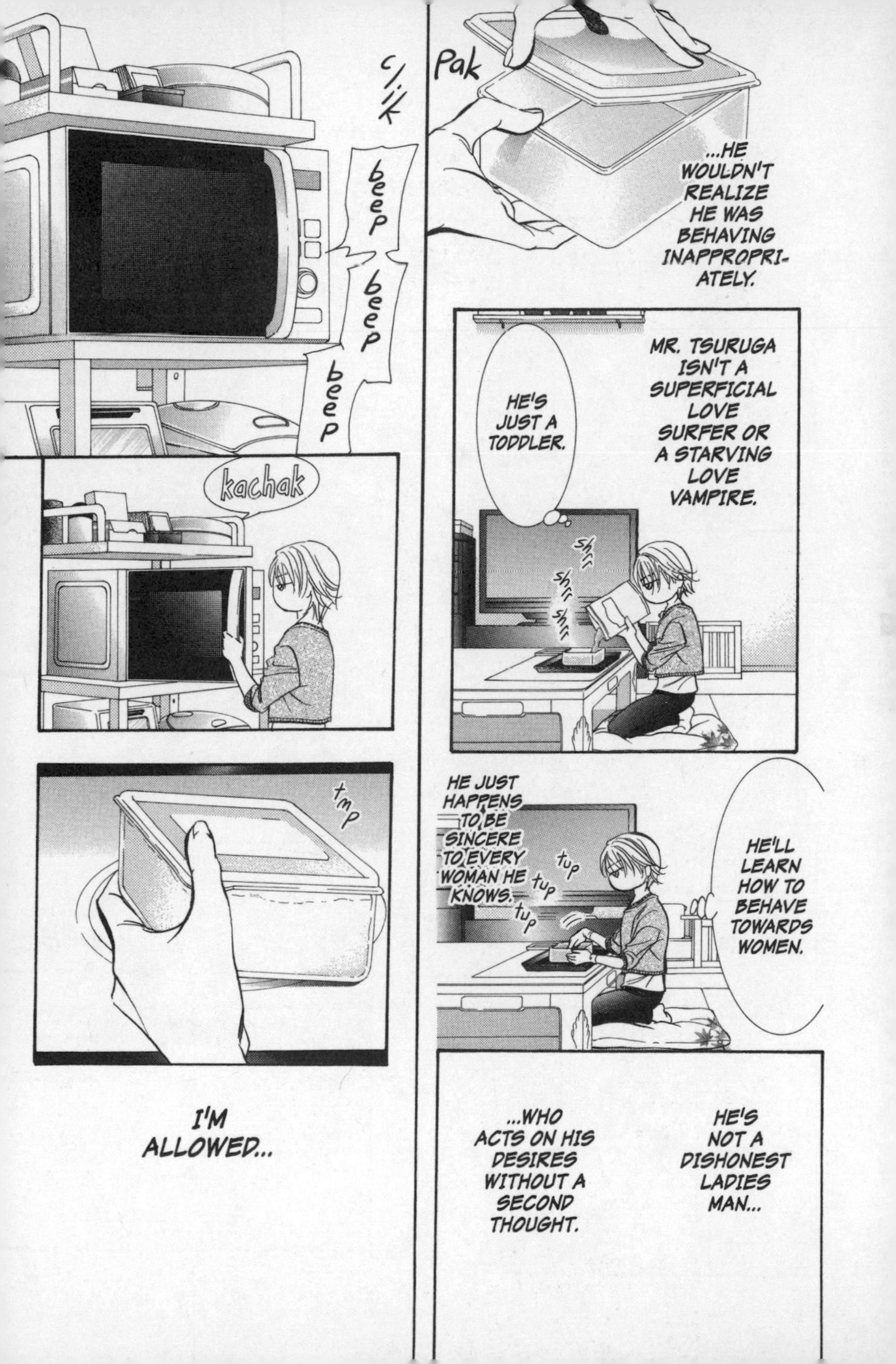
Pak
...HE WOULDN'T REALIZE HE WAS BEHAVING INAPPROPRIATELY.
MR. TSURUGA ISN'T A SUPERFICIAL LOVE SURFER OR A STARVING LOVE VAMPIRE.
HE'S JUST A TODDLER.
shrr shrr shrr
HE'LL LEARN HOW TO BEHAVE TOWARDS WOMEN.
HE JUST HAPPENS TO BE SINCERE TO EVERY WOMAN HE KNOWS.
tup tup tup
HE'S NOT A DISHONEST LADIES MAN...
...WHO ACTS ON HIS DESIRES WITHOUT A SECOND THOUGHT.
c/ik
beep beep beep
kachak
tmp
I'M ALLOWED...

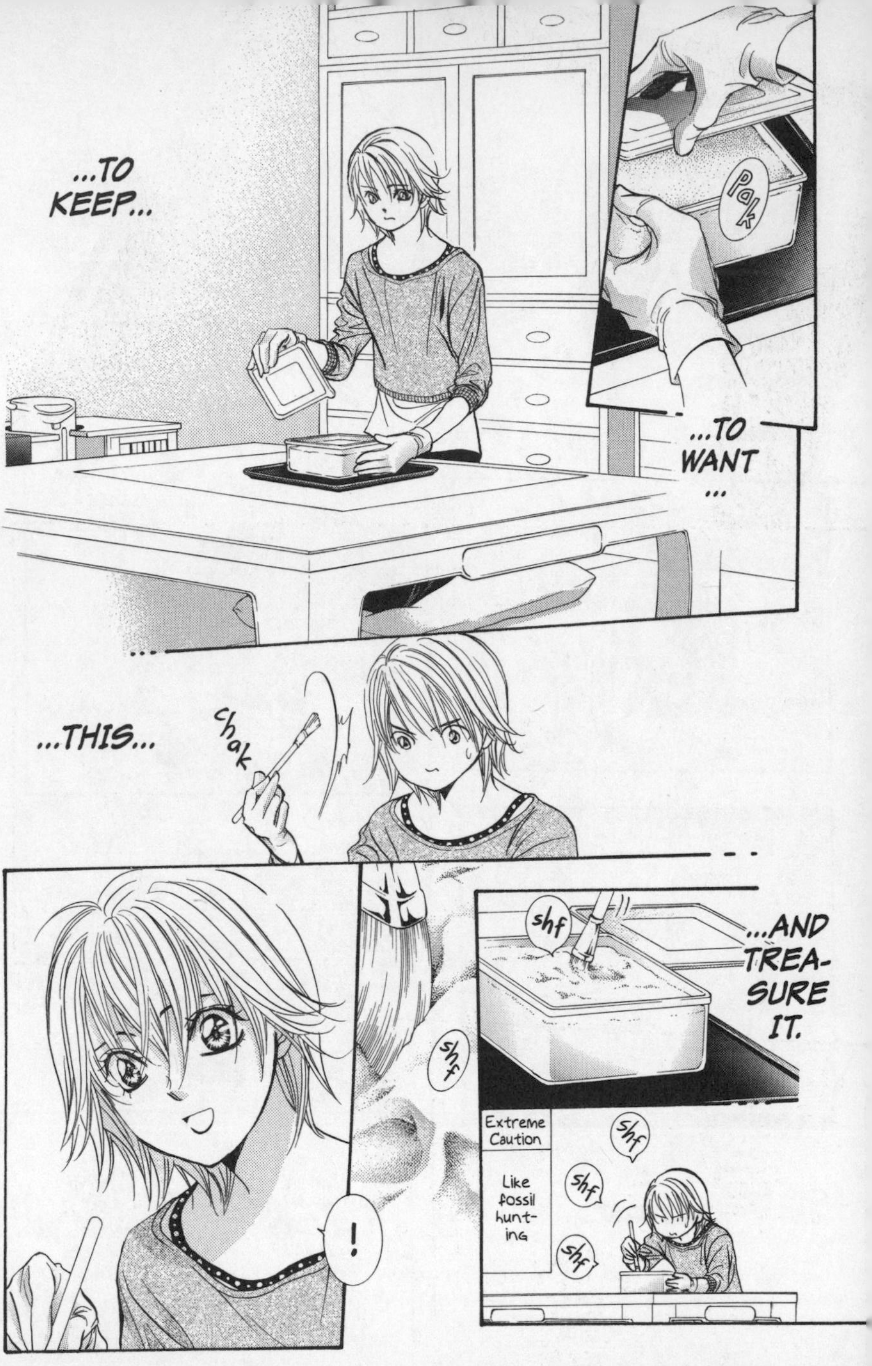
Pak
...TO WANT...
...TO KEEP...
...
...THIS...
chak
shf
...AND TREASURE IT.
Extreme Caution
Like fossil hunting
shf
shf
shf
shf
!

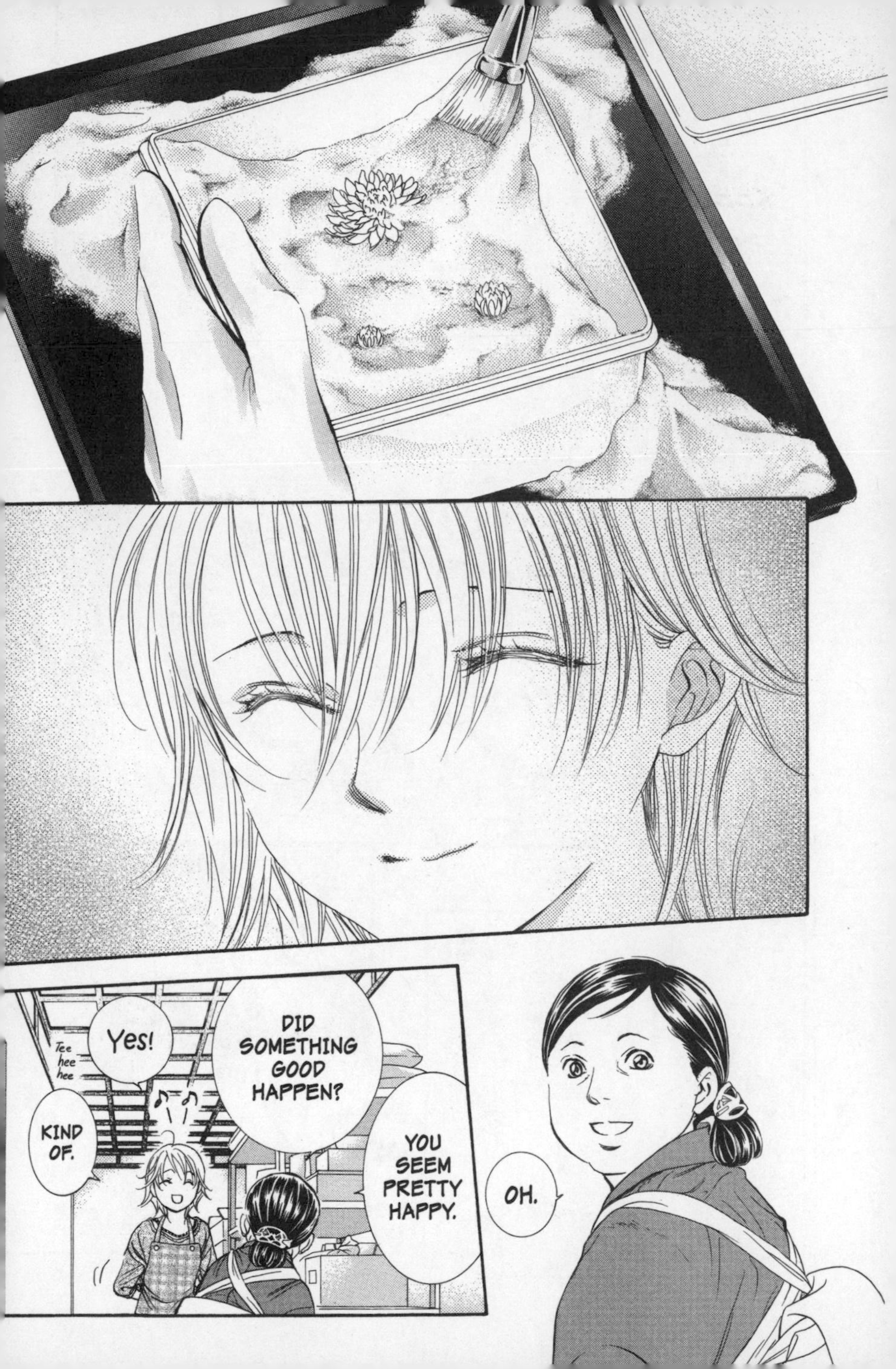
OH.
YOU SEEM PRETTY HAPPY.
DID SOMETHING GOOD HAPPEN?
Yes!
Tee hee hee
KIND OF.

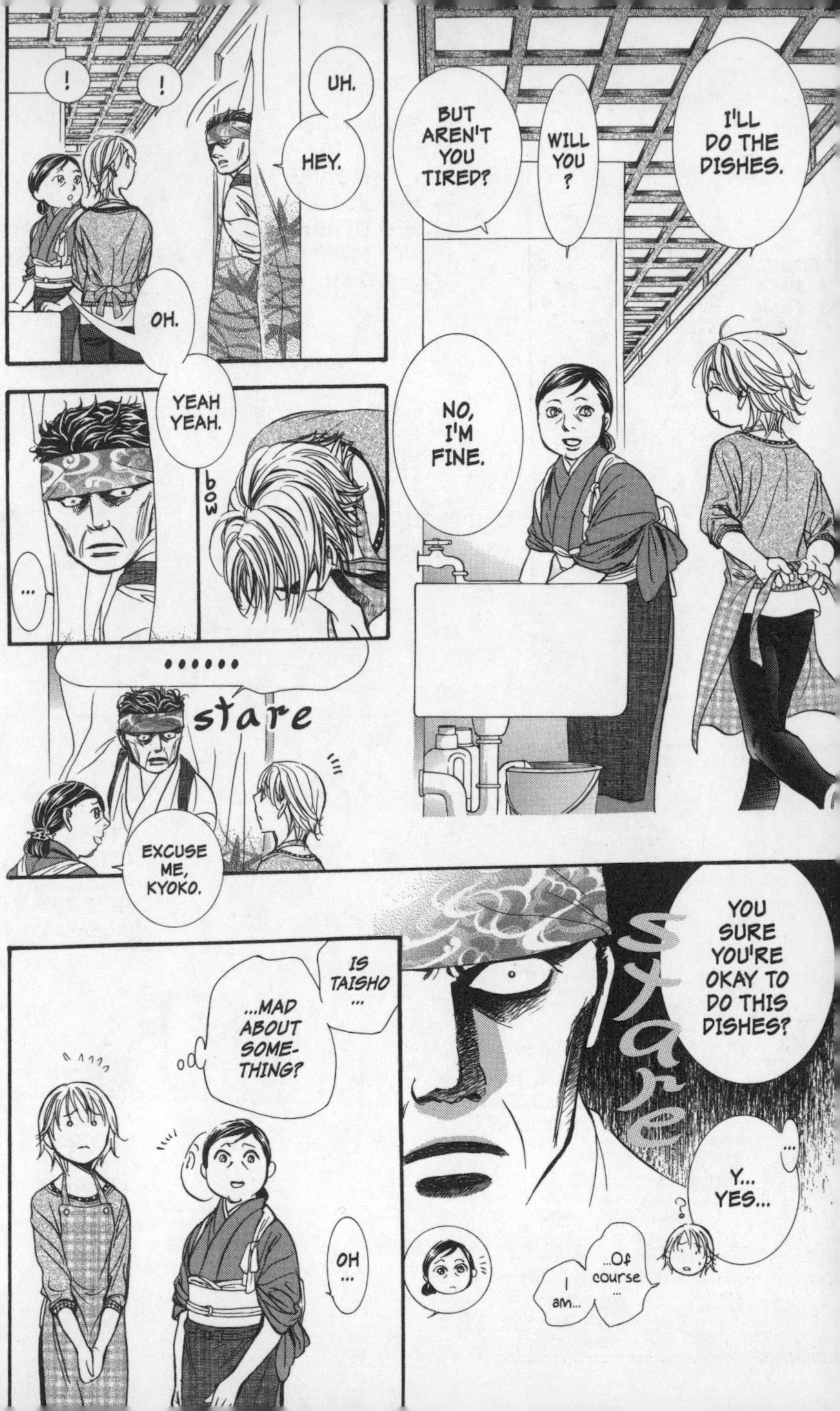
I'LL DO THE DISHES.
WILL YOU ?
BUT AREN'T YOU TIRED?
NO, I'M FINE.
!
!
UH.
HEY.
OH.
YEAH YEAH.
bow
...
......
stare
EXCUSE ME, KYOKO.
YOU SURE YOU'RE OKAY TO DO THIS DISHES?
stare
...
Y... YES...
...Of course ...
I am...
IS TAISHO ...
...MAD ABOUT SOME-THING?
OH ...

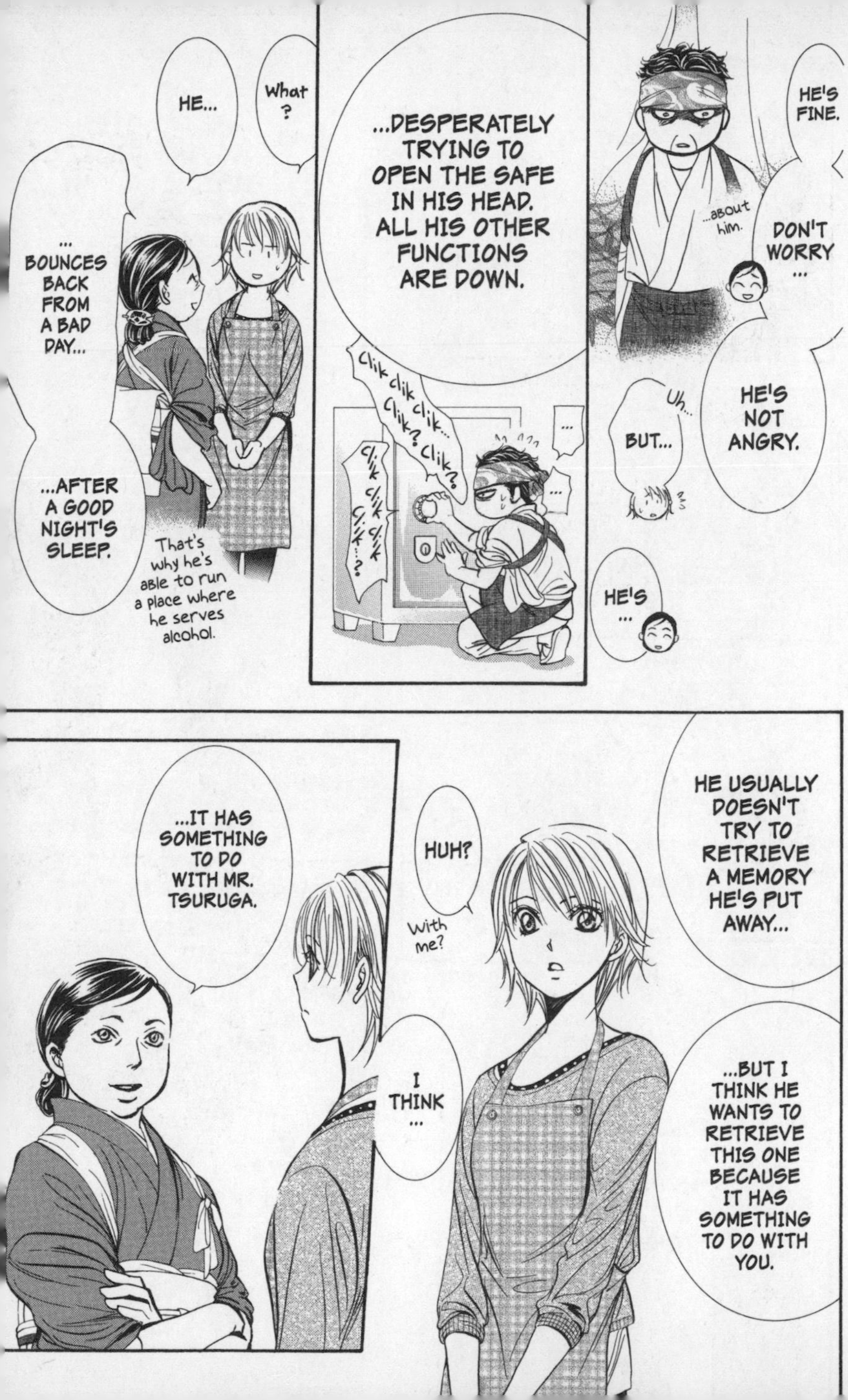
HE'S FINE.
DON'T WORRY ...
...about him.
HE'S NOT ANGRY.
Uh...
BUT...
HE'S ...
...DESPERATELY TRYING TO OPEN THE SAFE IN HIS HEAD. ALL HIS OTHER FUNCTIONS ARE DOWN.
...
...
Clik clik clik... Clik? Clik?
Clik clik clik clik...?
What ?
HE...
... BOUNCES BACK FROM A BAD DAY...
...AFTER A GOOD NIGHT'S SLEEP.
That's why he's able to run a place where he serves alcohol.
HE USUALLY DOESN'T TRY TO RETRIEVE A MEMORY HE'S PUT AWAY...
...BUT I THINK HE WANTS TO RETRIEVE THIS ONE BECAUSE IT HAS SOMETHING TO DO WITH YOU.
HUH?
With me?
I THINK ...
...IT HAS SOMETHING TO DO WITH MR. TSURUGA.

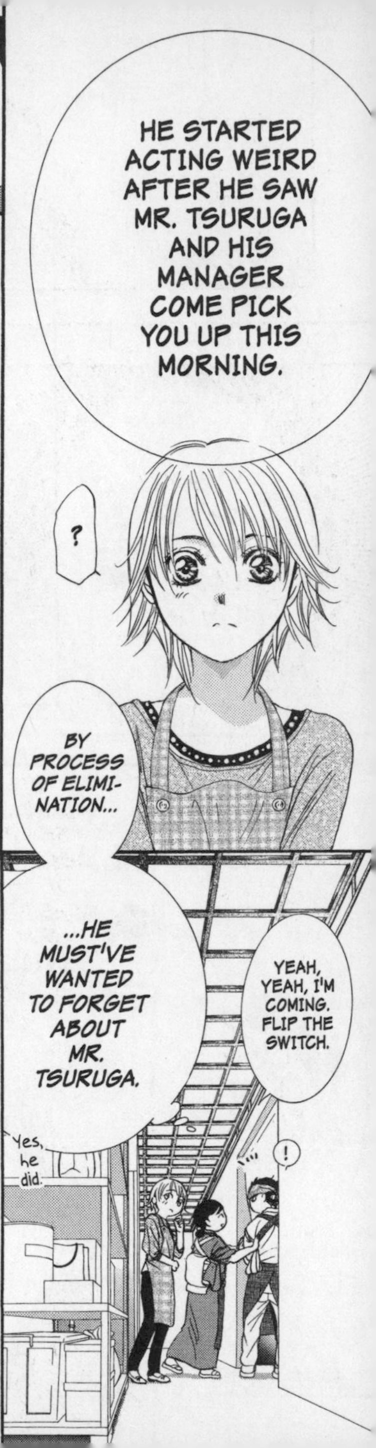
HE STARTED ACTING WEIRD AFTER HE SAW MR. TSURUGA AND HIS MANAGER COME PICK YOU UP THIS MORNING.
?
BY PROCESS OF ELIMINATION...
...HE MUST'VE WANTED TO FORGET ABOUT MR. TSURUGA.
YEAH, YEAH, I'M COMING. FLIP THE SWITCH.
!
Yes, he did.

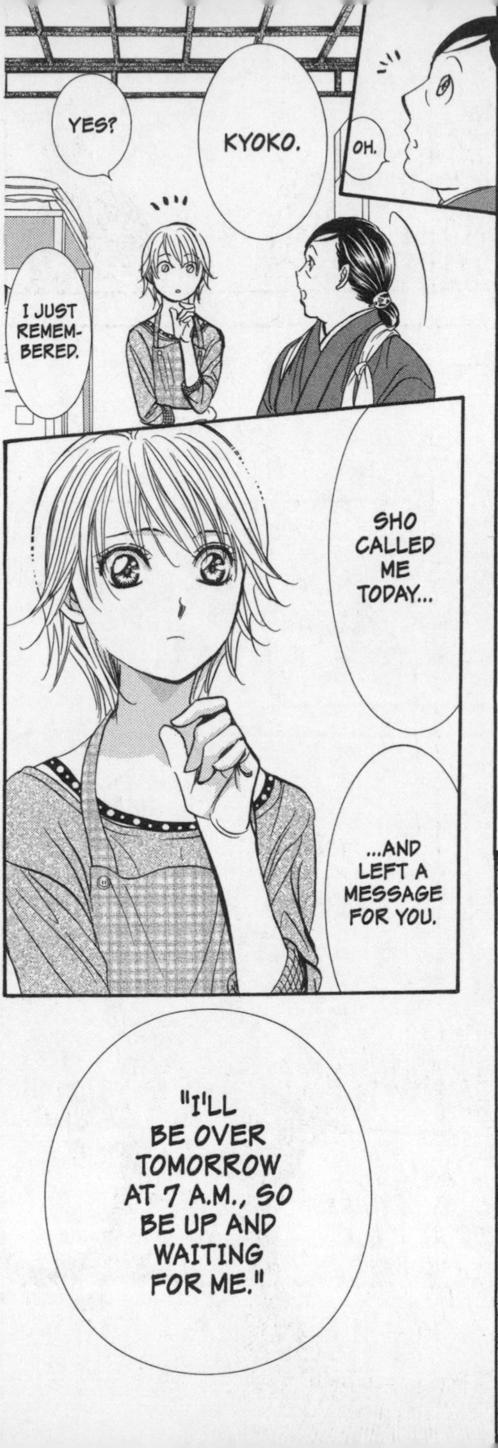
OH.
KYOKO.
YES?
I JUST REMEMBERED.
SHO CALLED ME TODAY...
...AND LEFT A MESSAGE FOR YOU.
"I'LL BE OVER TOMORROW AT 7 A.M., SO BE UP AND WAITING FOR ME."

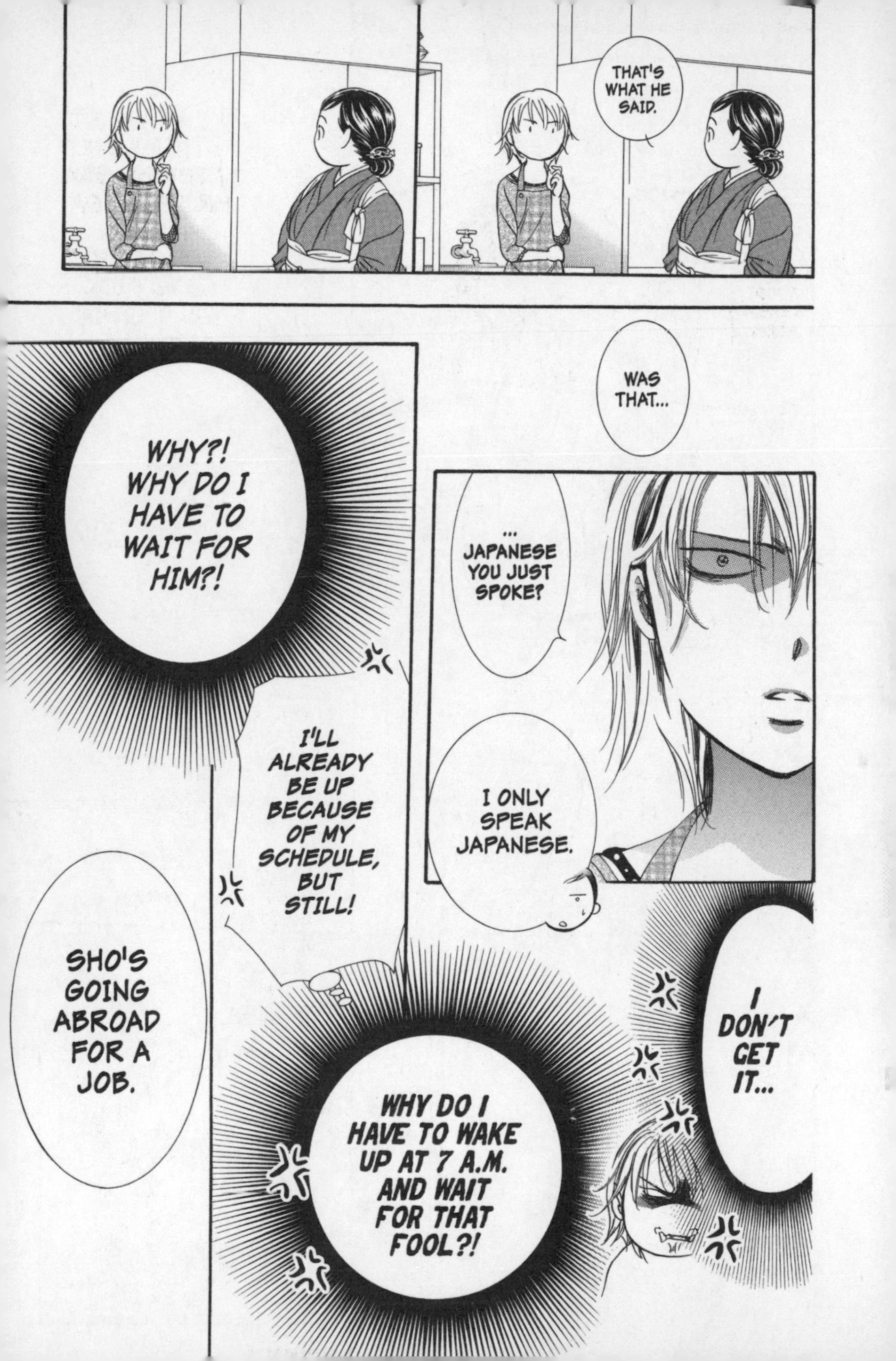

THAT'S WHAT HE SAID.
WAS THAT...
... JAPANESE YOU JUST SPOKE?
I ONLY SPEAK JAPANESE.
I DON'T GET IT...
WHY DO I HAVE TO WAKE UP AT 7 A.M. AND WAIT FOR THAT FOOL?!
I'LL ALREADY BE UP BECAUSE OF MY SCHEDULE, BUT STILL!
WHY?! WHY DO I HAVE TO WAIT FOR HIM?!
SHO'S GOING ABROAD FOR A JOB.

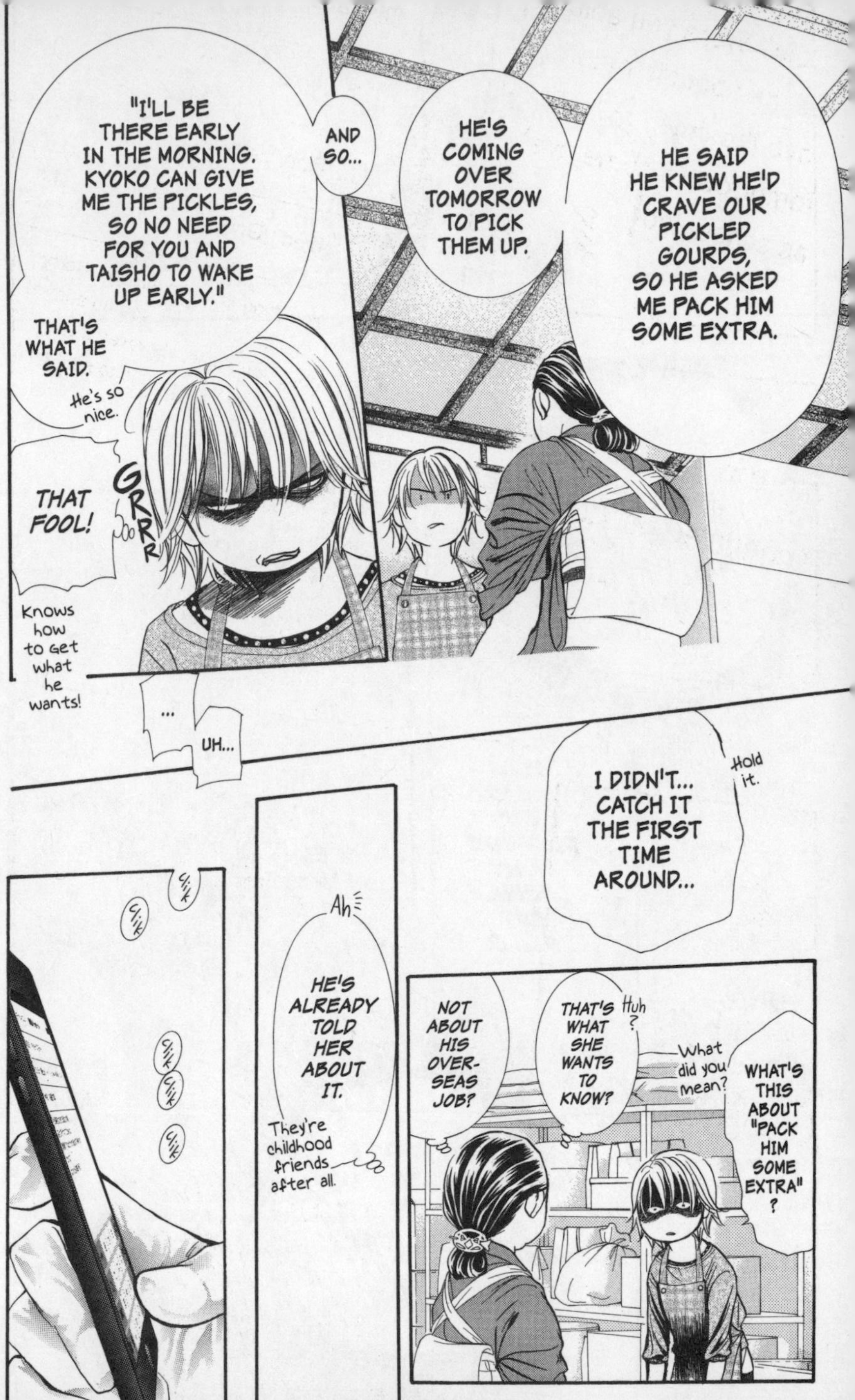

HE SAID HE KNEW HE'D CRAVE OUR PICKLED GOURDS, SO HE ASKED ME PACK HIM SOME EXTRA.
HE'S COMING OVER TOMORROW TO PICK THEM UP.
AND SO...
"I'LL BE THERE EARLY IN THE MORNING. KYOKO CAN GIVE ME THE PICKLES, SO NO NEED FOR YOU AND TAISHO TO WAKE UP EARLY."
THAT'S WHAT HE SAID.
He's so nice.
THAT FOOL!
GRRRR
Knows how to get what he wants!
...
UH...
I DIDN'T... CATCH IT THE FIRST TIME AROUND...
Hold it.
WHAT'S THIS ABOUT "PACK HIM SOME EXTRA"?
What did you mean?
Huh?
THAT'S WHAT SHE WANTS TO KNOW?
NOT ABOUT HIS OVER-SEAS JOB?
Ah
HE'S ALREADY TOLD HER ABOUT IT.
They're childhood friends after all.
clik
clik
clik
clik
clik
clik

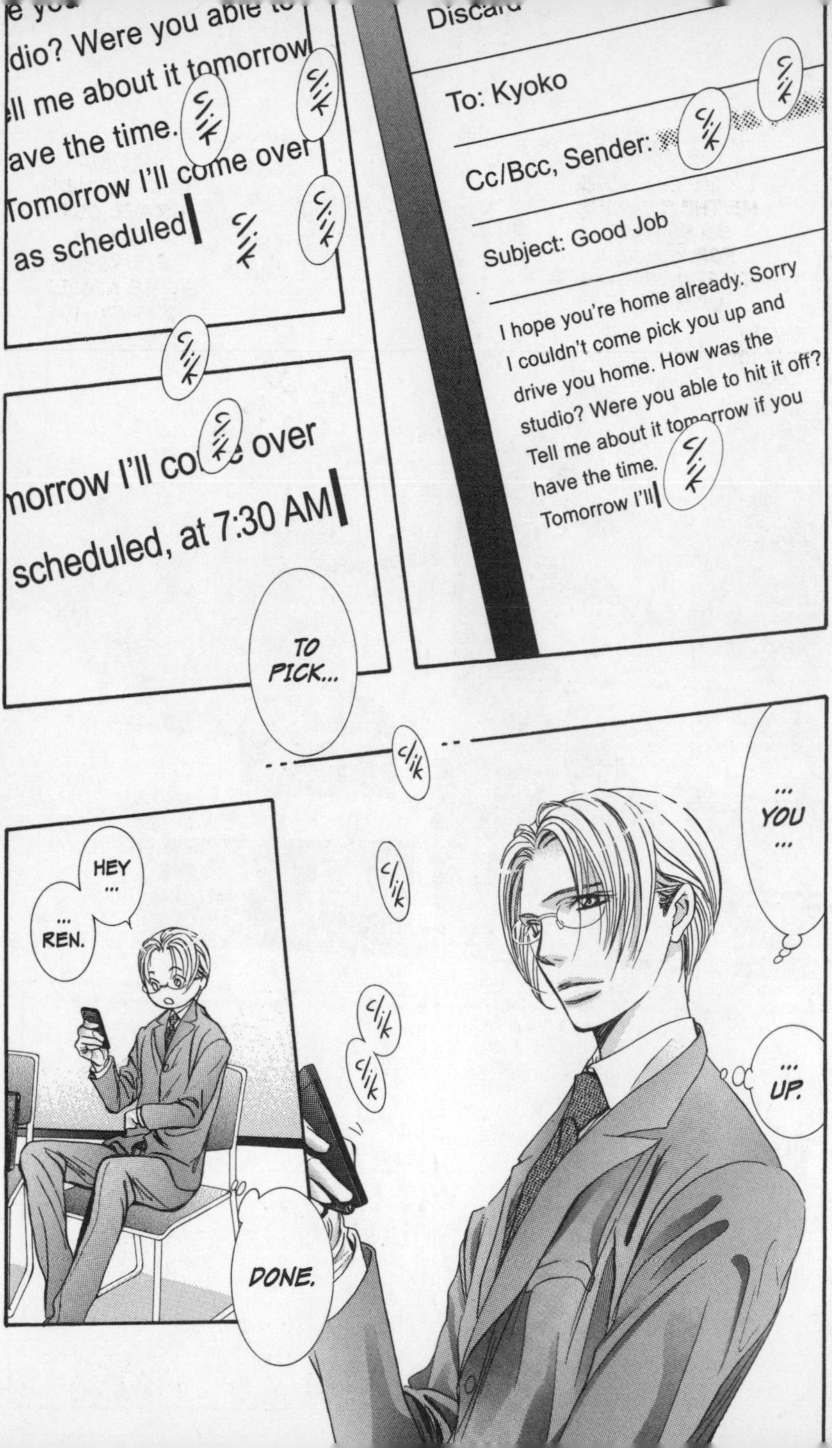

Discard
To: Kyoko
clik
Cc/Bcc, Sender:
clik
Subject: Good Job
I hope you're home already. Sorry I couldn't come pick you up and drive you home. How was the studio? Were you able to hit it off? Tell me about it tomorrow if you have the time.
Tomorrow I'll
clik
dio? Were you able to
ll me about it tomorrow
ave the time.
Tomorrow I'll come over
as scheduled
clik
clik
clik
clik
clik
morrow I'll co e over
scheduled, at 7:30 AM
clik
TO PICK...
clik
... YOU ...
clik
clik
clik
... UP.
DONE.
HEY ...
... REN.

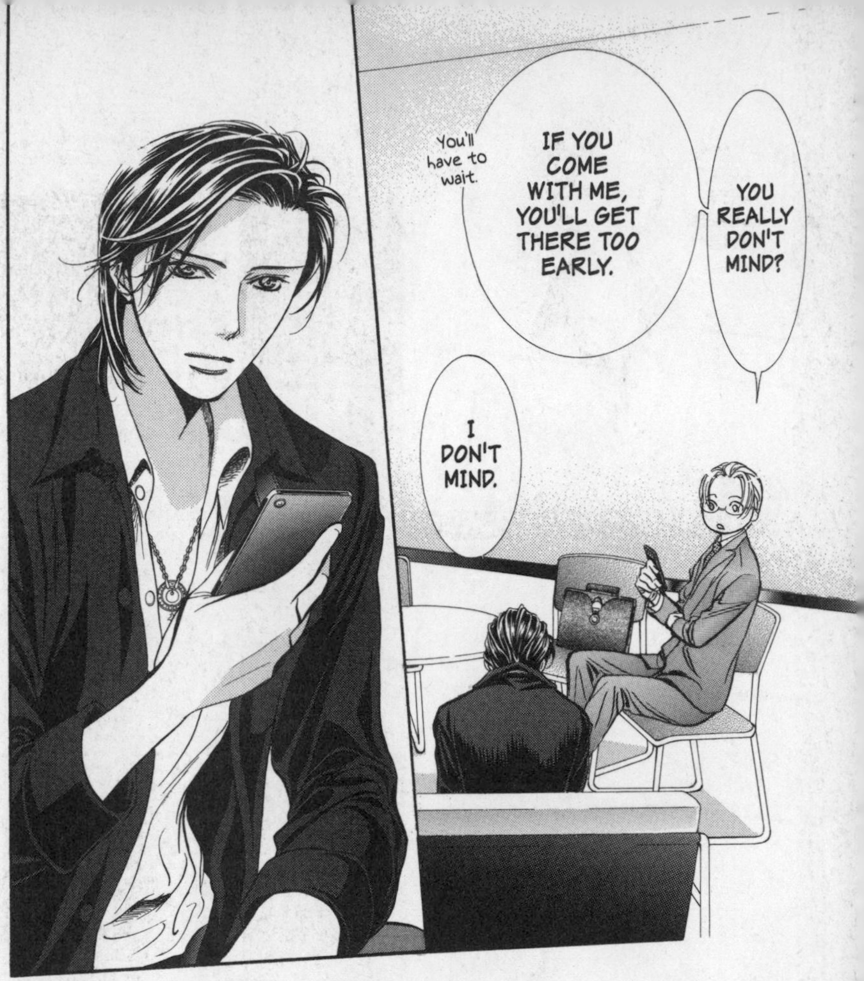
YOU REALLY DON'T MIND?
IF YOU COME WITH ME, YOU'LL GET THERE TOO EARLY.
You'll have to wait.
I DON'T MIND.

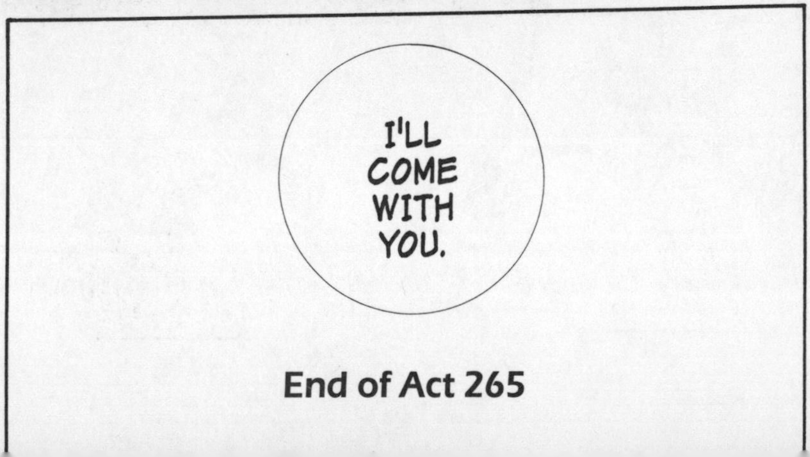
I'LL COME WITH YOU.

End of Act 265

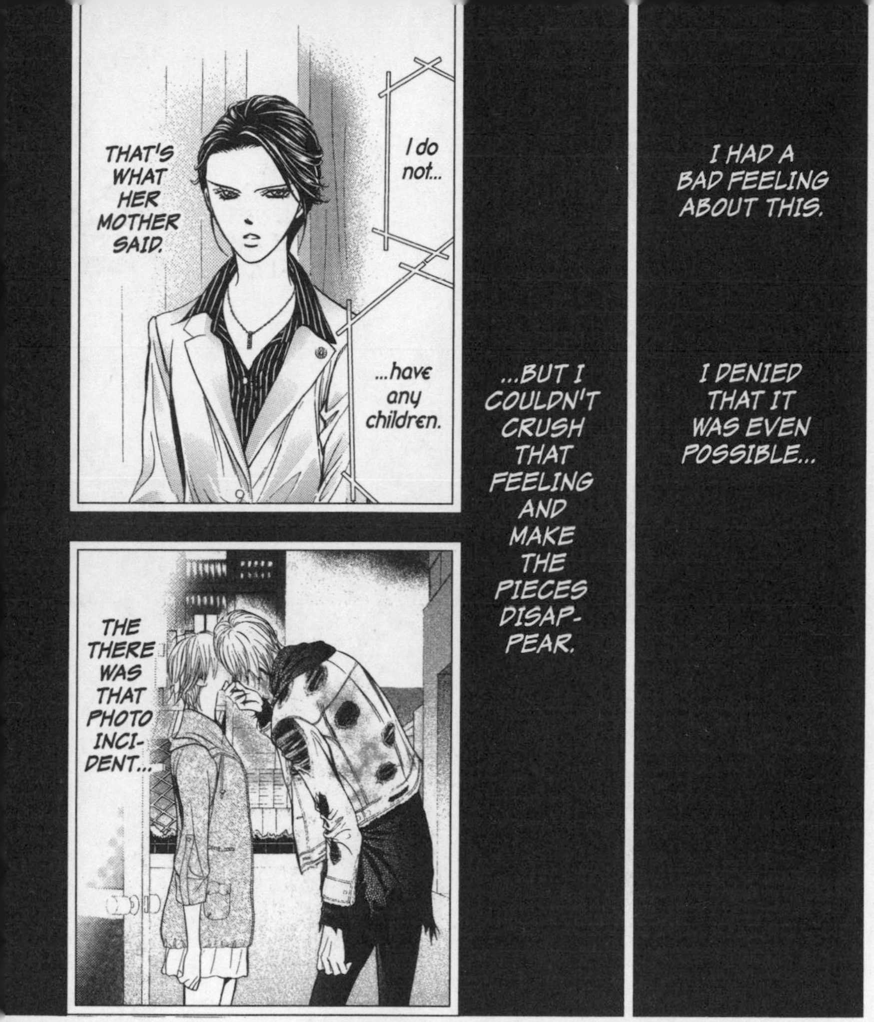
I HAD A BAD FEELING ABOUT THIS.
I DENIED THAT IT WAS EVEN POSSIBLE...
...BUT I COULDN'T CRUSH THAT FEELING AND MAKE THE PIECES DISAP-PEAR.
I do not...
...have any children.
THAT'S WHAT HER MOTHER SAID.
THE THERE WAS THAT PHOTO INCI-DENT...
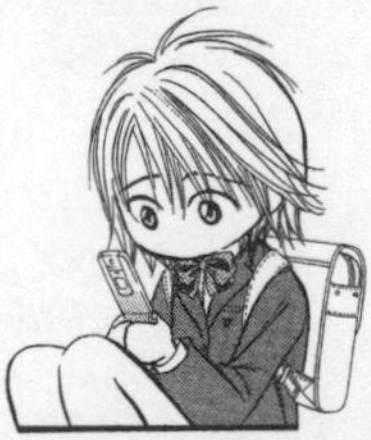

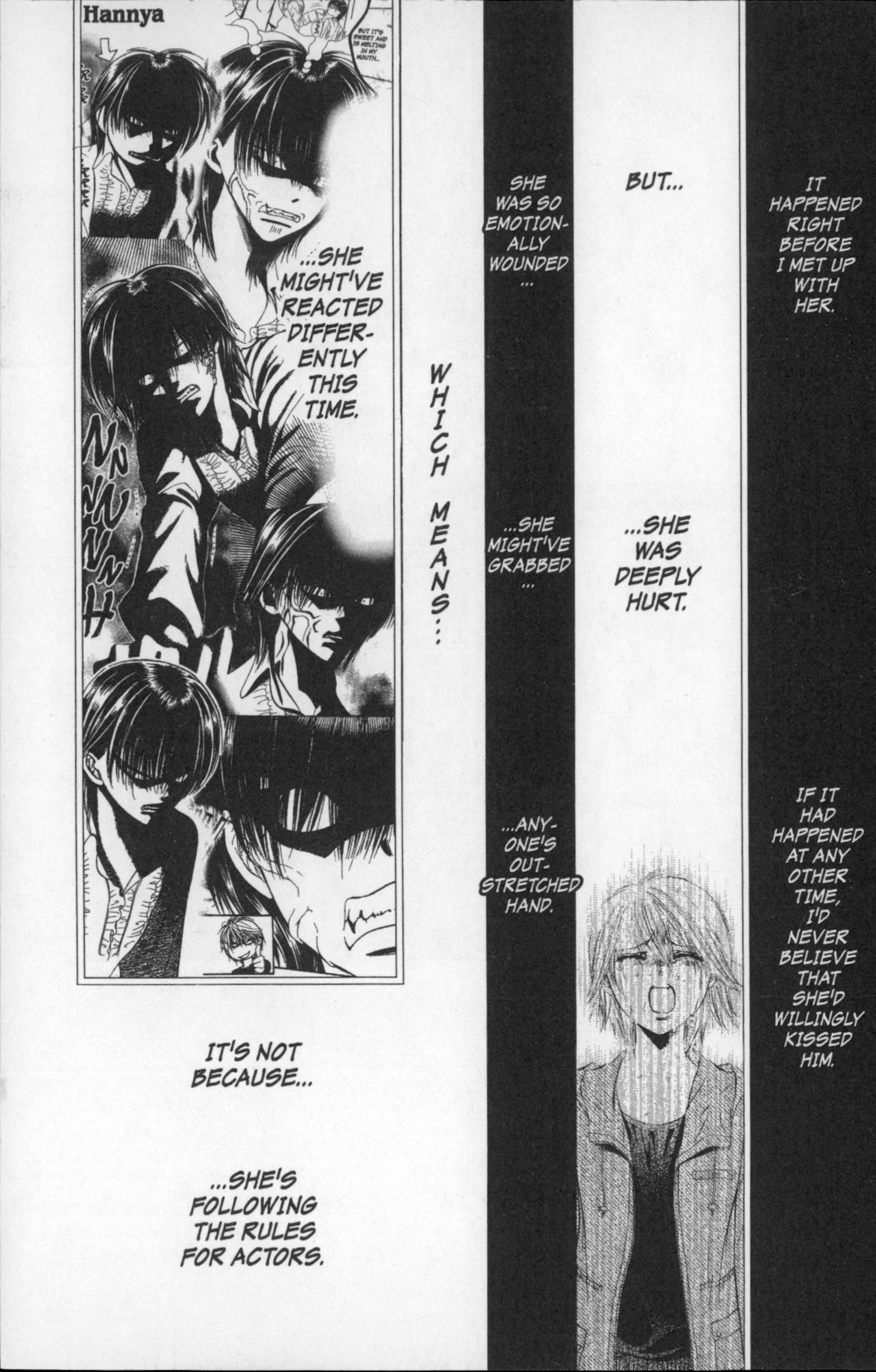
IT HAPPENED RIGHT BEFORE I MET UP WITH HER.
IF IT HAD HAPPENED AT ANY OTHER TIME, I'D NEVER BELIEVE THAT SHE'D WILLINGLY KISSED HIM.
BUT...
...SHE WAS DEEPLY HURT.
SHE WAS SO EMOTIONALLY WOUNDED...
...SHE MIGHT'VE GRABBED...
...ANYONE'S OUTSTRETCHED HAND.
WHICH MEANS...
Hannya
BUT IT'S SWEET AND IS MELTING IN MY MOUTH...
...SHE MIGHT'VE REACTED DIFFERENTLY THIS TIME.
IT'S NOT BECAUSE...
...SHE'S FOLLOWING THE RULES FOR ACTORS.

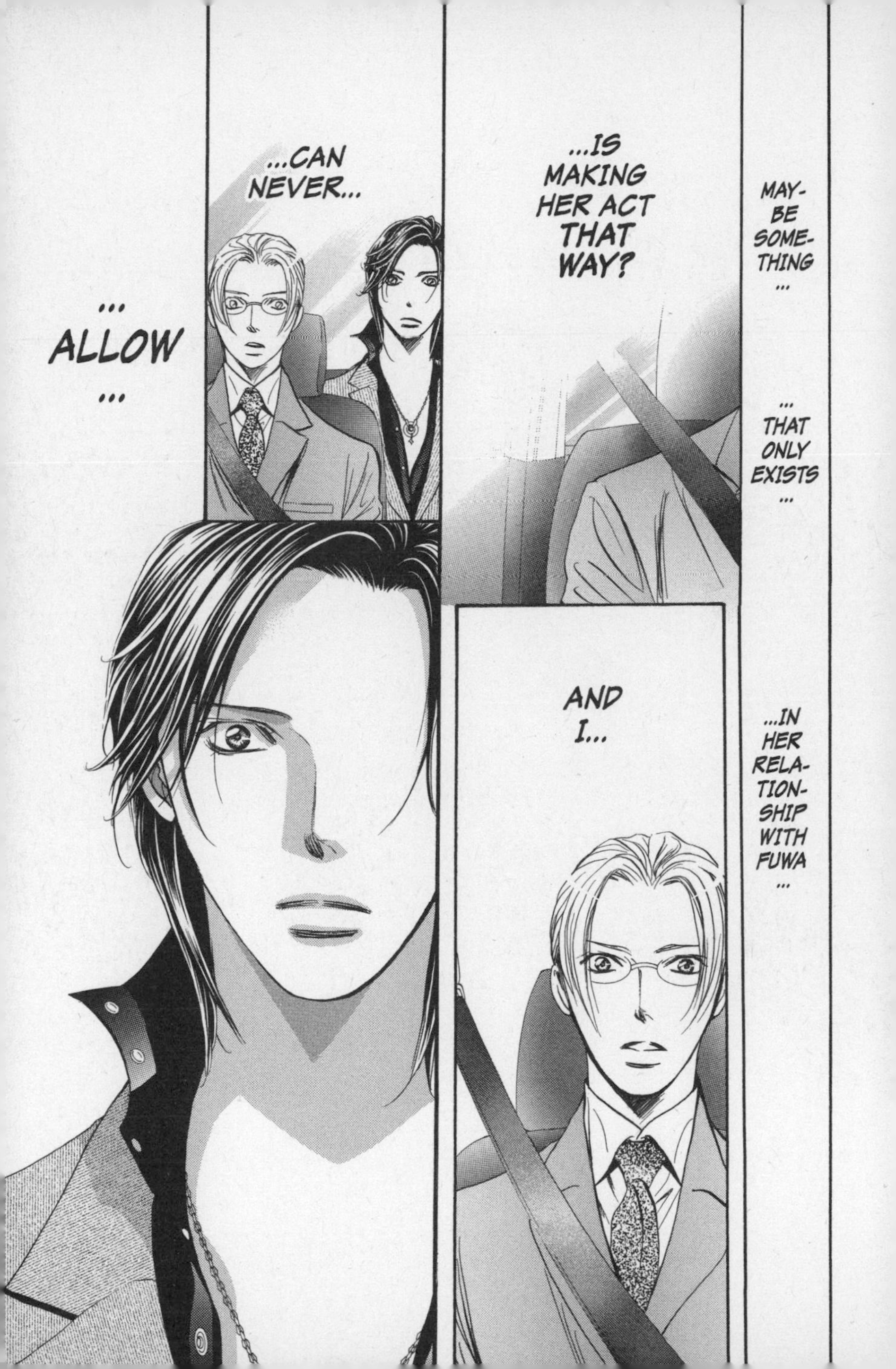
MAY-BE SOME-THING ...
... THAT ONLY EXISTS ...
...IN HER RELA-TION-SHIP WITH FUWA ...
...IS MAKING HER ACT THAT WAY?
...CAN NEVER...
... ALLOW ...
AND I...

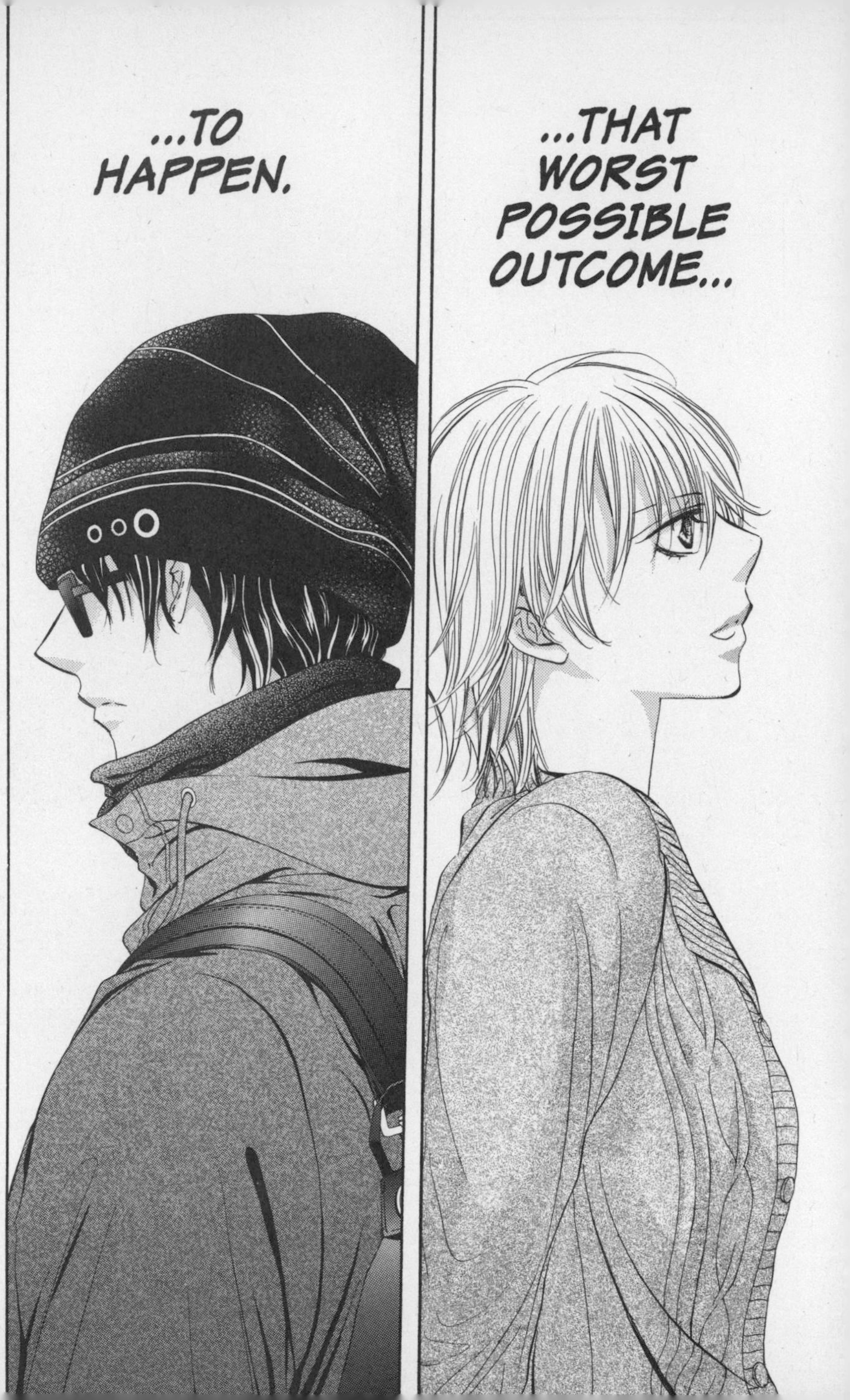
...THAT WORST POSSIBLE OUTCOME...
...TO HAPPEN.

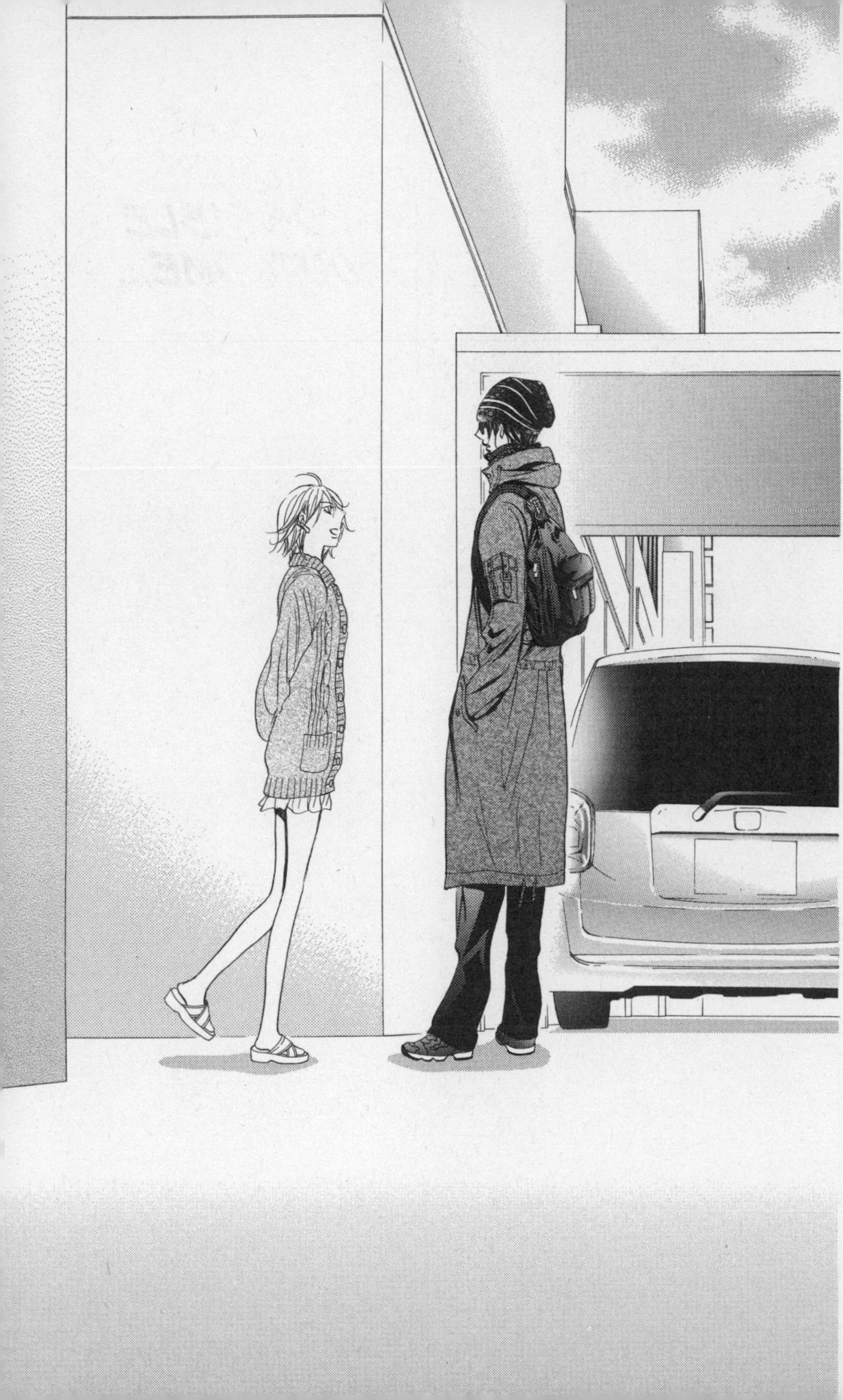

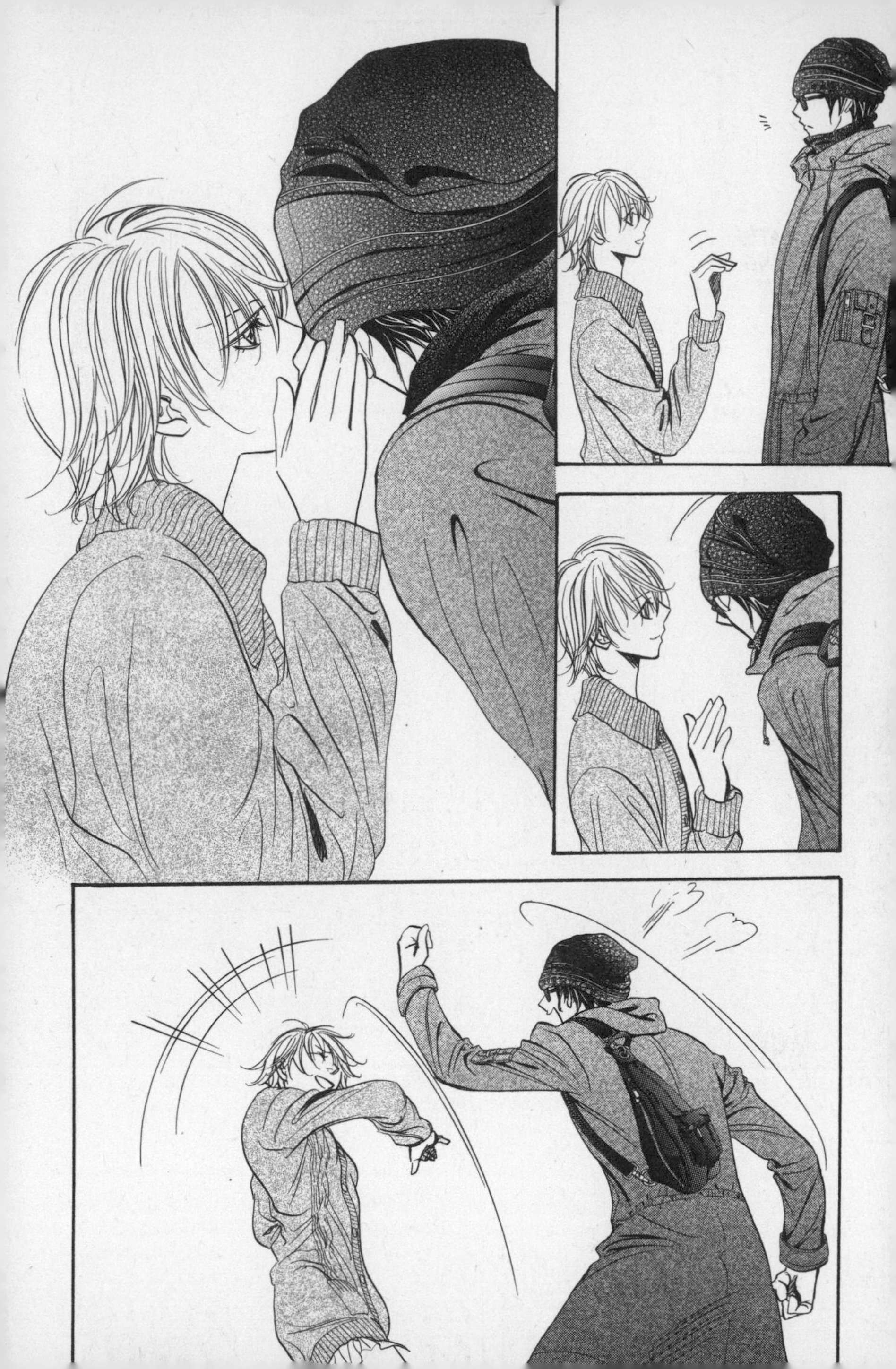

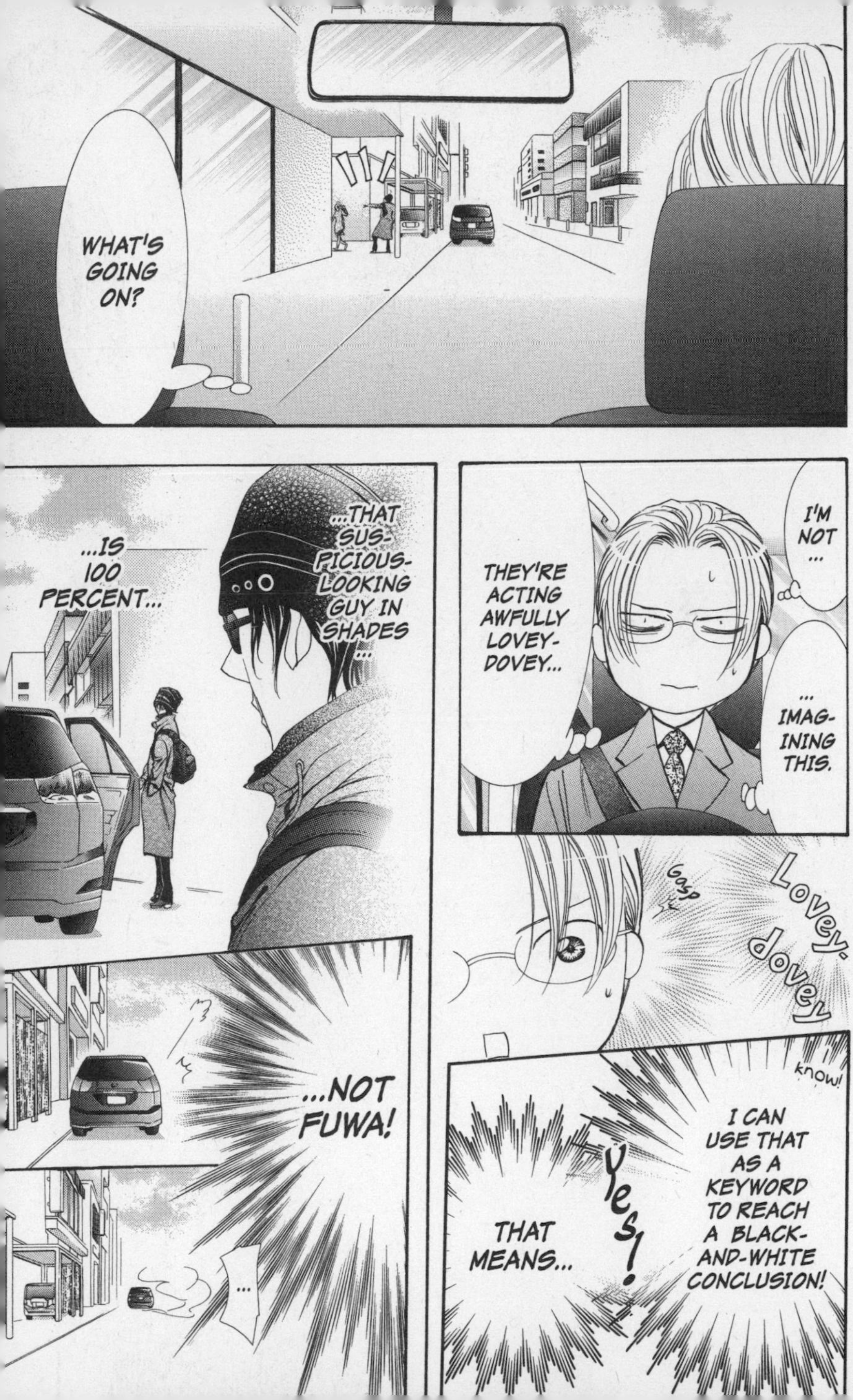
WHAT'S GOING ON?
I'M NOT...
THEY'RE ACTING AWFULLY LOVEY-DOVEY...
...IMAGINING THIS.
Lovey-dovey
Gasp
know!
I CAN USE THAT AS A KEYWORD TO REACH A BLACK-AND-WHITE CONCLUSION!
Yes!
THAT MEANS...
...THAT SUS-PICIOUS-LOOKING GUY IN SHADES...
...IS 100 PERCENT...
...NOT FUWA!
...

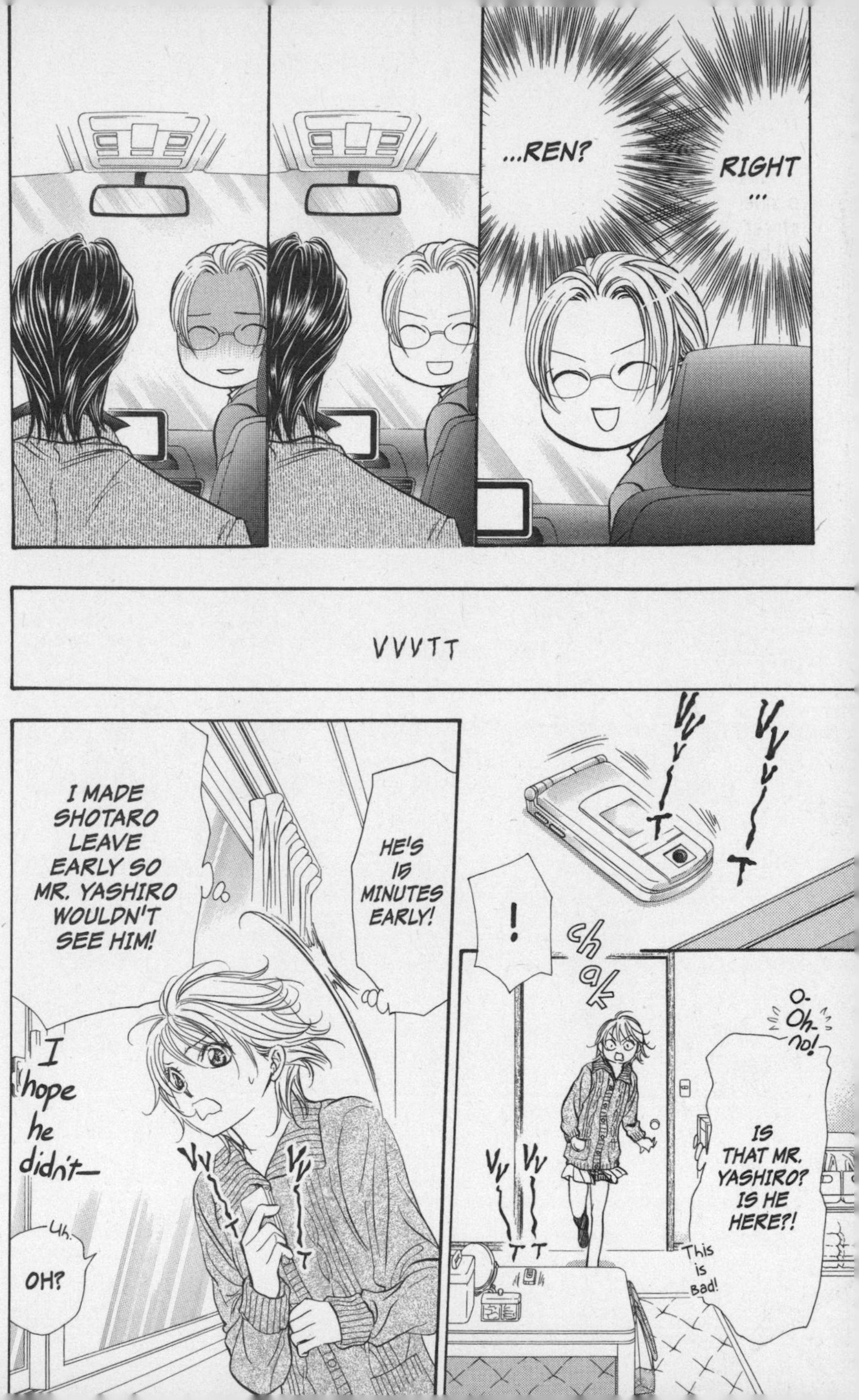
RIGHT ...
...REN?
VVVTT
VVVVT
VVVVT
!
chak
O-Oh-no!
IS THAT MR. YASHIRO? IS HE HERE?!
This is bad!
VV T
VV T
HE'S 15 MINUTES EARLY!
I MADE SHOTARO LEAVE EARLY SO MR. YASHIRO WOULDN'T SEE HIM!
I hope he didn't—
VV T
VV T
Uh.
OH?

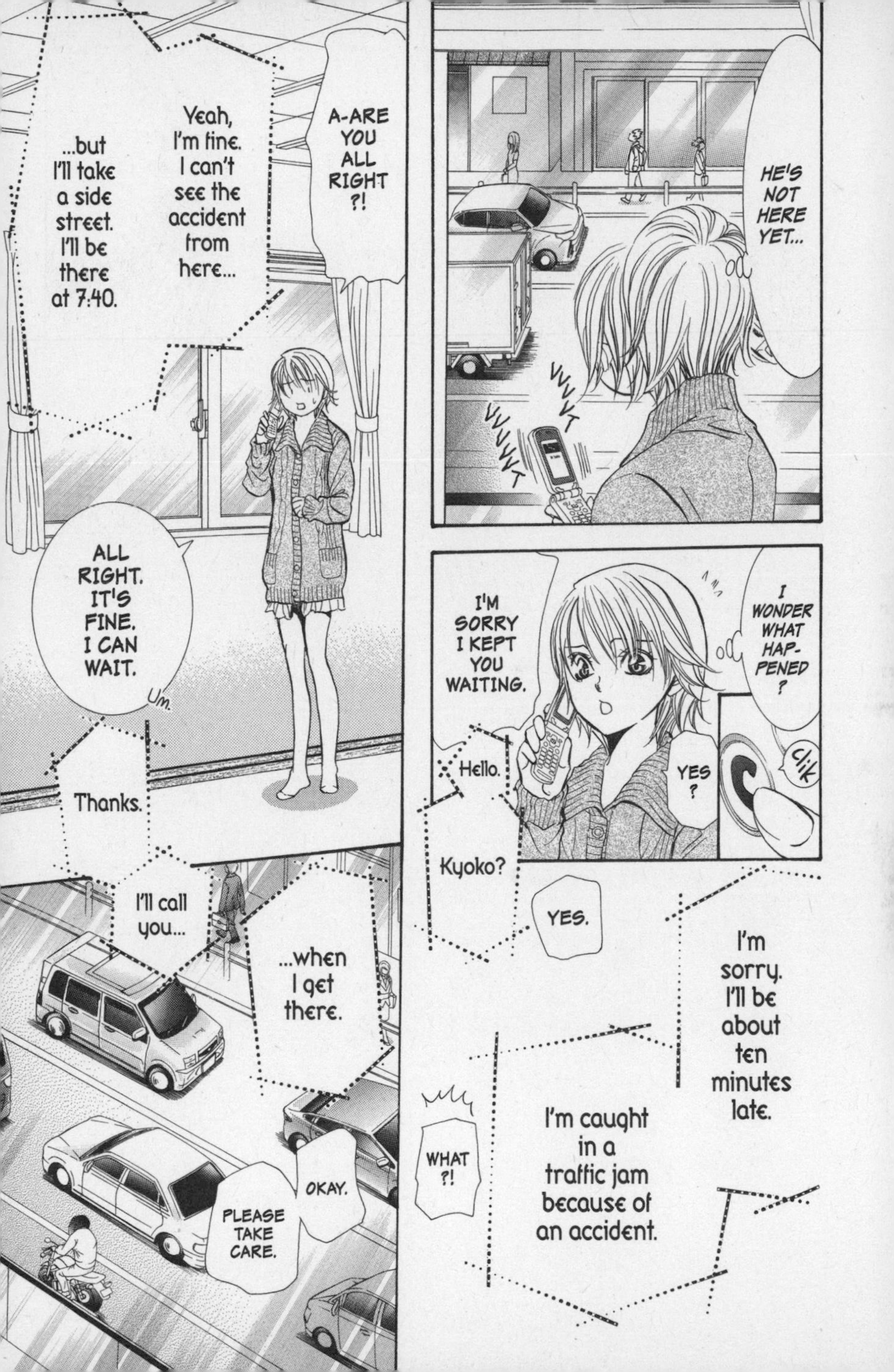

HE'S NOT HERE YET...
VVVVT
VVVVVT
I WONDER WHAT HAP-PENED?
CLIK
YES?
I'M SORRY I KEPT YOU WAITING.
Hello.
Kyoko?
YES.
I'm sorry. I'll be about ten minutes late.
I'm caught in a traffic jam because of an accident.
WHAT?!
A-ARE YOU ALL RIGHT?!
Yeah, I'm fine. I can't see the accident from here...
...but I'll take a side street. I'll be there at 7:40.
ALL RIGHT. IT'S FINE. I CAN WAIT.
Um.
Thanks.
I'll call you...
...when I get there.
OKAY.
PLEASE TAKE CARE.

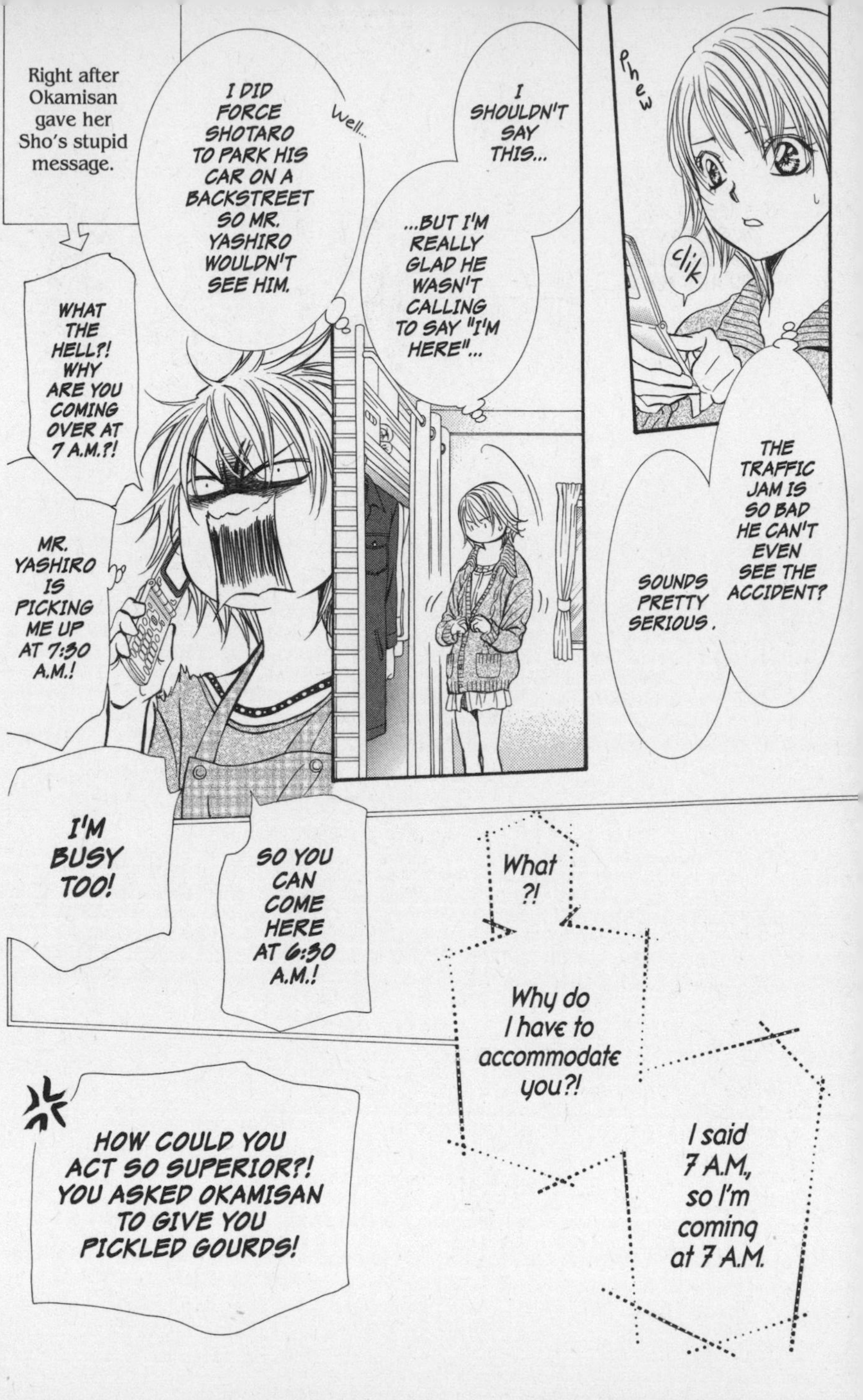
Phew
clik
THE TRAFFIC JAM IS SO BAD HE CAN'T EVEN SEE THE ACCIDENT?
SOUNDS PRETTY SERIOUS.
I SHOULDN'T SAY THIS...
...BUT I'M REALLY GLAD HE WASN'T CALLING TO SAY "I'M HERE"...
Well...
I DID FORCE SHOTARO TO PARK HIS CAR ON A BACKSTREET SO MR. YASHIRO WOULDN'T SEE HIM.
Right after Okamisan gave her Sho's stupid message.
WHAT THE HELL?! WHY ARE YOU COMING OVER AT 7 A.M.?!
MR. YASHIRO IS PICKING ME UP AT 7:30 A.M.!
I'M BUSY TOO!
SO YOU CAN COME HERE AT 6:30 A.M.!
What?!
Why do I have to accommodate you?!
I said 7 A.M., so I'm coming at 7 A.M.
HOW COULD YOU ACT SO SUPERIOR?! YOU ASKED OKAMISAN TO GIVE YOU PICKLED GOURDS!

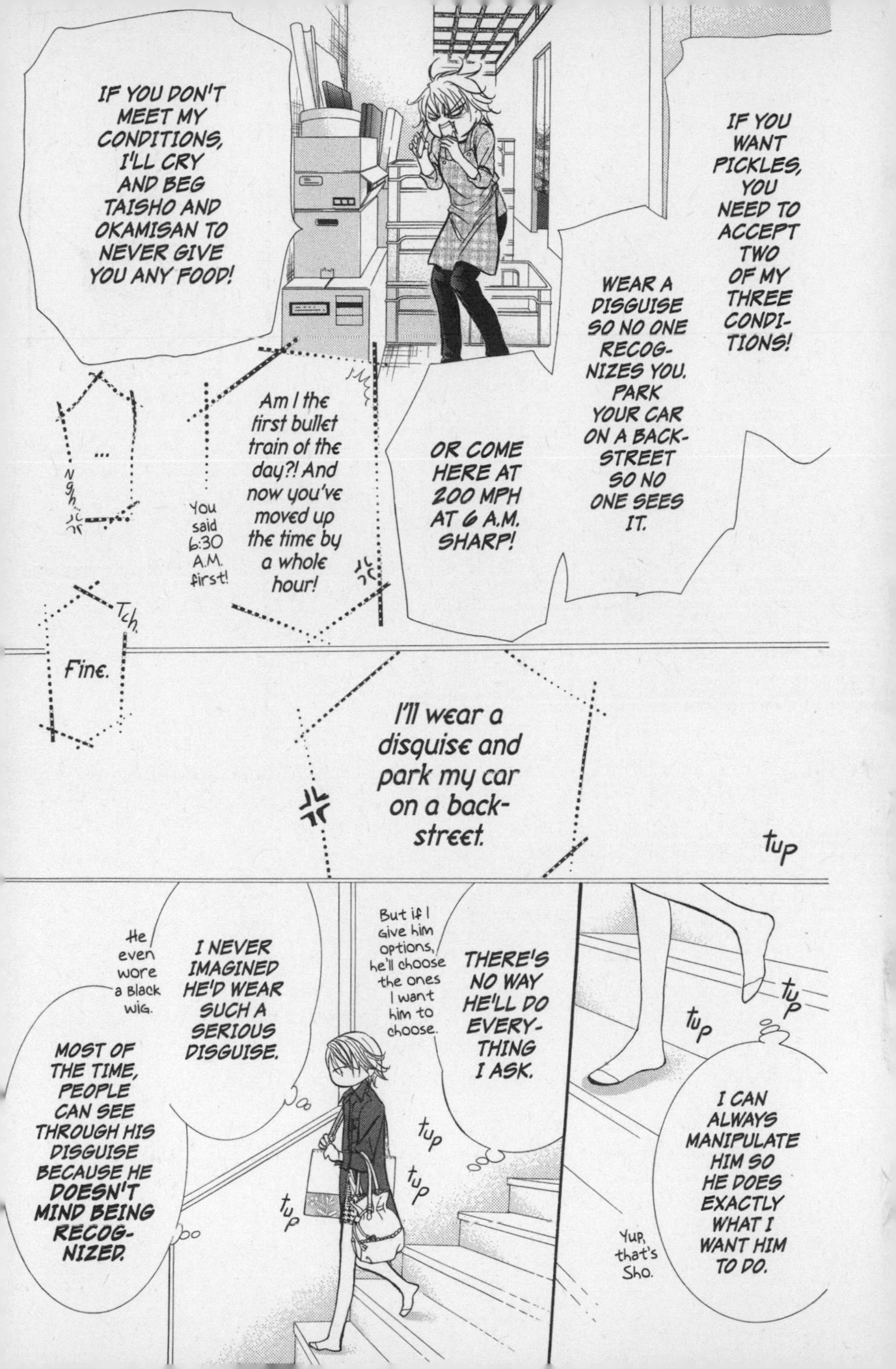
IF YOU WANT PICKLES, YOU NEED TO ACCEPT TWO OF MY THREE CONDITIONS!
WEAR A DISGUISE SO NO ONE RECOGNIZES YOU. PARK YOUR CAR ON A BACKSTREET SO NO ONE SEES IT.
OR COME HERE AT 200 MPH AT 6 A.M. SHARP!
IF YOU DON'T MEET MY CONDITIONS, I'LL CRY AND BEG TAISHO AND OKAMISAN TO NEVER GIVE YOU ANY FOOD!
Am I the first bullet train of the day?! And now you've moved up the time by a whole hour!
You said 6:30 A.M. first!
...
Ngh...
Tch.
Fine.
I'll wear a disguise and park my car on a backstreet.
tup
tup
tup
I CAN ALWAYS MANIPULATE HIM SO HE DOES EXACTLY WHAT I WANT HIM TO DO.
Yup, that's Sho.
THERE'S NO WAY HE'LL DO EVERYTHING I ASK.
But if I give him options, he'll choose the ones I want him to choose.
I NEVER IMAGINED HE'D WEAR SUCH A SERIOUS DISGUISE.
He even wore a black wig.
MOST OF THE TIME, PEOPLE CAN SEE THROUGH HIS DISGUISE BECAUSE HE DOESN'T MIND BEING RECOGNIZED.
tup
tup
tup

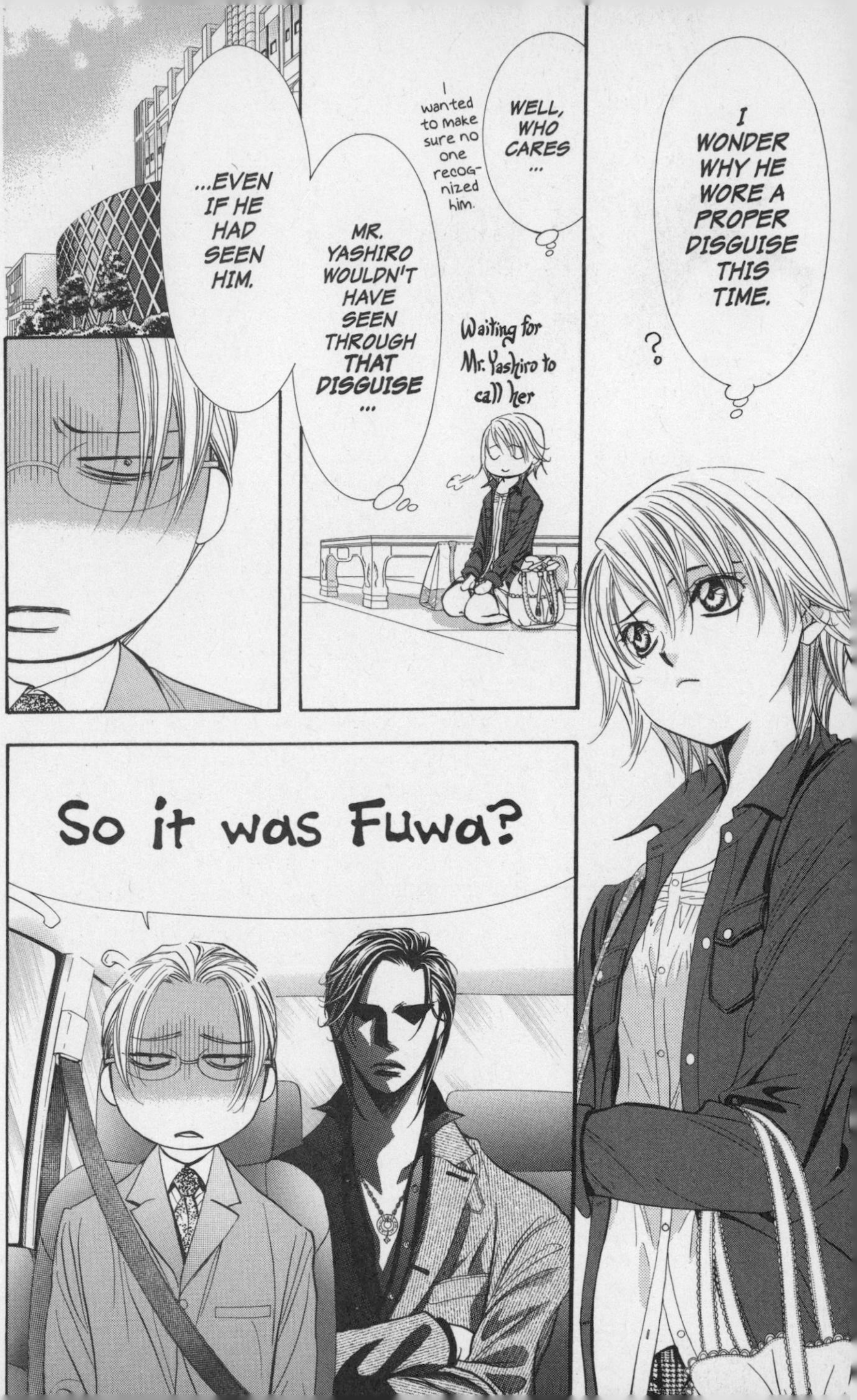
I WONDER WHY HE WORE A PROPER DISGUISE THIS TIME.
?
WELL, WHO CARES...
I wanted to make sure no one recognized him.
Waiting for Mr. Yashiro to call her
MR. YASHIRO WOULDN'T HAVE SEEN THROUGH THAT DISGUISE...
...EVEN IF HE HAD SEEN HIM.
So it was Fuwa?

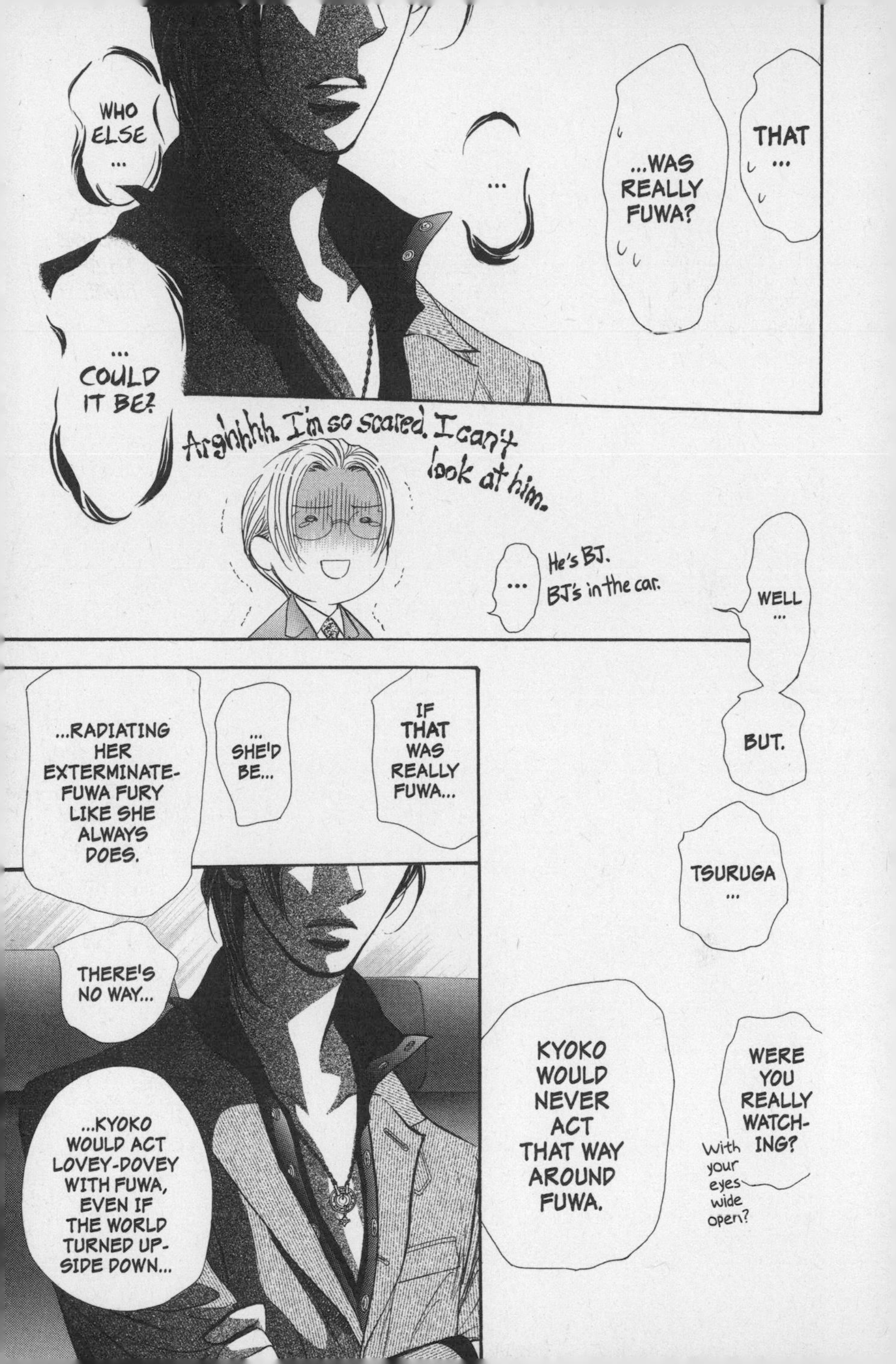

THAT...
...WAS REALLY FUWA?
...
WHO ELSE...
...COULD IT BE?
WELL...
Arghhhh. I'm so scared. I can't look at him.
...
He's BJ. BJ's in the car.
BUT.
TSURUGA...
IF THAT WAS REALLY FUWA...
...SHE'D BE...
...RADIATING HER EXTERMINATE-FUWA FURY LIKE SHE ALWAYS DOES.
THERE'S NO WAY...
...KYOKO WOULD ACT LOVEY-DOVEY WITH FUWA, EVEN IF THE WORLD TURNED UP-SIDE DOWN...
WERE YOU REALLY WATCH-ING?
With your eyes wide open?
KYOKO WOULD NEVER ACT THAT WAY AROUND FUWA.

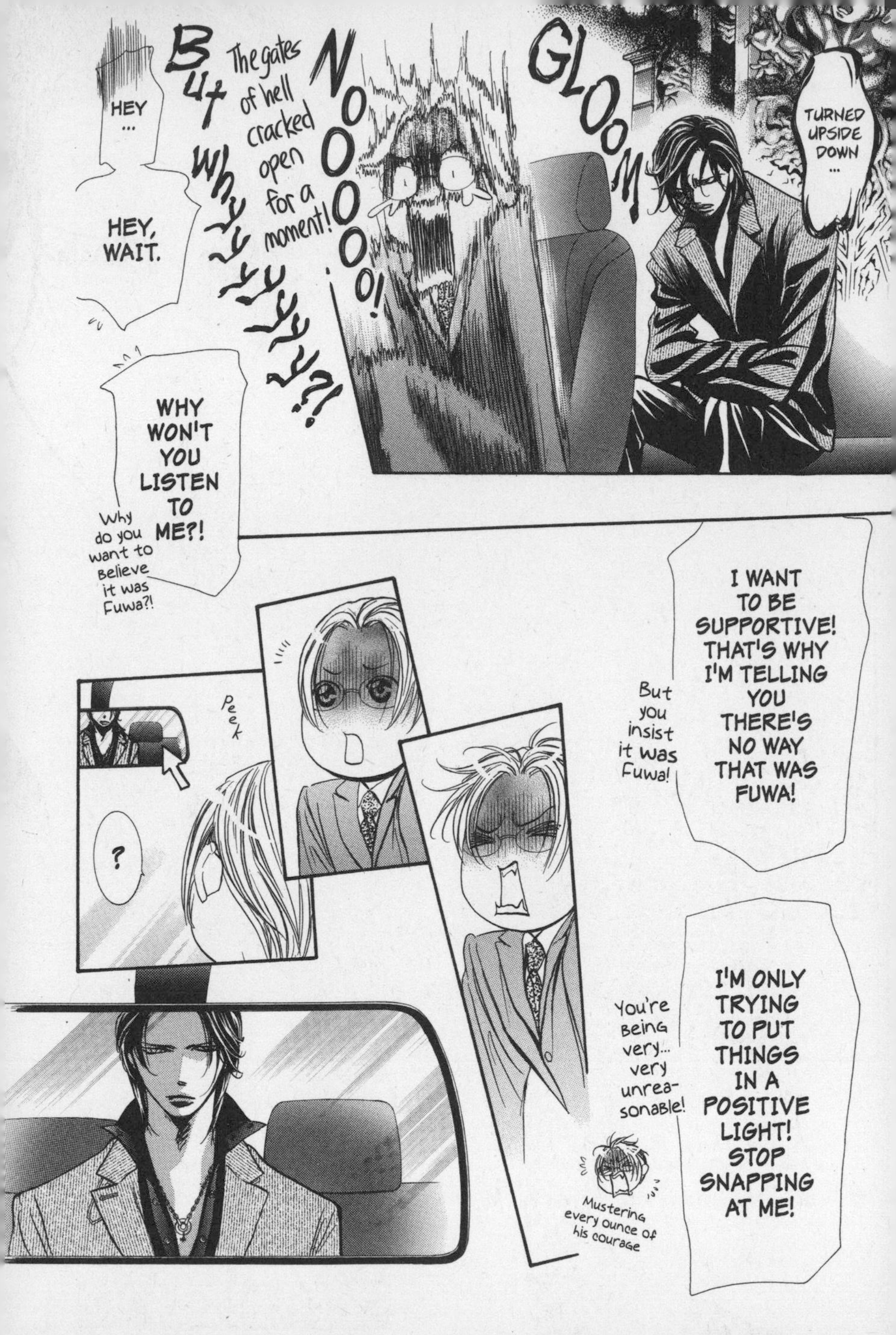
TURNED UPSIDE DOWN ...
GLOOM
NOOOOOO!
The gates of hell cracked open for a moment!
But whyyyyyyy?!
HEY ...
HEY, WAIT.
WHY WON'T YOU LISTEN TO ME?!
Why do you want to believe it was Fuwa?!
I WANT TO BE SUPPORTIVE! THAT'S WHY I'M TELLING YOU THERE'S NO WAY THAT WAS FUWA!
But you insist it was Fuwa!
Peek
?
I'M ONLY TRYING TO PUT THINGS IN A POSITIVE LIGHT! STOP SNAPPING AT ME!
You're being very... very unreasonable!
Mustering every ounce of his courage

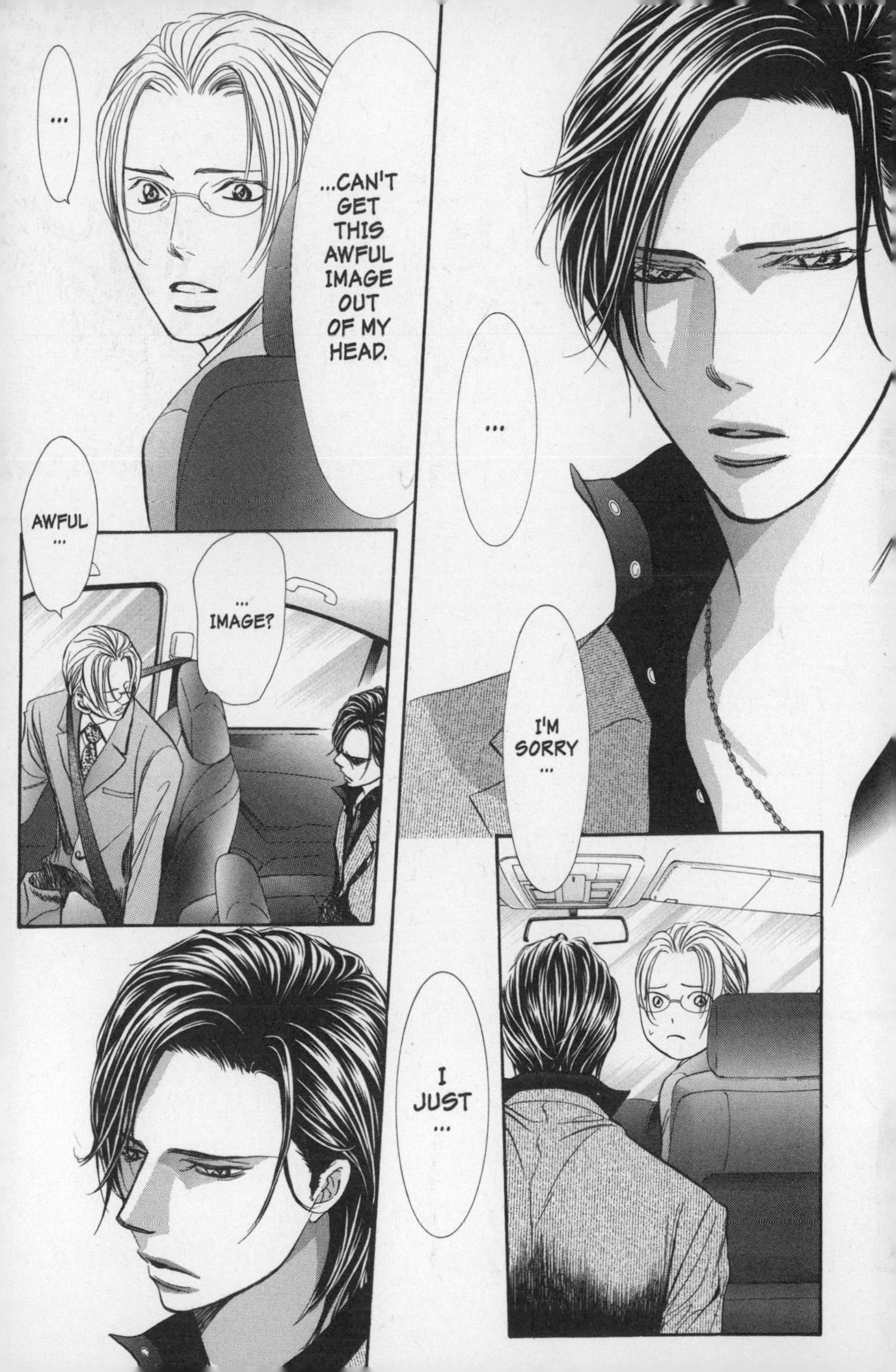
...
I'M SORRY ...
...CAN'T GET THIS AWFUL IMAGE OUT OF MY HEAD.
...
AWFUL ...
... IMAGE?
I JUST ...

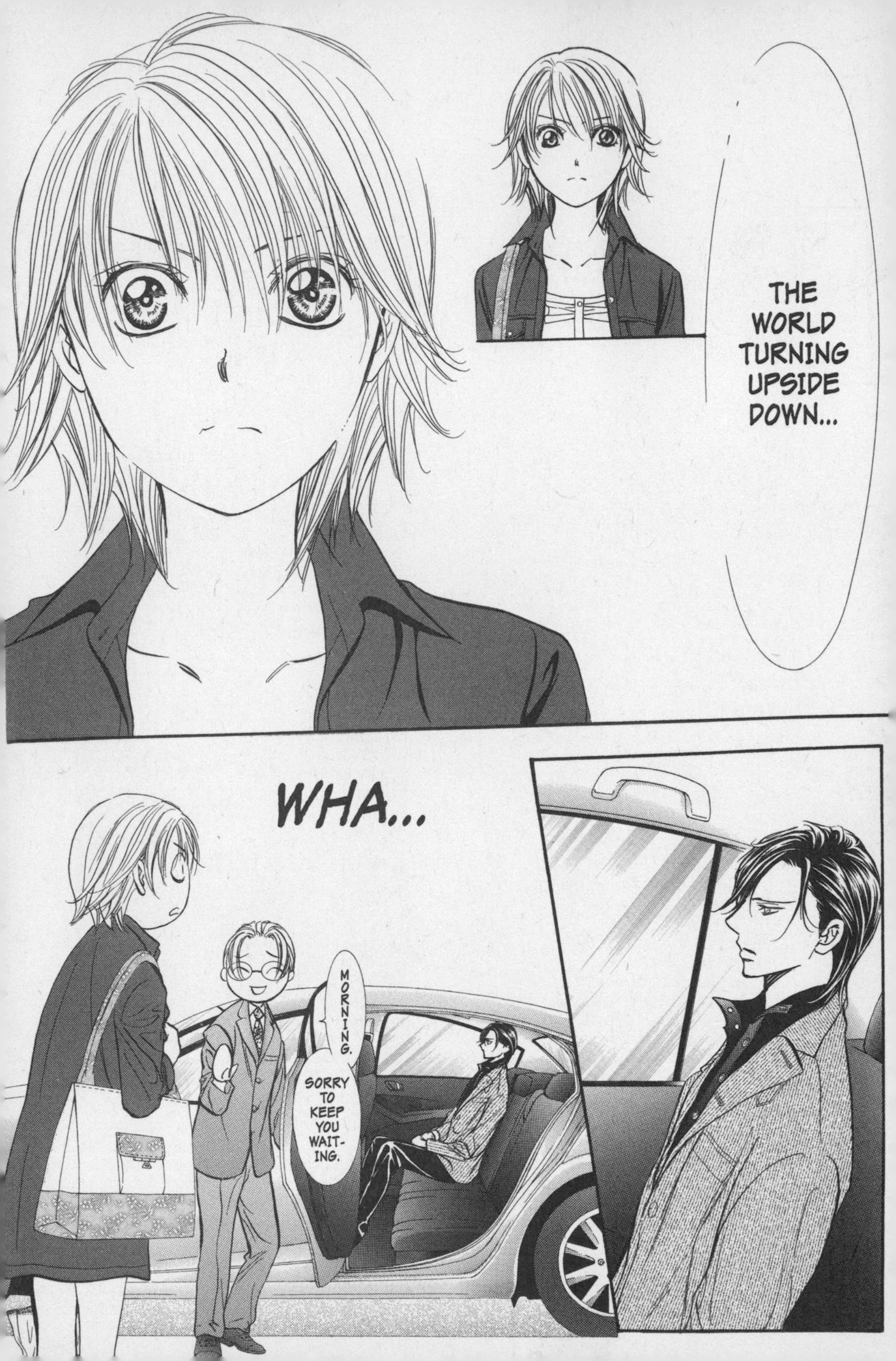

THE WORLD TURNING UPSIDE DOWN...
WHA...
MORNING.
SORRY TO KEEP YOU WAIT-ING.

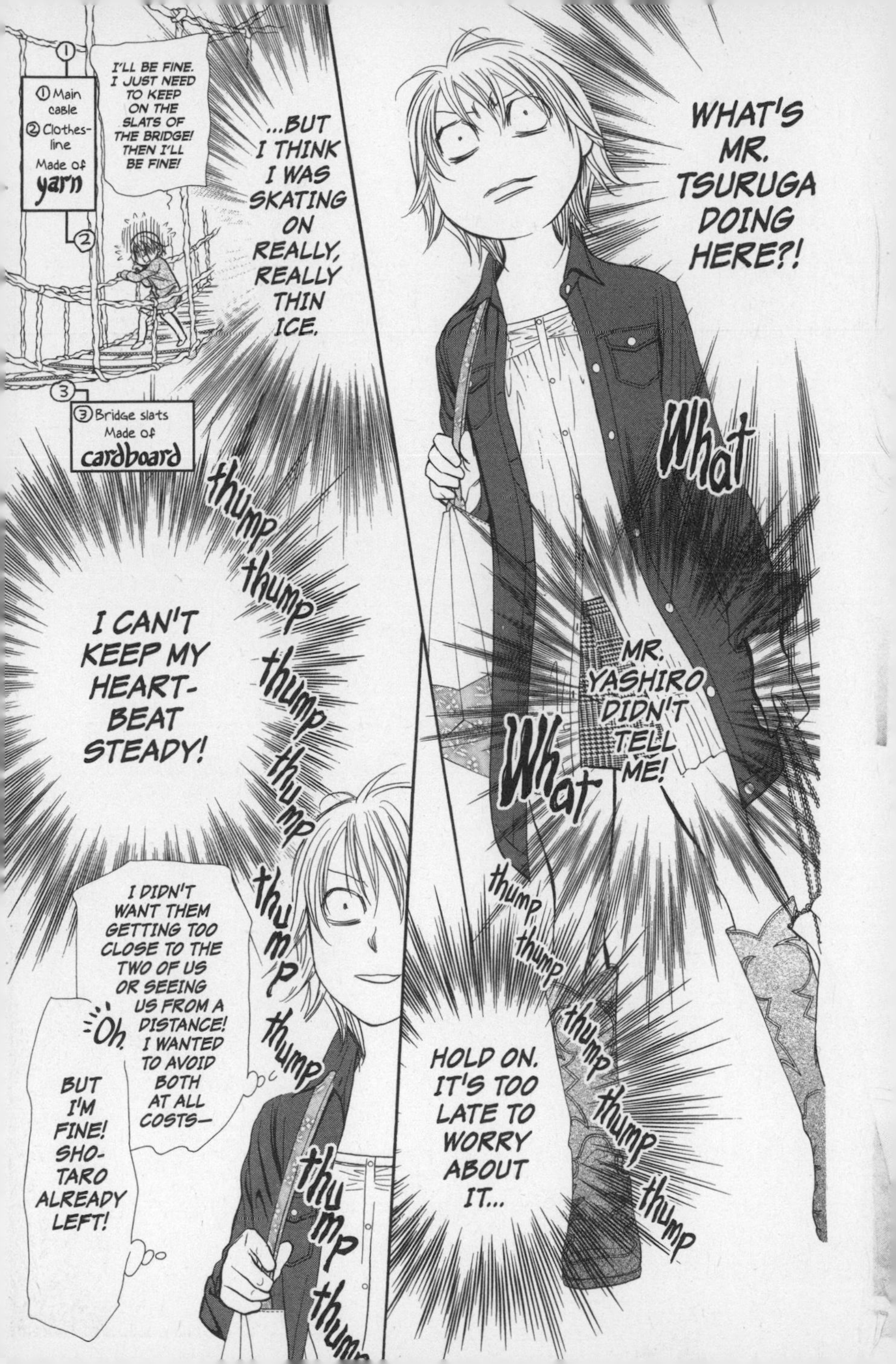
WHAT'S MR. TSURUGA DOING HERE?!
What
What
MR. YASHIRO DIDN'T TELL ME!
thump thump
thump thump thump
HOLD ON. IT'S TOO LATE TO WORRY ABOUT IT...
...BUT I THINK I WAS SKATING ON REALLY, REALLY THIN ICE.
I'LL BE FINE. I JUST NEED TO KEEP ON THE SLATS OF THE BRIDGE! THEN I'LL BE FINE!
① Main cable
② Clothes-line
Made of yarn
③ Bridge slats
Made of cardboard
thump thump thump thump thump thump thump thump thump thump
I CAN'T KEEP MY HEART-BEAT STEADY!
I DIDN'T WANT THEM GETTING TOO CLOSE TO THE TWO OF US OR SEEING US FROM A DISTANCE! I WANTED TO AVOID BOTH AT ALL COSTS—
Oh.
BUT I'M FINE! SHO-TARO ALREADY LEFT!

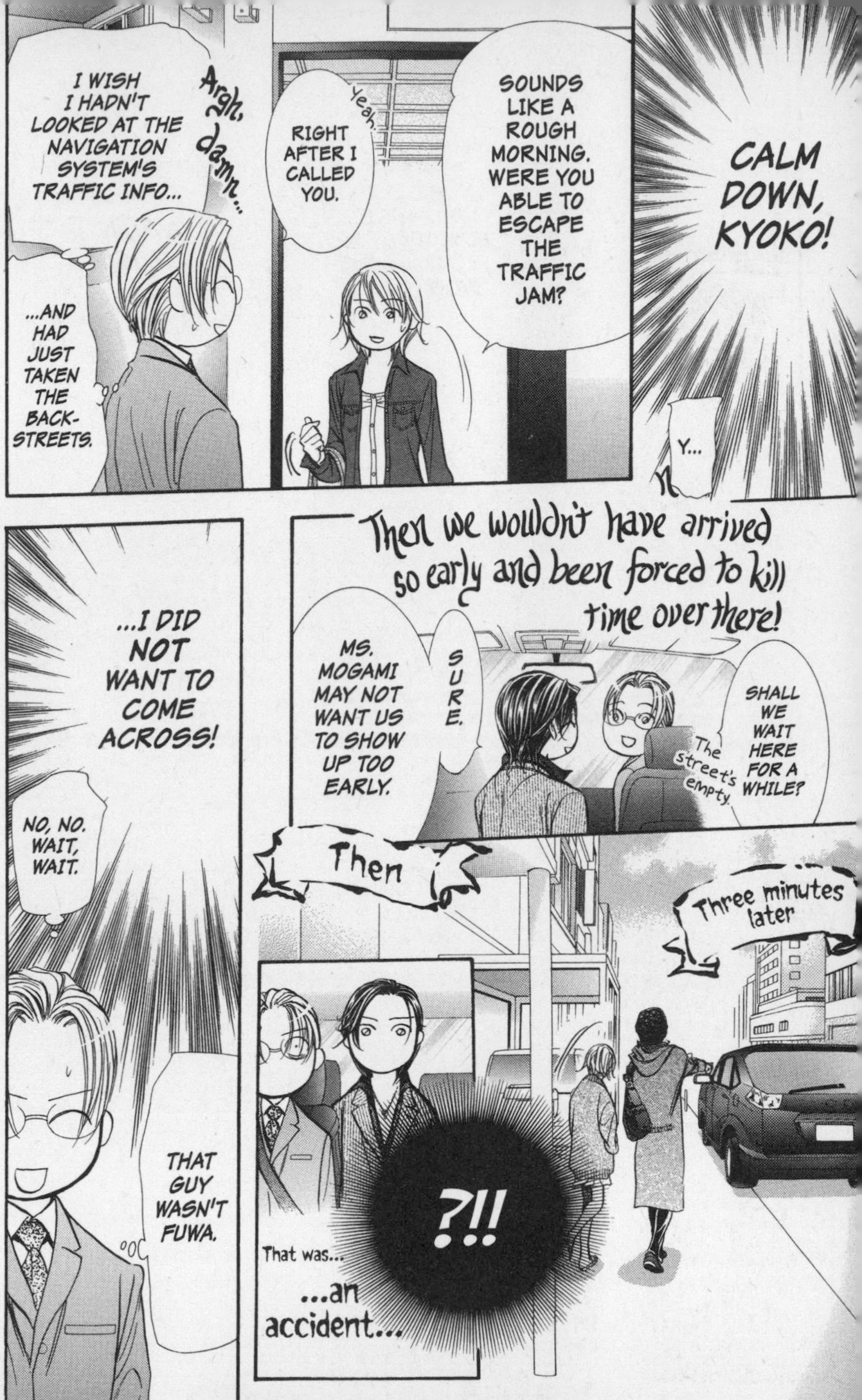
CALM DOWN, KYOKO!
Y...
SOUNDS LIKE A ROUGH MORNING. WERE YOU ABLE TO ESCAPE THE TRAFFIC JAM?
Yeah.
RIGHT AFTER I CALLED YOU.
Argh, damn...
I WISH I HADN'T LOOKED AT THE NAVIGATION SYSTEM'S TRAFFIC INFO...
...AND HAD JUST TAKEN THE BACK-STREETS.
Then we wouldn't have arrived so early and been forced to kill time over there!
SHALL WE WAIT HERE FOR A WHILE?
The street's empty.
SURE.
MS. MOGAMI MAY NOT WANT US TO SHOW UP TOO EARLY.
Then
Three minutes later
?!!
That was...
...an accident...
...I DID NOT WANT TO COME ACROSS!
NO, NO. WAIT, WAIT.
THAT GUY WASN'T FUWA.

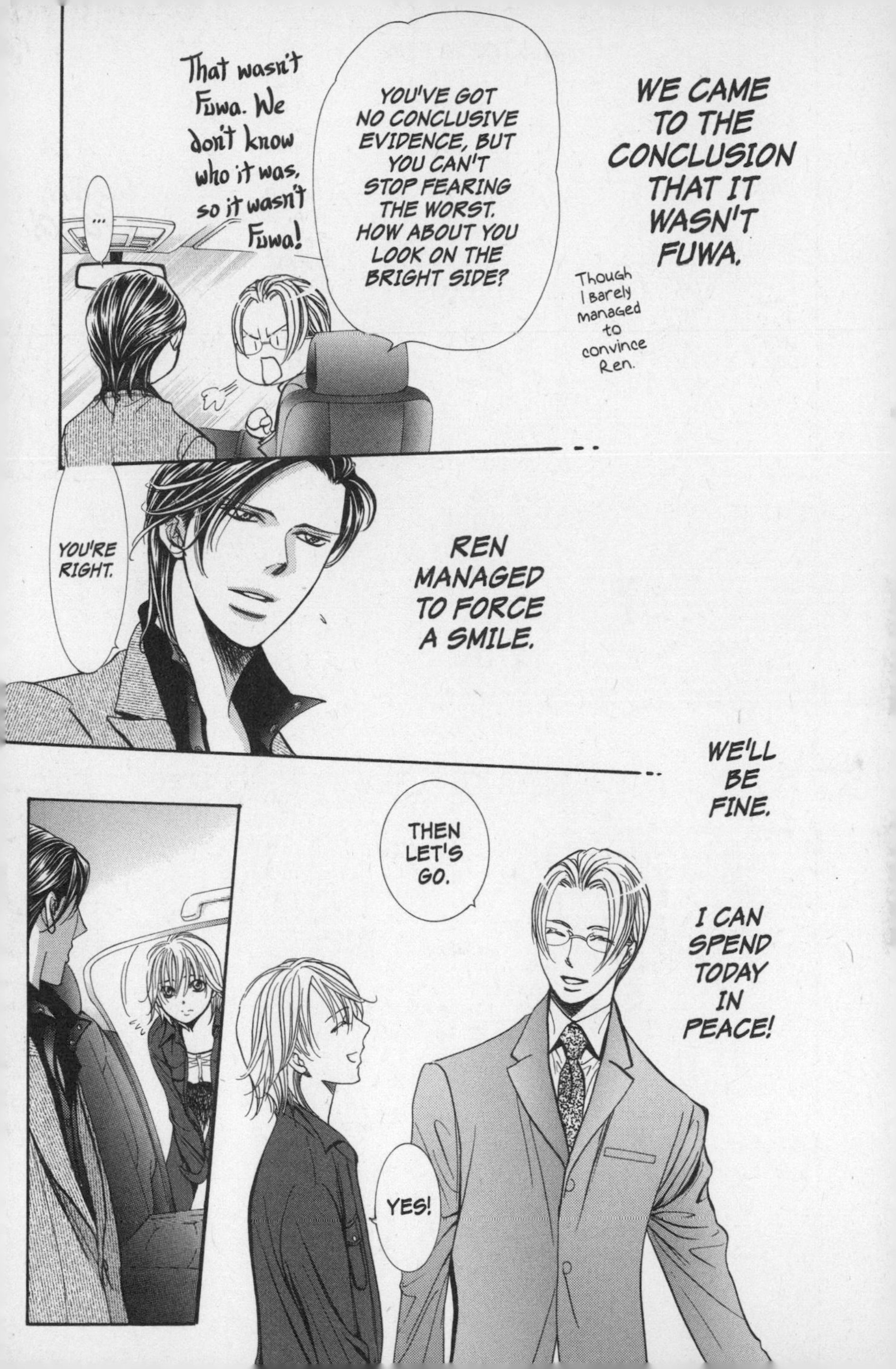
WE CAME TO THE CONCLUSION THAT IT WASN'T FUWA.
Though I barely managed to convince Ren.
YOU'VE GOT NO CONCLUSIVE EVIDENCE, BUT YOU CAN'T STOP FEARING THE WORST. HOW ABOUT YOU LOOK ON THE BRIGHT SIDE?
That wasn't Fuwa. We don't know who it was, so it wasn't Fuwa!
...
REN MANAGED TO FORCE A SMILE.
YOU'RE RIGHT.
WE'LL BE FINE.
I CAN SPEND TODAY IN PEACE!
THEN LET'S GO.
YES!

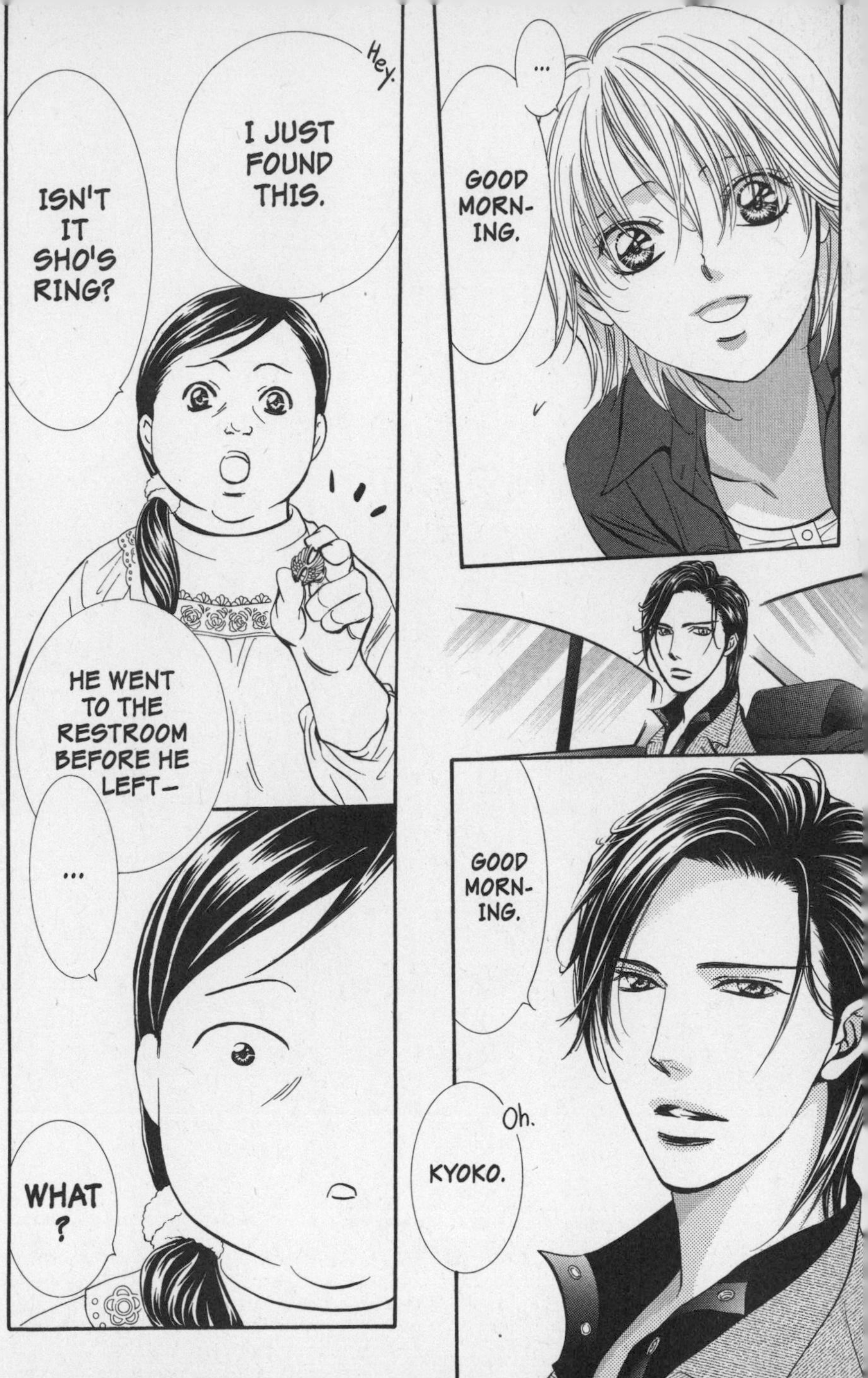
...
GOOD MORN-ING.
GOOD MORN-ING.
Oh.
KYOKO.
Hey.
I JUST FOUND THIS.
ISN'T IT SHO'S RING?
HE WENT TO THE RESTROOM BEFORE HE LEFT—
...
WHAT?

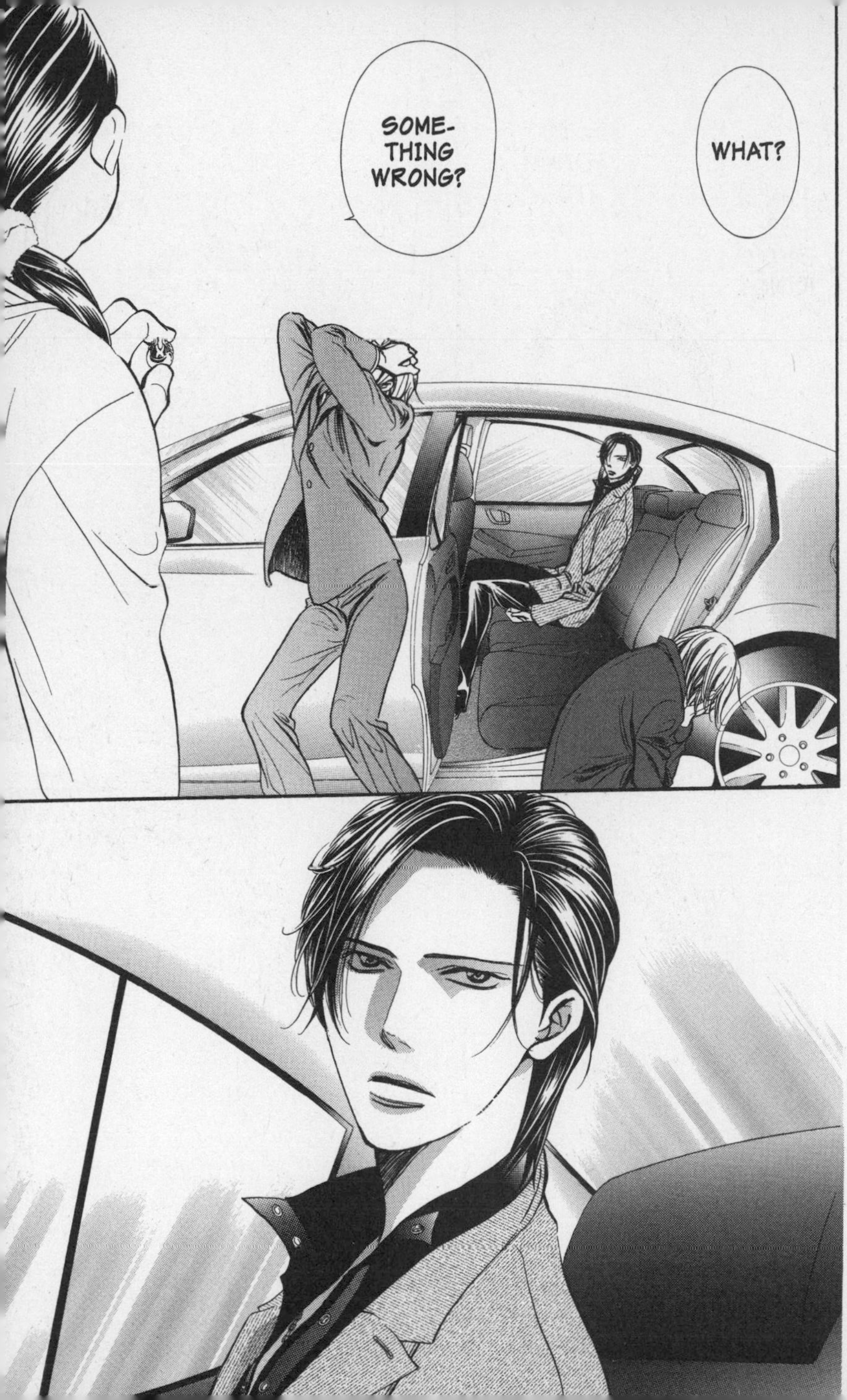
WHAT?
SOME-
THING
WRONG?

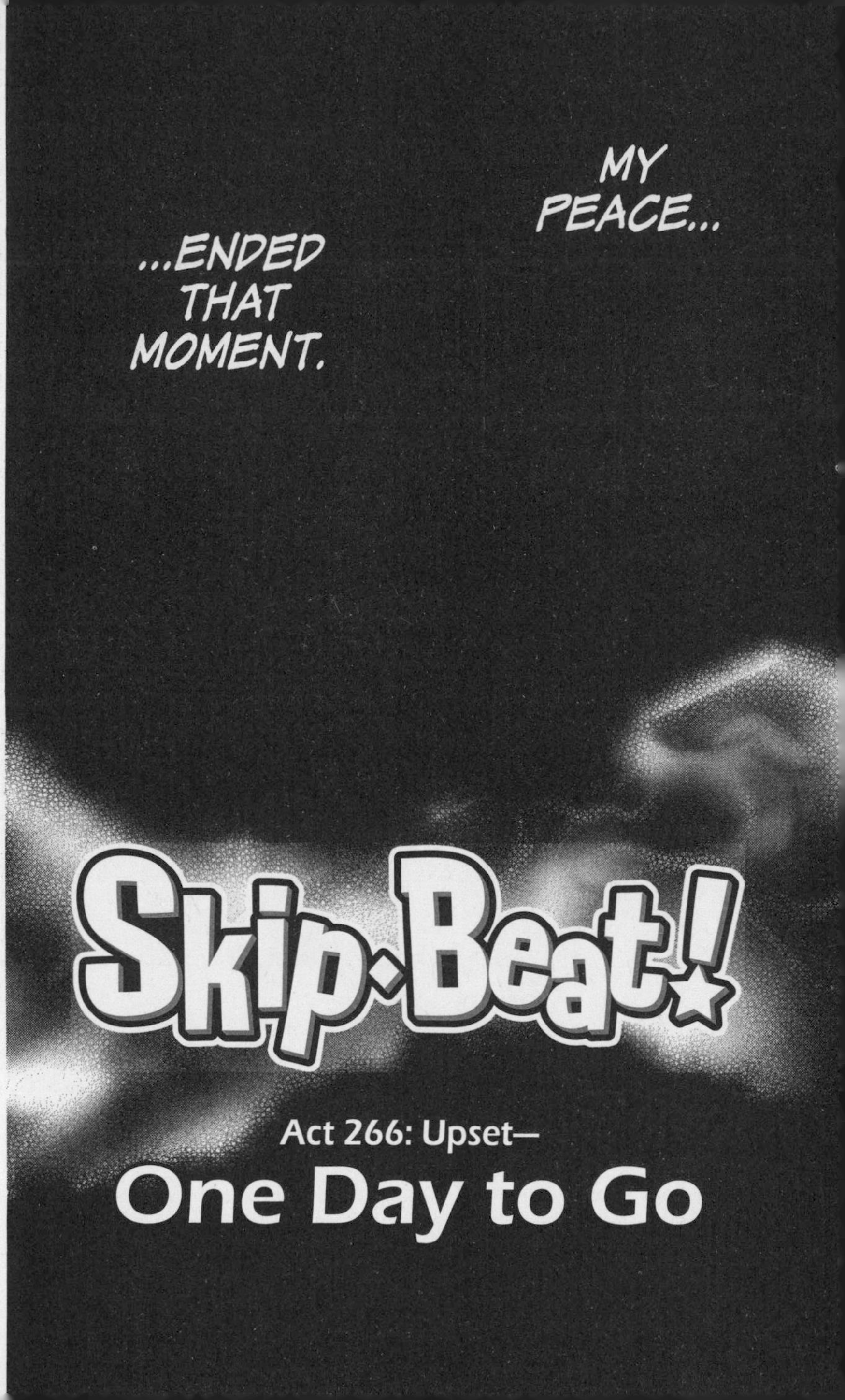
MY PEACE...
...ENDED THAT MOMENT.
Skip·Beat!
Act 266: Upset—
One Day to Go

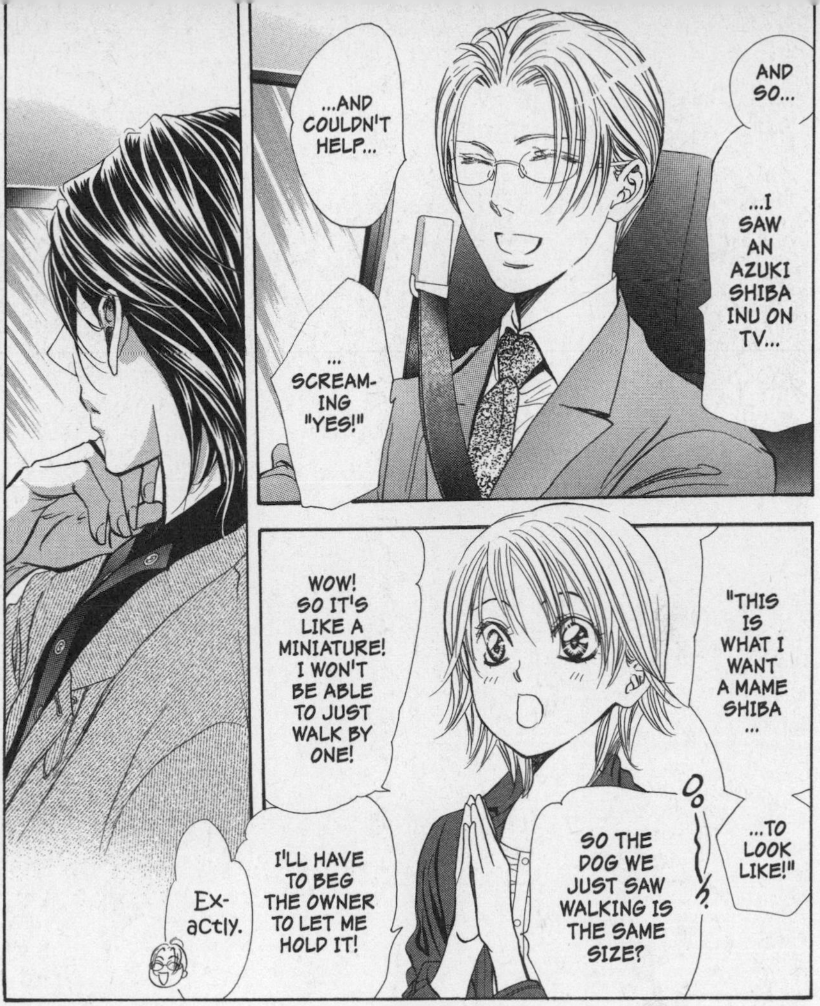
AND SO...
...I SAW AN AZUKI SHIBA INU ON TV...
...AND COULDN'T HELP...
... SCREAMING "YES!"
"THIS IS WHAT I WANT A MAME SHIBA ...
...TO LOOK LIKE!"
SO THE DOG WE JUST SAW WALKING IS THE SAME SIZE?
WOW! SO IT'S LIKE A MINIATURE! I WON'T BE ABLE TO JUST WALK BY ONE!
I'LL HAVE TO BEG THE OWNER TO LET ME HOLD IT!
Ex-actly.

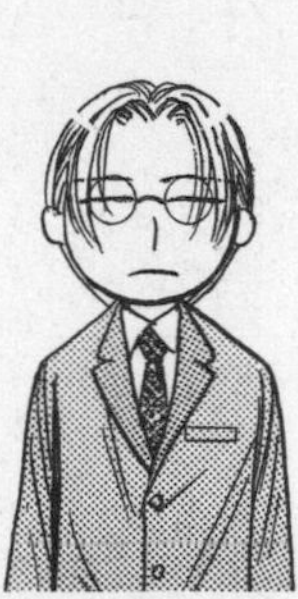

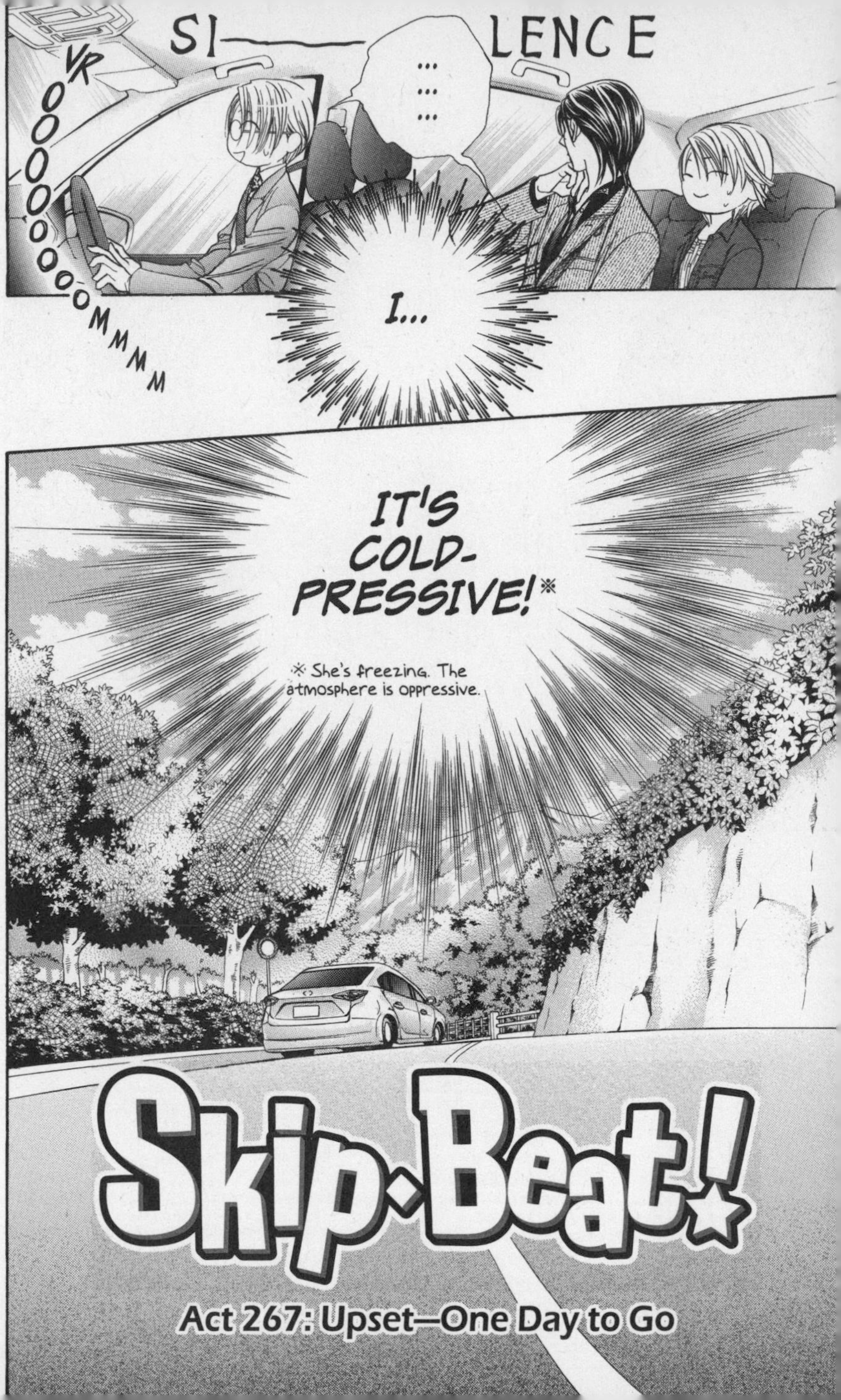

SI— —LENCE
...
...
...
VROOOOOOOOOOOOOOMMMMM
I...
IT'S COLD-PRESSIVE!※
※ She's freezing. The atmosphere is oppressive.
Skip·Beat!
Act 267: Upset—One Day to Go

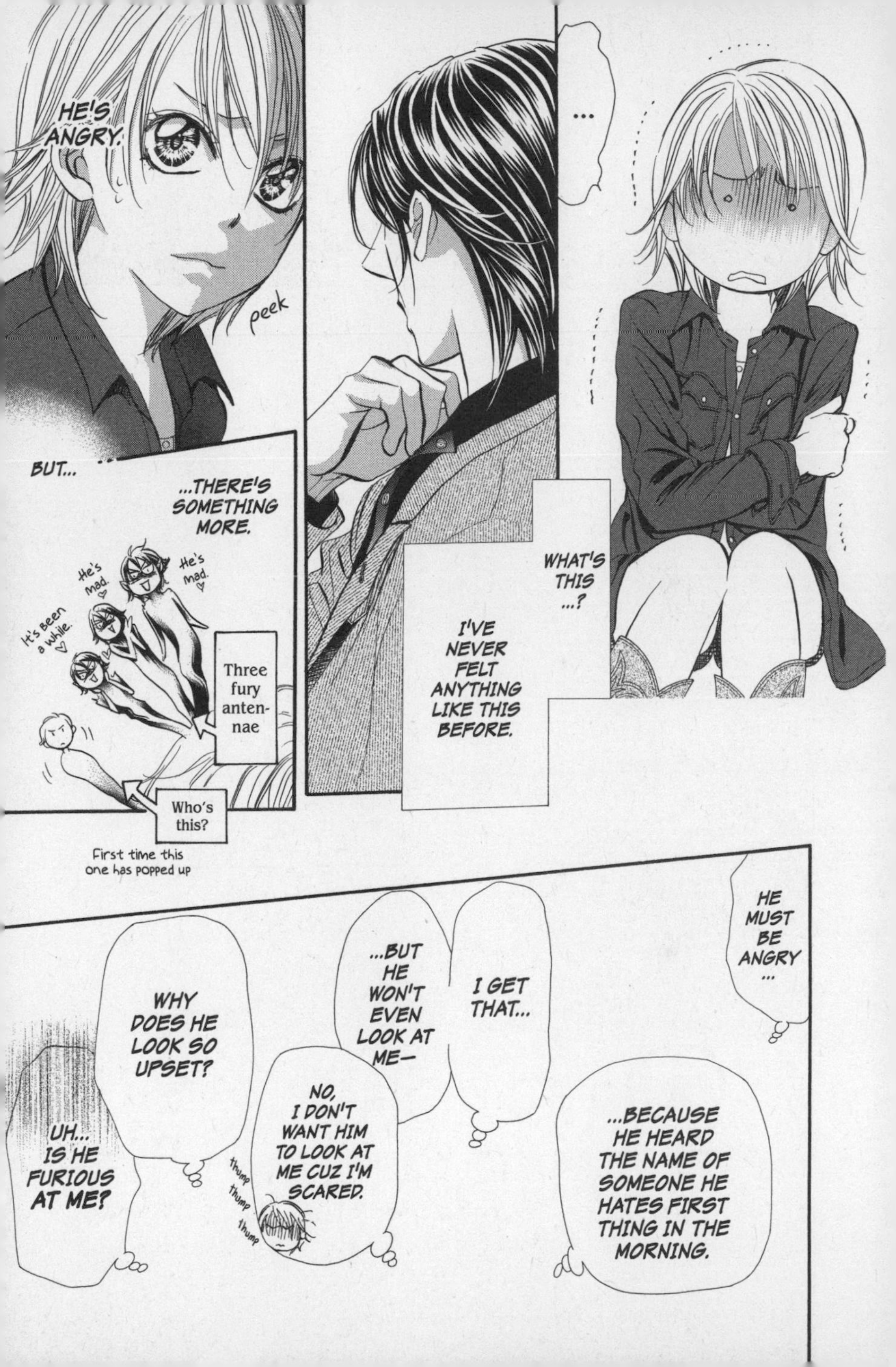
...
WHAT'S THIS ...?
I'VE NEVER FELT ANYTHING LIKE THIS BEFORE.
HE'S ANGRY.
peek
BUT...
...THERE'S SOMETHING MORE.
He's mad.
He's mad.
It's been a while.
Three fury antennae
Who's this?
First time this one has popped up
HE MUST BE ANGRY...
...BECAUSE HE HEARD THE NAME OF SOMEONE HE HATES FIRST THING IN THE MORNING.
I GET THAT...
...BUT HE WON'T EVEN LOOK AT ME—
NO, I DON'T WANT HIM TO LOOK AT ME CUZ I'M SCARED.
thump thump thump
WHY DOES HE LOOK SO UPSET?
UH... IS HE FURIOUS AT ME?

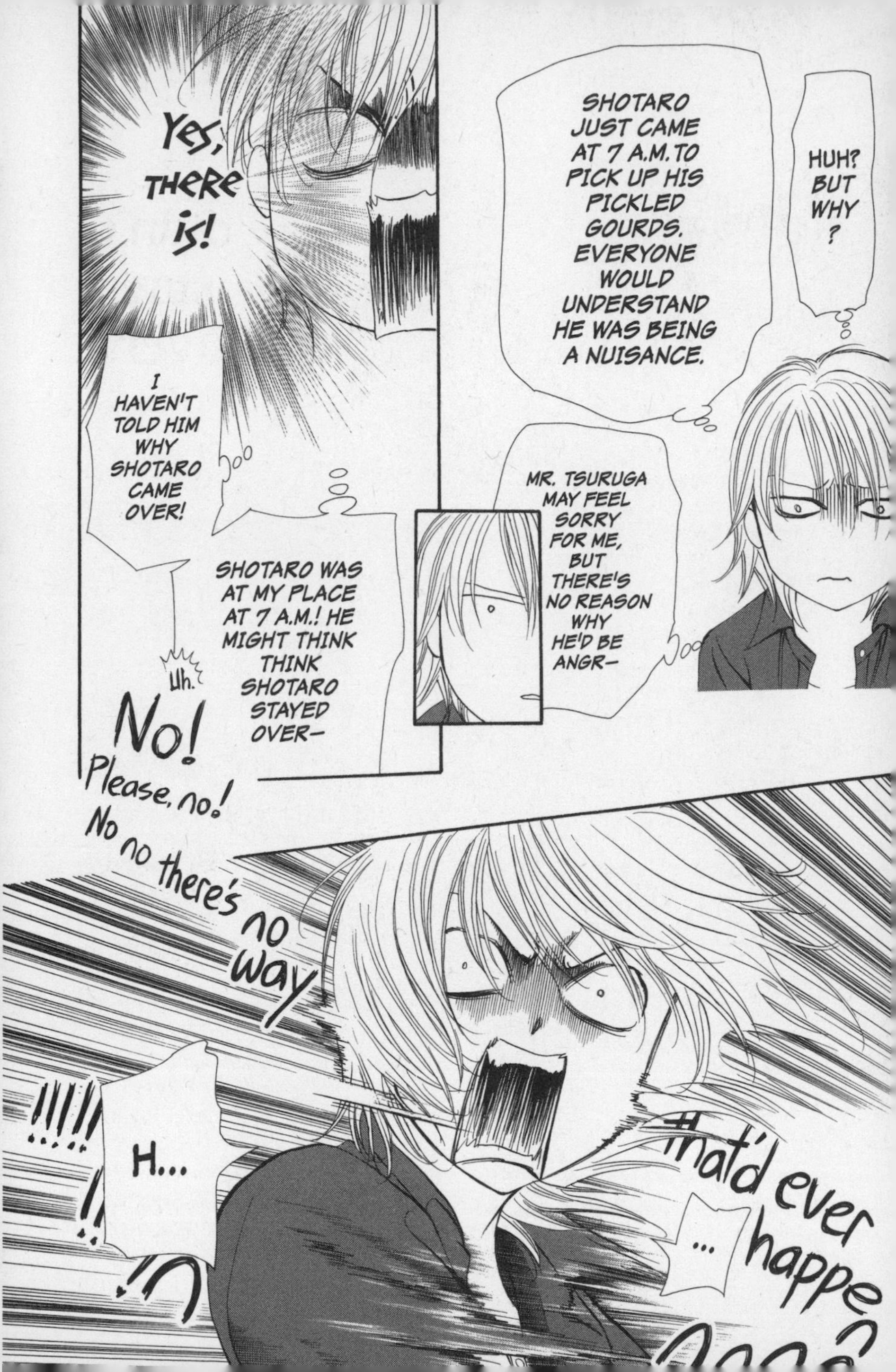
HUH? BUT WHY?
SHOTARO JUST CAME AT 7 A.M. TO PICK UP HIS PICKLED GOURDS. EVERYONE WOULD UNDERSTAND HE WAS BEING A NUISANCE.
MR. TSURUGA MAY FEEL SORRY FOR ME, BUT THERE'S NO REASON WHY HE'D BE ANGR—
Yes, there is!
I HAVEN'T TOLD HIM WHY SHOTARO CAME OVER!
SHOTARO WAS AT MY PLACE AT 7 A.M.! HE MIGHT THINK THINK SHOTARO STAYED OVER—
Uh.
No! Please, no! No no there's no way
that'd ever happe—
...
H...
!!!!!!

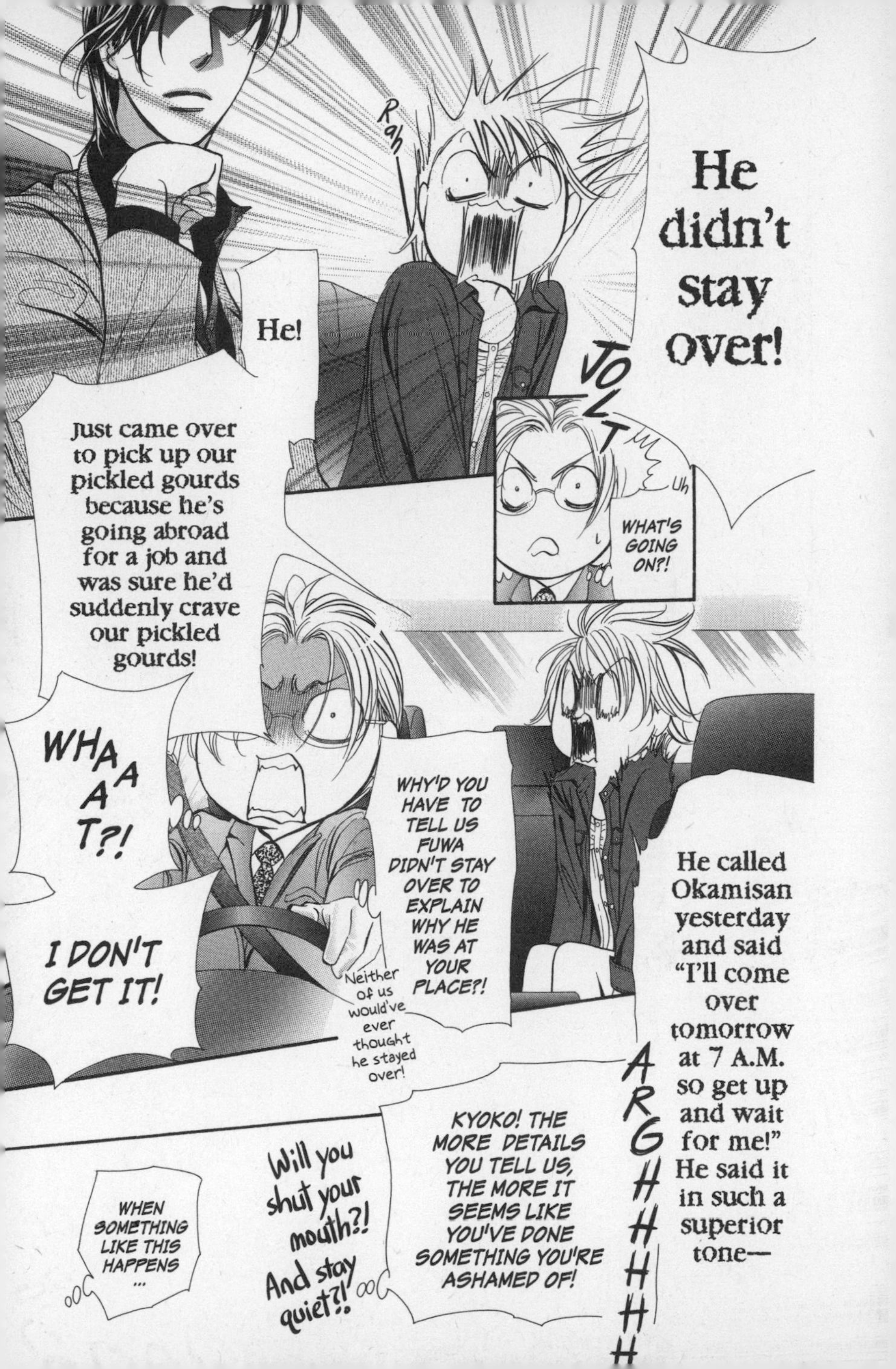
Rah
He didn't stay over!
JOLT
Uh
WHAT'S GOING ON?!
He!
Just came over to pick up our pickled gourds because he's going abroad for a job and was sure he'd suddenly crave our pickled gourds!
He called Okamisan yesterday and said "I'll come over tomorrow at 7 A.M. so get up and wait for me!" He said it in such a superior tone—
ARGHHHHHHH
WHY'D YOU HAVE TO TELL US FUWA DIDN'T STAY OVER TO EXPLAIN WHY HE WAS AT YOUR PLACE?!
Neither of us would've ever thought he stayed over!
WHAAAT?!
I DON'T GET IT!
KYOKO! THE MORE DETAILS YOU TELL US, THE MORE IT SEEMS LIKE YOU'VE DONE SOMETHING YOU'RE ASHAMED OF!
Will you shut your mouth?! And stay quiet?!
WHEN SOMETHING LIKE THIS HAPPENS ...

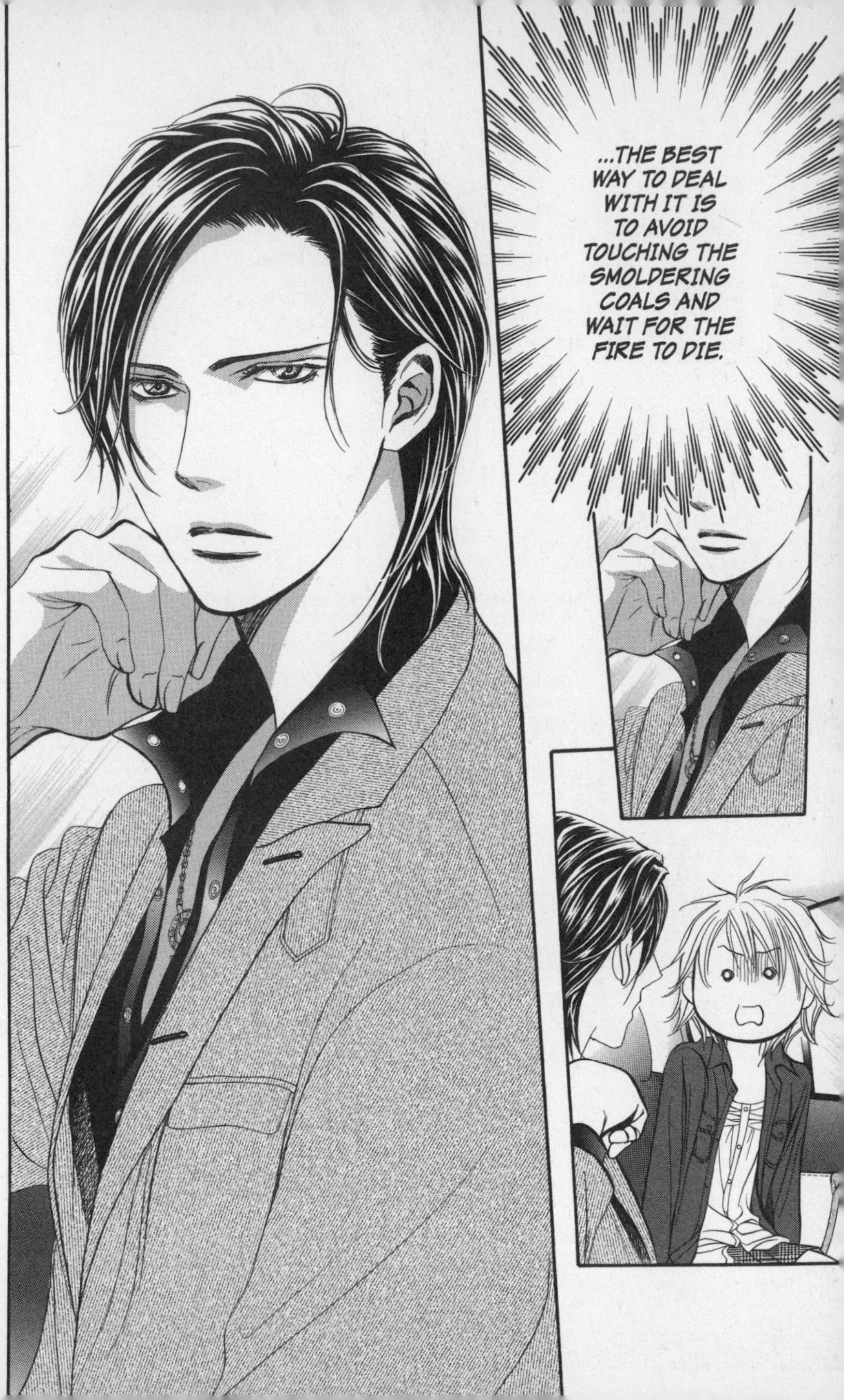
...THE BEST WAY TO DEAL WITH IT IS TO AVOID TOUCHING THE SMOLDERING COALS AND WAIT FOR THE FIRE TO DIE.

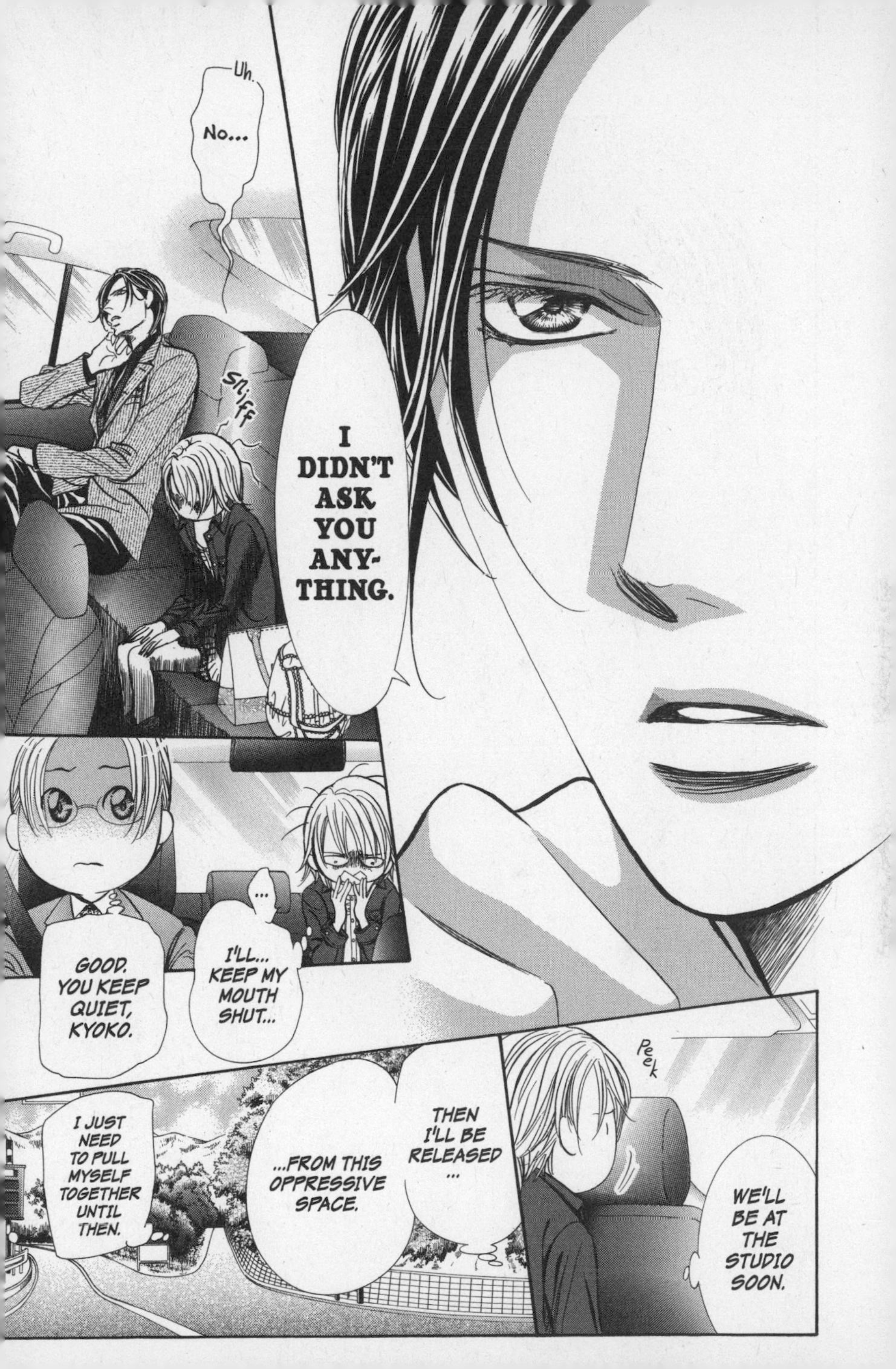
I DIDN'T ASK YOU ANY-THING.
Uh. No...
Sniff
...
I'LL... KEEP MY MOUTH SHUT...
GOOD. YOU KEEP QUIET, KYOKO.
Peek
WE'LL BE AT THE STUDIO SOON.
THEN I'LL BE RELEASED ...
...FROM THIS OPPRESSIVE SPACE.
I JUST NEED TO PULL MYSELF TOGETHER UNTIL THEN.

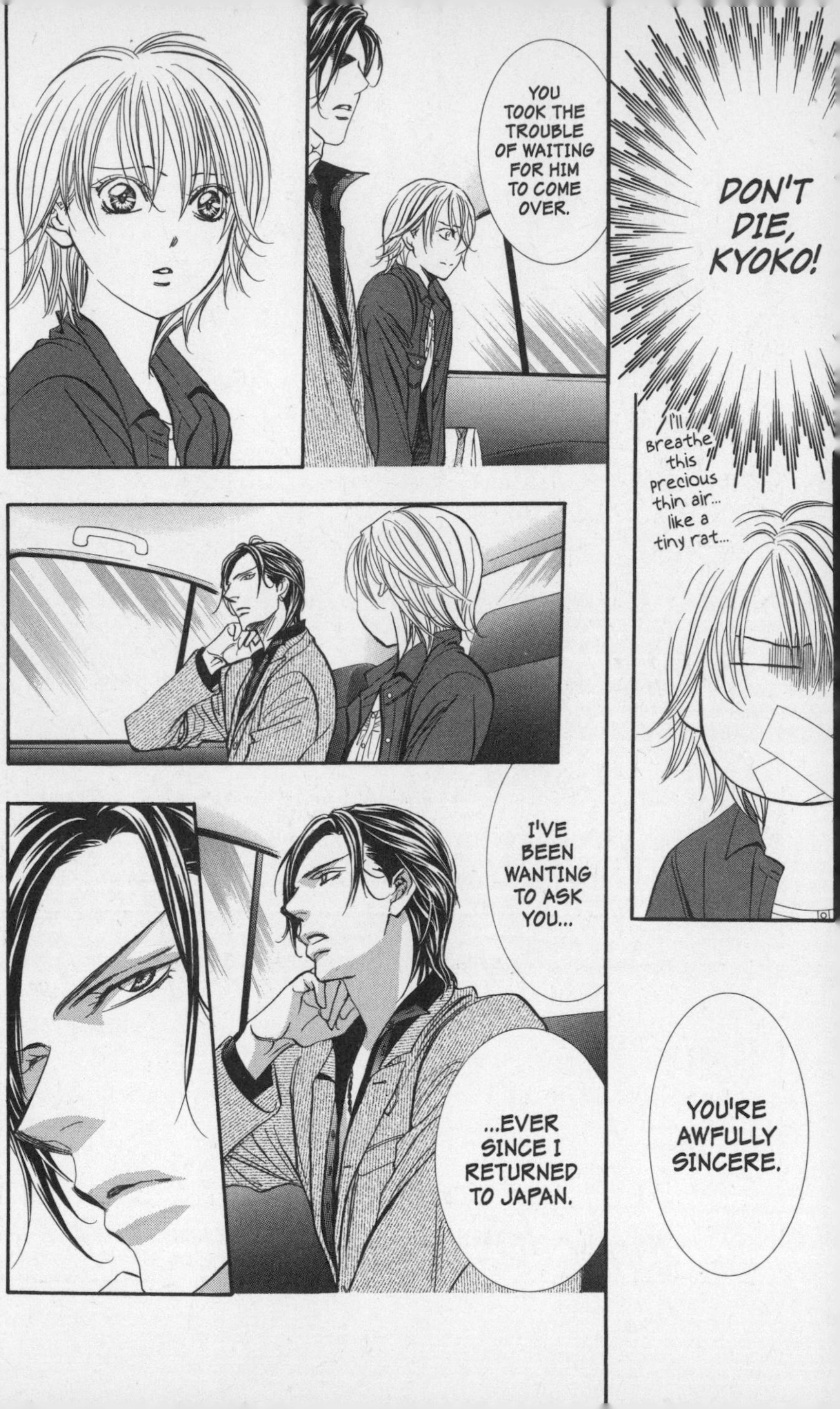
DON'T DIE, KYOKO!
I'll Breathe this precious thin air... like a tiny rat...
YOU'RE AWFULLY SINCERE.
YOU TOOK THE TROUBLE OF WAITING FOR HIM TO COME OVER.
I'VE BEEN WANTING TO ASK YOU...
...EVER SINCE I RETURNED TO JAPAN.

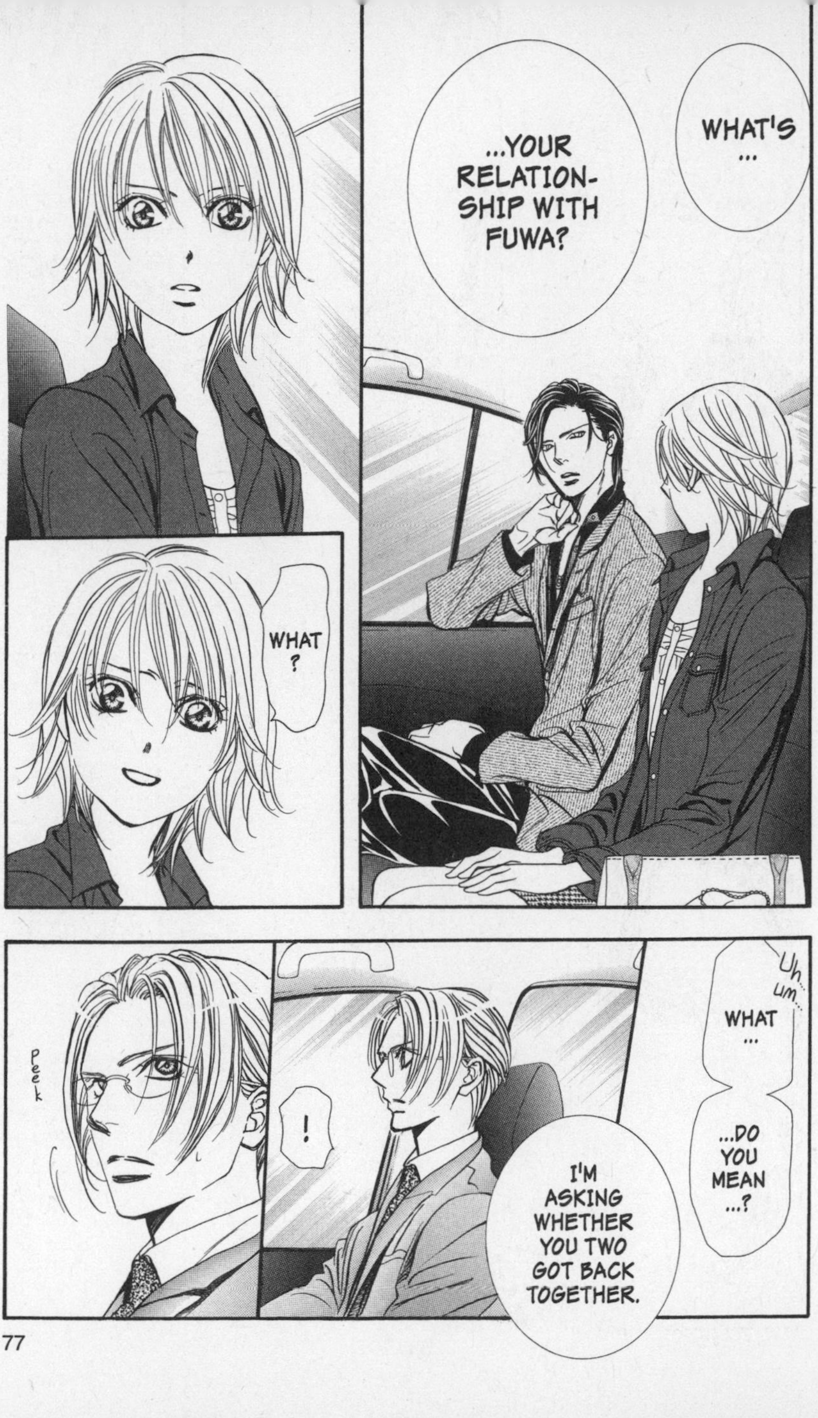
WHAT'S ...
...YOUR RELATION-SHIP WITH FUWA?
WHAT?
Uh... um...
WHAT ... ...DO YOU MEAN ...?
I'M ASKING WHETHER YOU TWO GOT BACK TOGETHER.
!
Peek

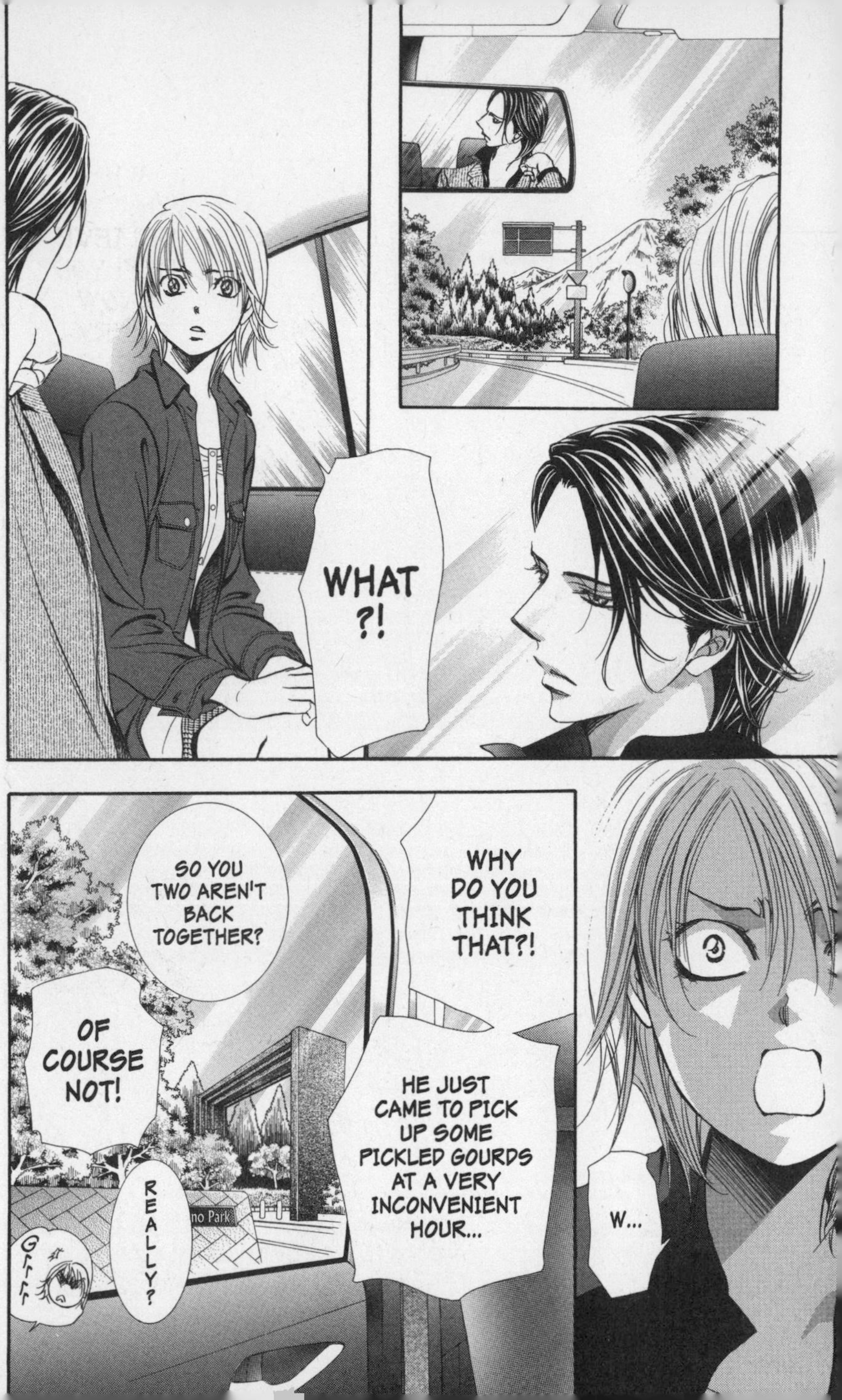
WHAT ?!
W...
WHY DO YOU THINK THAT?!
SO YOU TWO AREN'T BACK TOGETHER?
HE JUST CAME TO PICK UP SOME PICKLED GOURDS AT A VERY INCONVENIENT HOUR...
OF COURSE NOT!
REALLY?
Grrrr

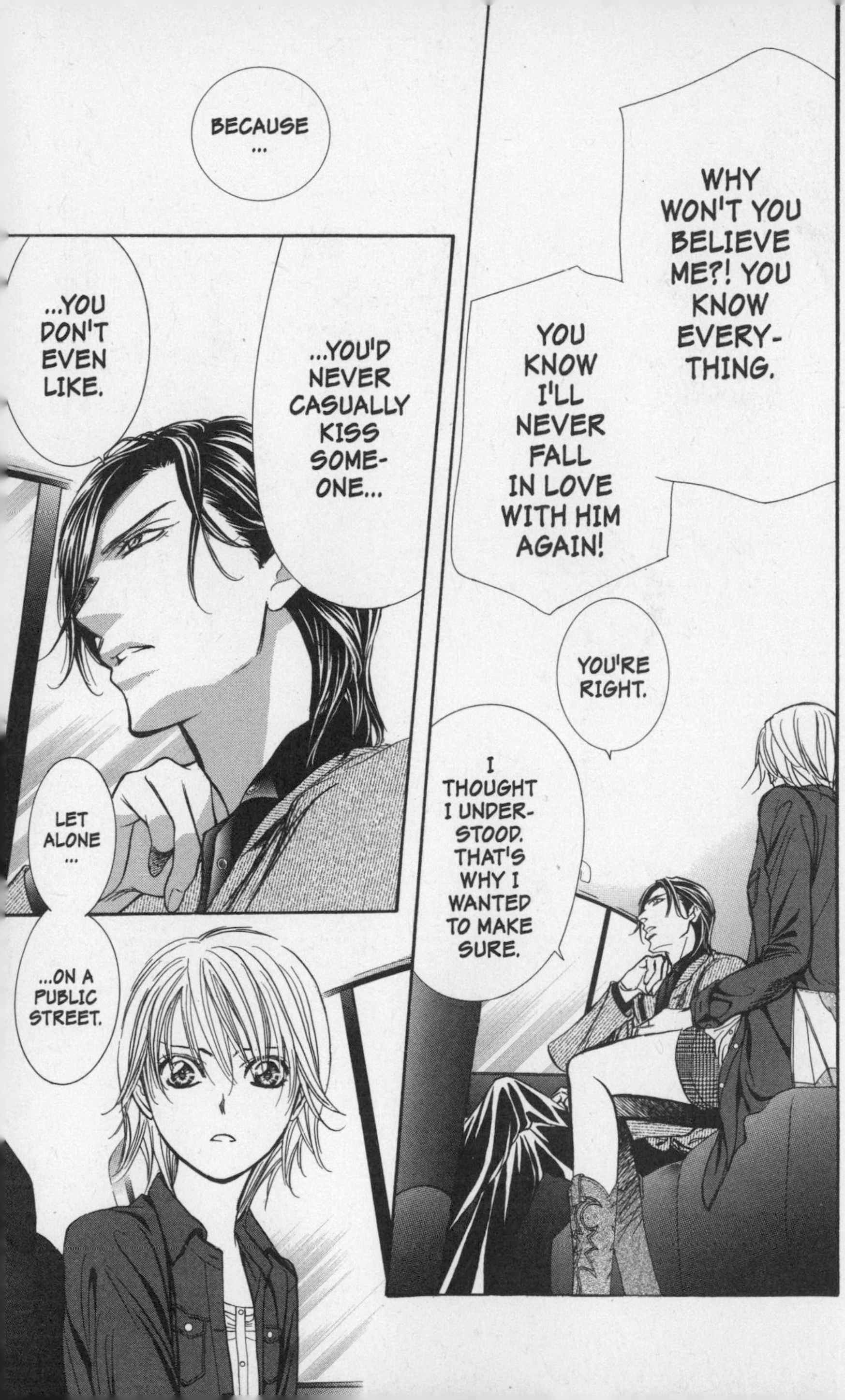
WHY WON'T YOU BELIEVE ME?! YOU KNOW EVERY-THING.
YOU KNOW I'LL NEVER FALL IN LOVE WITH HIM AGAIN!
YOU'RE RIGHT.
I THOUGHT I UNDER-STOOD. THAT'S WHY I WANTED TO MAKE SURE.
BECAUSE ...
...YOU'D NEVER CASUALLY KISS SOME-ONE...
...YOU DON'T EVEN LIKE.
LET ALONE ...
...ON A PUBLIC STREET.

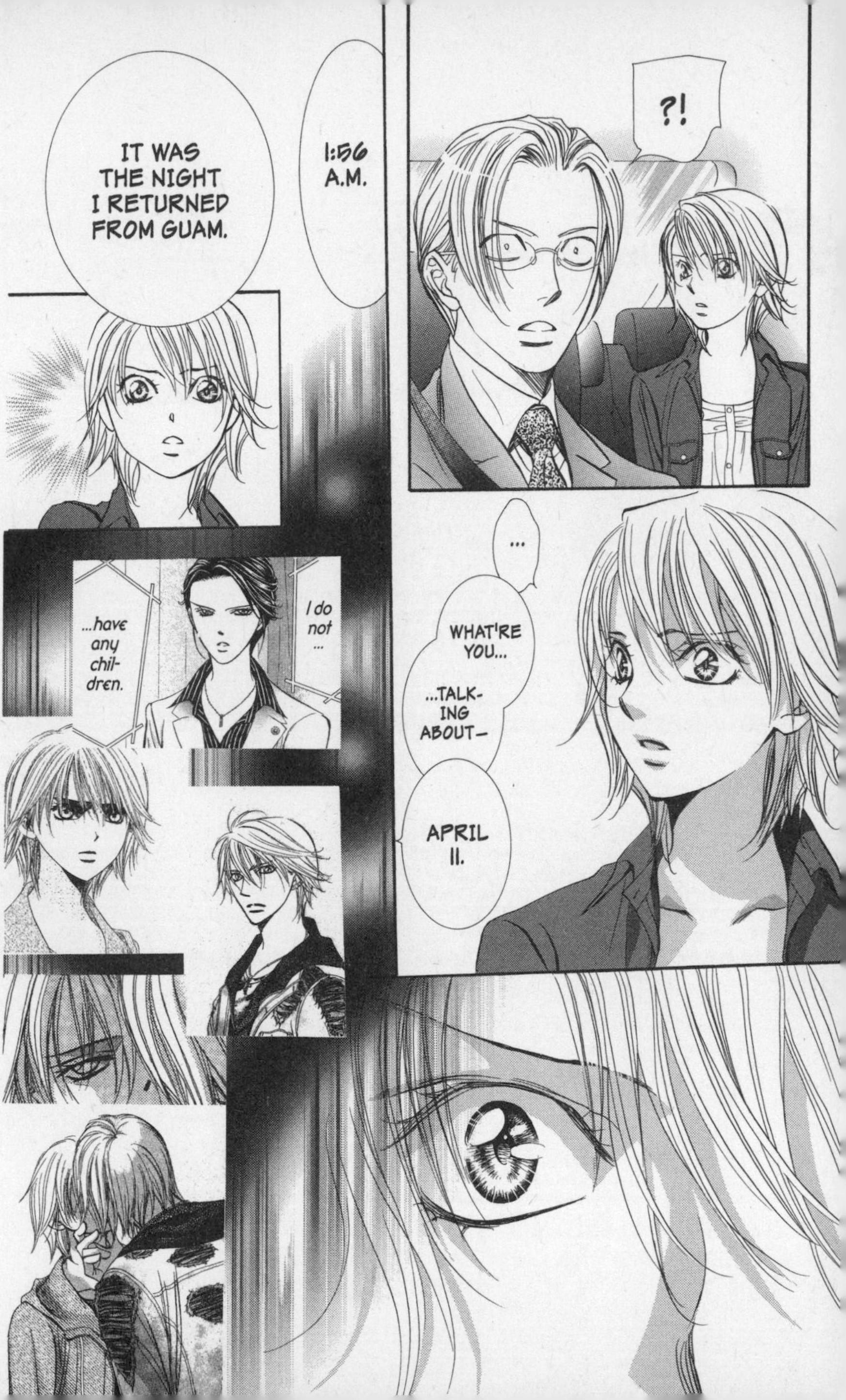
?!
...
WHAT'RE YOU...
...TALKING ABOUT—
APRIL 11.
1:56 A.M.
IT WAS THE NIGHT I RETURNED FROM GUAM.
I do not ...
...have any children.

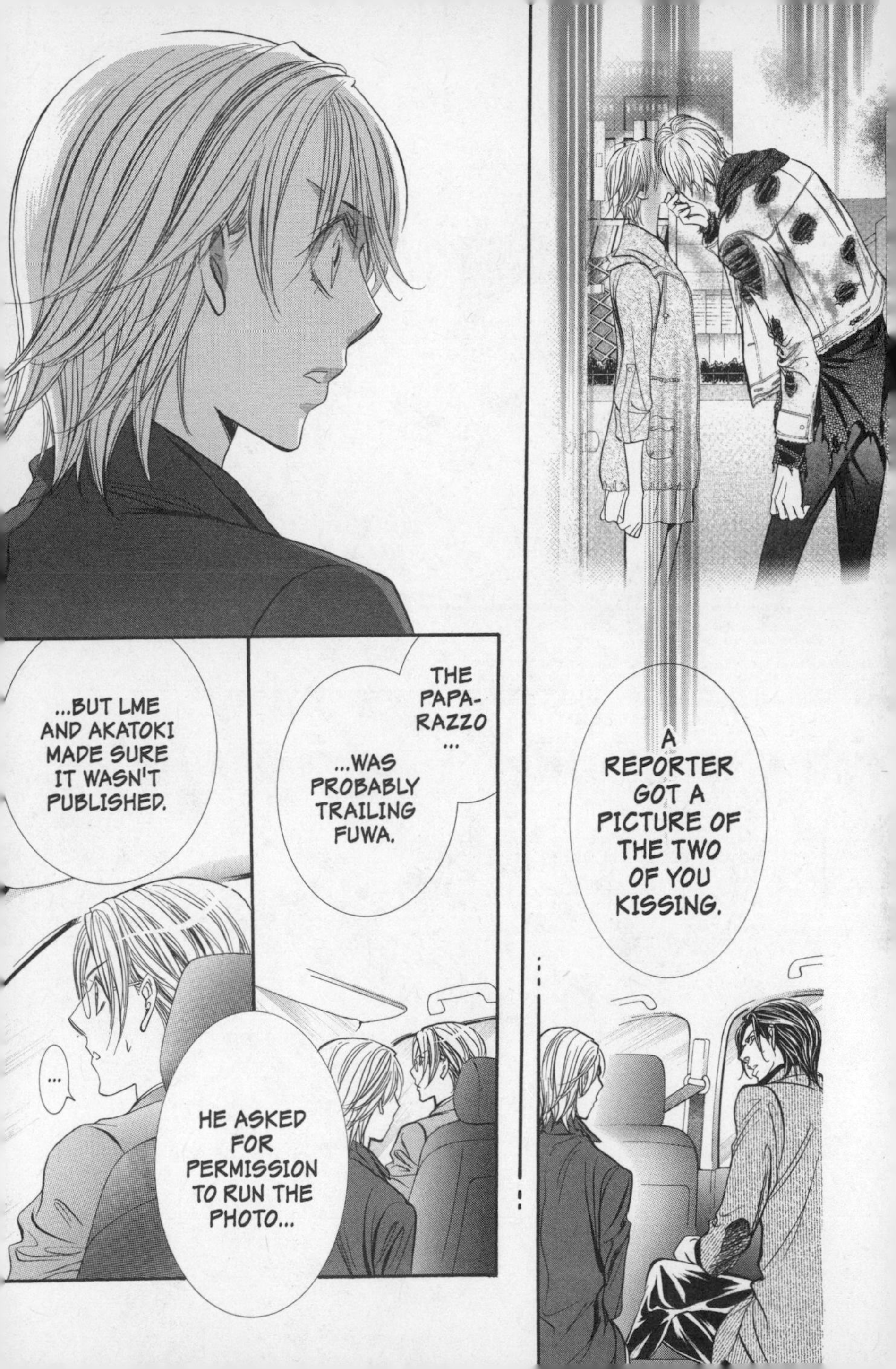
A REPORTER GOT A PICTURE OF THE TWO OF YOU KISSING.
THE PAPARAZZO...
...WAS PROBABLY TRAILING FUWA.
HE ASKED FOR PERMISSION TO RUN THE PHOTO...
...BUT LME AND AKATOKI MADE SURE IT WASN'T PUBLISHED.
...

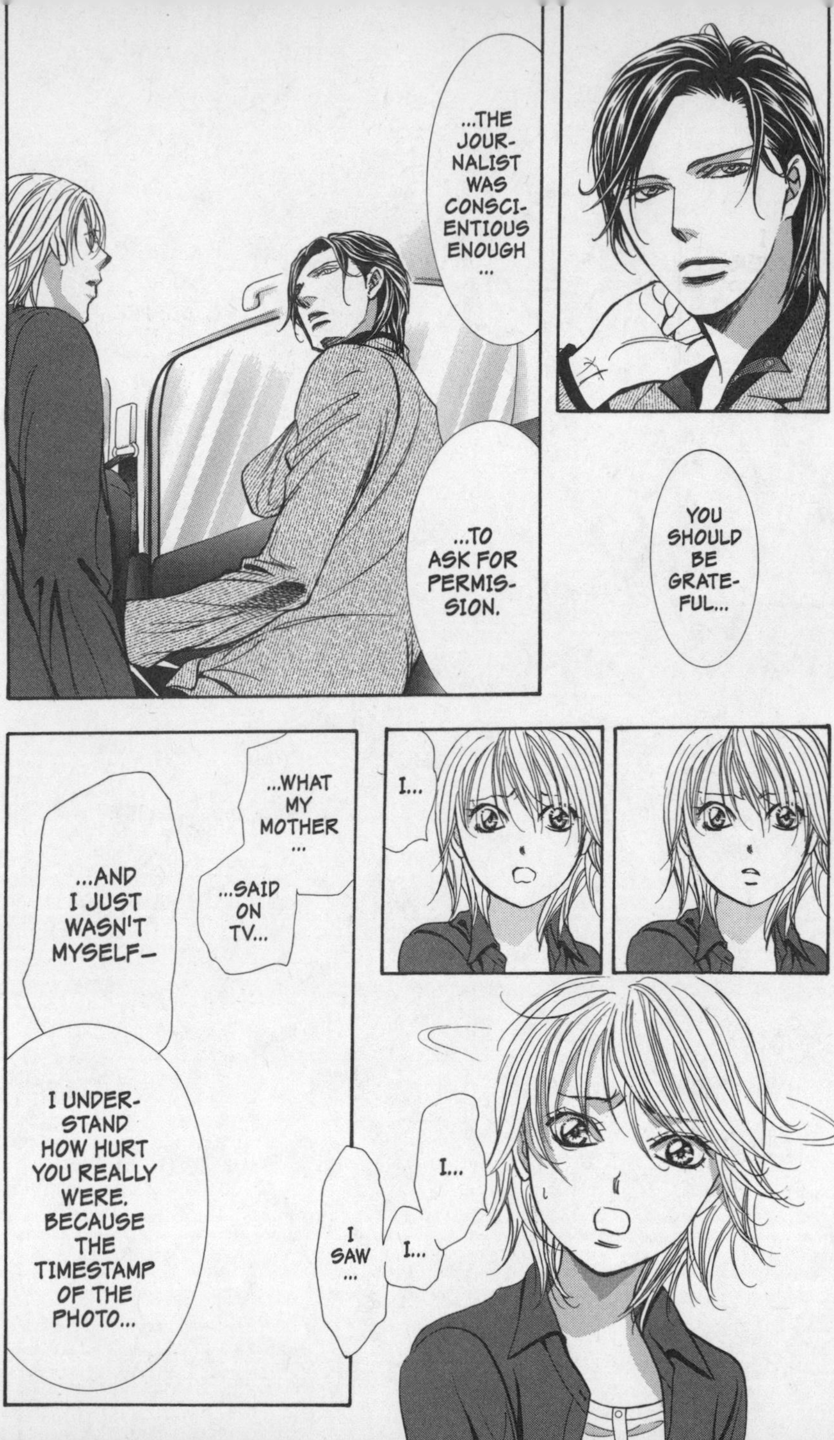
YOU SHOULD BE GRATE-FUL...
...THE JOUR-NALIST WAS CONSCI-ENTIOUS ENOUGH ...
...TO ASK FOR PERMIS-SION.
I...
I...
I...
I SAW ...
...WHAT MY MOTHER ...
...SAID ON TV...
...AND I JUST WASN'T MYSELF—
I UNDER-STAND HOW HURT YOU REALLY WERE. BECAUSE THE TIMESTAMP OF THE PHOTO...

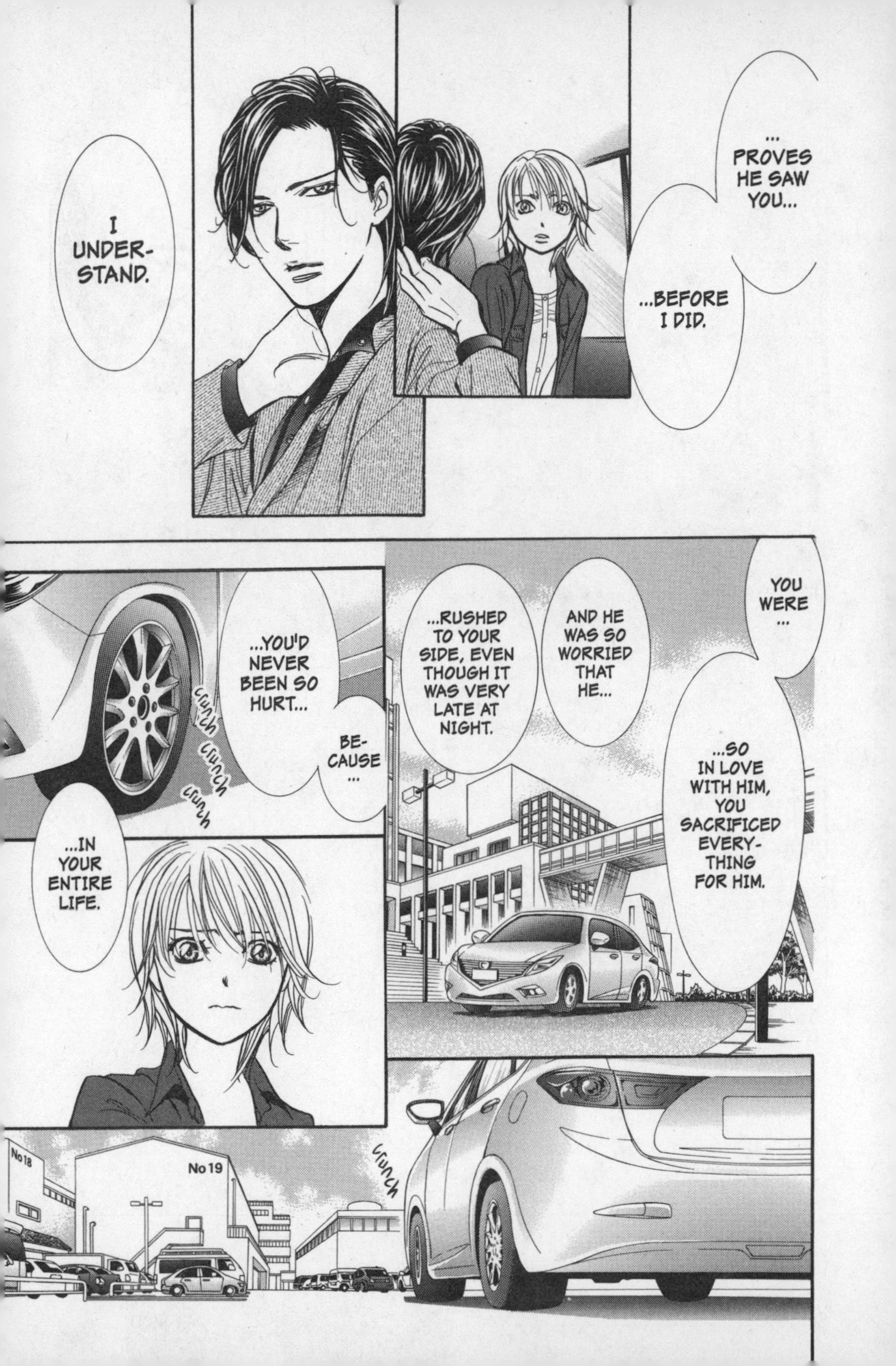
... PROVES HE SAW YOU...
...BEFORE I DID.
I UNDER-STAND.
YOU WERE ...
...SO IN LOVE WITH HIM, YOU SACRIFICED EVERY-THING FOR HIM.
AND HE WAS SO WORRIED THAT HE...
...RUSHED TO YOUR SIDE, EVEN THOUGH IT WAS VERY LATE AT NIGHT.
BE-CAUSE ...
...YOU'D NEVER BEEN SO HURT...
crunch crunch crunch
...IN YOUR ENTIRE LIFE.
crunch
No 19
No 18

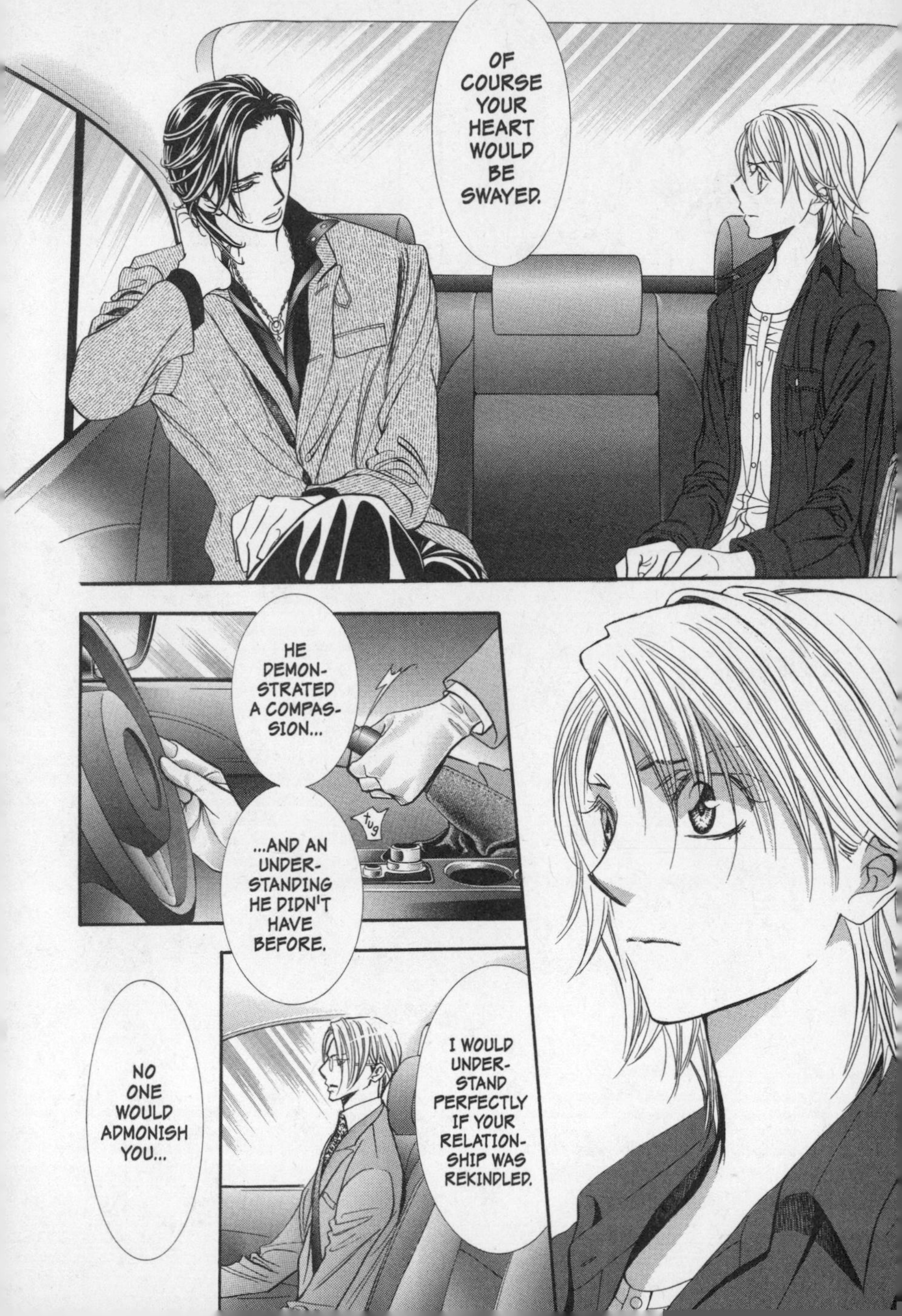
OF COURSE YOUR HEART WOULD BE SWAYED.
HE DEMON-STRATED A COMPAS-SION...
tug
...AND AN UNDER-STANDING HE DIDN'T HAVE BEFORE.
I WOULD UNDER-STAND PERFECTLY IF YOUR RELATION-SHIP WAS REKINDLED.
NO ONE WOULD ADMONISH YOU...

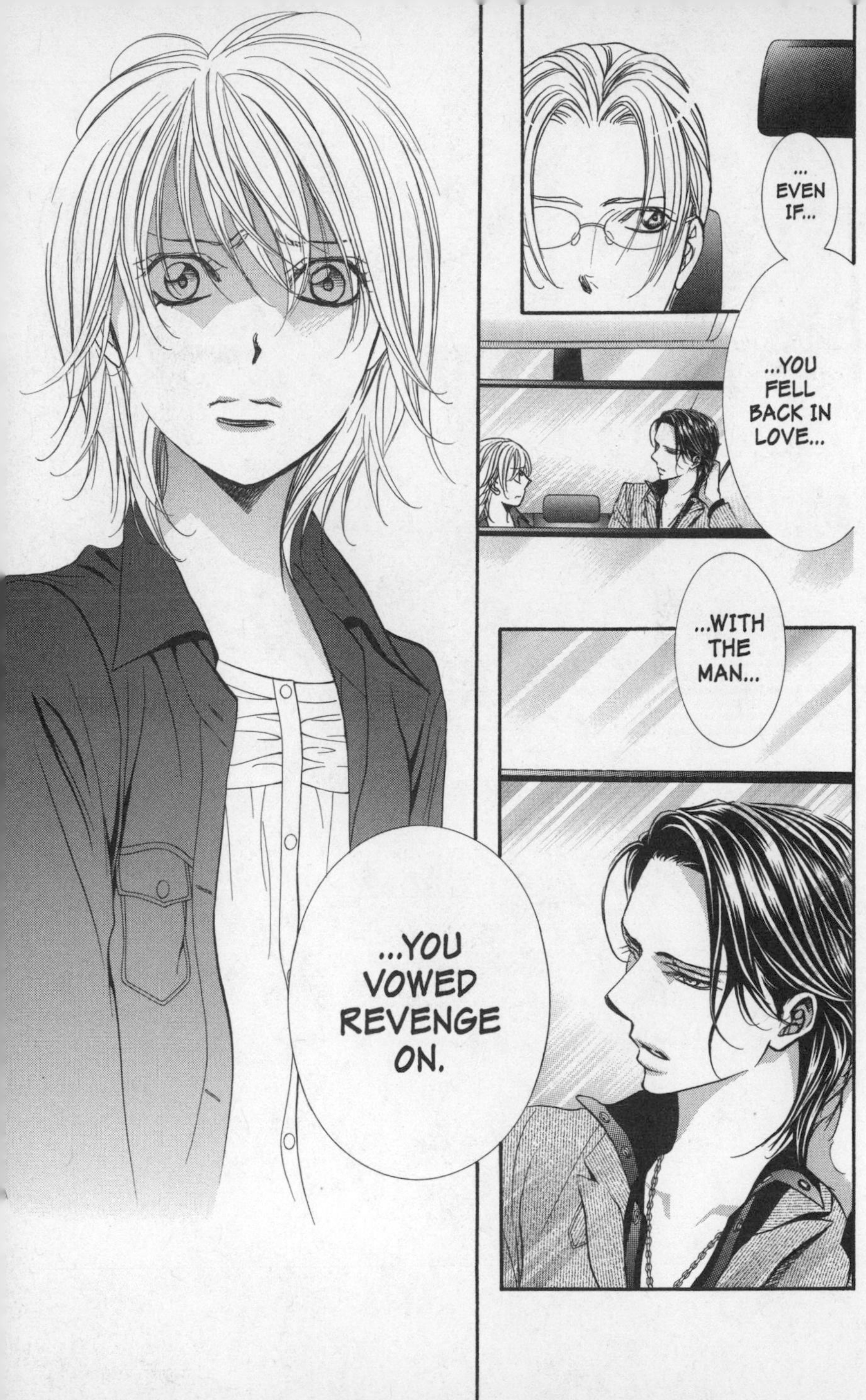

...EVEN IF...
...YOU FELL BACK IN LOVE...
...WITH THE MAN...
...YOU VOWED REVENGE ON.

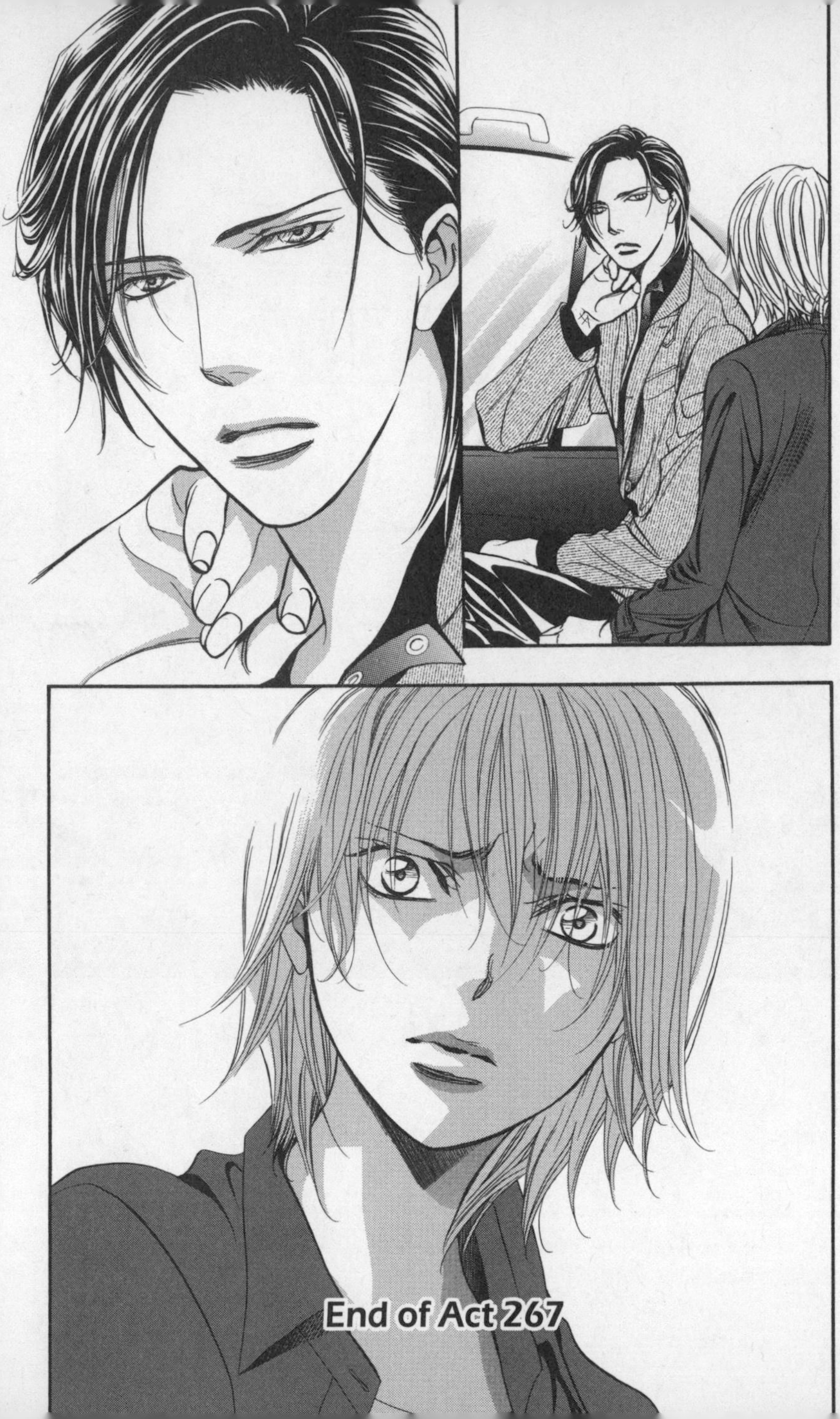
End of Act 267

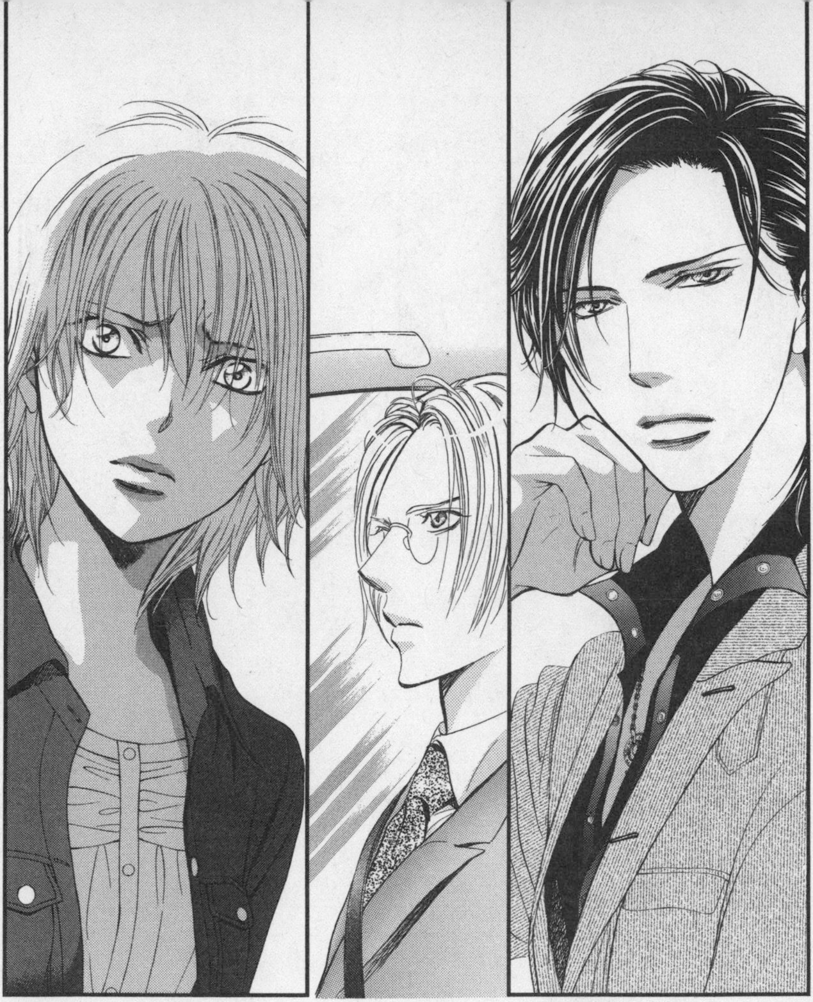

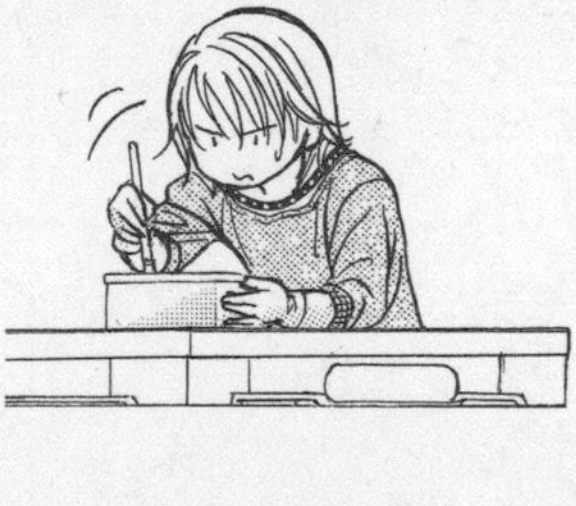

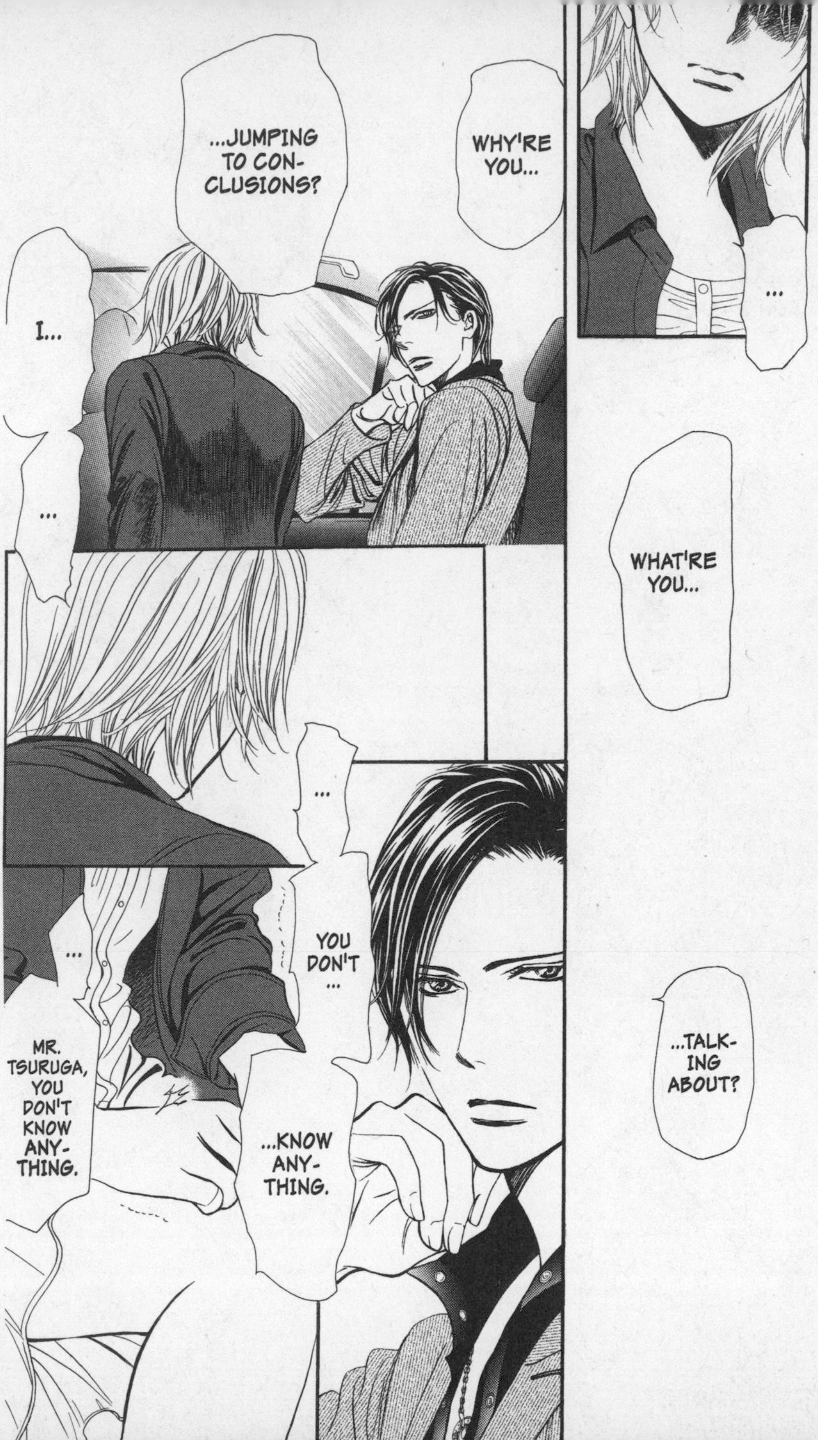
...
WHAT'RE YOU...
...TALKING ABOUT?
WHY'RE YOU...
...JUMPING TO CONCLUSIONS?
I...
...
...
YOU DON'T ...
...KNOW ANYTHING.
...
MR. TSURUGA, YOU DON'T KNOW ANYTHING.

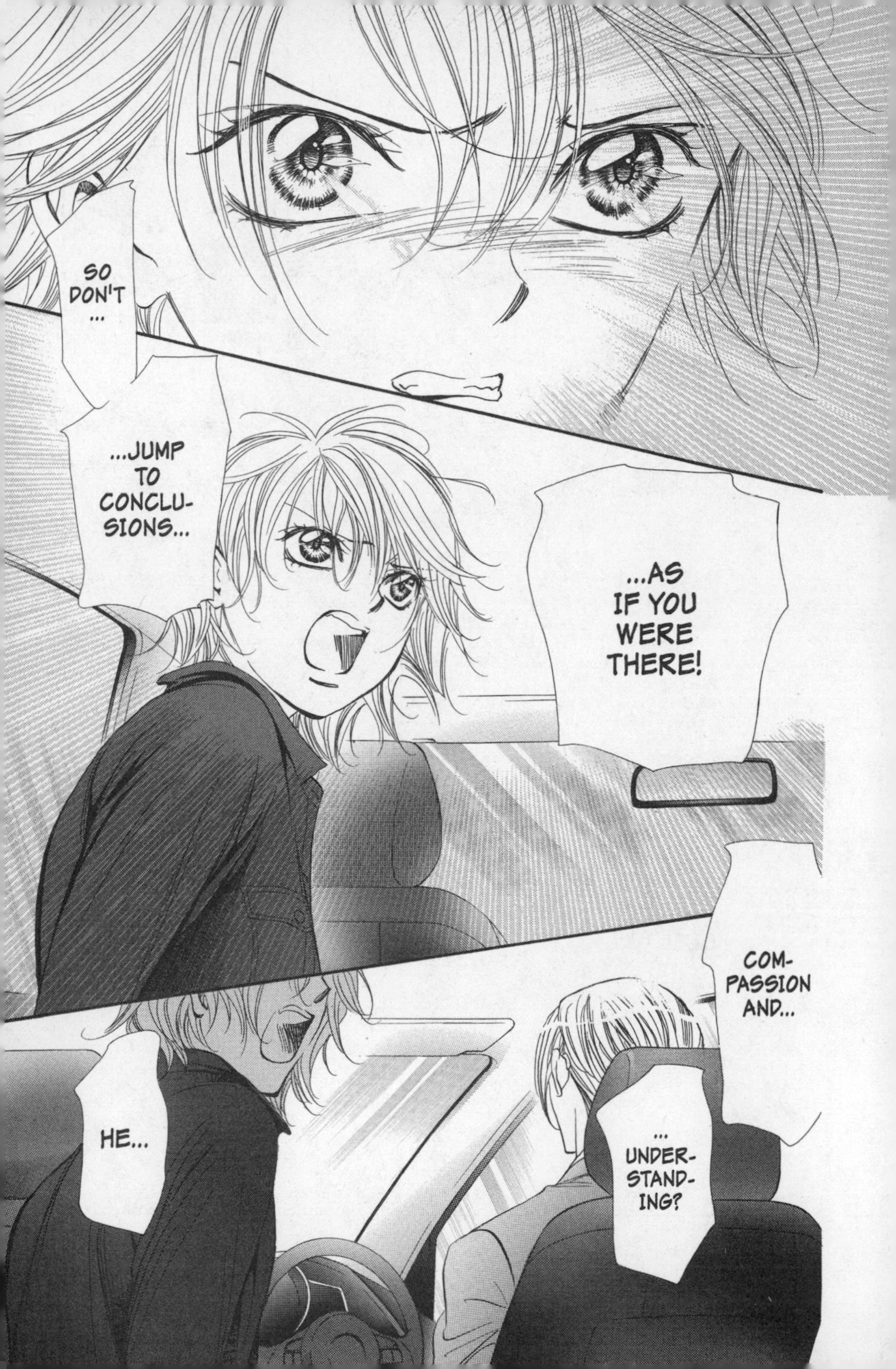
SO DON'T ...
...JUMP TO CONCLUSIONS...
...AS IF YOU WERE THERE!
COMPASSION AND...
... UNDERSTANDING?
HE...

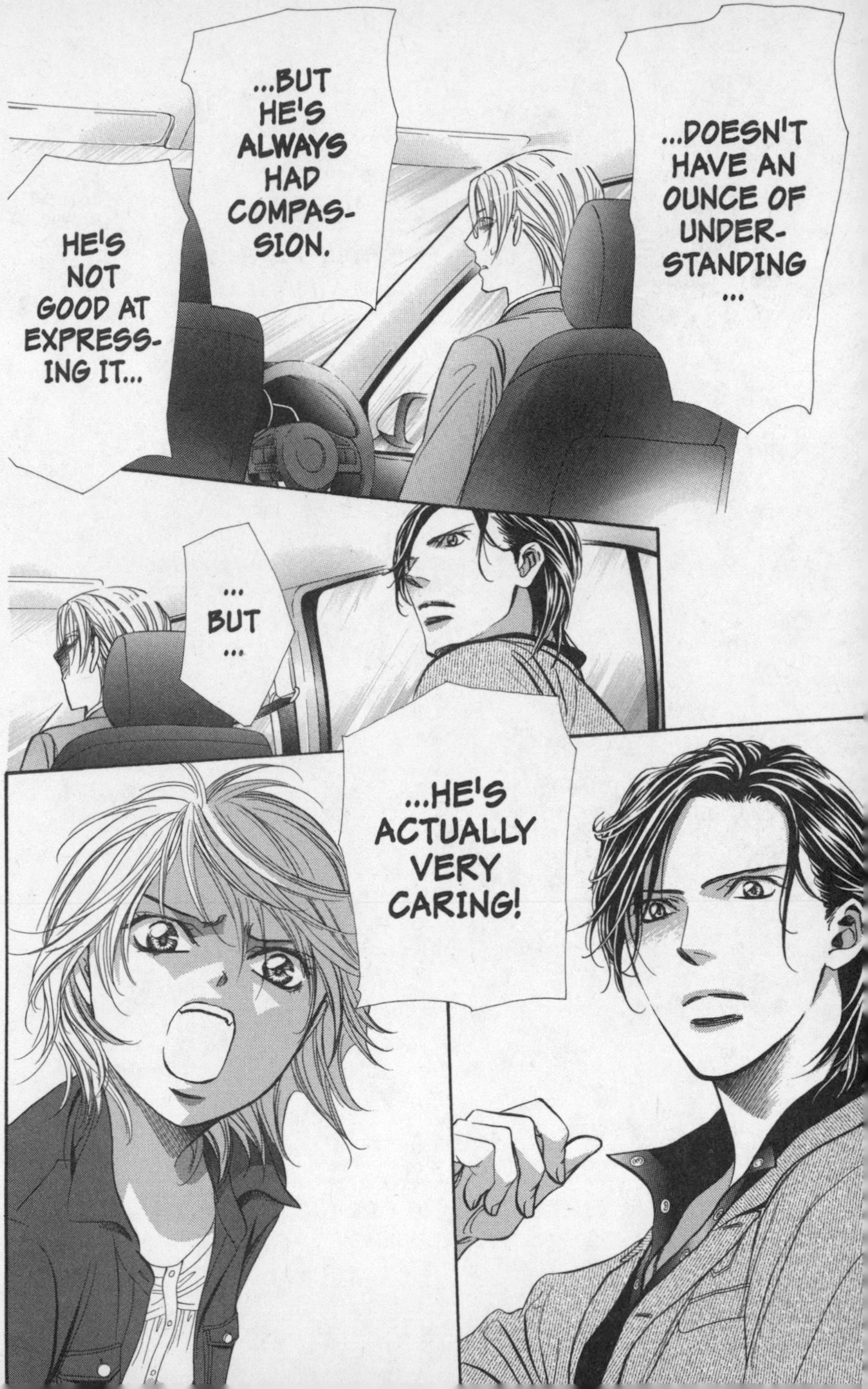
...DOESN'T HAVE AN OUNCE OF UNDER-STANDING ...
...BUT HE'S ALWAYS HAD COMPAS-SION.
HE'S NOT GOOD AT EXPRESS-ING IT...
... BUT ...
...HE'S ACTUALLY VERY CARING!

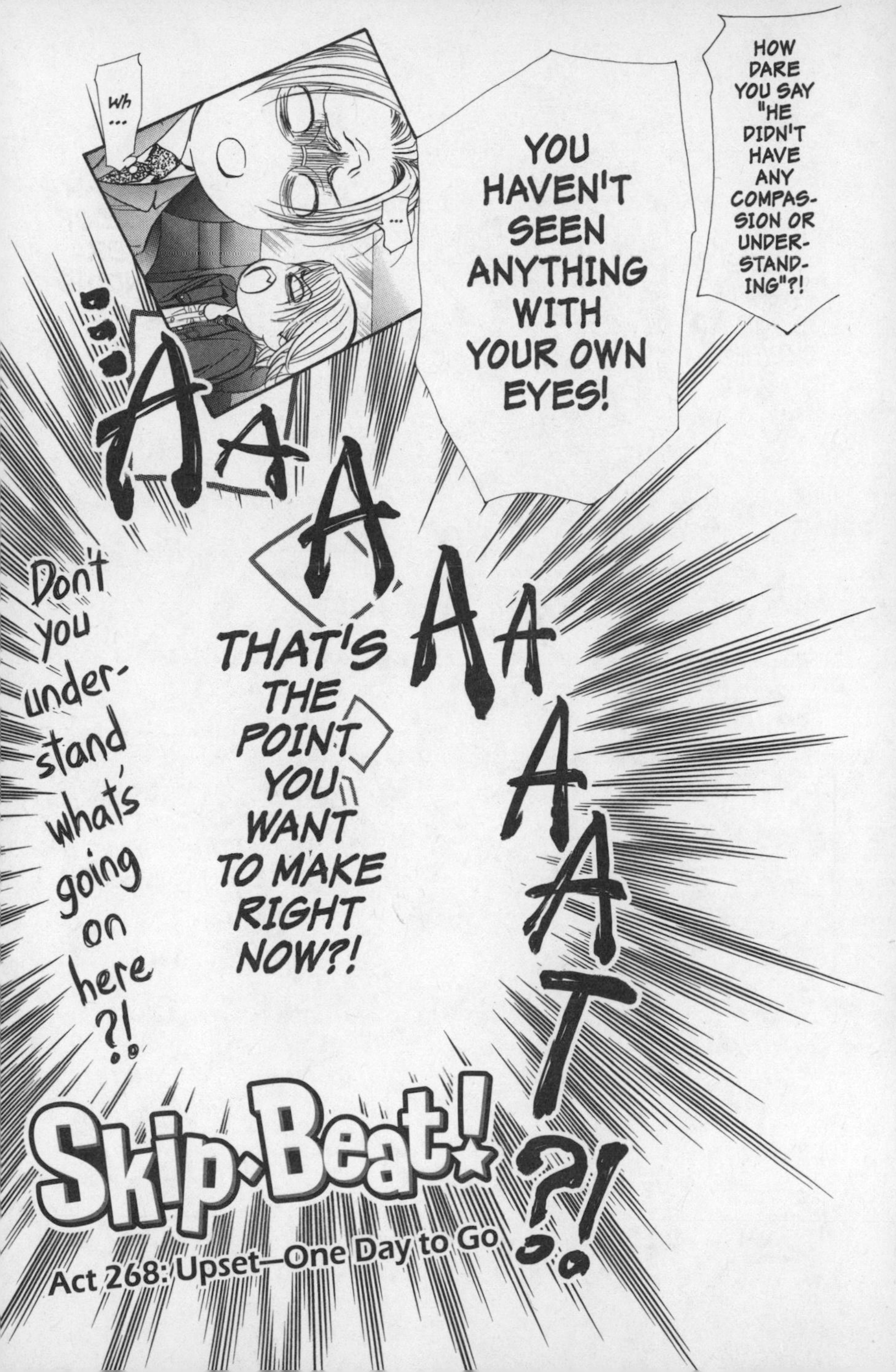
HOW DARE YOU SAY "HE DIDN'T HAVE ANY COMPASSION OR UNDERSTANDING"?!
YOU HAVEN'T SEEN ANYTHING WITH YOUR OWN EYES!
...
Wh...
AAAAAAT
THAT'S THE POINT YOU WANT TO MAKE RIGHT NOW?!
Don't you understand what's going on here?!
?!
Skip·Beat!
Act 268: Upset—One Day to Go

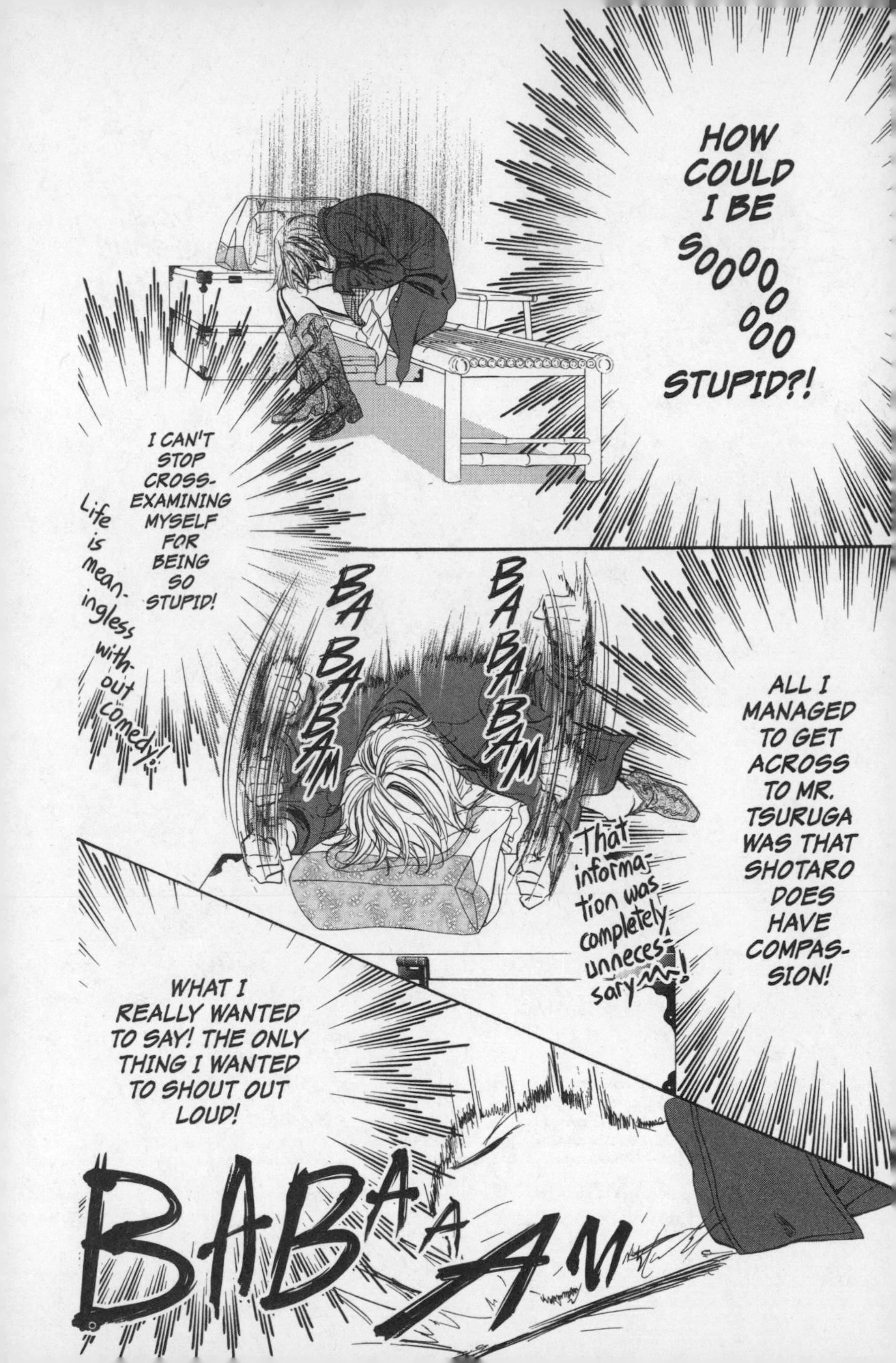
HOW COULD I BE SOOOOOOOOO STUPID?!
I CAN'T STOP CROSS-EXAMINING MYSELF FOR BEING SO STUPID!
Life is meaningless without comedy!
BABABABAM
BABABAM
ALL I MANAGED TO GET ACROSS TO MR. TSURUGA WAS THAT SHOTARO DOES HAVE COMPASSION!
That information was completely unnecessary~!
WHAT I REALLY WANTED TO SAY! THE ONLY THING I WANTED TO SHOUT OUT LOUD!
BABAAAM

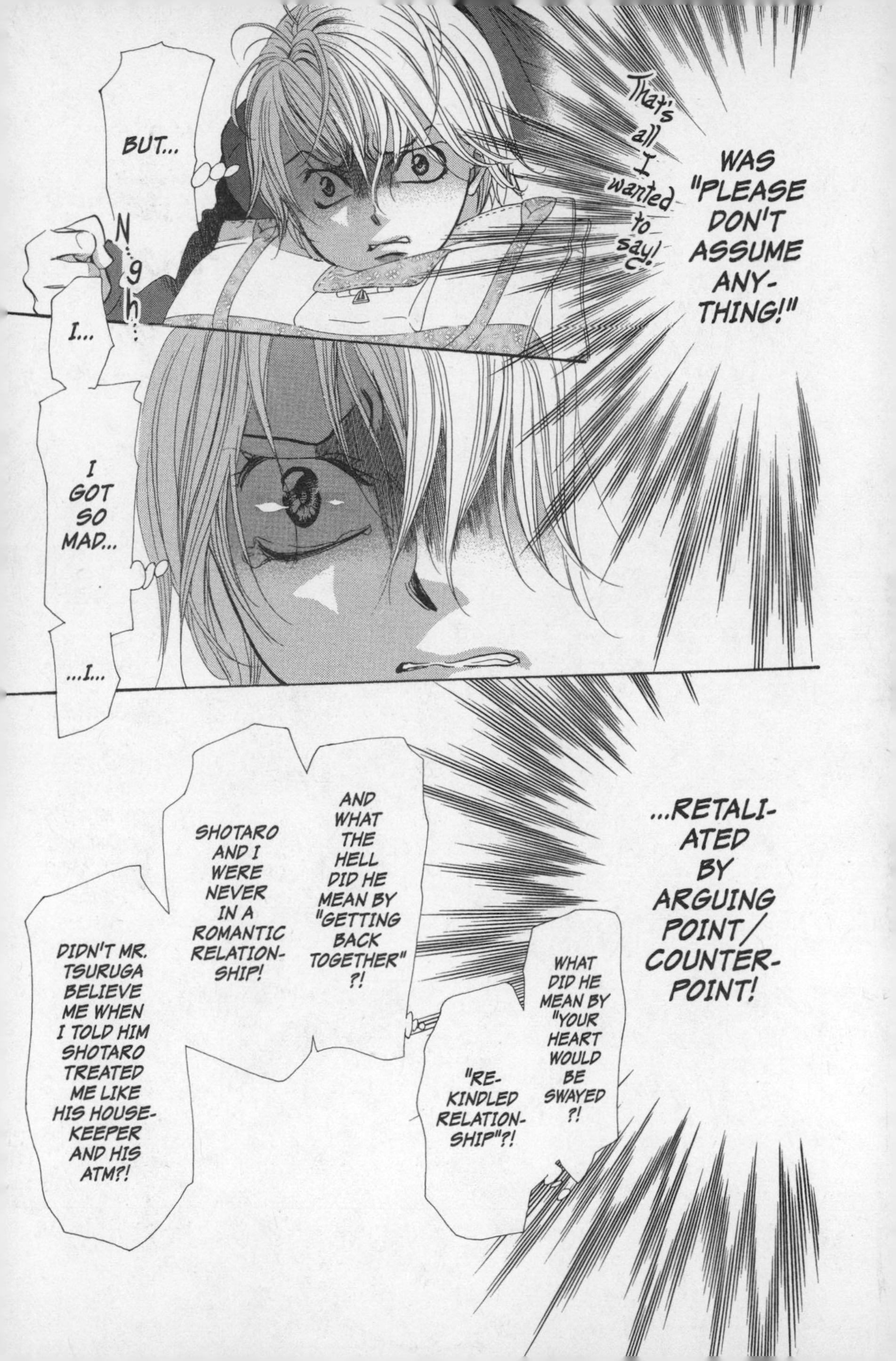
WAS "PLEASE DON'T ASSUME ANY-THING!"
That's all I wanted to say!
BUT...
Ngh...
I...
I GOT SO MAD...
...I...
...RETALI-ATED BY ARGUING POINT/COUNTER-POINT!
WHAT DID HE MEAN BY "YOUR HEART WOULD BE SWAYED"?!
"RE-KINDLED RELATION-SHIP"?!
AND WHAT THE HELL DID HE MEAN BY "GETTING BACK TOGETHER"?!
SHOTARO AND I WERE NEVER IN A ROMANTIC RELATION-SHIP!
DIDN'T MR. TSURUGA BELIEVE ME WHEN I TOLD HIM SHOTARO TREATED ME LIKE HIS HOUSE-KEEPER AND HIS ATM?!

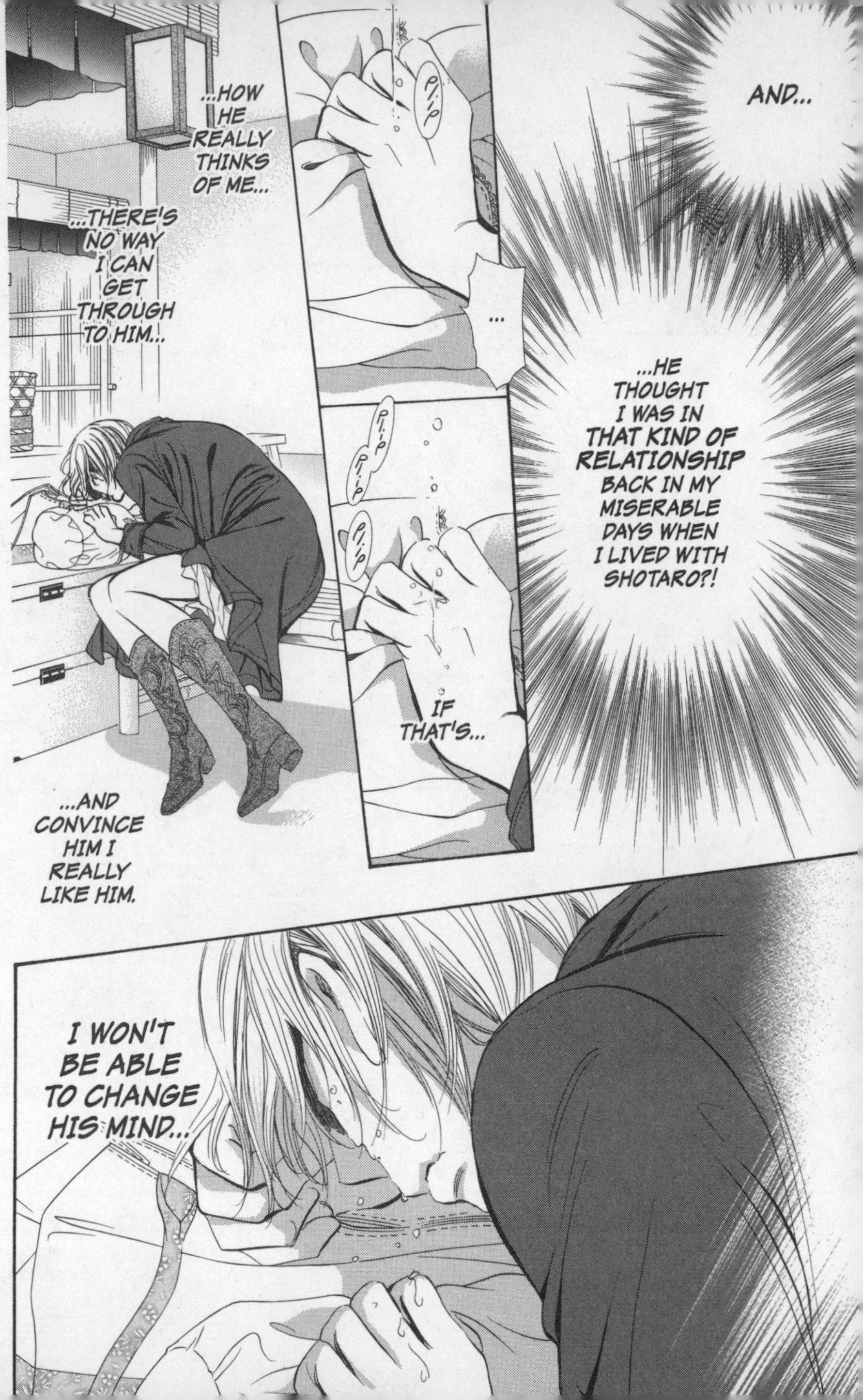

AND...
...HE THOUGHT I WAS IN THAT KIND OF RELATIONSHIP BACK IN MY MISERABLE DAYS WHEN I LIVED WITH SHOTARO?!
PLIP
...
PLIP
PLIP
PLIP
IF THAT'S...
...HOW HE REALLY THINKS OF ME...
...THERE'S NO WAY I CAN GET THROUGH TO HIM...
...AND CONVINCE HIM I REALLY LIKE HIM.
I WON'T BE ABLE TO CHANGE HIS MIND...

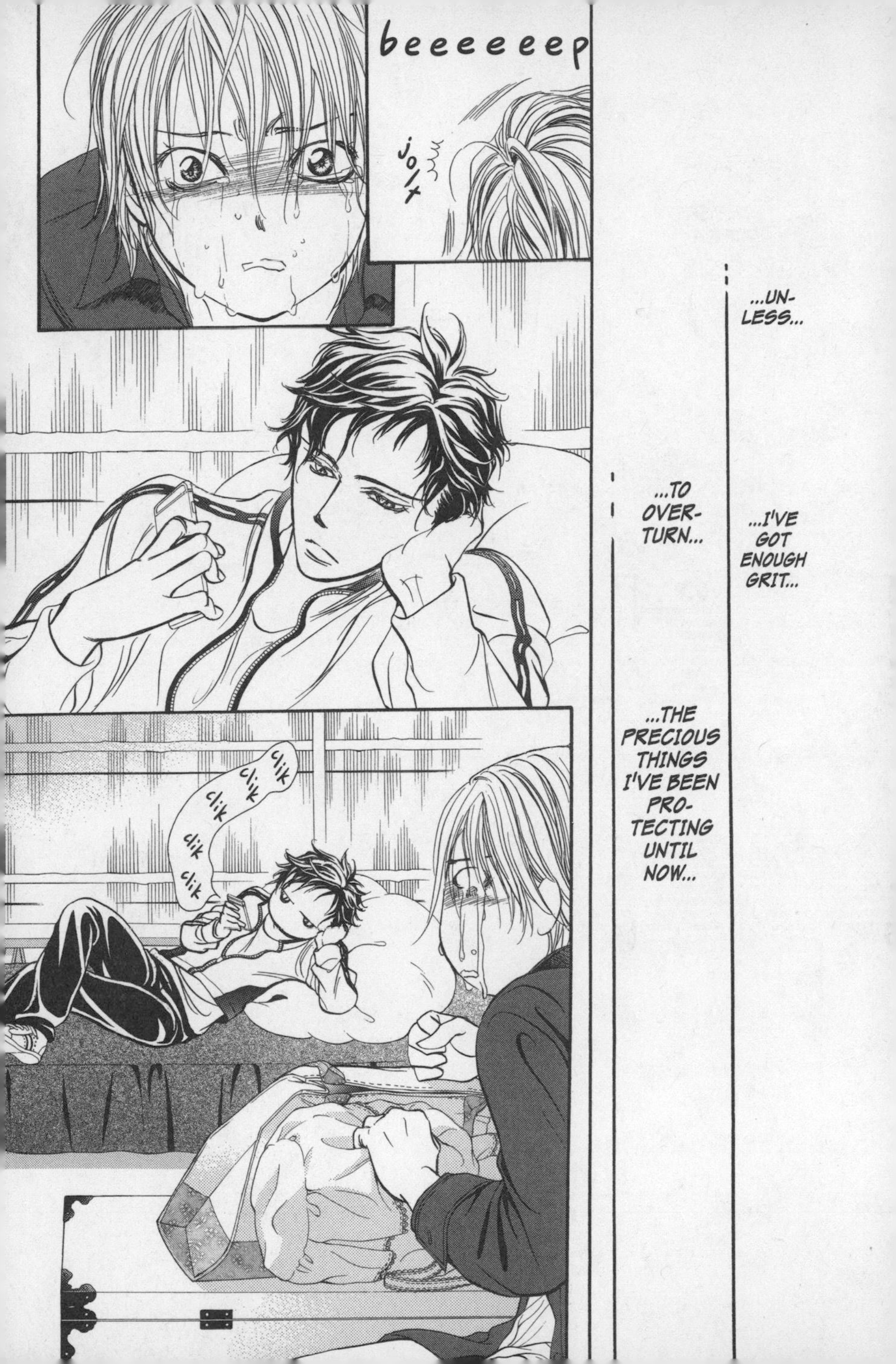
...UN-LESS...
...I'VE GOT ENOUGH GRIT...
...TO OVER-TURN...
...THE PRECIOUS THINGS I'VE BEEN PRO-TECTING UNTIL NOW...
beeeeeeep
jolt
clik clik clik clik clik

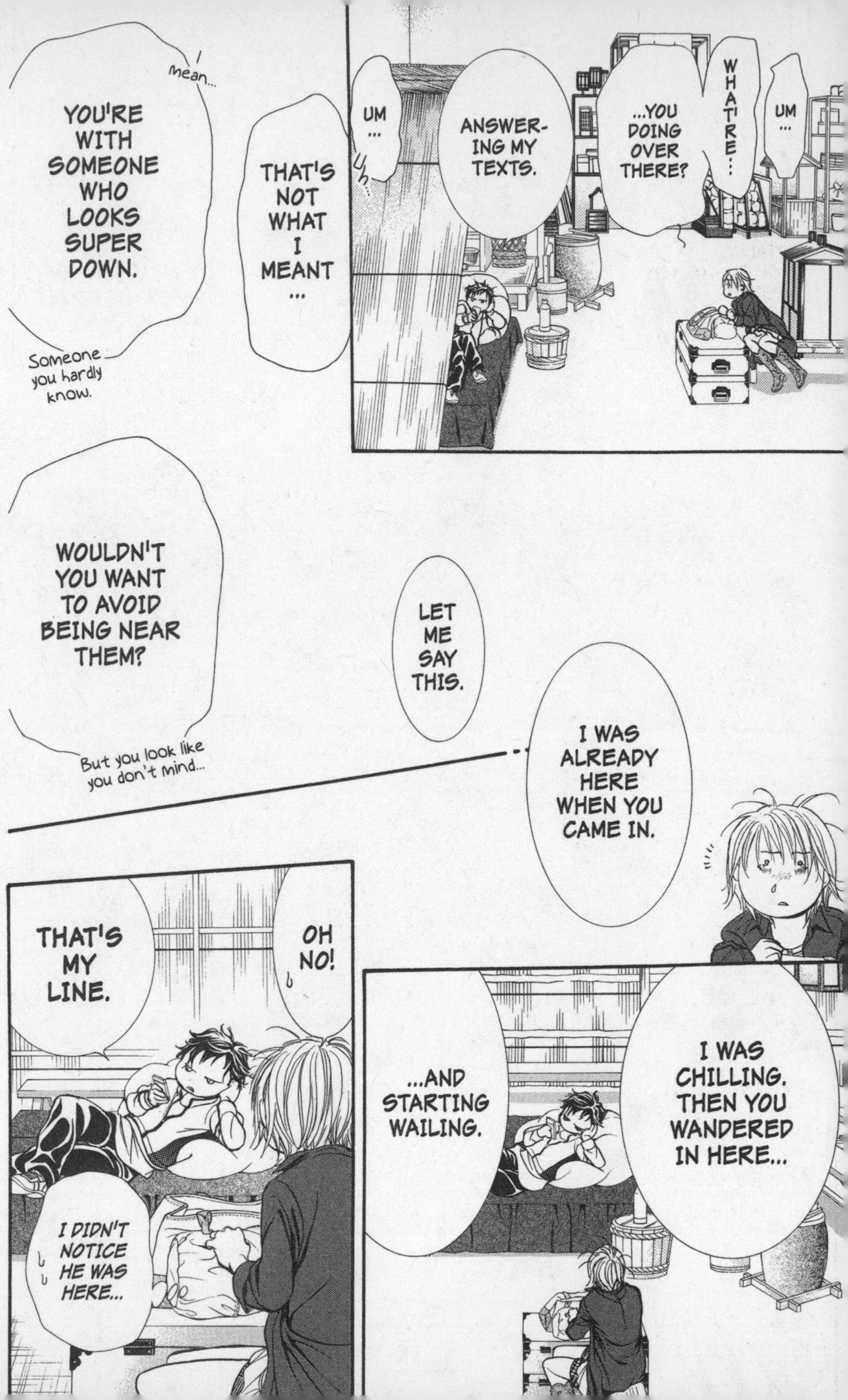
UM ...
WHAT'RE...
...YOU DOING OVER THERE?
ANSWERING MY TEXTS.
UM ...
Uh...
THAT'S NOT WHAT I MEANT ...
I mean...
YOU'RE WITH SOMEONE WHO LOOKS SUPER DOWN.
Someone you hardly know.
WOULDN'T YOU WANT TO AVOID BEING NEAR THEM?
But you look like you don't mind...
LET ME SAY THIS.
I WAS ALREADY HERE WHEN YOU CAME IN.
I WAS CHILLING. THEN YOU WANDERED IN HERE...
...AND STARTING WAILING.
OH NO!
THAT'S MY LINE.
I DIDN'T NOTICE HE WAS HERE...

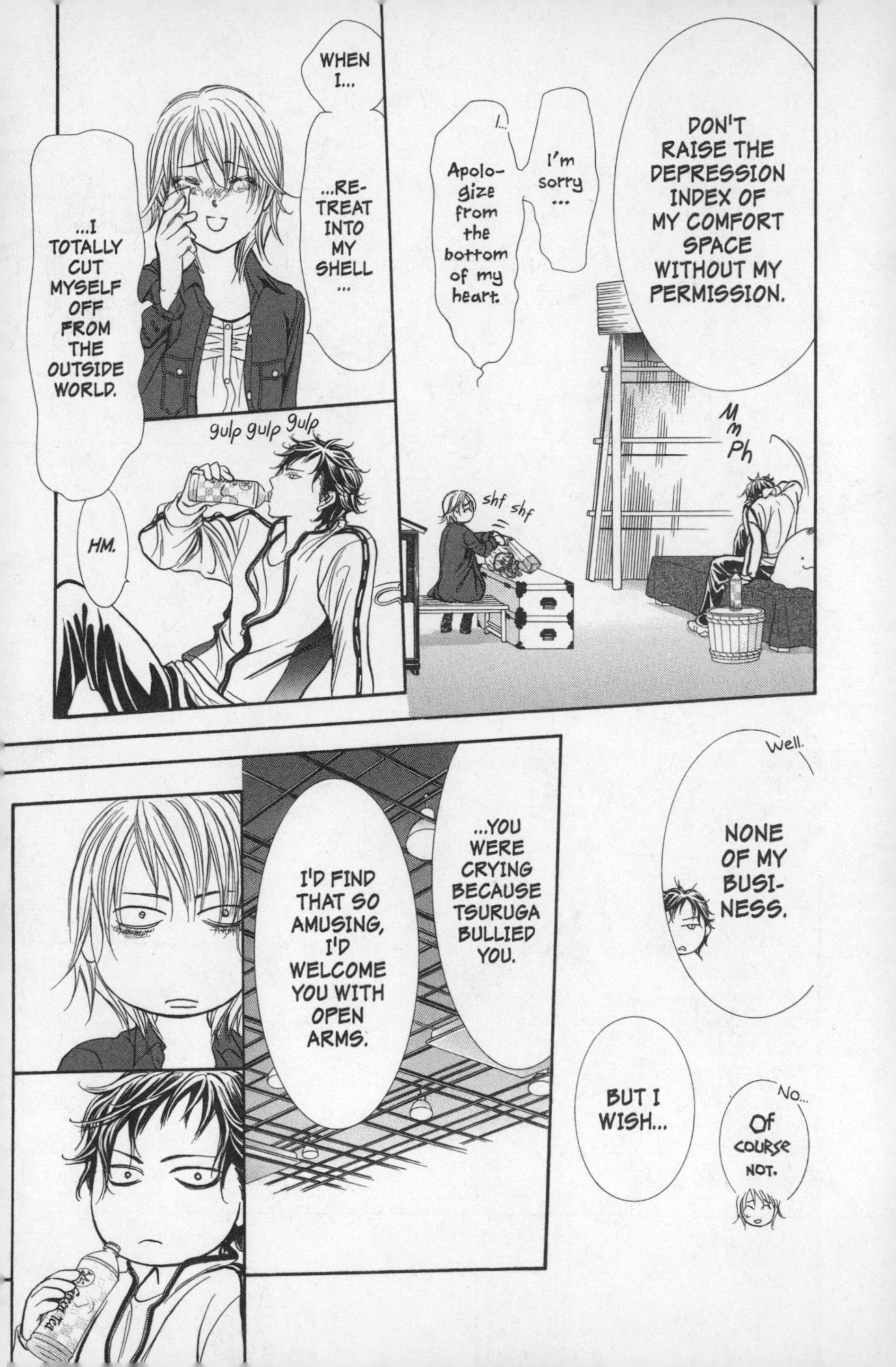
DON'T RAISE THE DEPRESSION INDEX OF MY COMFORT SPACE WITHOUT MY PERMISSION.
MmPh
I...
I'm sorry...
Apologize from the bottom of my heart.
shf shf
WHEN I...
...RETREAT INTO MY SHELL...
...I TOTALLY CUT MYSELF OFF FROM THE OUTSIDE WORLD.
gulp gulp gulp
HM.
Well.
NONE OF MY BUSINESS.
BUT I WISH...
No...
Of course not.
...YOU WERE CRYING BECAUSE TSURUGA BULLIED YOU.
I'D FIND THAT SO AMUSING, I'D WELCOME YOU WITH OPEN ARMS.

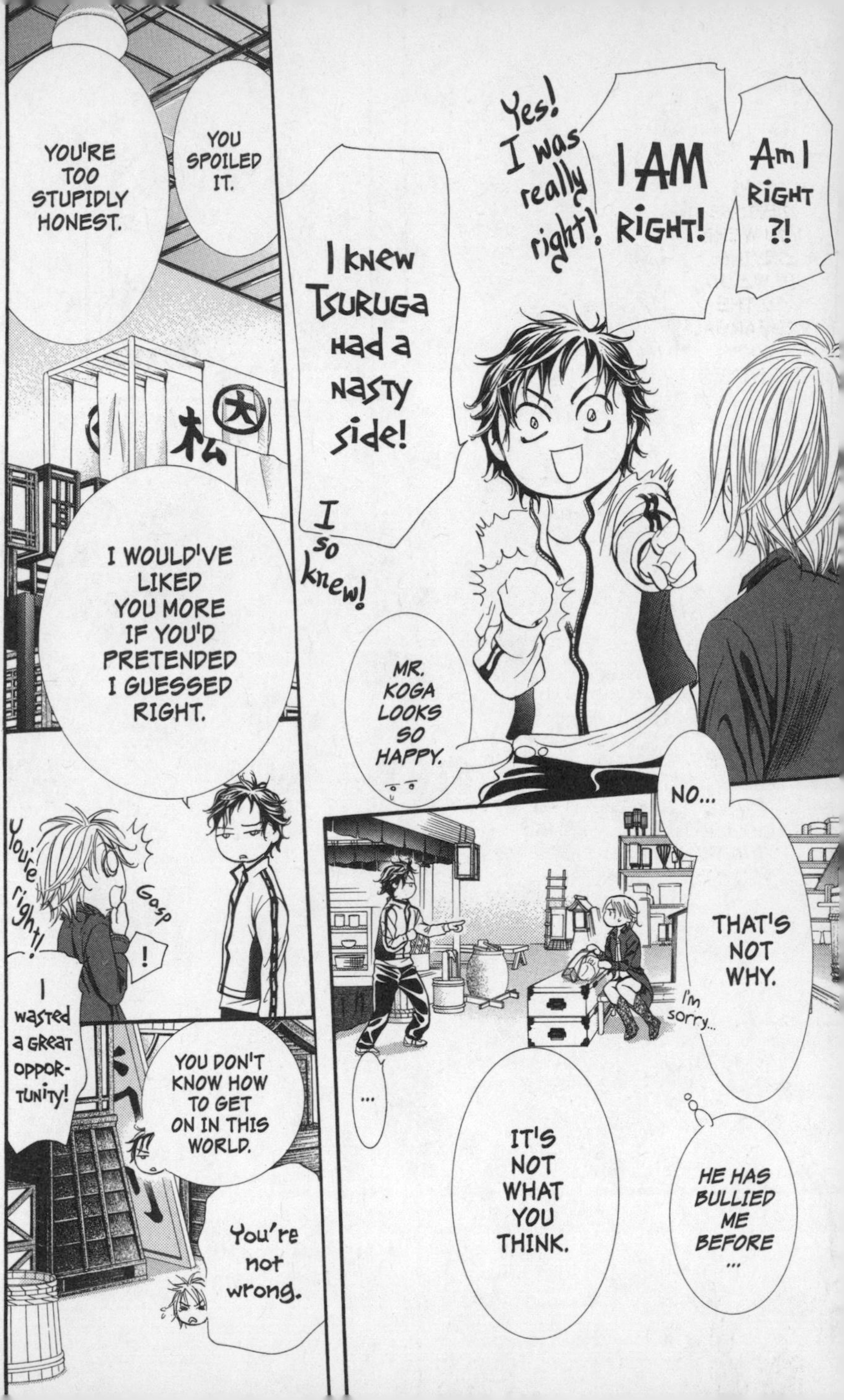
Am I RIGHT ?!
I AM RIGHT!
Yes! I was really right!
I knew Tsuruga had a nasty side!
I so knew!
MR. KOGA LOOKS SO HAPPY.
NO...
THAT'S NOT WHY.
I'm sorry...
HE HAS BULLIED ME BEFORE ...
IT'S NOT WHAT YOU THINK.
...
YOU SPOILED IT.
YOU'RE TOO STUPIDLY HONEST.
I WOULD'VE LIKED YOU MORE IF YOU'D PRETENDED I GUESSED RIGHT.
Gasp
!
You're right!!
I wasted a great opportunity!
YOU DON'T KNOW HOW TO GET ON IN THIS WORLD.
You're not wrong.

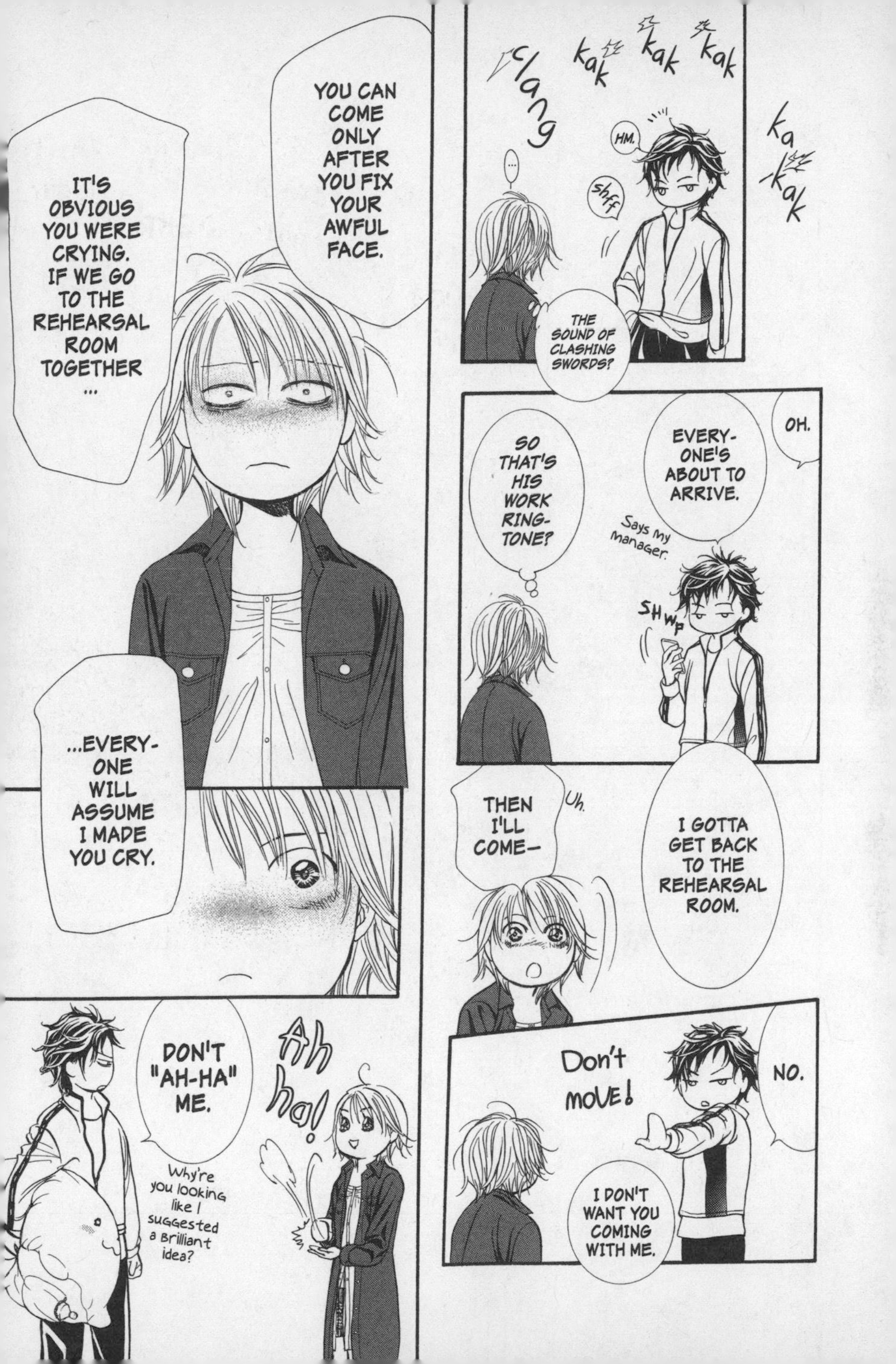
clang
kak kak kak
kakak
HM.
shff
...
THE SOUND OF CLASHING SWORDS?
OH.
EVERY-ONE'S ABOUT TO ARRIVE.
Says my manager.
SO THAT'S HIS WORK RING-TONE?
SHWP
I GOTTA GET BACK TO THE REHEARSAL ROOM.
Uh.
THEN I'LL COME—
NO.
Don't move!
I DON'T WANT YOU COMING WITH ME.
YOU CAN COME ONLY AFTER YOU FIX YOUR AWFUL FACE.
IT'S OBVIOUS YOU WERE CRYING. IF WE GO TO THE REHEARSAL ROOM TOGETHER ...
...EVERY-ONE WILL ASSUME I MADE YOU CRY.
Ah ha!
DON'T "AH-HA" ME.
Why're you looking like I suggested a brilliant idea?

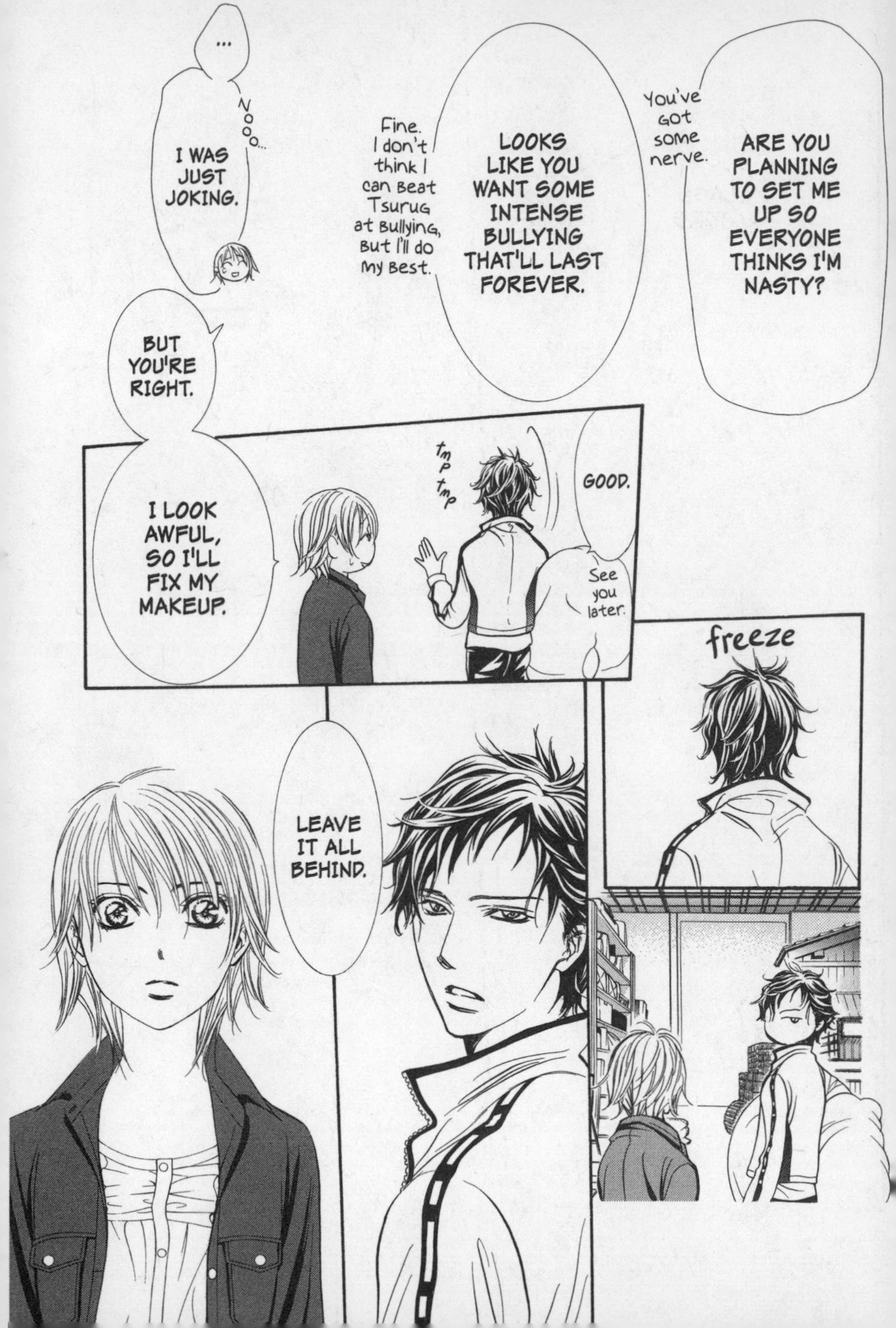
You've got some nerve.
ARE YOU PLANNING TO SET ME UP SO EVERYONE THINKS I'M NASTY?
LOOKS LIKE YOU WANT SOME INTENSE BULLYING THAT'LL LAST FOREVER.
Fine. I don't think I can beat Tsurug at bullying, but I'll do my best.
...
Nooo...
I WAS JUST JOKING.
BUT YOU'RE RIGHT.
I LOOK AWFUL, SO I'LL FIX MY MAKEUP.
GOOD.
See you later.
tmp tmp
freeze
LEAVE IT ALL BEHIND.

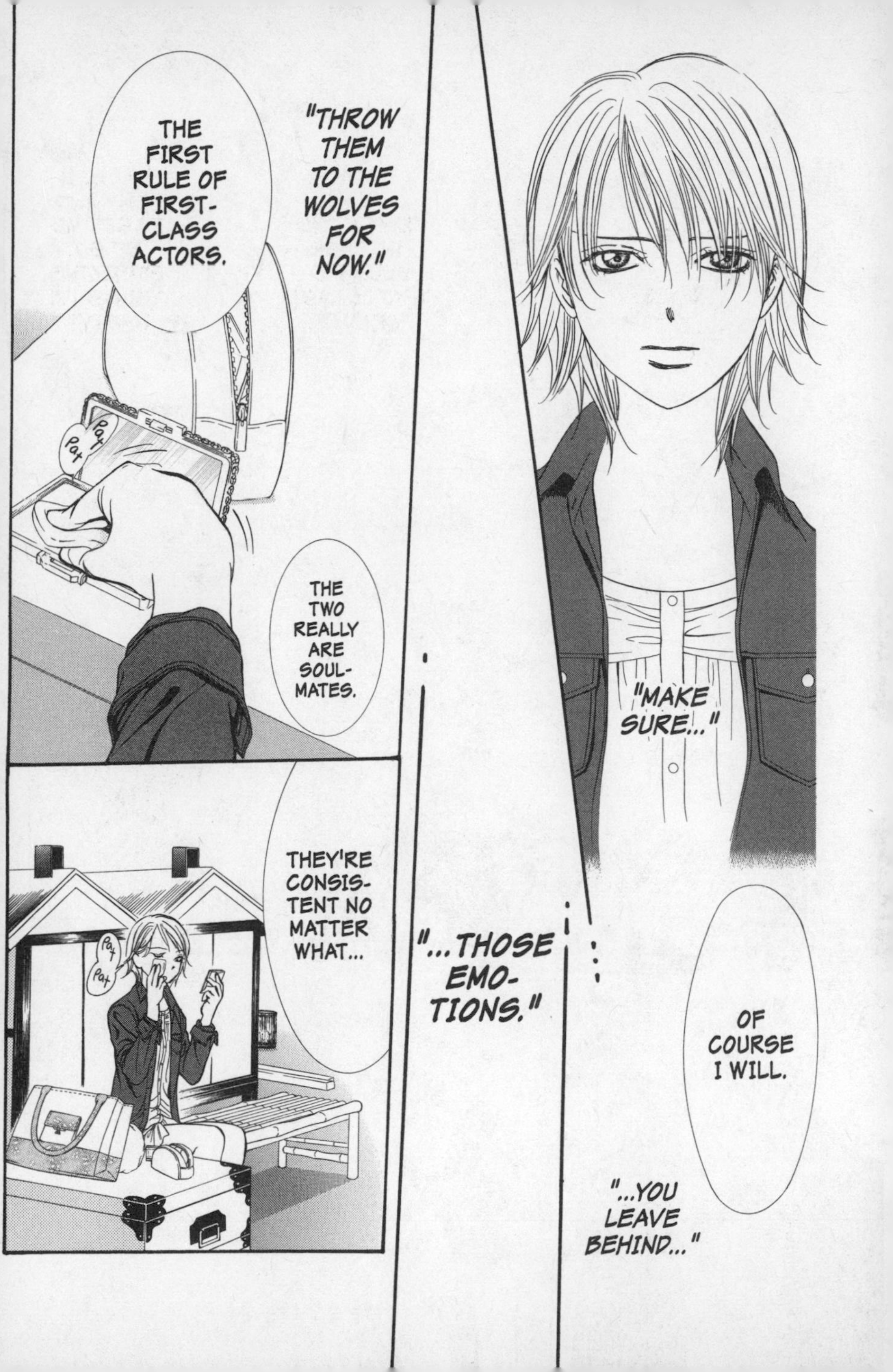
"MAKE SURE..."
"...YOU LEAVE BEHIND..."
"...THOSE EMOTIONS."
OF COURSE I WILL.
"THROW THEM TO THE WOLVES FOR NOW."
THE FIRST RULE OF FIRST-CLASS ACTORS.
Pat Pat
THE TWO REALLY ARE SOULMATES.
THEY'RE CONSISTENT NO MATTER WHAT...
Pat Pat

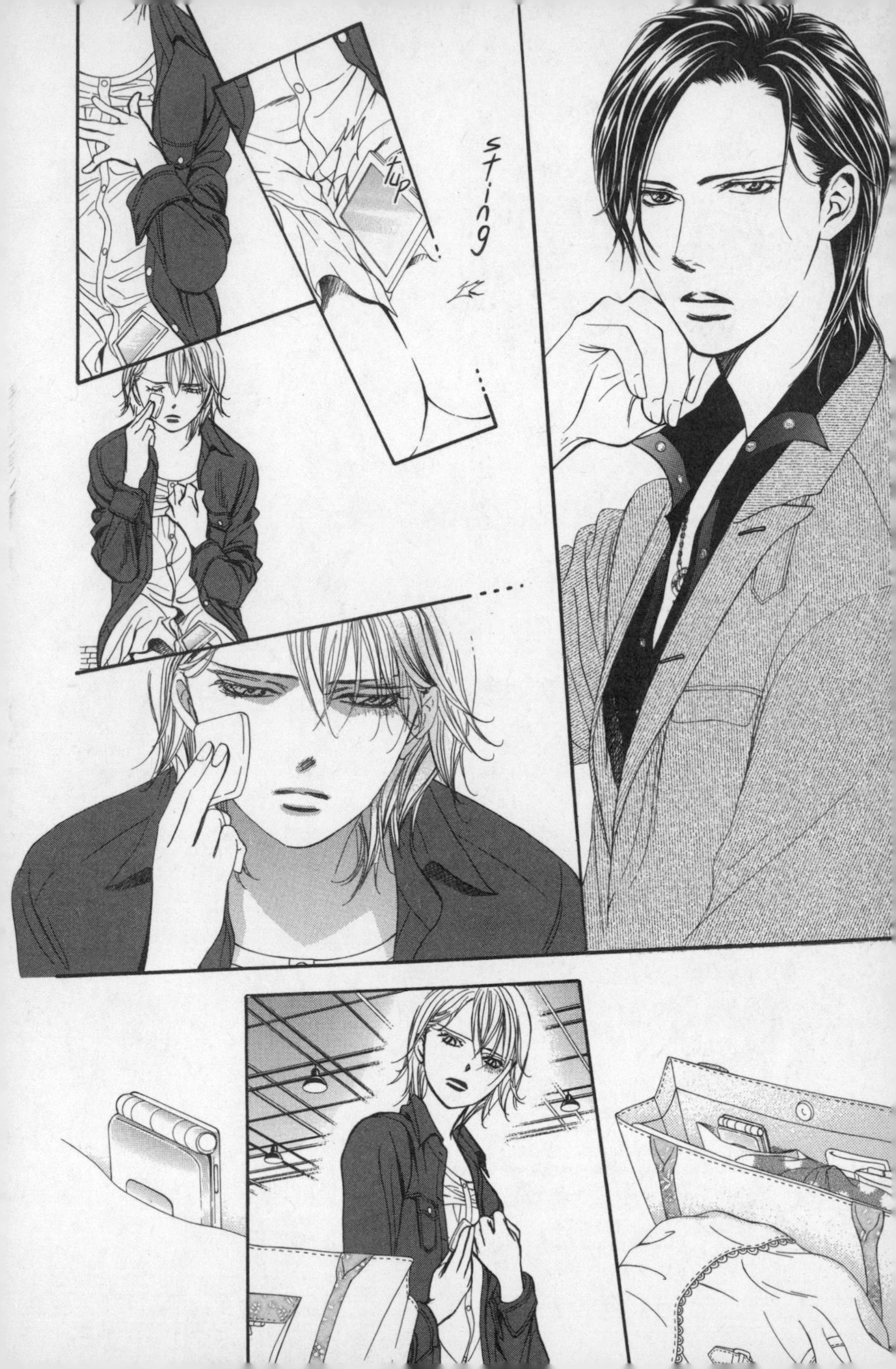
sting
tup

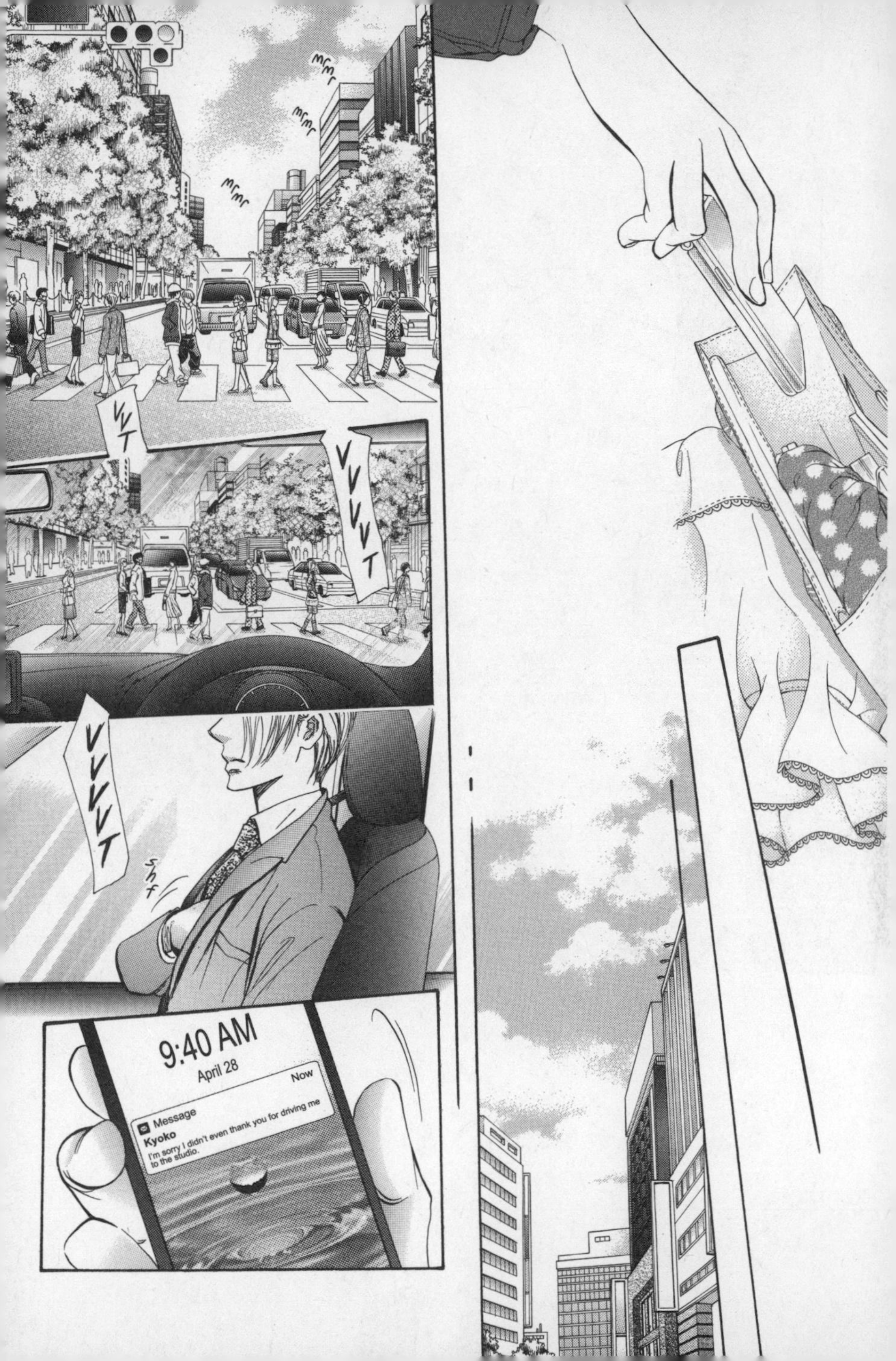
mrmr
mrmr
mrmr
VVT
VVVVVT
VVVVVT
shf
9:40 AM
April 28
Now
Message
Kyoko
I'm sorry I didn't even thank you for driving me to the studio.

End of Act 268

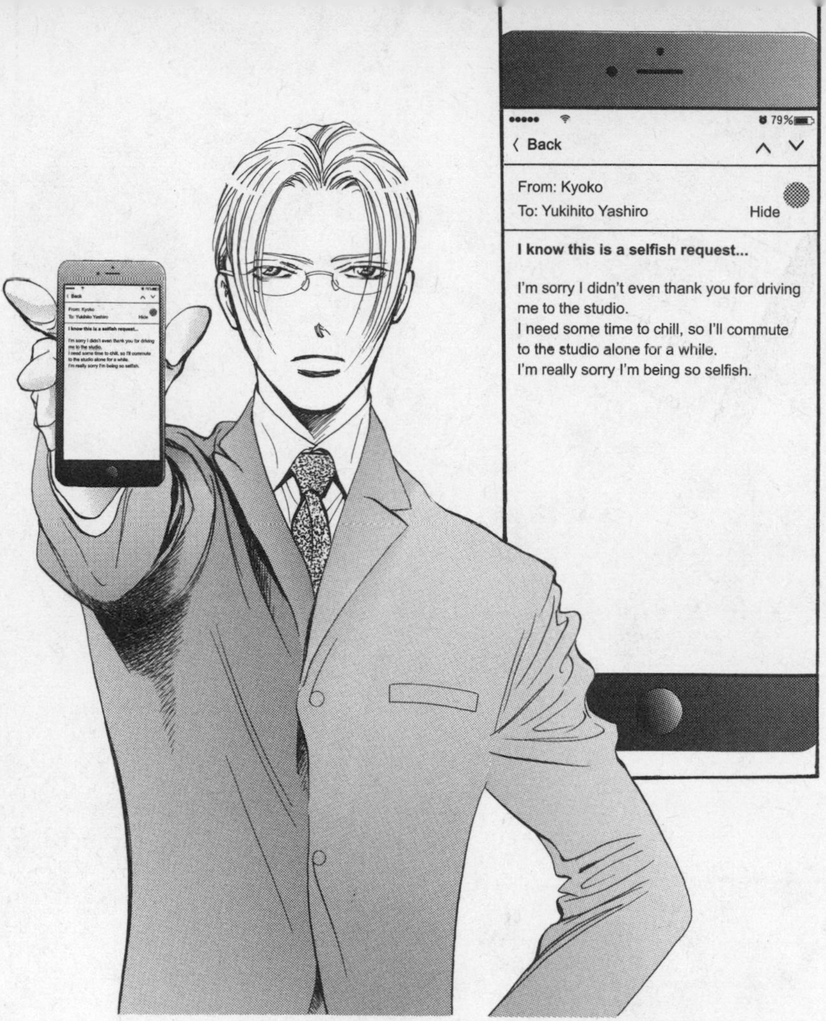
79%
Back
From: Kyoko
To: Yukihito Yashiro
Hide
I know this is a selfish request...
I'm sorry I didn't even thank you for driving me to the studio.
I need some time to chill, so I'll commute to the studio alone for a while.
I'm really sorry I'm being so selfish.

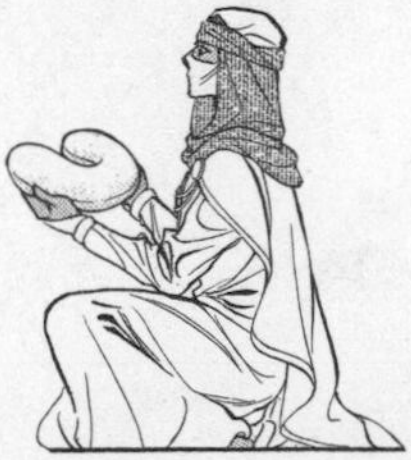

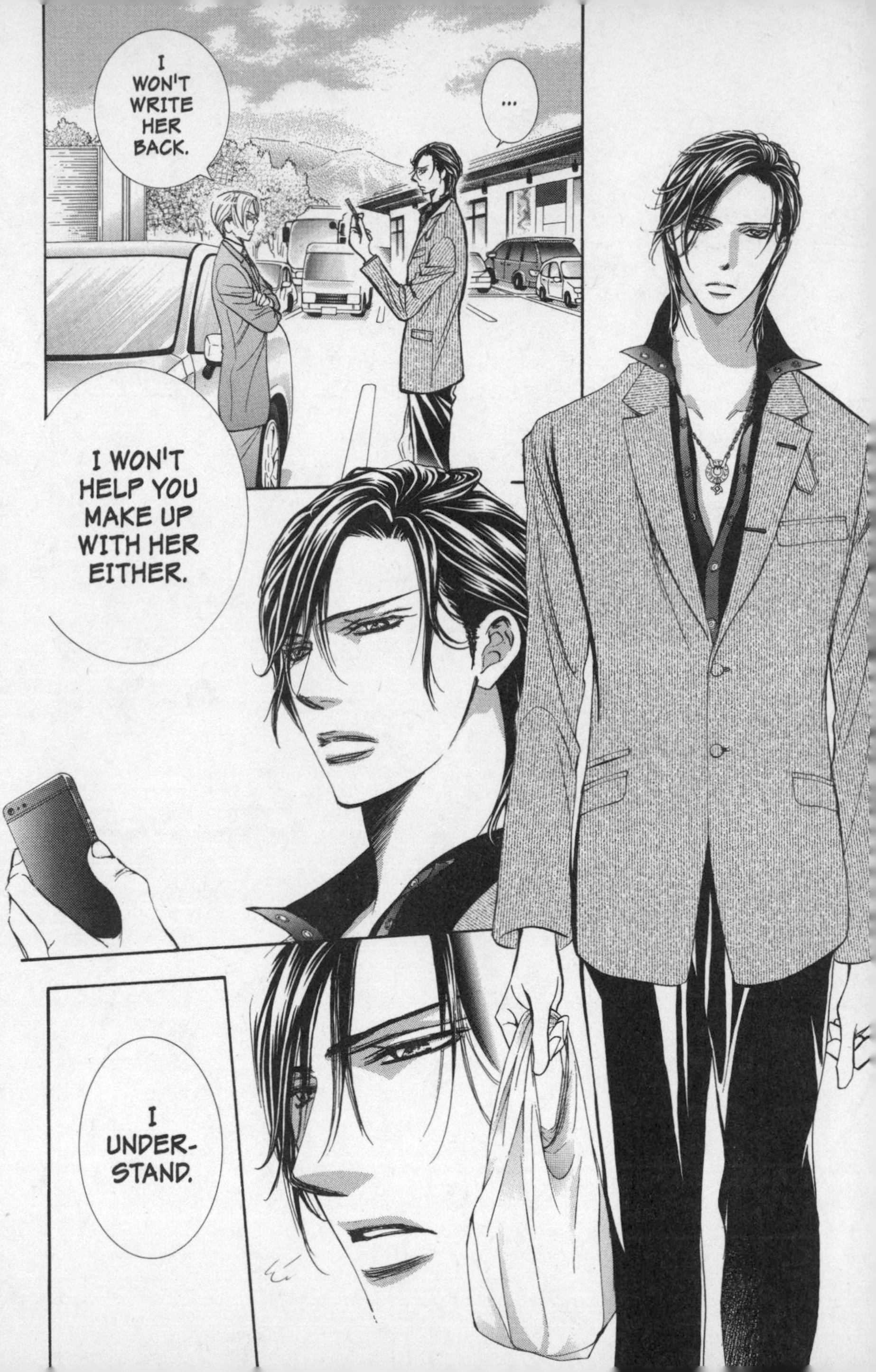
...
I WON'T WRITE HER BACK.
I WON'T HELP YOU MAKE UP WITH HER EITHER.
I UNDER-STAND.

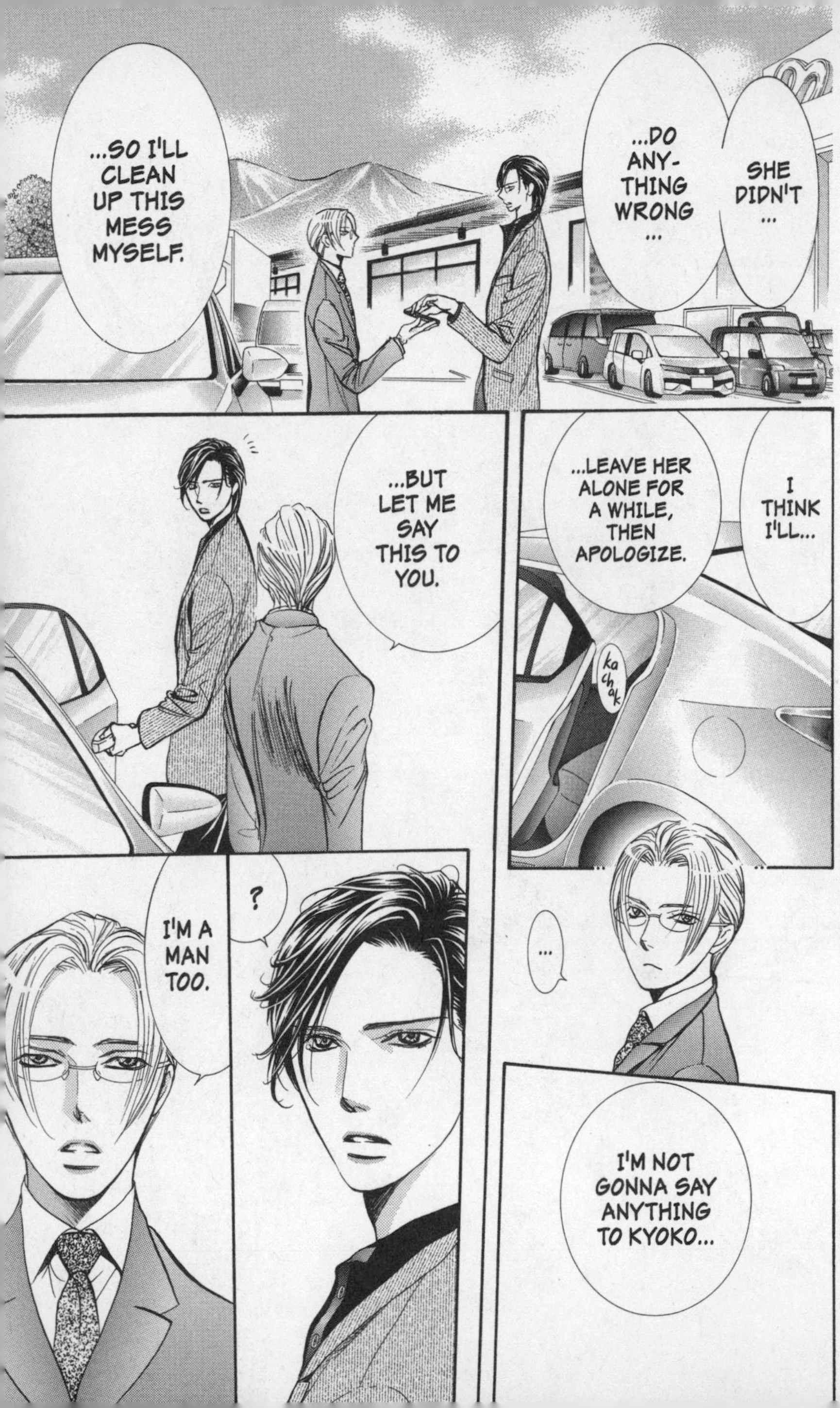
SHE DIDN'T ...
...DO ANY-THING WRONG ...
...SO I'LL CLEAN UP THIS MESS MYSELF.
I THINK I'LL...
...LEAVE HER ALONE FOR A WHILE, THEN APOLOGIZE.
kachak
...BUT LET ME SAY THIS TO YOU.
...
I'M NOT GONNA SAY ANYTHING TO KYOKO...
?
I'M A MAN TOO.

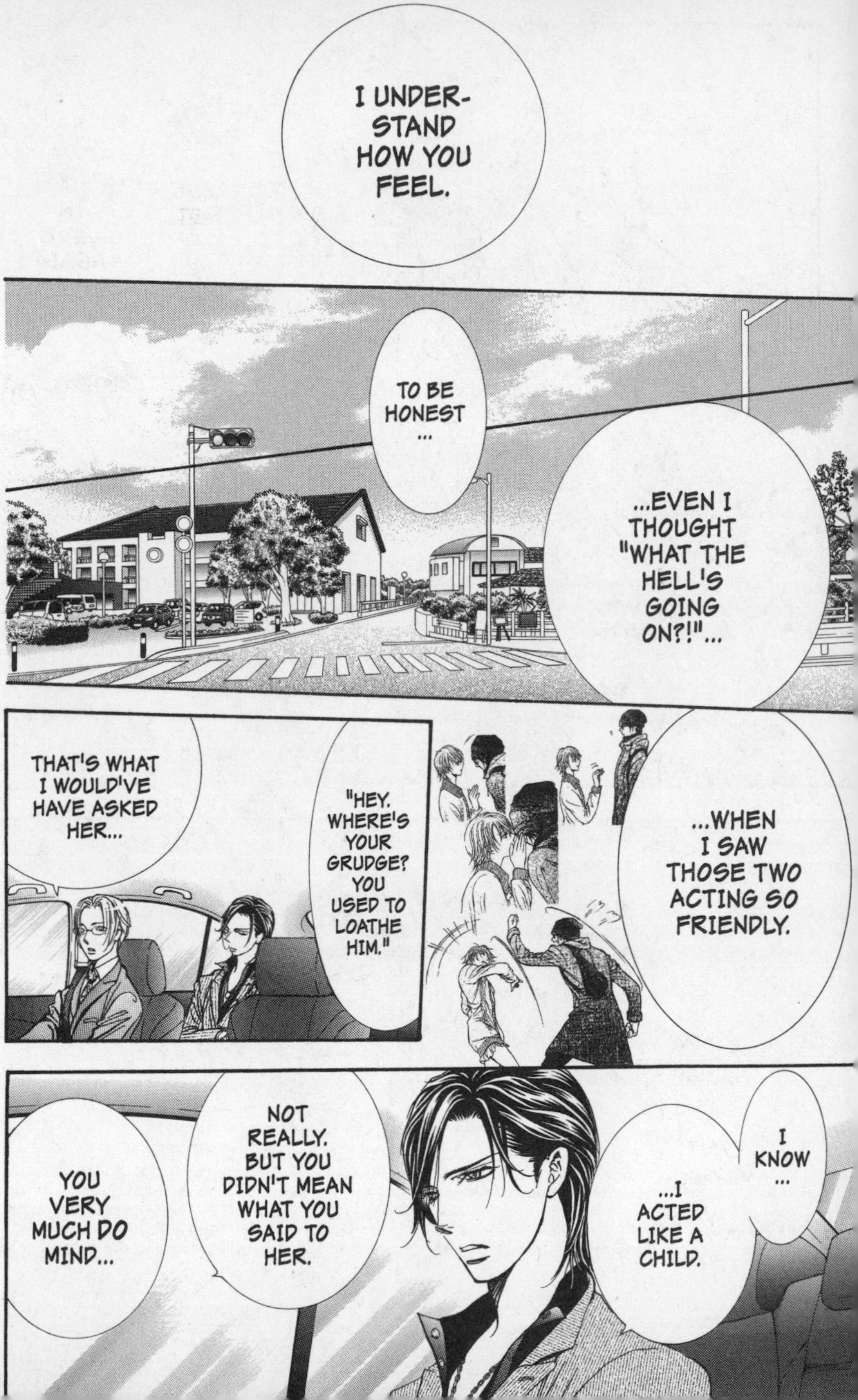
I UNDER-STAND HOW YOU FEEL.
TO BE HONEST ...
...EVEN I THOUGHT "WHAT THE HELL'S GOING ON?!"...
...WHEN I SAW THOSE TWO ACTING SO FRIENDLY.
"HEY. WHERE'S YOUR GRUDGE? YOU USED TO LOATHE HIM."
THAT'S WHAT I WOULD'VE HAVE ASKED HER...
I KNOW ...
...I ACTED LIKE A CHILD.
NOT REALLY. BUT YOU DIDN'T MEAN WHAT YOU SAID TO HER.
YOU VERY MUCH DO MIND...

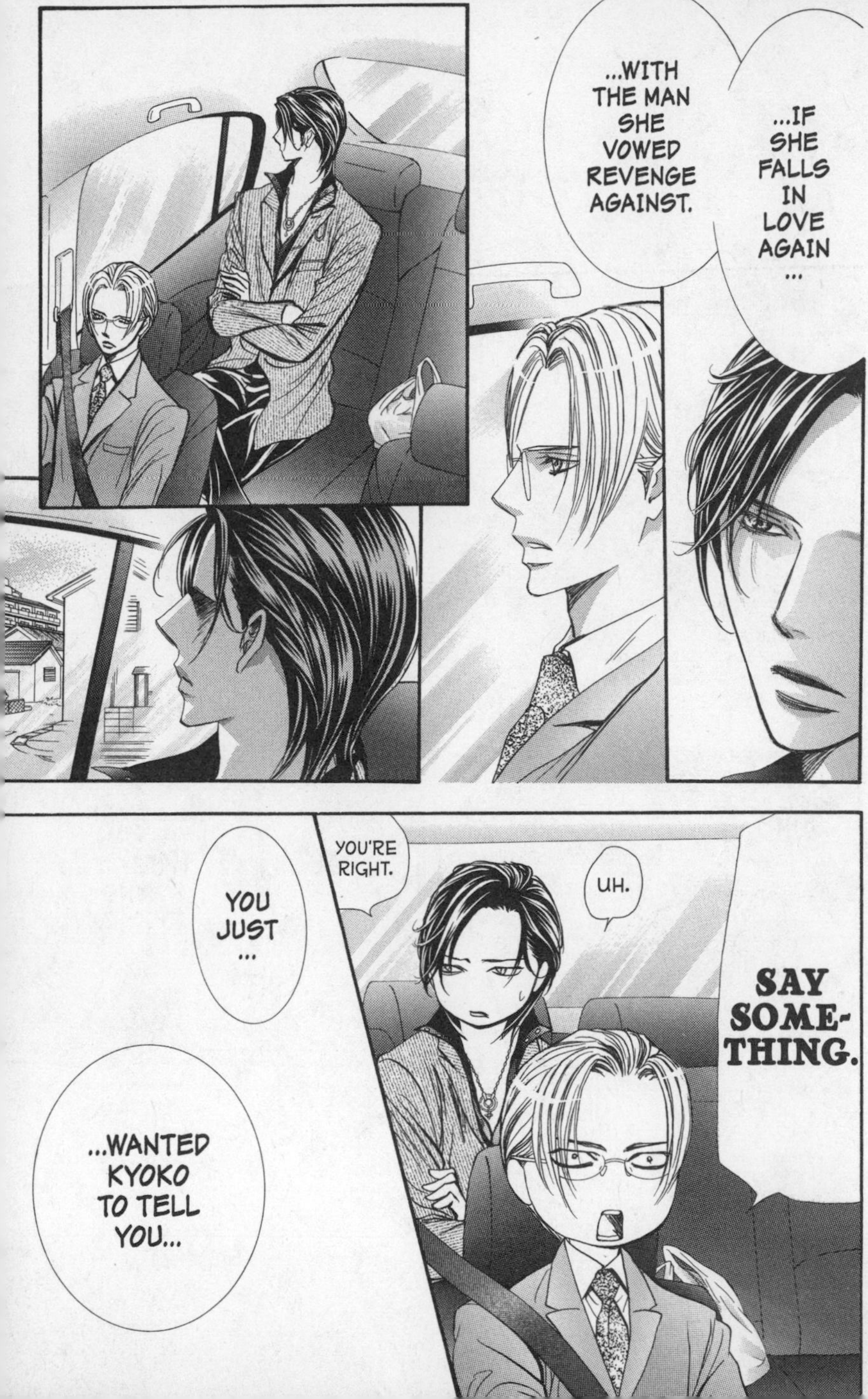
...IF SHE FALLS IN LOVE AGAIN...
...WITH THE MAN SHE VOWED REVENGE AGAINST.
SAY SOMETHING.
UH.
YOU'RE RIGHT.
YOU JUST...
...WANTED KYOKO TO TELL YOU...

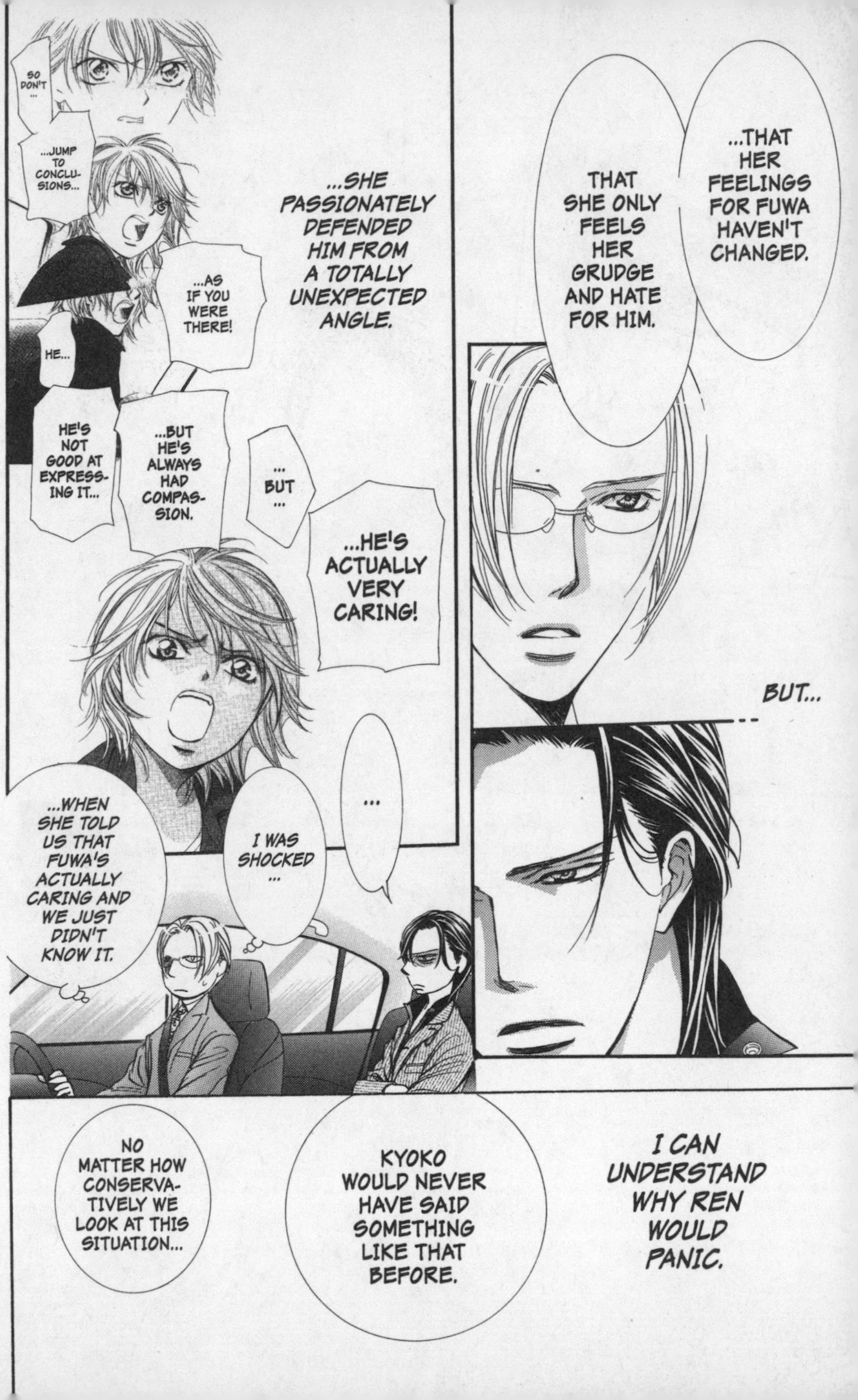

...THAT HER FEELINGS FOR FUWA HAVEN'T CHANGED.
THAT SHE ONLY FEELS HER GRUDGE AND HATE FOR HIM.
BUT...
...SHE PASSIONATELY DEFENDED HIM FROM A TOTALLY UNEXPECTED ANGLE.
SO DON'T...
...JUMP TO CONCLUSIONS...
...AS IF YOU WERE THERE!
HE...
HE'S NOT GOOD AT EXPRESSING IT...
...BUT HE'S ALWAYS HAD COMPASSION.
... BUT ...
...HE'S ACTUALLY VERY CARING!
...
I WAS SHOCKED...
...WHEN SHE TOLD US THAT FUWA'S ACTUALLY CARING AND WE JUST DIDN'T KNOW IT.
I CAN UNDERSTAND WHY REN WOULD PANIC.
KYOKO WOULD NEVER HAVE SAID SOMETHING LIKE THAT BEFORE.
NO MATTER HOW CONSERVATIVELY WE LOOK AT THIS SITUATION...

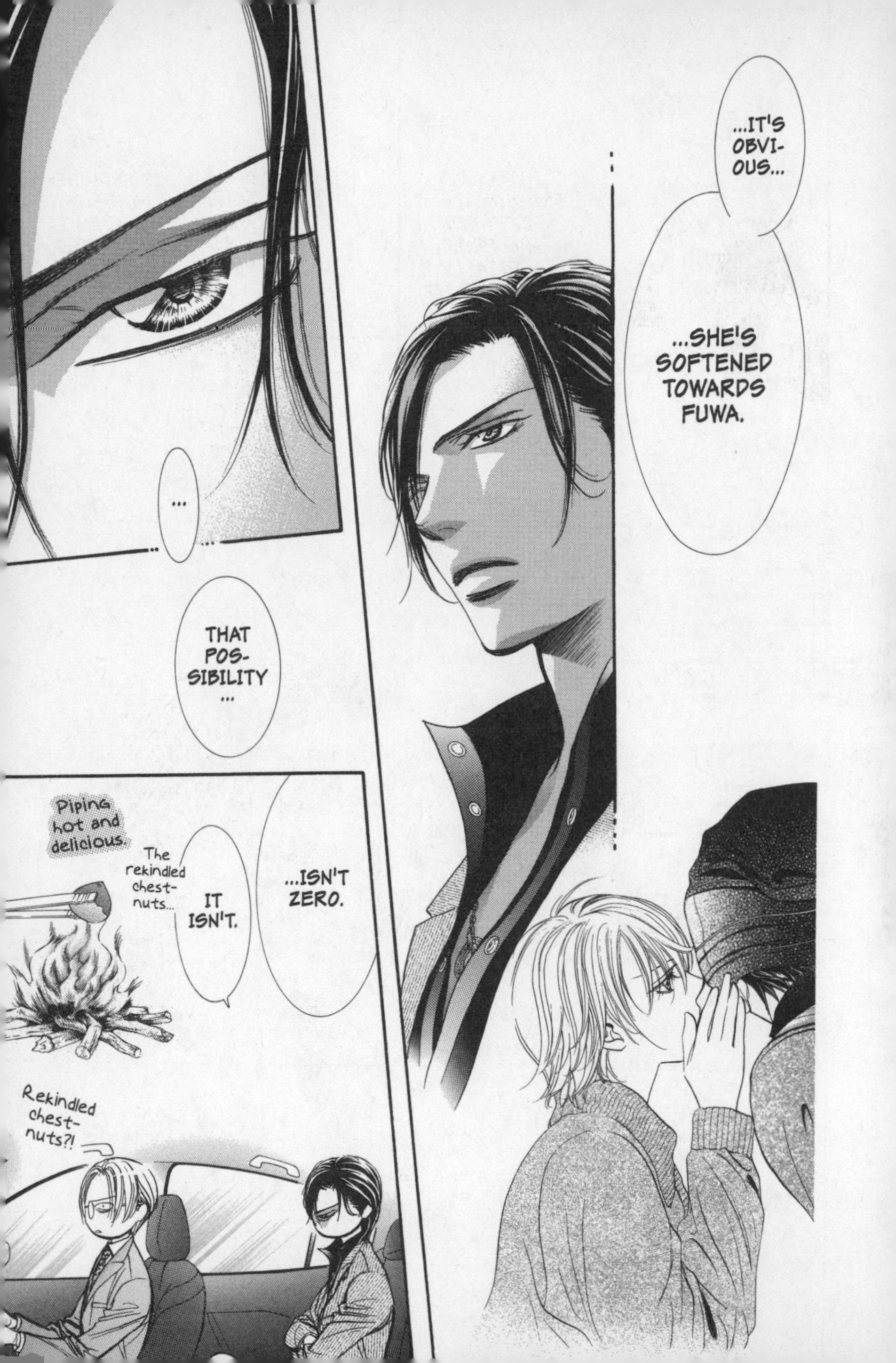
...IT'S OBVIOUS...
...SHE'S SOFTENED TOWARDS FUWA.
...
THAT POSSIBILITY...
...ISN'T ZERO.
IT ISN'T.
The rekindled chest-nuts...
Piping hot and delicious.
Rekindled chest-nuts?!

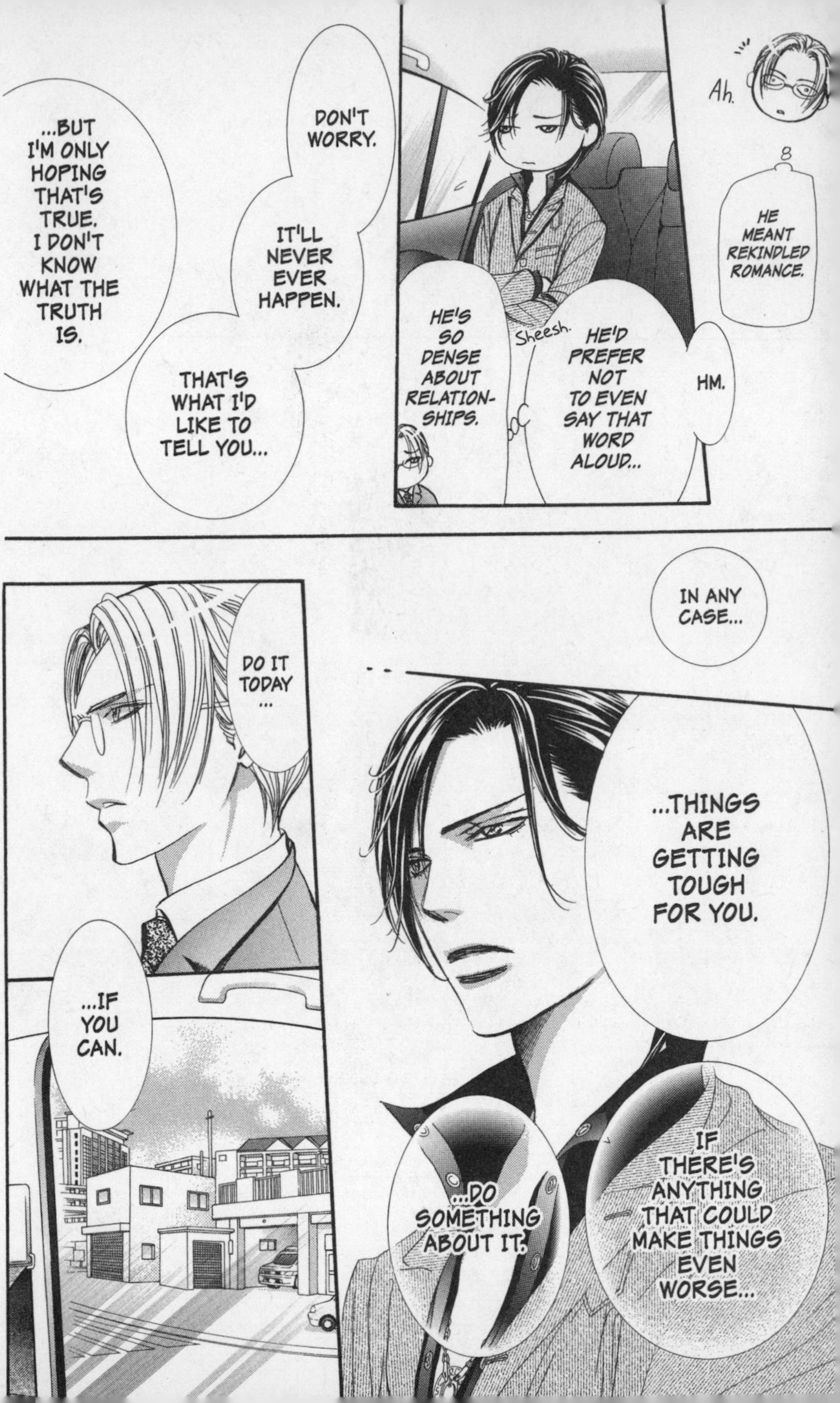
Ah.
HE MEANT REKINDLED ROMANCE.
HM.
HE'D PREFER NOT TO EVEN SAY THAT WORD ALOUD...
Sheesh.
HE'S SO DENSE ABOUT RELATIONSHIPS.
DON'T WORRY.
IT'LL NEVER EVER HAPPEN.
THAT'S WHAT I'D LIKE TO TELL YOU...
...BUT I'M ONLY HOPING THAT'S TRUE. I DON'T KNOW WHAT THE TRUTH IS.
IN ANY CASE...
...THINGS ARE GETTING TOUGH FOR YOU.
IF THERE'S ANYTHING THAT COULD MAKE THINGS EVEN WORSE...
...DO SOMETHING ABOUT IT.
DO IT TODAY...
...IF YOU CAN.

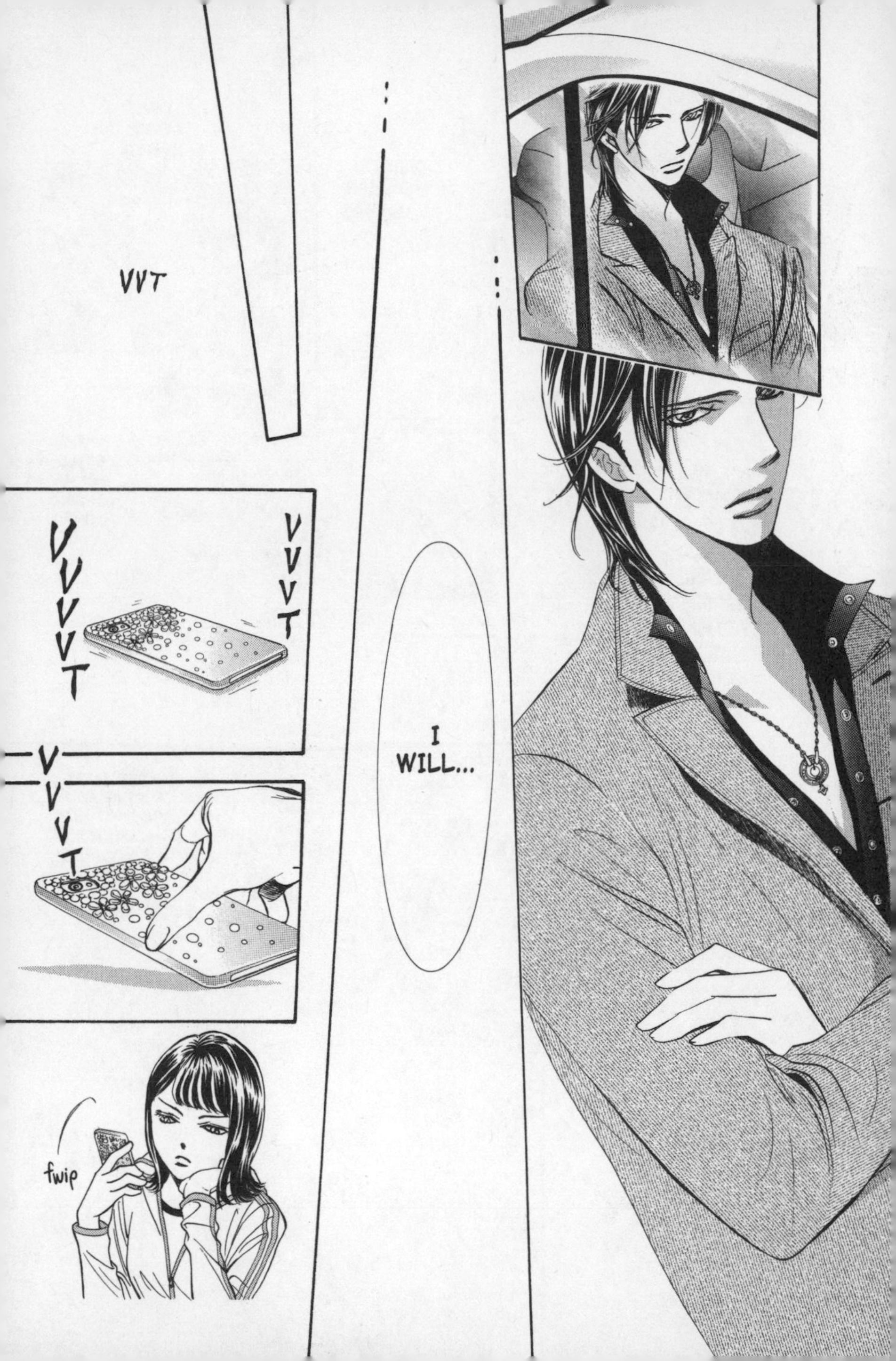

I WILL...
VVT
VVVVT
VVVT
VVVVT
fwip

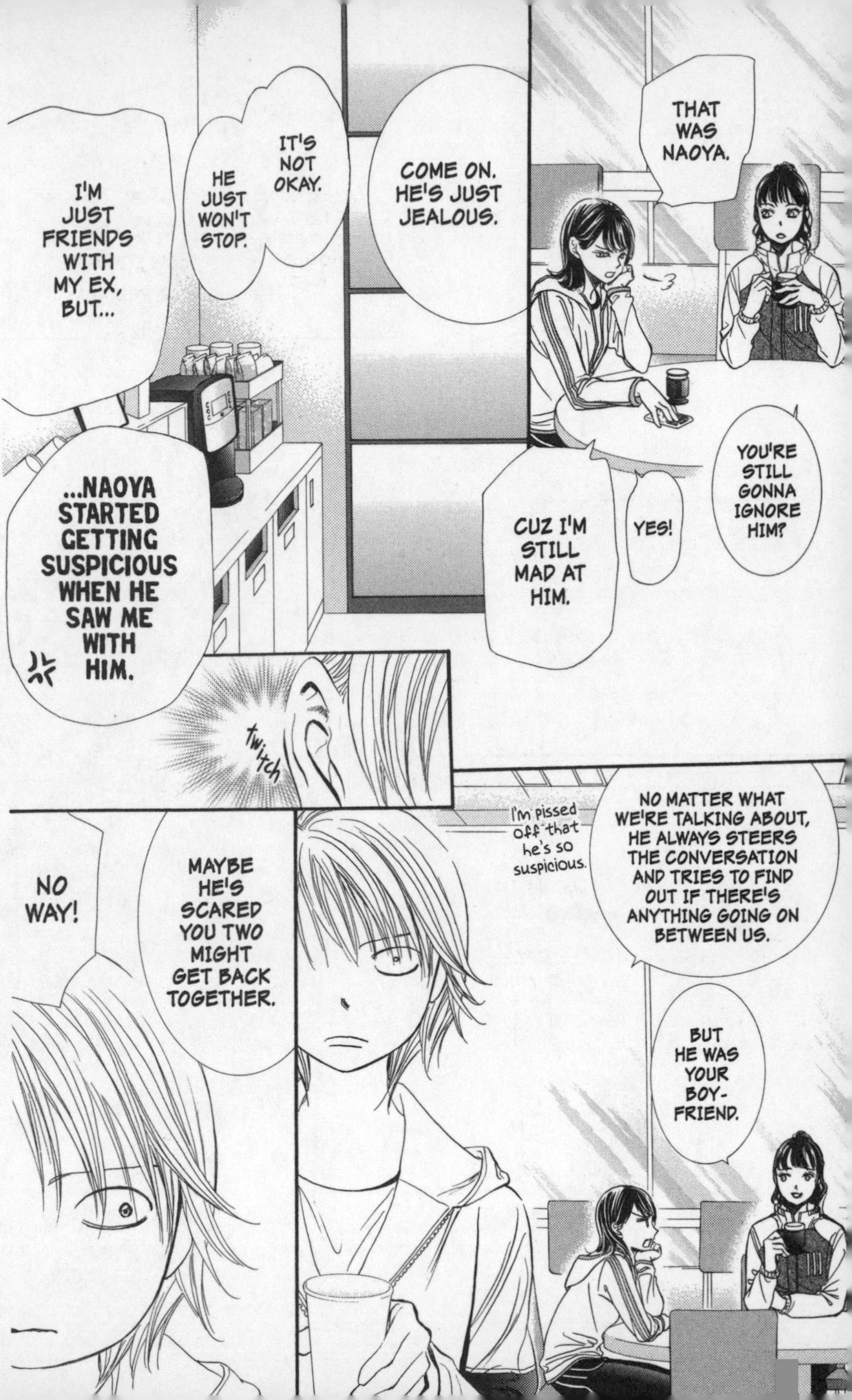
THAT WAS NAOYA.
YOU'RE STILL GONNA IGNORE HIM?
YES!
CUZ I'M STILL MAD AT HIM.
COME ON. HE'S JUST JEALOUS.
IT'S NOT OKAY.
HE JUST WON'T STOP.
I'M JUST FRIENDS WITH MY EX, BUT...
...NAOYA STARTED GETTING SUSPICIOUS WHEN HE SAW ME WITH HIM.
twitch
NO MATTER WHAT WE'RE TALKING ABOUT, HE ALWAYS STEERS THE CONVERSATION AND TRIES TO FIND OUT IF THERE'S ANYTHING GOING ON BETWEEN US.
I'm pissed off that he's so suspicious.
BUT HE WAS YOUR BOY-FRIEND.
MAYBE HE'S SCARED YOU TWO MIGHT GET BACK TOGETHER.
NO WAY!

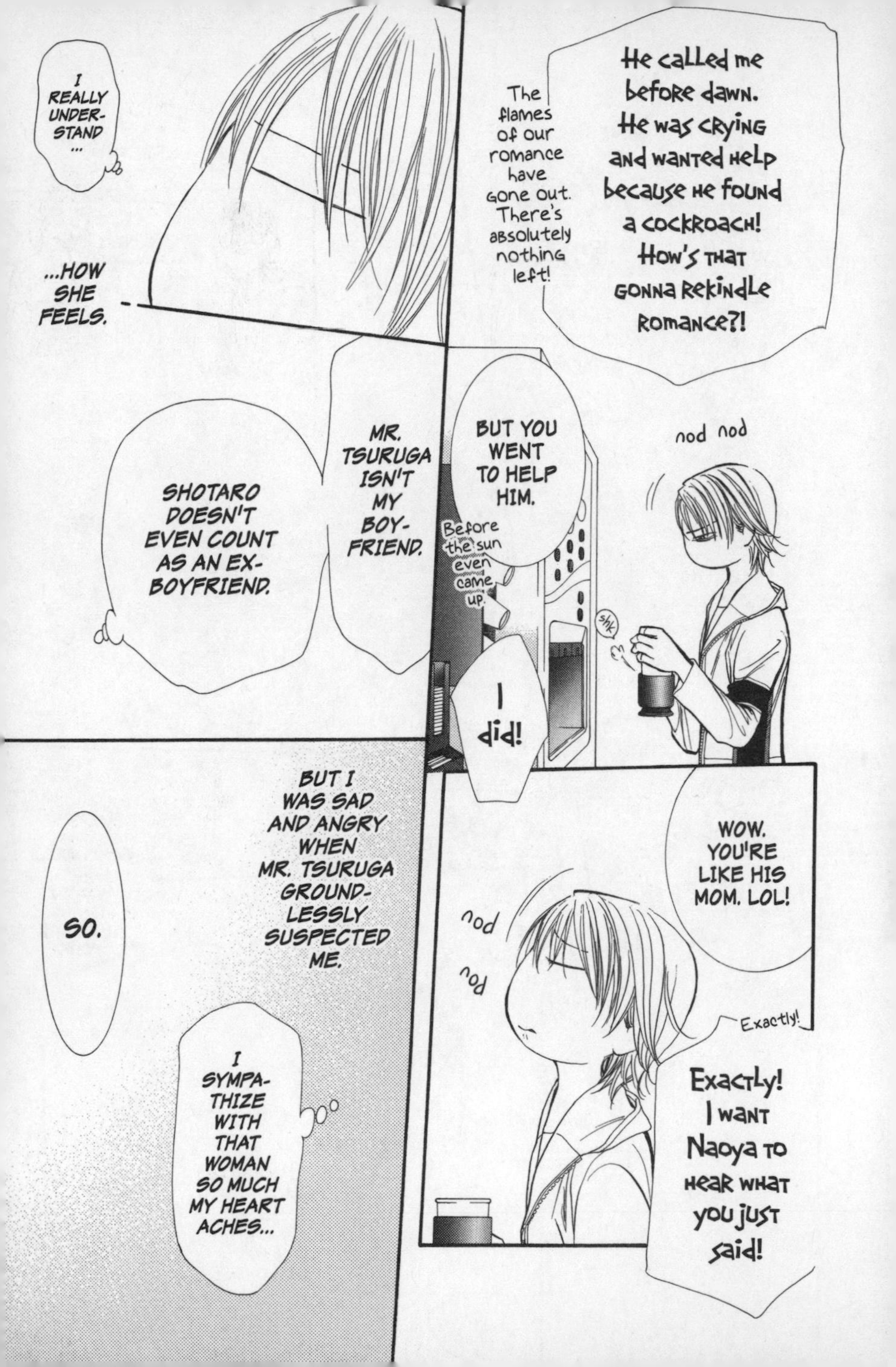
He called me before dawn. He was crying and wanted help because he found a cockroach! How's that gonna rekindle romance?!
The flames of our romance have gone out. There's absolutely nothing left!
I really under-stand ...
...how she feels.
But you went to help him.
nod nod
Before the sun even came up.
shk
I did!
Mr. Tsuruga isn't my boy-friend.
Shotaro doesn't even count as an ex-boyfriend.
Wow. You're like his mom. LOL!
nod nod
Exactly!
Exactly! I want Naoya to hear what you just said!
But I was sad and angry when Mr. Tsuruga ground-lessly suspected me.
So.
I sympa-thize with that woman so much my heart aches...

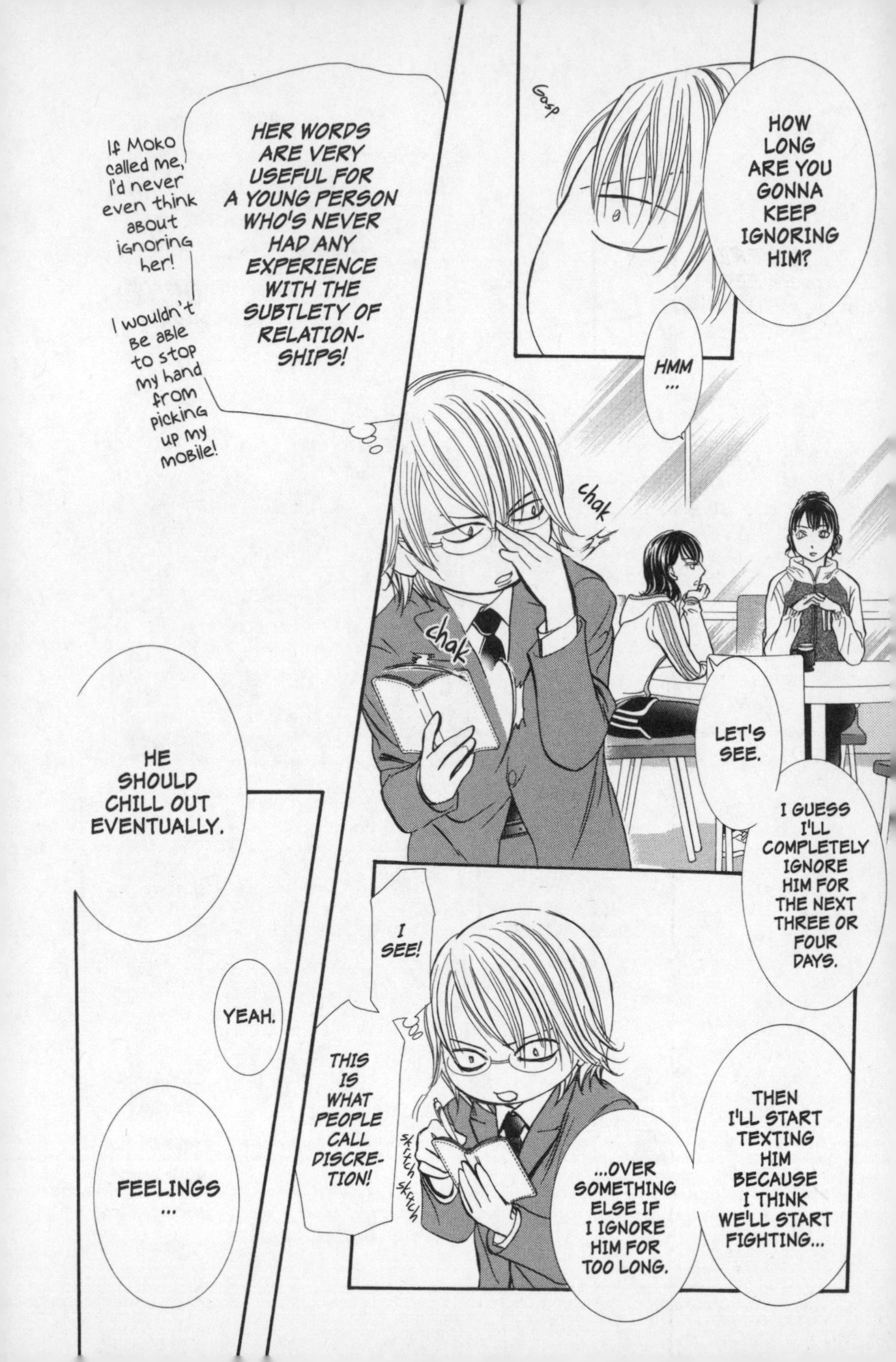
Gasp
HOW LONG ARE YOU GONNA KEEP IGNORING HIM?
HER WORDS ARE VERY USEFUL FOR A YOUNG PERSON WHO'S NEVER HAD ANY EXPERIENCE WITH THE SUBTLETY OF RELATION-SHIPS!
If Moko called me, I'd never even think about ignoring her!
I wouldn't be able to stop my hand from picking up my mobile!
HMM...
chak
chak
LET'S SEE.
I GUESS I'LL COMPLETELY IGNORE HIM FOR THE NEXT THREE OR FOUR DAYS.
THEN I'LL START TEXTING HIM BECAUSE I THINK WE'LL START FIGHTING...
...OVER SOMETHING ELSE IF I IGNORE HIM FOR TOO LONG.
I SEE!
THIS IS WHAT PEOPLE CALL DISCRE-TION!
skritch skritch
HE SHOULD CHILL OUT EVENTUALLY.
YEAH.
FEELINGS...

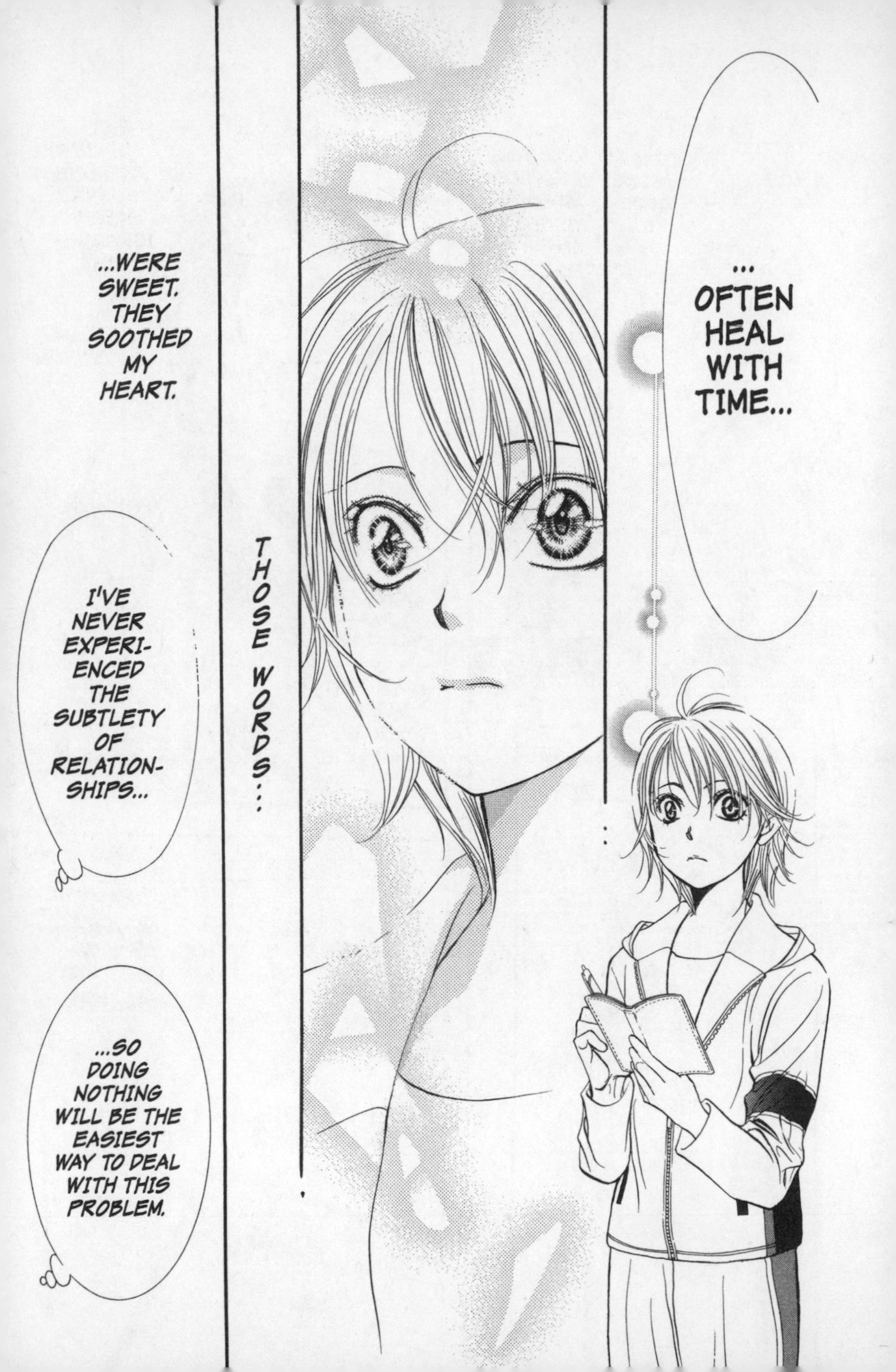
... OFTEN HEAL WITH TIME...
THOSE WORDS...
...WERE SWEET. THEY SOOTHED MY HEART.
I'VE NEVER EXPERIENCED THE SUBTLETY OF RELATIONSHIPS...
...SO DOING NOTHING WILL BE THE EASIEST WAY TO DEAL WITH THIS PROBLEM.

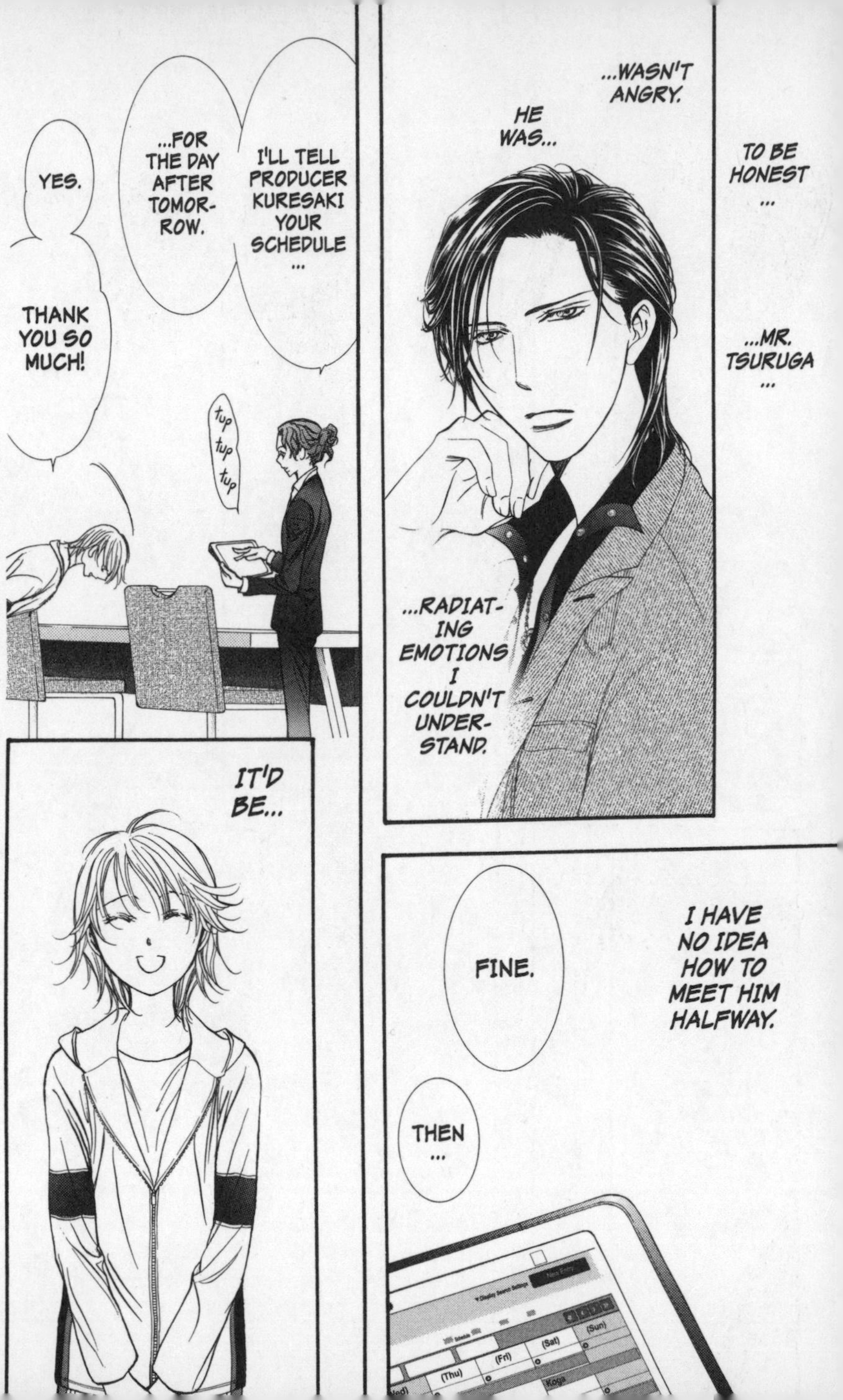
TO BE HONEST ...
...MR. TSURUGA ...
...WASN'T ANGRY.
HE WAS...
...RADIATING-ING EMOTIONS I COULDN'T UNDER-STAND.
I'LL TELL PRODUCER KURESAKI YOUR SCHEDULE ...
...FOR THE DAY AFTER TOMOR-ROW.
YES.
THANK YOU SO MUCH!
tup tup tup
I HAVE NO IDEA HOW TO MEET HIM HALFWAY.
FINE.
THEN ...
(Sun)
(Sat)
(Fri)
(Thu)
Koga
IT'D BE...

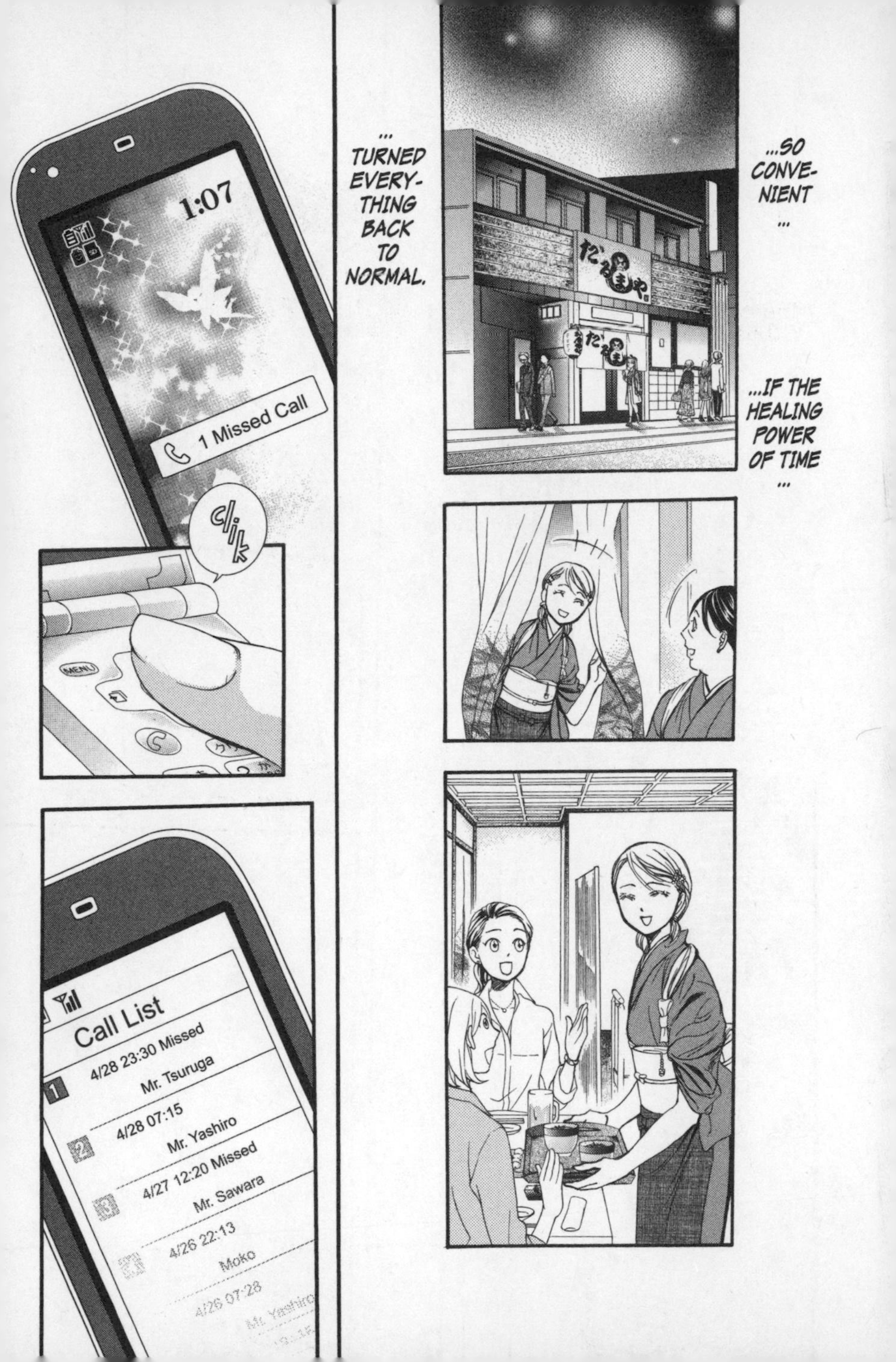
...SO CONVENIENT...
...IF THE HEALING POWER OF TIME...
...TURNED EVERYTHING BACK TO NORMAL.
だるまや
1:07
1 Missed Call
clik
MENU
Call List
4/28 23:30 Missed
Mr. Tsuruga
4/28 07:15
Mr. Yashiro
4/27 12:20 Missed
Mr. Sawara
4/26 22:13
Moko
4/26 07:28
Mr. Yashiro

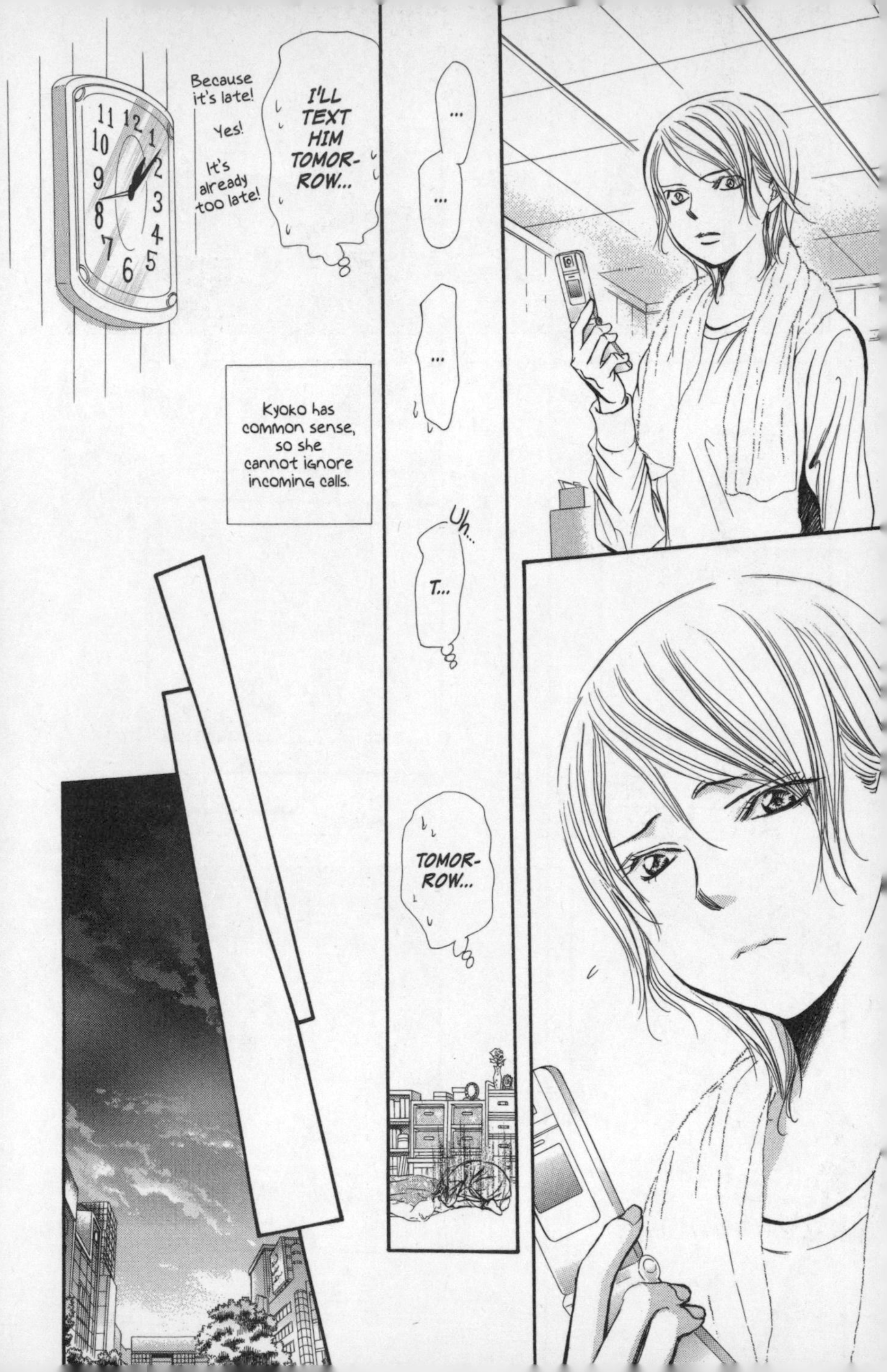
...
...
...
Uh... T...
TOMOR-ROW...
I'LL TEXT HIM TOMOR-ROW...
Because it's late!
Yes!
It's already too late!
Kyoko has common sense, so she cannot ignore incoming calls.

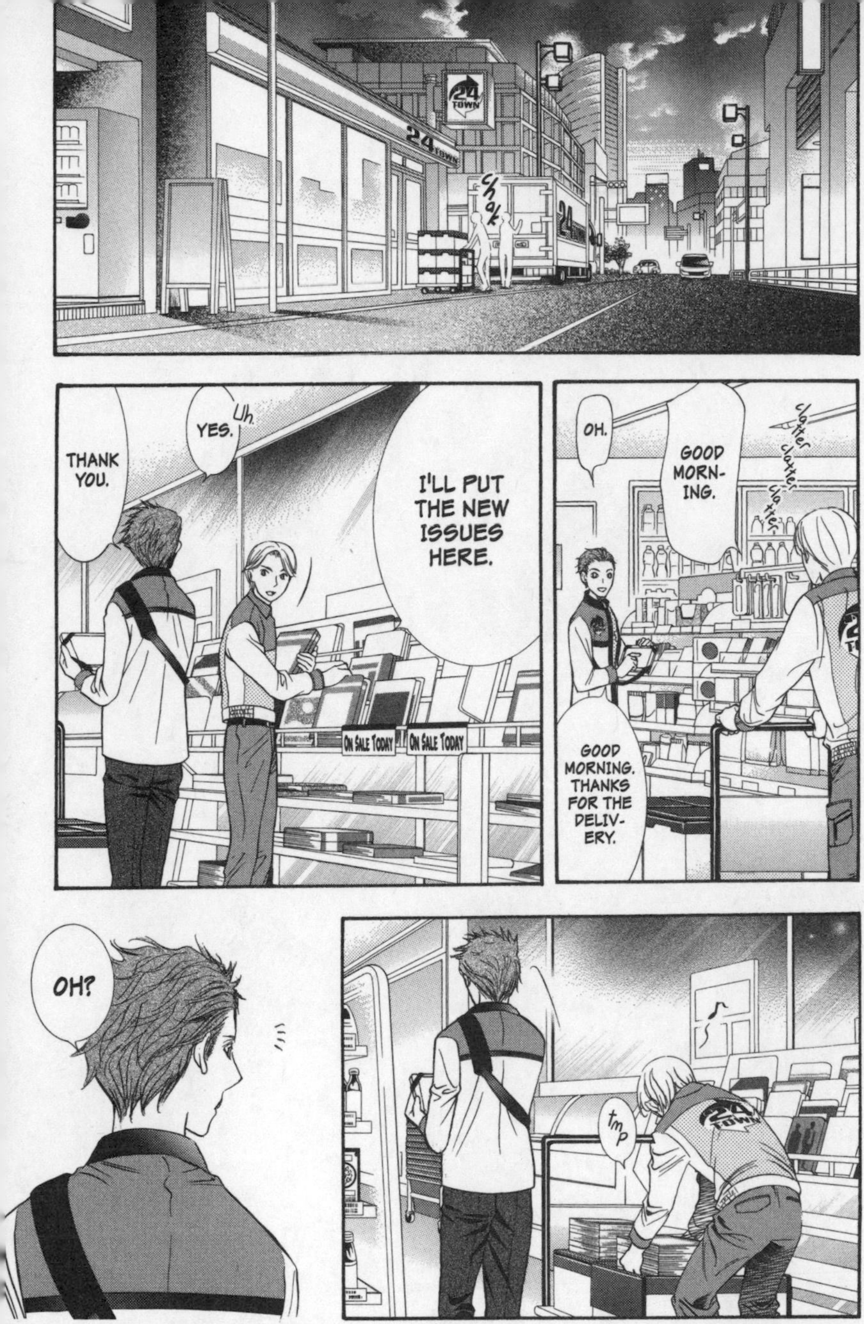
chak
OH.
GOOD MORNING.
clatter clatter clatter
GOOD MORNING. THANKS FOR THE DELIVERY.
I'LL PUT THE NEW ISSUES HERE.
Uh. YES.
THANK YOU.
ON SALE TODAY
ON SALE TODAY
tmp
OH?

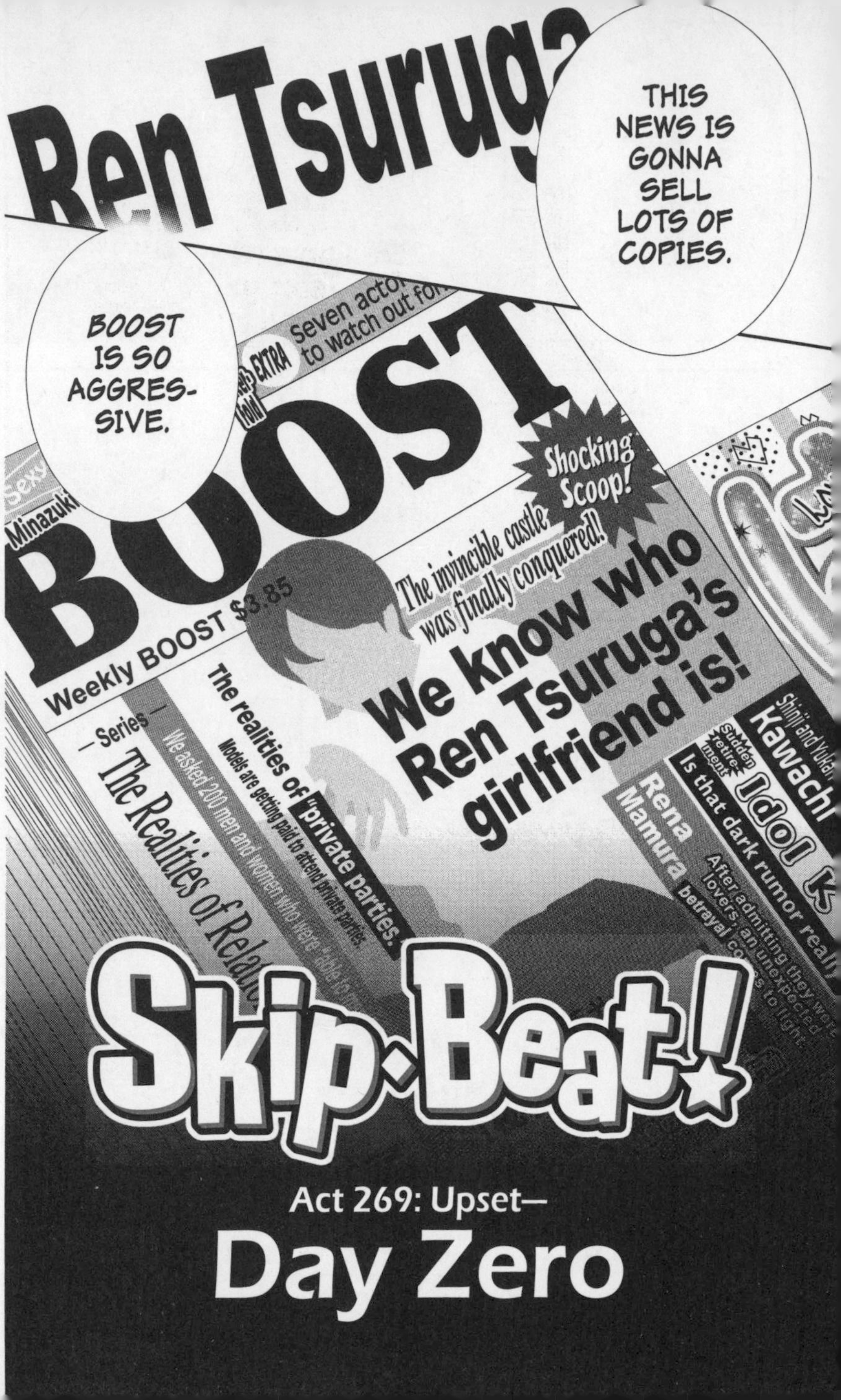
Ren Tsuruga
THIS NEWS IS GONNA SELL LOTS OF COPIES.
BOOST IS SO AGGRES-SIVE.
Seven actors to watch out for
EXTRA
BOOST
Shocking Scoop!
Minazuki
Weekly BOOST $3.85
The invincible castle was finally conquered!
We know who Ren Tsuruga's girlfriend is!
The realities of "private parties."
Models are getting paid to attend private parties.
—Series—
The Realities of Relatio
We asked 200 men and women who were
Rena Mamura
Is that dark rumor really
Sudden retirements
Idol
Kawachi
After admitting they were lovers, an unexpected betrayal comes to light.
Skip·Beat!
Act 269: Upset—
Day Zero

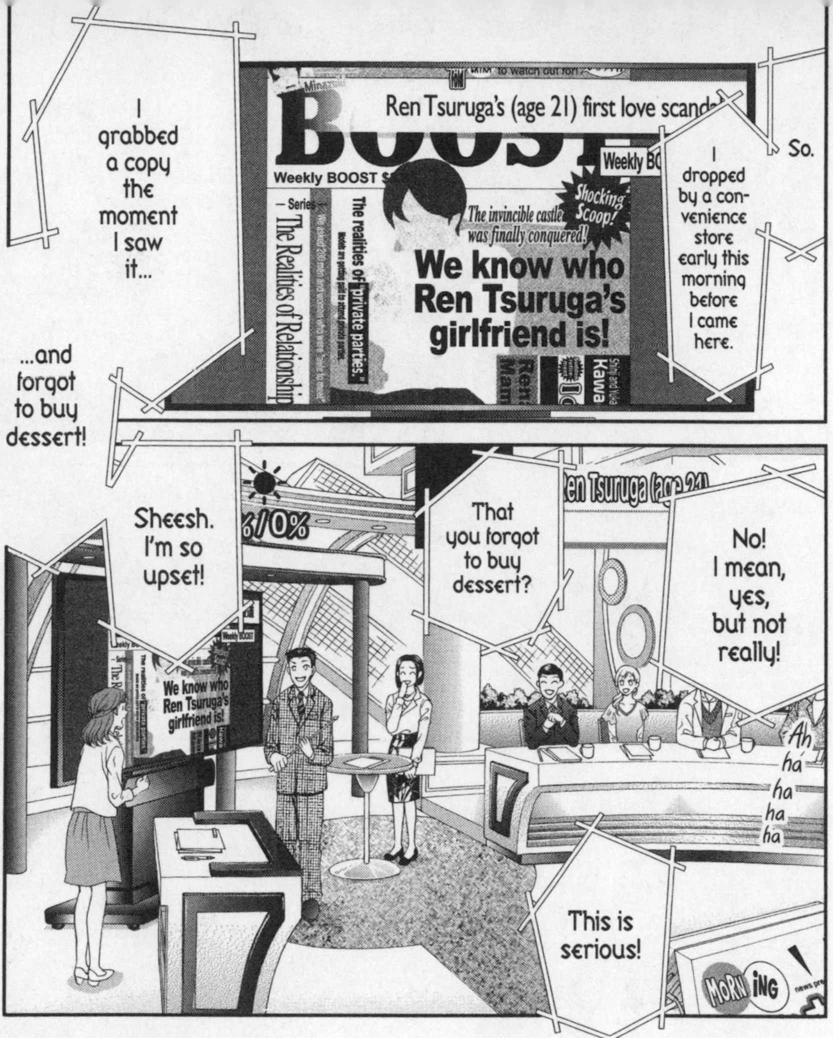
Ren Tsuruga's (age 21) first love scandal
BOOST
Weekly BOOST
Shocking Scoop!
The invincible castle was finally conquered!
We know who Ren Tsuruga's girlfriend is!
The realities of "private parties."
The Realities of Relationship
So.
I dropped by a con-venience store early this morning before I came here.
I grabbed a copy the moment I saw it...
...and forgot to buy dessert!
Sheesh. I'm so upset!
That you forgot to buy dessert?
No! I mean, yes, but not really!
This is serious!
Ren Tsuruga (age 21)
We know who Ren Tsuruga's girlfriend is!
Ah ha ha ha ha ha
MORNING
%/0%

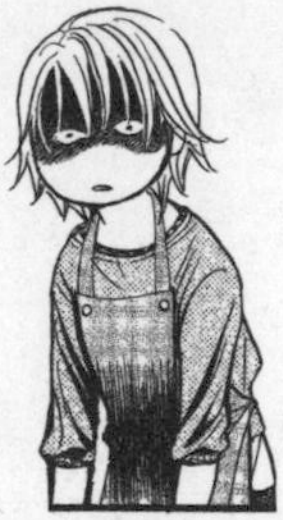

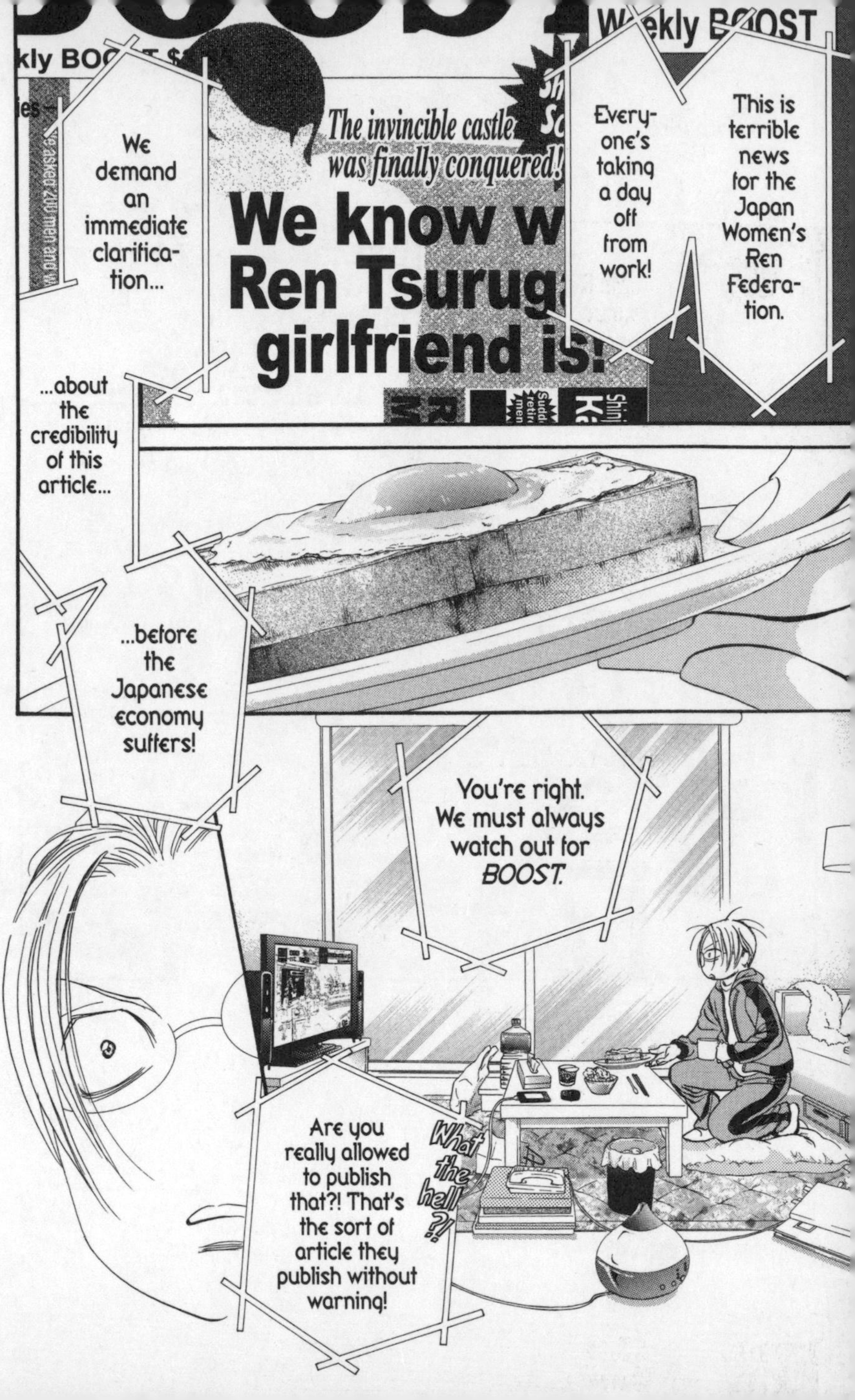

Weekly BOOST
This is terrible news for the Japan Women's Ren Federation.
Everyone's taking a day off from work!
The invincible castle was finally conquered!!
We know w
Ren Tsuruga
girlfriend is!
We demand an immediate clarification...
...about the credibility of this article...
...before the Japanese economy suffers!
You're right. We must always watch out for *BOOST.*
What the hell?!
Are you really allowed to publish that?! That's the sort of article they publish without warning!

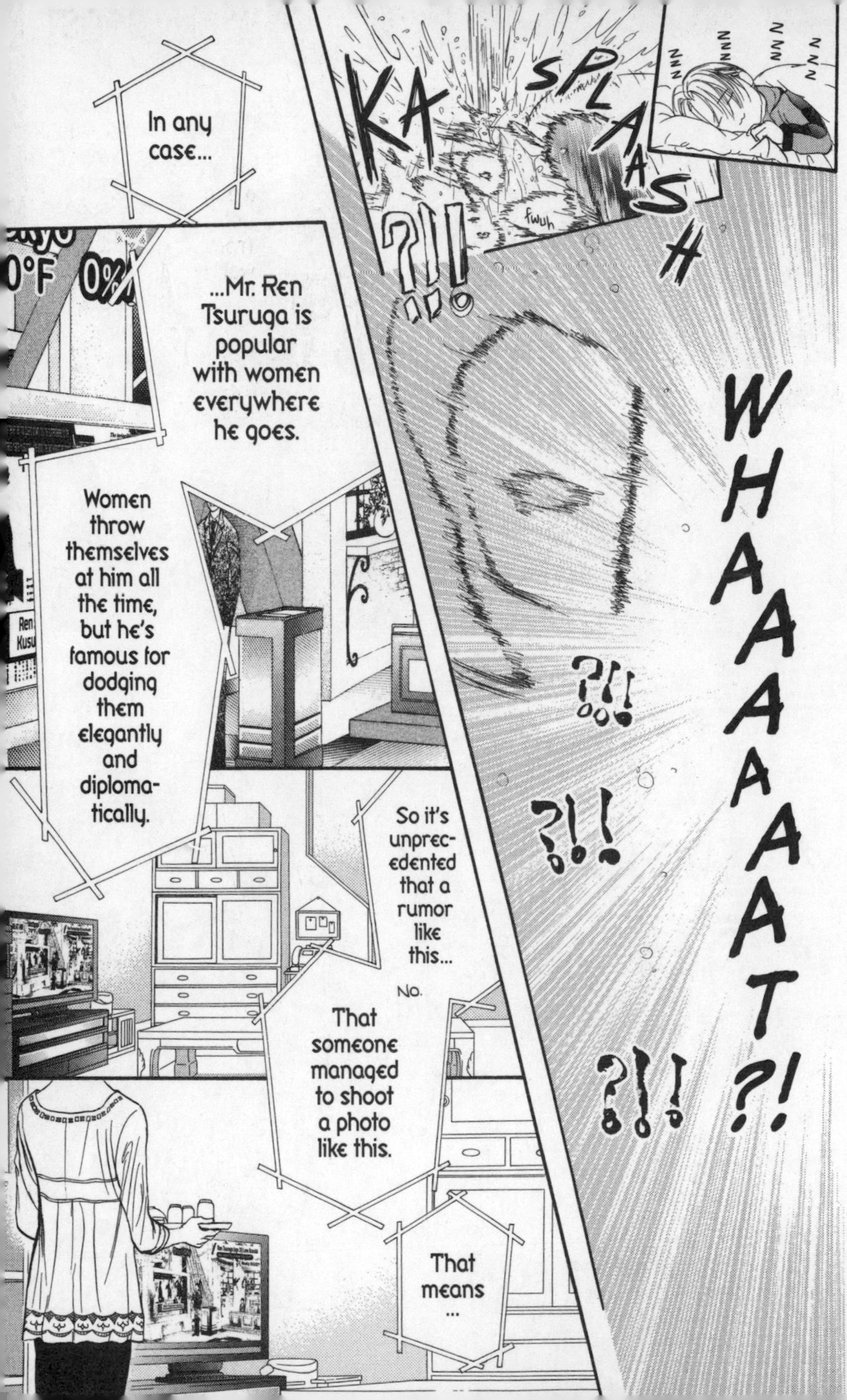

ZZZ
ZZZ
ZZZ
ZZZ
KASPLAASH
fwuh
?!!
WHAAAAAT?!
?!!
?!!
?!!
In any case...
...Mr. Ren Tsuruga is popular with women everywhere he goes.
Women throw themselves at him all the time, but he's famous for dodging them elegantly and diplomatically.
So it's unprecedented that a rumor like this...
No.
That someone managed to shoot a photo like this.
That means ...

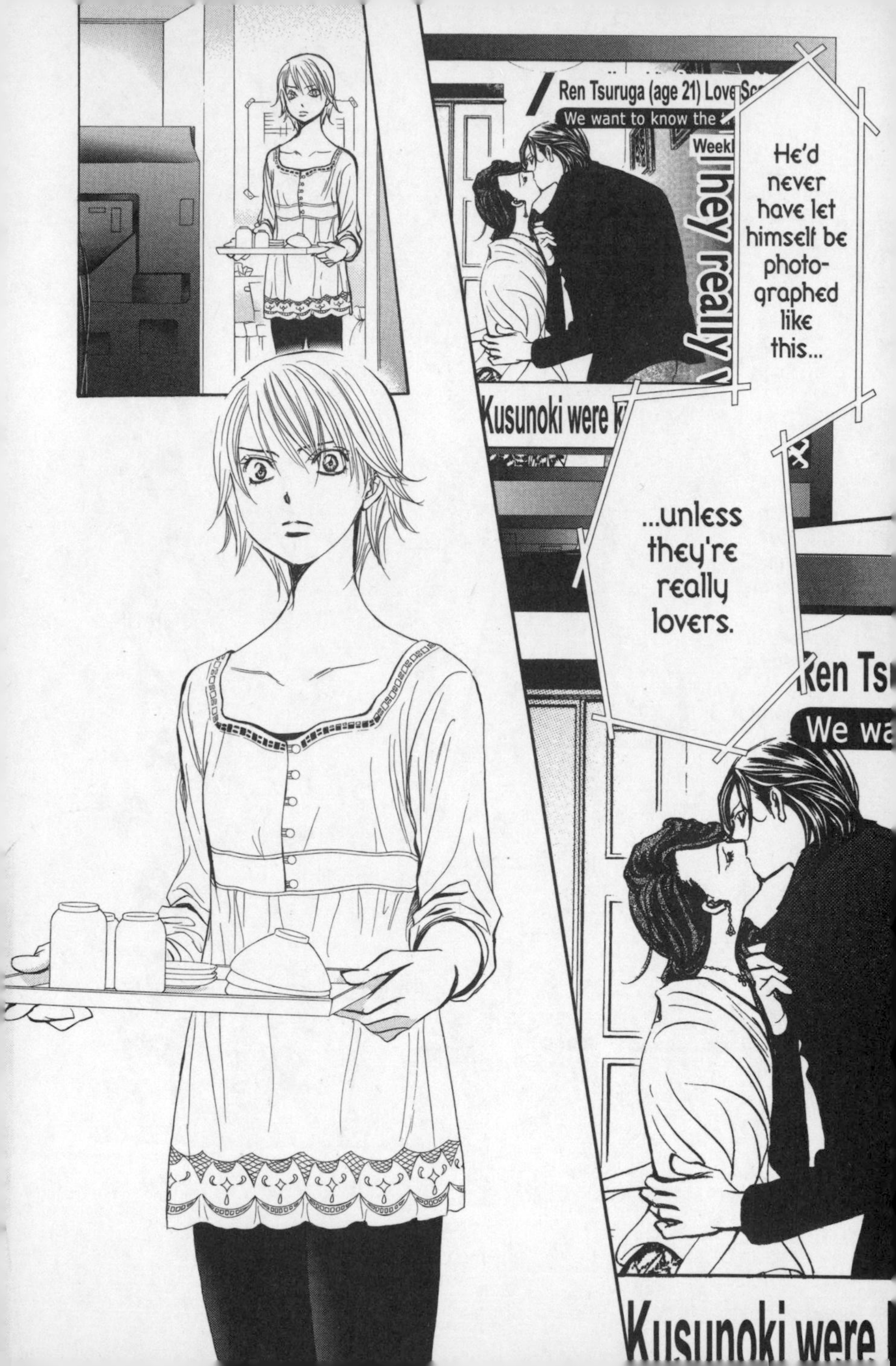
Ren Tsuruga (age 21) Love
We want to know the
They really
Kusunoki were
He'd never have let himself be photo-graphed like this...
...unless they're really lovers.
Ren Ts
We wa
Kusunoki were

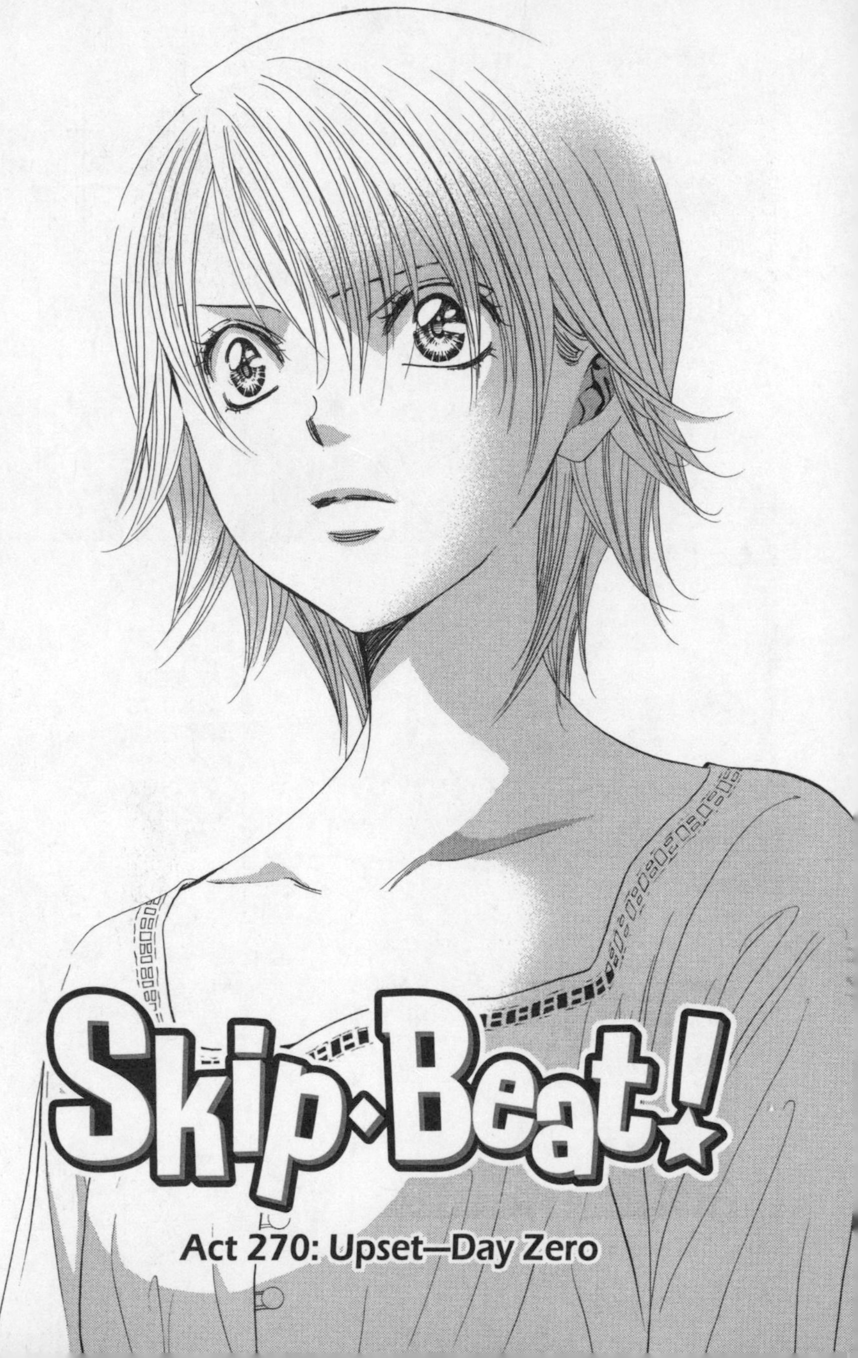
Skip·Beat!
Act 270: Upset—Day Zero

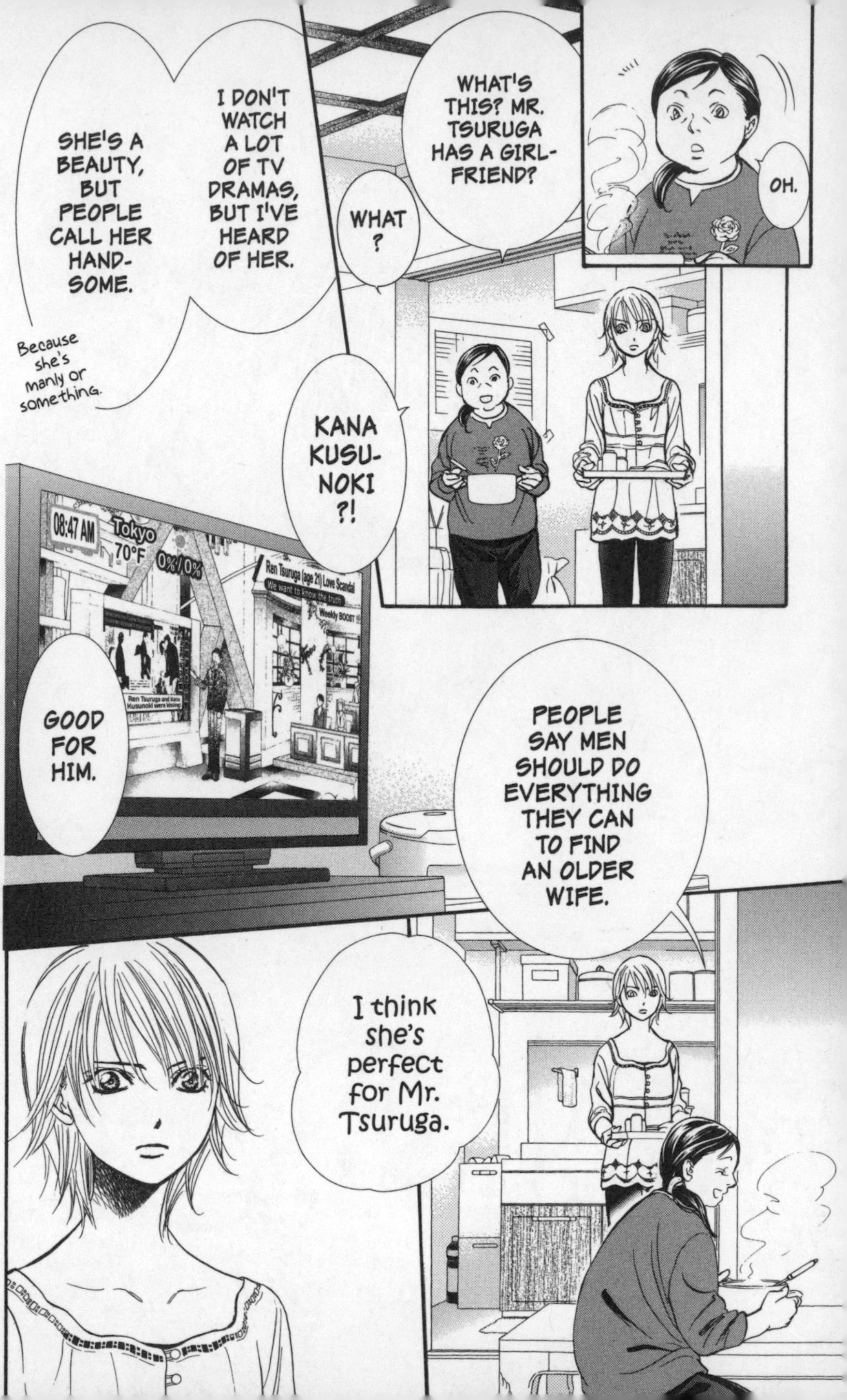
OH.
WHAT'S THIS? MR. TSURUGA HAS A GIRL-FRIEND?
WHAT ?
KANA KUSU-NOKI ?!
I DON'T WATCH A LOT OF TV DRAMAS, BUT I'VE HEARD OF HER.
SHE'S A BEAUTY, BUT PEOPLE CALL HER HAND-SOME.
Because she's manly or something.
08:47 AM
Tokyo 70°F
0%/0%
Ren Tsuruga (age 21) Love Scandal
We want to know the truth.
Weekly BOOST
Ren Tsuruga and Kana Kusunoki were kissing!
GOOD FOR HIM.
PEOPLE SAY MEN SHOULD DO EVERYTHING THEY CAN TO FIND AN OLDER WIFE.
I think she's perfect for Mr. Tsuruga.

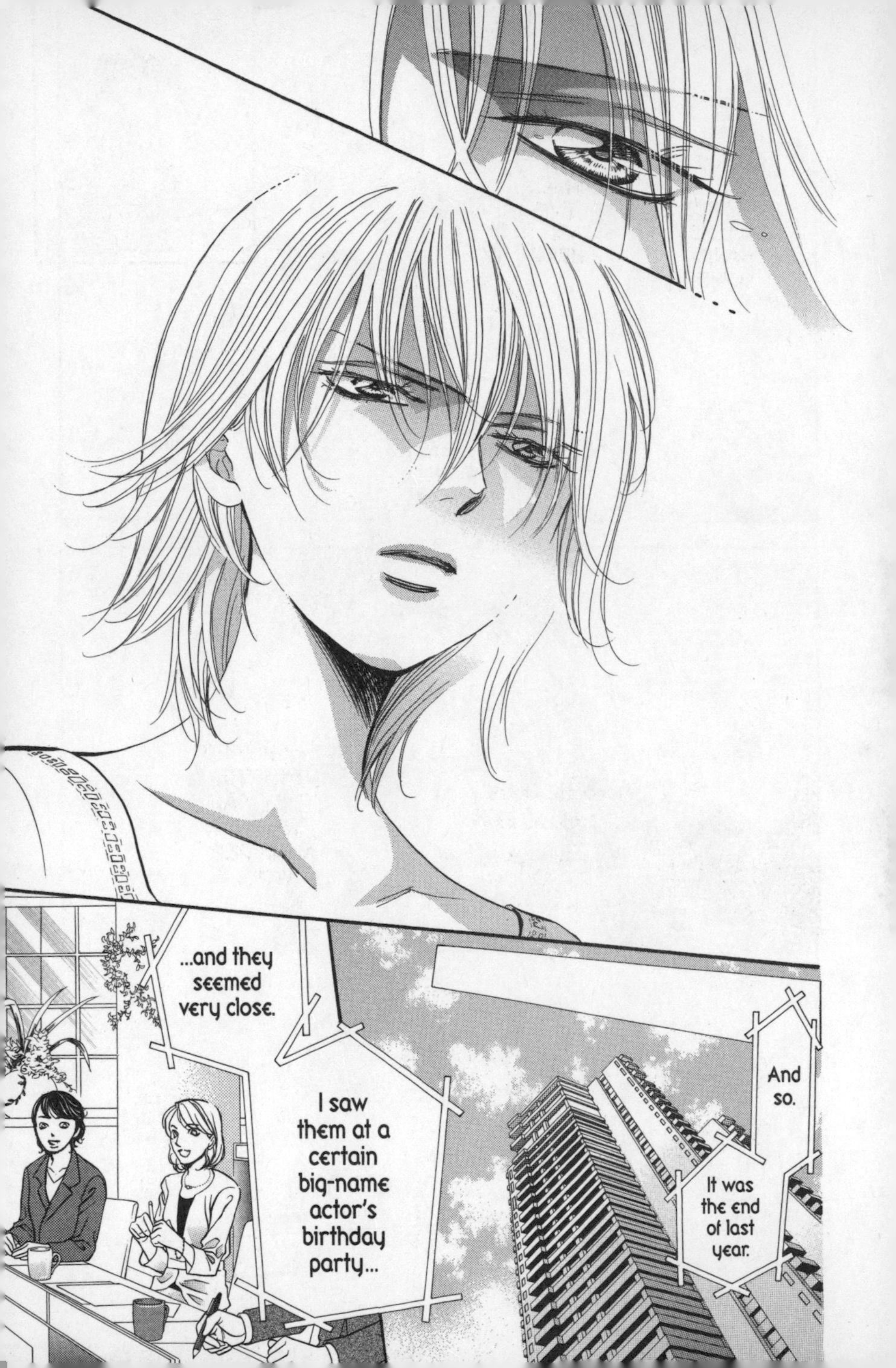
And so.
It was the end of last year.
I saw them at a certain big-name actor's birthday party...
...and they seemed very close.

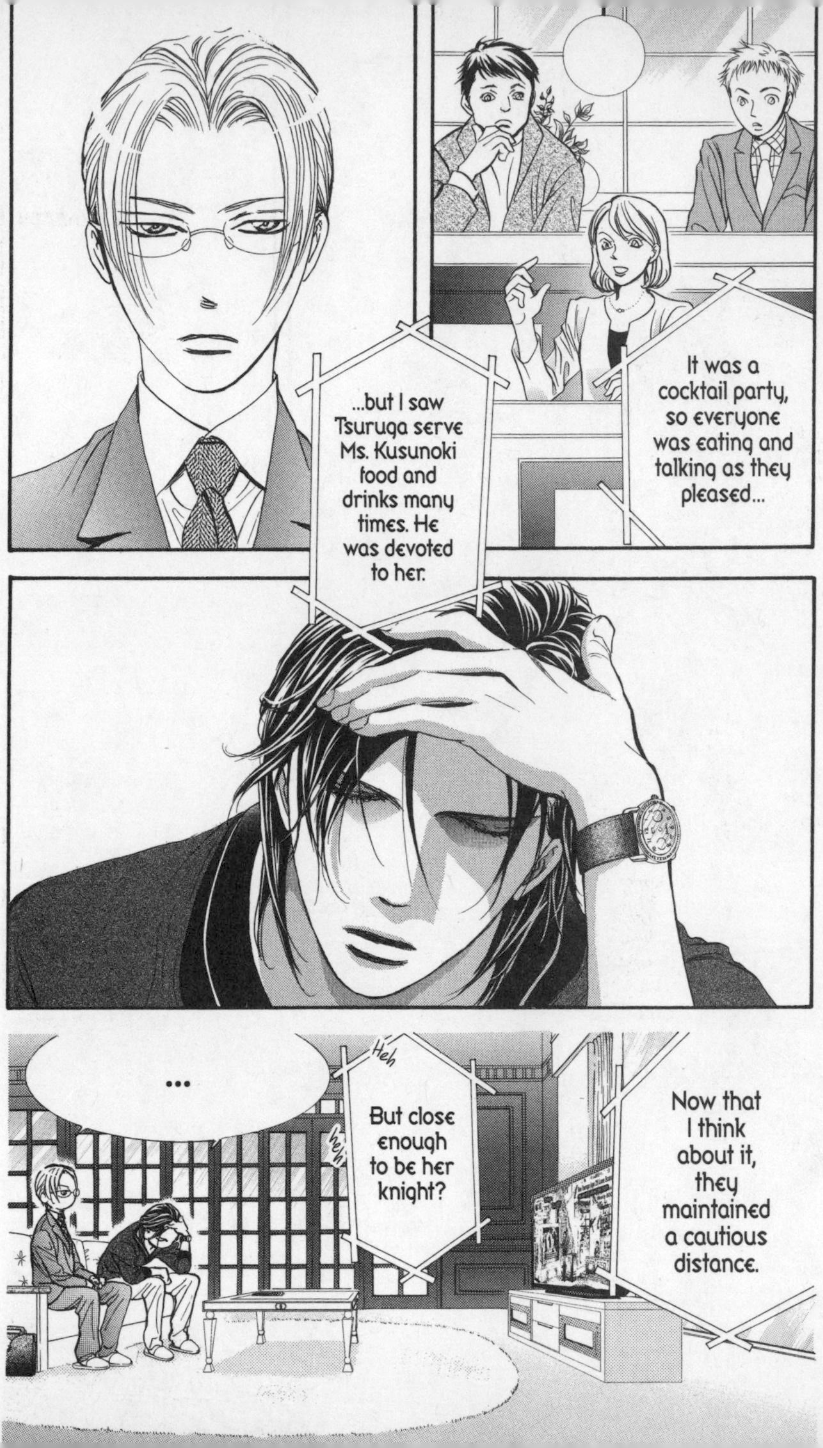
It was a cocktail party, so everyone was eating and talking as they pleased...
...but I saw Tsuruga serve Ms. Kusunoki food and drinks many times. He was devoted to her.
Now that I think about it, they maintained a cautious distance.
Heh
Heh
But close enough to be her knight?
...

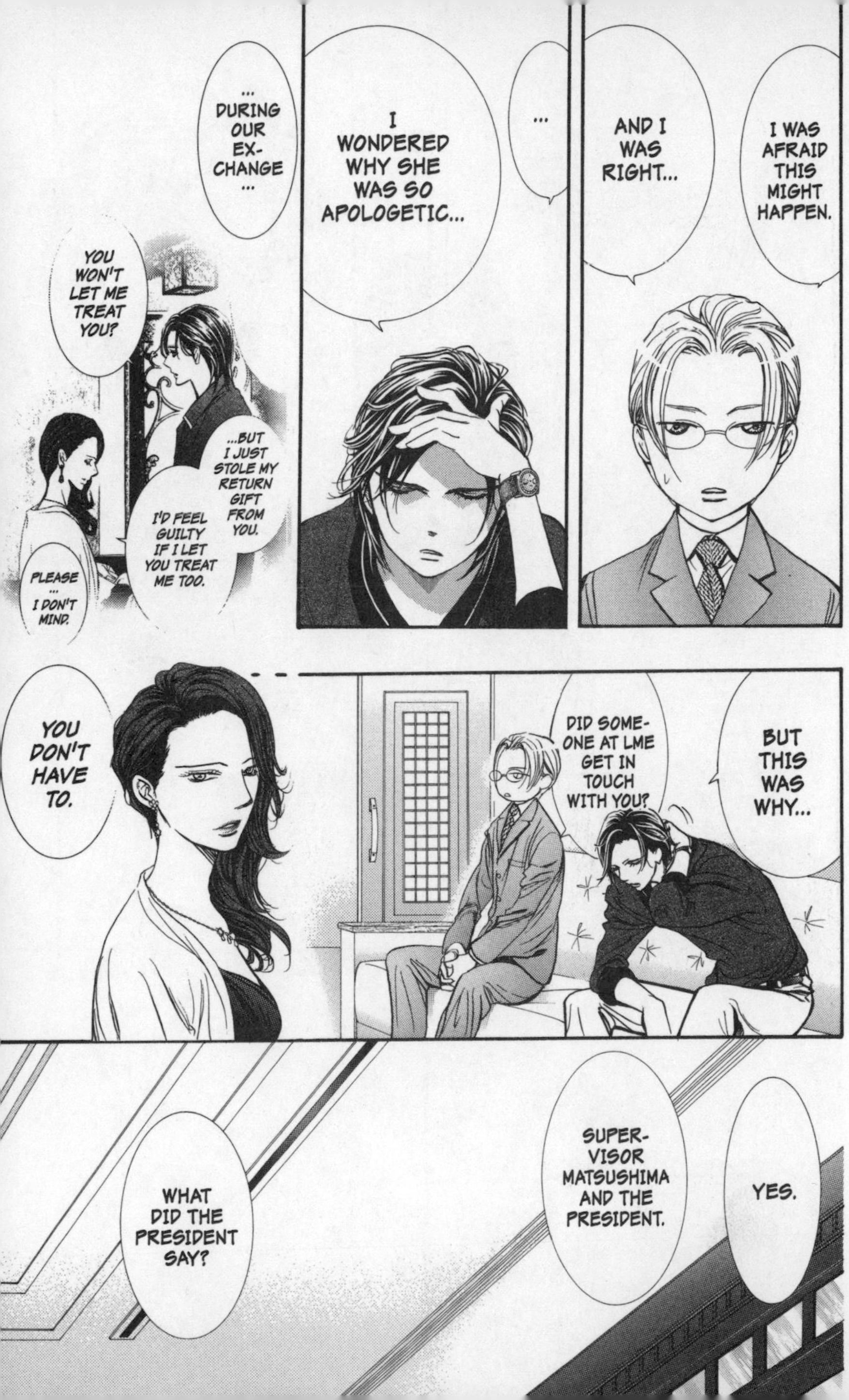
I WAS AFRAID THIS MIGHT HAPPEN.
AND I WAS RIGHT...
...
I WONDERED WHY SHE WAS SO APOLOGETIC...
... DURING OUR EX-CHANGE ...
YOU WON'T LET ME TREAT YOU?
...BUT I JUST STOLE MY RETURN GIFT FROM YOU.
I'D FEEL GUILTY IF I LET YOU TREAT ME TOO.
PLEASE ... I DON'T MIND.
BUT THIS WAS WHY...
DID SOME-ONE AT LME GET IN TOUCH WITH YOU?
YOU DON'T HAVE TO.
YES.
SUPER-VISOR MATSUSHIMA AND THE PRESIDENT.
WHAT DID THE PRESIDENT SAY?

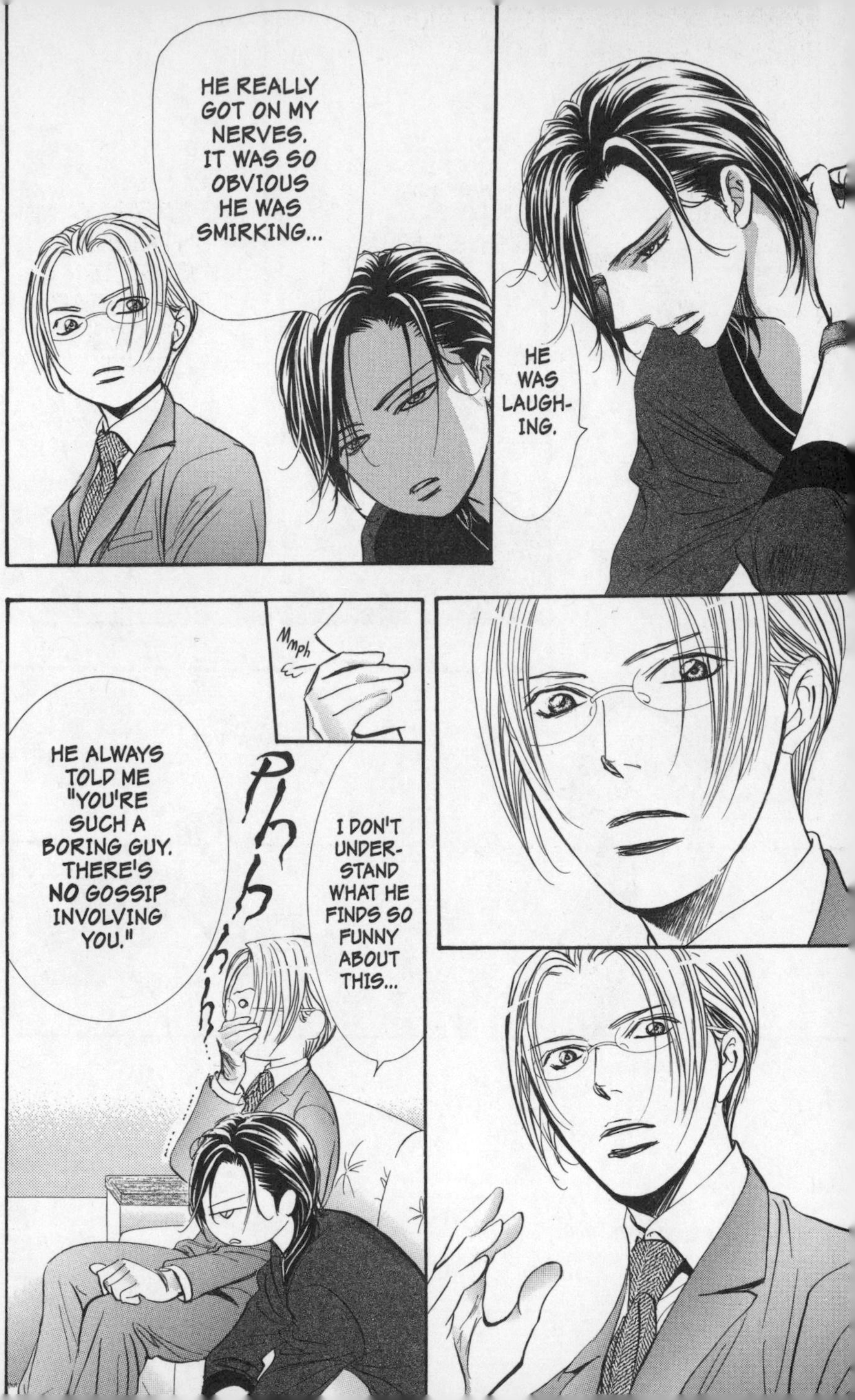
HE WAS LAUGH-ING.
HE REALLY GOT ON MY NERVES. IT WAS SO OBVIOUS HE WAS SMIRKING...
Mmph
Phhhh...
I DON'T UNDER-STAND WHAT HE FINDS SO FUNNY ABOUT THIS...
HE ALWAYS TOLD ME "YOU'RE SUCH A BORING GUY. THERE'S NO GOSSIP INVOLVING YOU."

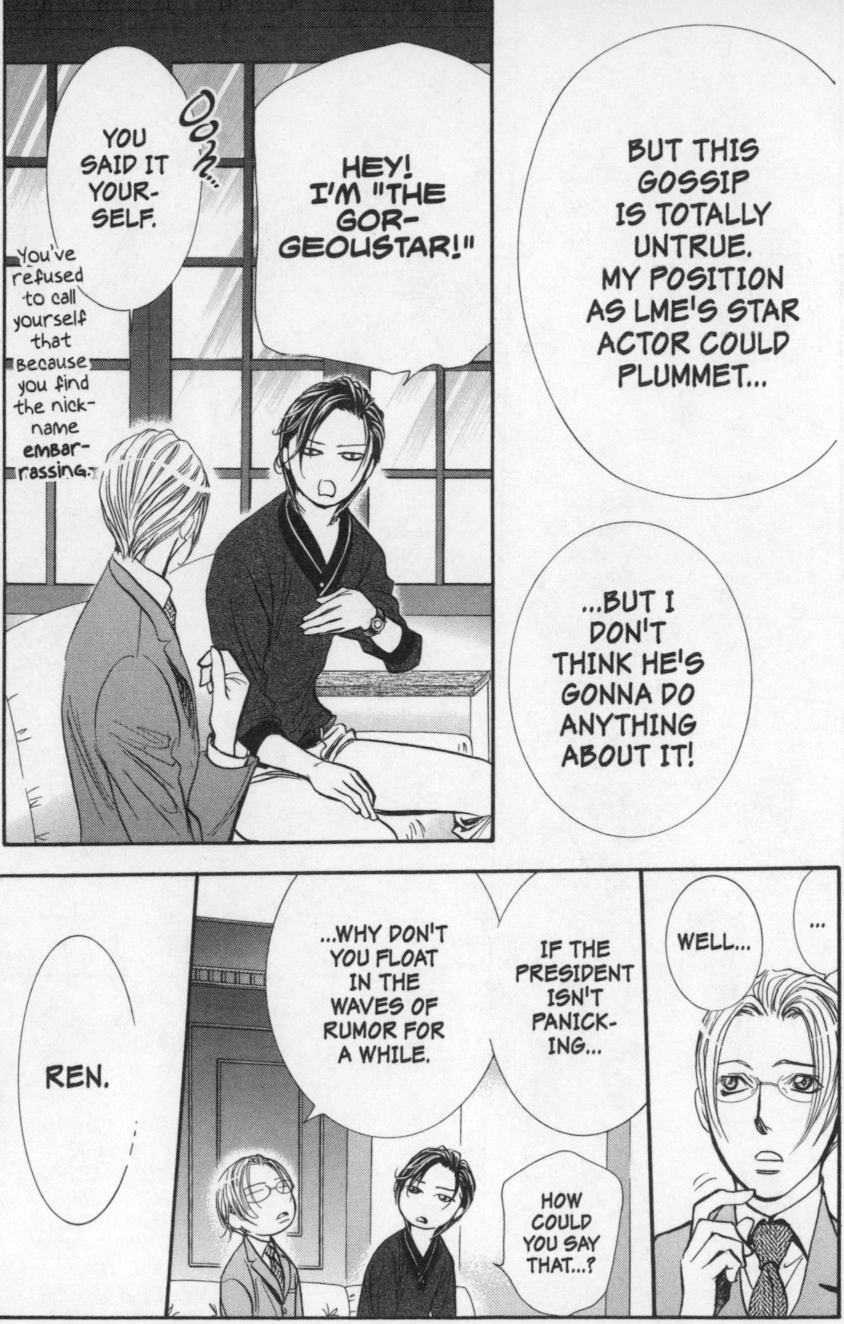
BUT THIS GOSSIP IS TOTALLY UNTRUE. MY POSITION AS LME'S STAR ACTOR COULD PLUMMET...
...BUT I DON'T THINK HE'S GONNA DO ANYTHING ABOUT IT!
HEY! I'M "THE GORGEOUSTAR!"
Oooh...
YOU SAID IT YOURSELF.
You've refused to call yourself that because you find the nick-name embarrassing.
...
WELL...
IF THE PRESIDENT ISN'T PANICKING...
...WHY DON'T YOU FLOAT IN THE WAVES OF RUMOR FOR A WHILE.
HOW COULD YOU SAY THAT...?
REN.

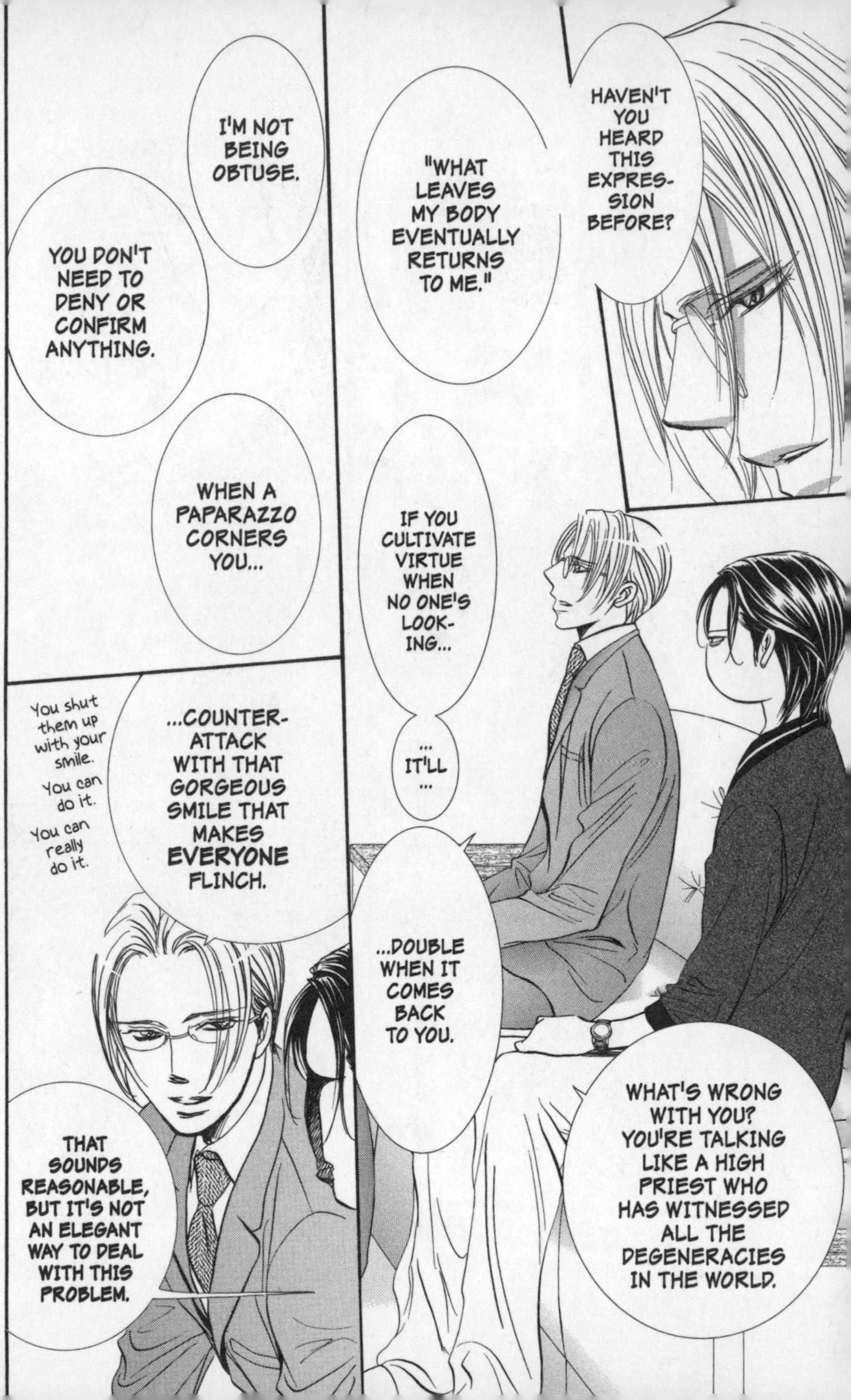
HAVEN'T YOU HEARD THIS EXPRESSION BEFORE?
"WHAT LEAVES MY BODY EVENTUALLY RETURNS TO ME."
IF YOU CULTIVATE VIRTUE WHEN NO ONE'S LOOKING...
...IT'LL...
...DOUBLE WHEN IT COMES BACK TO YOU.
WHAT'S WRONG WITH YOU? YOU'RE TALKING LIKE A HIGH PRIEST WHO HAS WITNESSED ALL THE DEGENERACIES IN THE WORLD.
I'M NOT BEING OBTUSE.
YOU DON'T NEED TO DENY OR CONFIRM ANYTHING.
WHEN A PAPARAZZO CORNERS YOU...
...COUNTER-ATTACK WITH THAT GORGEOUS SMILE THAT MAKES EVERYONE FLINCH.
You shut them up with your smile.
You can do it.
You can really do it.
THAT SOUNDS REASONABLE, BUT IT'S NOT AN ELEGANT WAY TO DEAL WITH THIS PROBLEM.

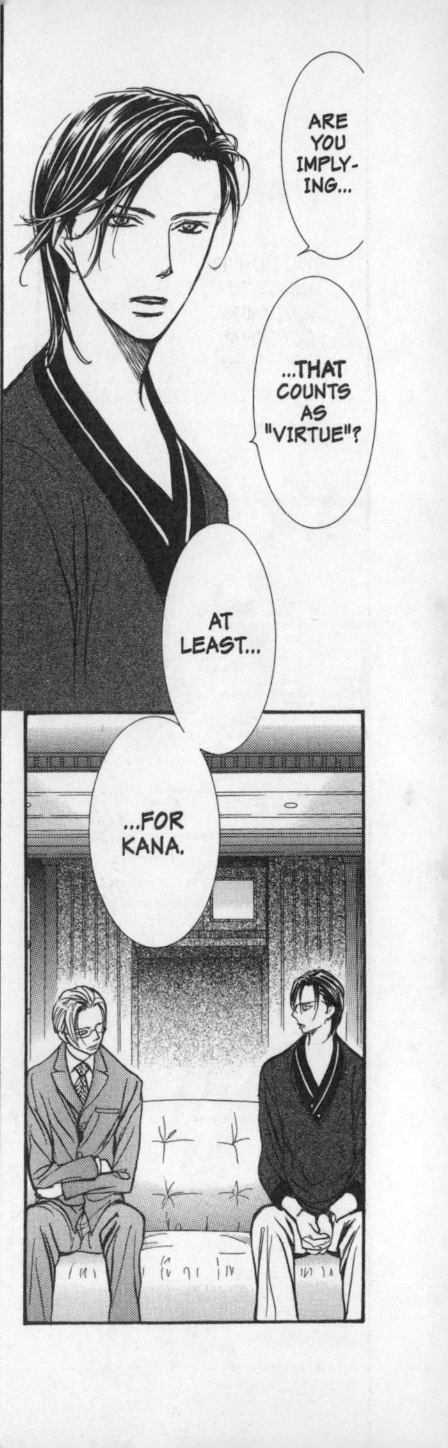
ARE YOU IMPLYING...
...THAT COUNTS AS "VIRTUE"?
AT LEAST...
...FOR KANA.

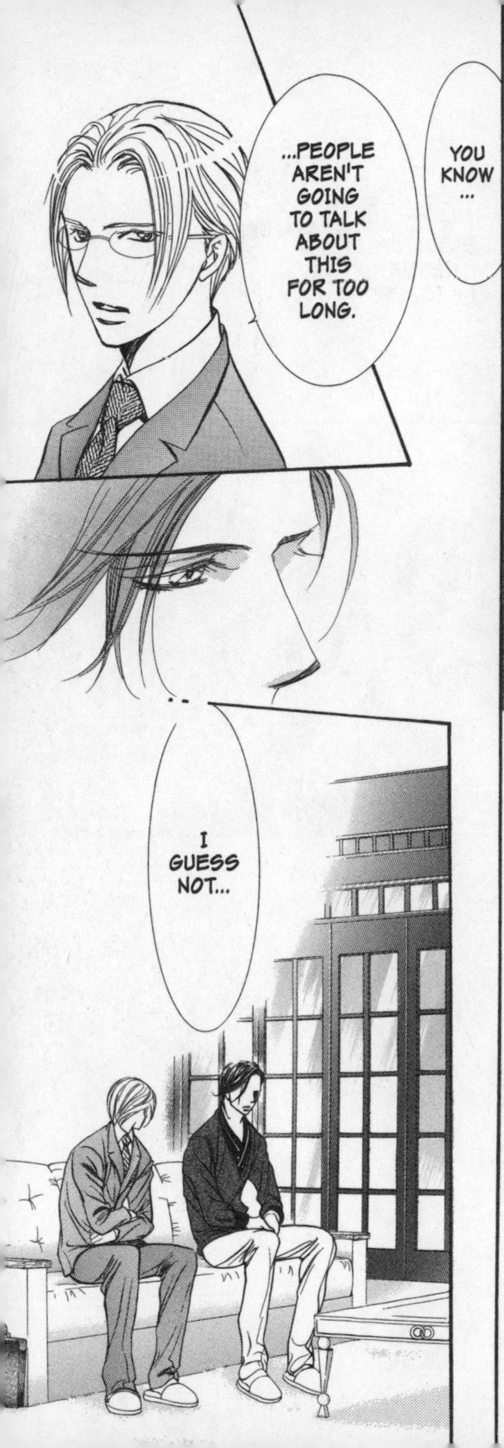
YOU KNOW ...
...PEOPLE AREN'T GOING TO TALK ABOUT THIS FOR TOO LONG.
..
I GUESS NOT...

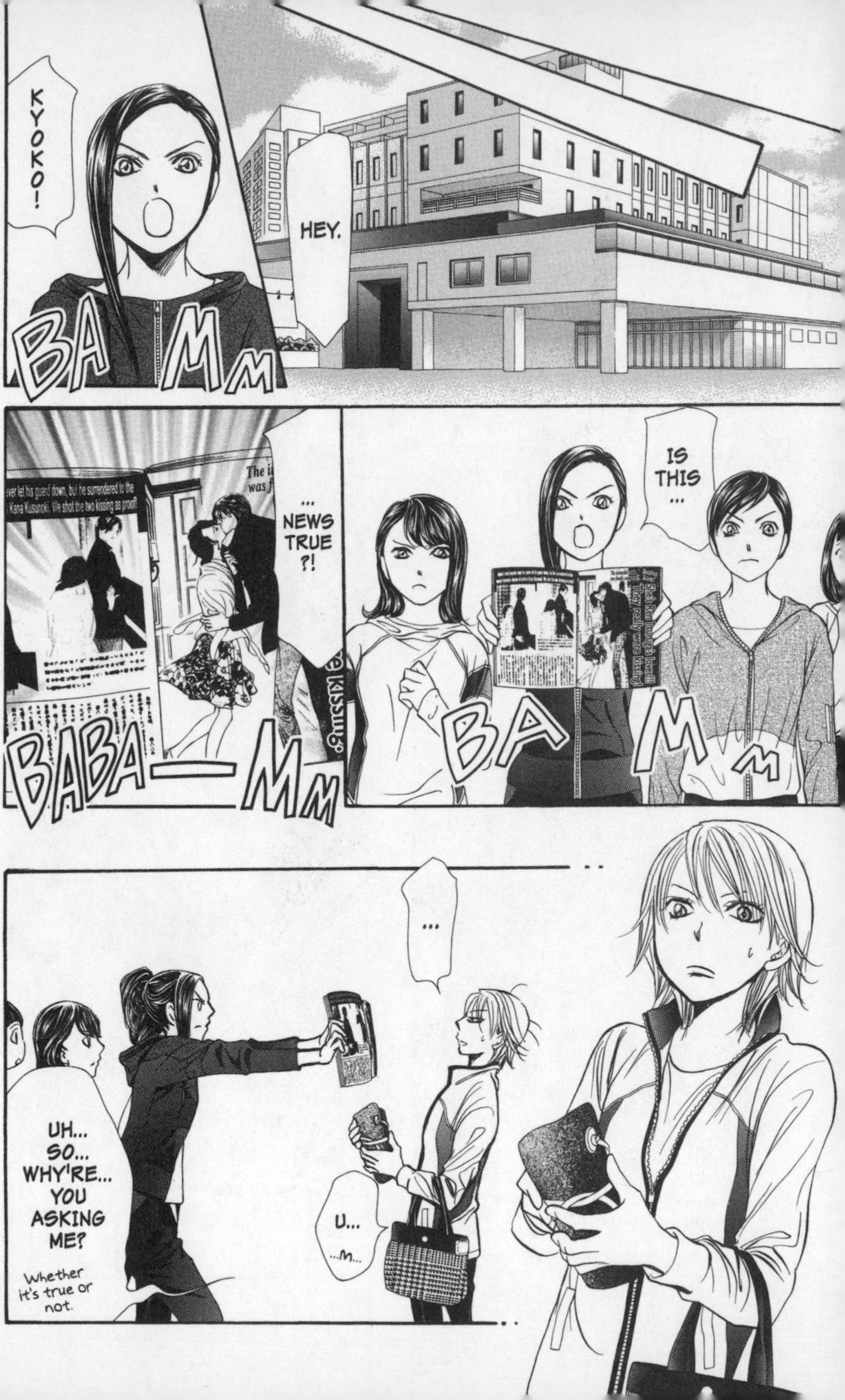
HEY.
KYOKO!
BAMM
IS THIS ...
BAMM
... NEWS TRUE?!
BABA—MM
...
U... ...M...
UH... SO... WHY'RE... YOU ASKING ME?
Whether it's true or not.

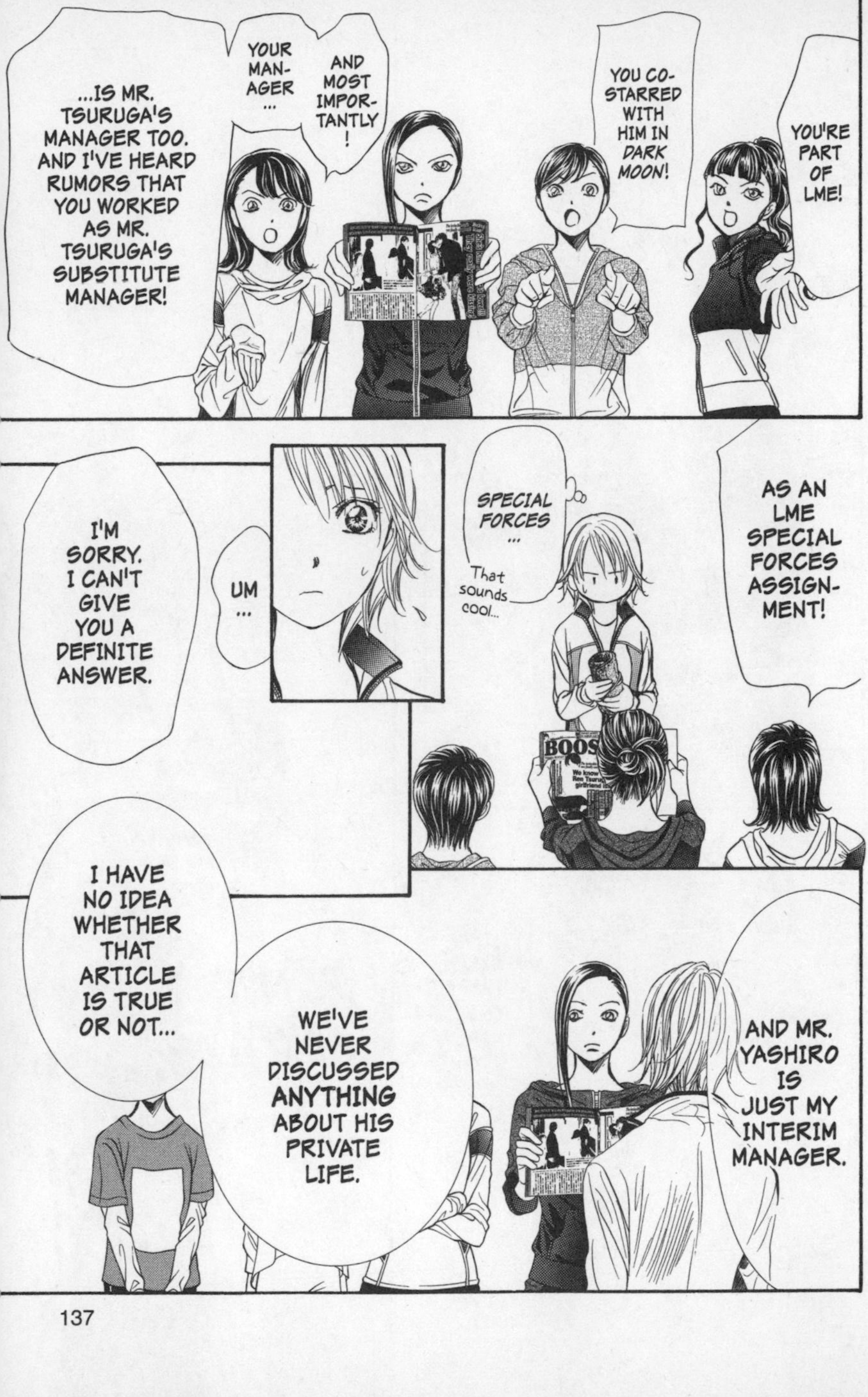
YOU'RE PART OF LME!
YOU CO-STARRED WITH HIM IN DARK MOON!
AND MOST IMPORTANTLY!
YOUR MANAGER...
...IS MR. TSURUGA'S MANAGER TOO. AND I'VE HEARD RUMORS THAT YOU WORKED AS MR. TSURUGA'S SUBSTITUTE MANAGER!
AS AN LME SPECIAL FORCES ASSIGNMENT!
SPECIAL FORCES...
That sounds cool...
UM...
I'M SORRY. I CAN'T GIVE YOU A DEFINITE ANSWER.
AND MR. YASHIRO IS JUST MY INTERIM MANAGER.
WE'VE NEVER DISCUSSED ANYTHING ABOUT HIS PRIVATE LIFE.
I HAVE NO IDEA WHETHER THAT ARTICLE IS TRUE OR NOT...

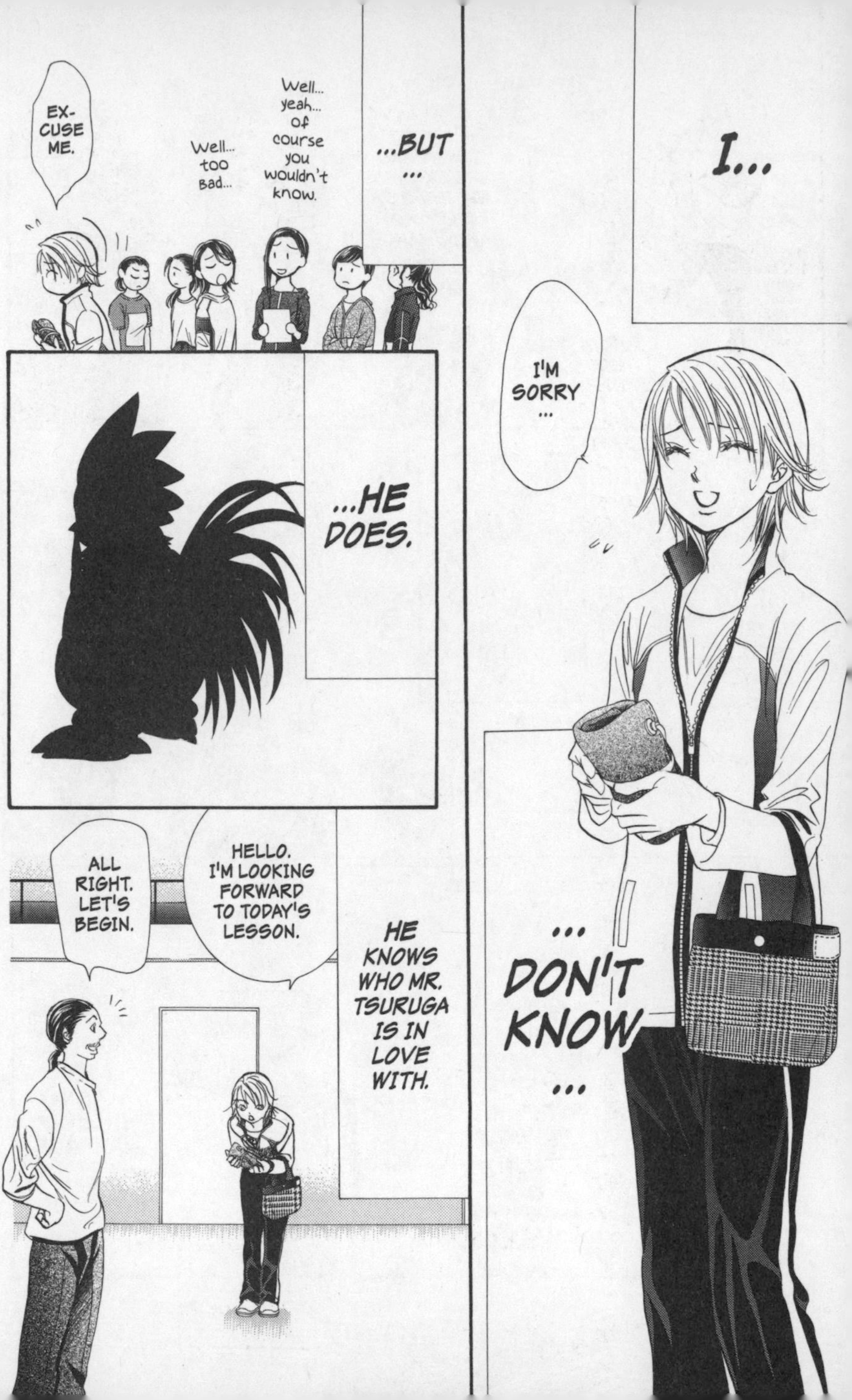
I...
I'M SORRY...
...DON'T KNOW...
...BUT...
Well... yeah... of course you wouldn't know.
Well... too bad...
EX-CUSE ME.
...HE DOES.
HE KNOWS WHO MR. TSURUGA IS IN LOVE WITH.
HELLO. I'M LOOKING FORWARD TO TODAY'S LESSON.
ALL RIGHT. LET'S BEGIN.

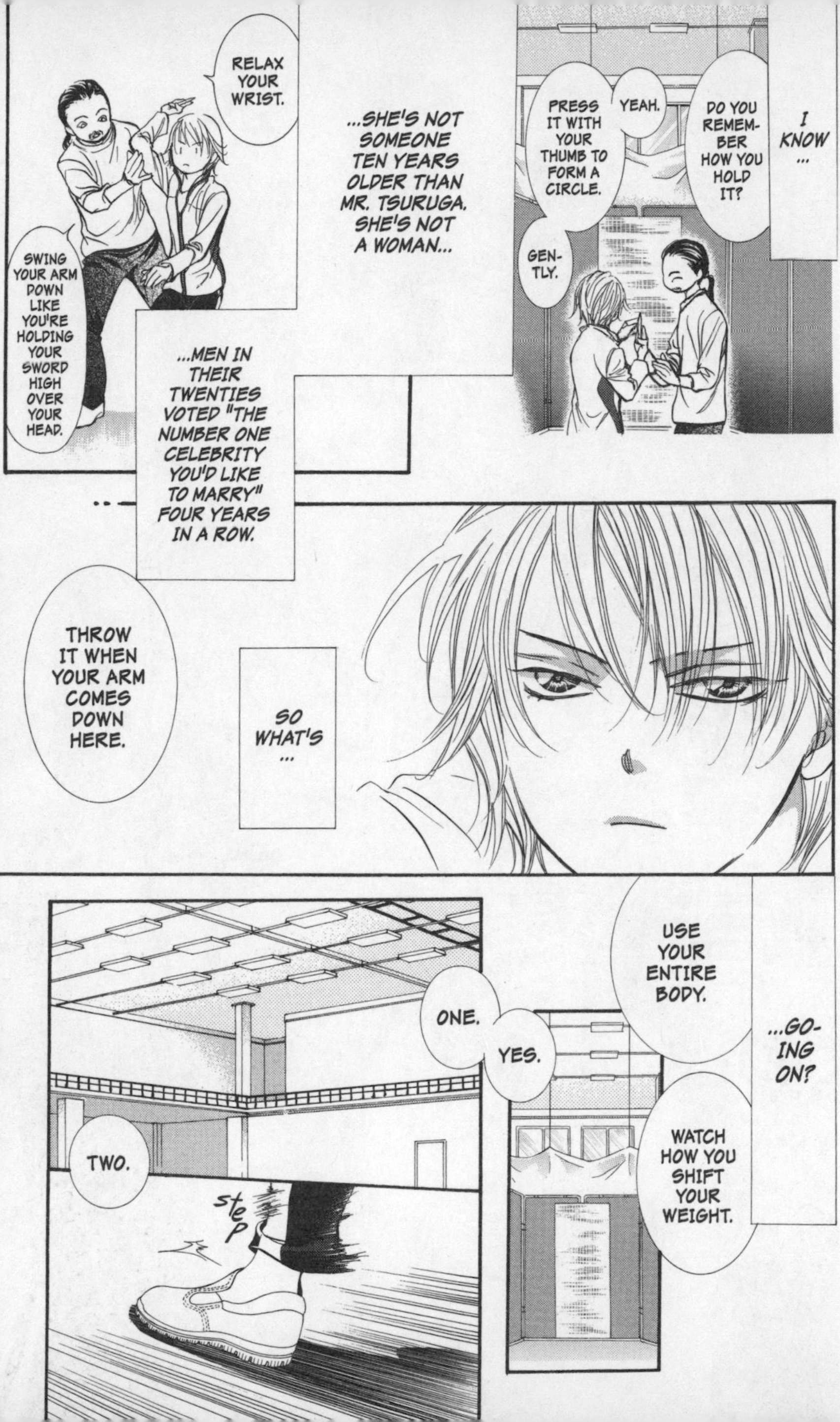
I KNOW ...
DO YOU REMEMBER HOW YOU HOLD IT?
YEAH.
PRESS IT WITH YOUR THUMB TO FORM A CIRCLE.
GENTLY.
...SHE'S NOT SOMEONE TEN YEARS OLDER THAN MR. TSURUGA. SHE'S NOT A WOMAN...
RELAX YOUR WRIST.
SWING YOUR ARM DOWN LIKE YOU'RE HOLDING YOUR SWORD HIGH OVER YOUR HEAD.
...MEN IN THEIR TWENTIES VOTED "THE NUMBER ONE CELEBRITY YOU'D LIKE TO MARRY" FOUR YEARS IN A ROW.
SO WHAT'S ...
THROW IT WHEN YOUR ARM COMES DOWN HERE.
...GO-ING ON?
USE YOUR ENTIRE BODY.
WATCH HOW YOU SHIFT YOUR WEIGHT.
YES.
ONE.
TWO.
step

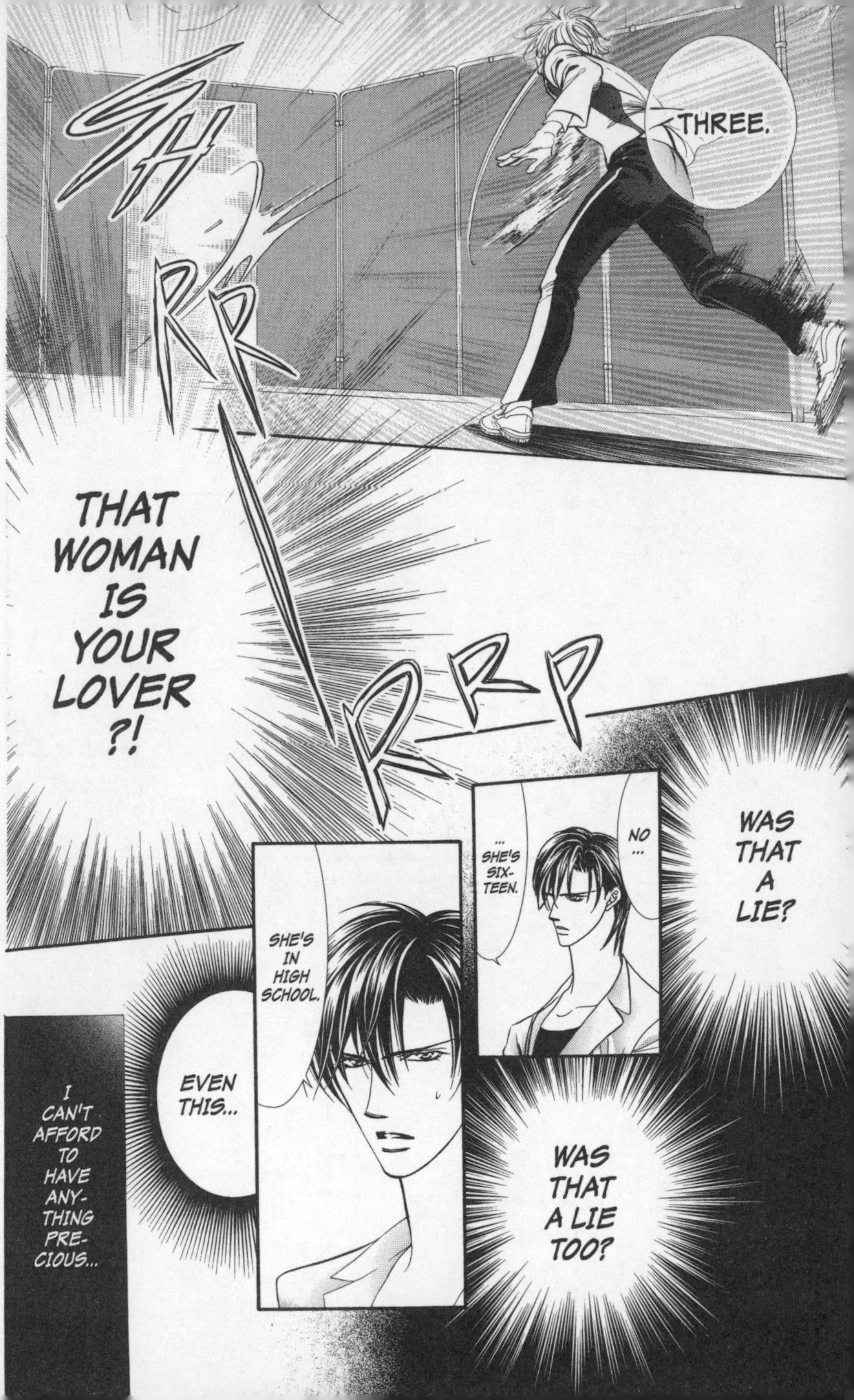
THREE.
SHRRRRP
THAT WOMAN IS YOUR LOVER?!
NO...
...SHE'S SIXTEEN.
WAS THAT A LIE?
SHE'S IN HIGH SCHOOL.
EVEN THIS...
WAS THAT A LIE TOO?
I CAN'T AFFORD TO HAVE ANYTHING PRECIOUS...

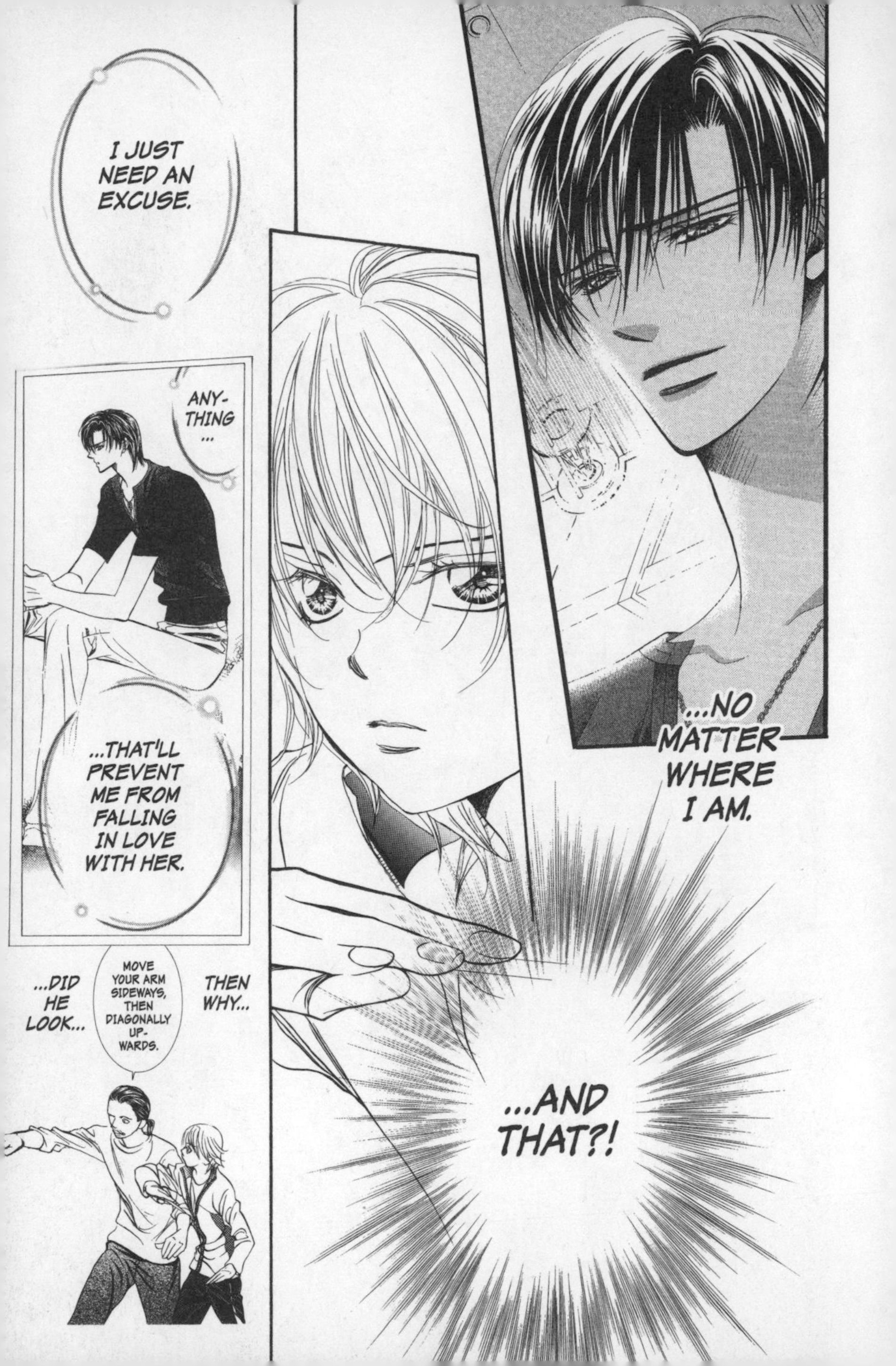
...NO MATTER WHERE I AM.
I JUST NEED AN EXCUSE.
ANY-THING...
...THAT'LL PREVENT ME FROM FALLING IN LOVE WITH HER.
THEN WHY...
MOVE YOUR ARM SIDEWAYS, THEN DIAGONALLY UP-WARDS.
...DID HE LOOK...
...AND THAT?!

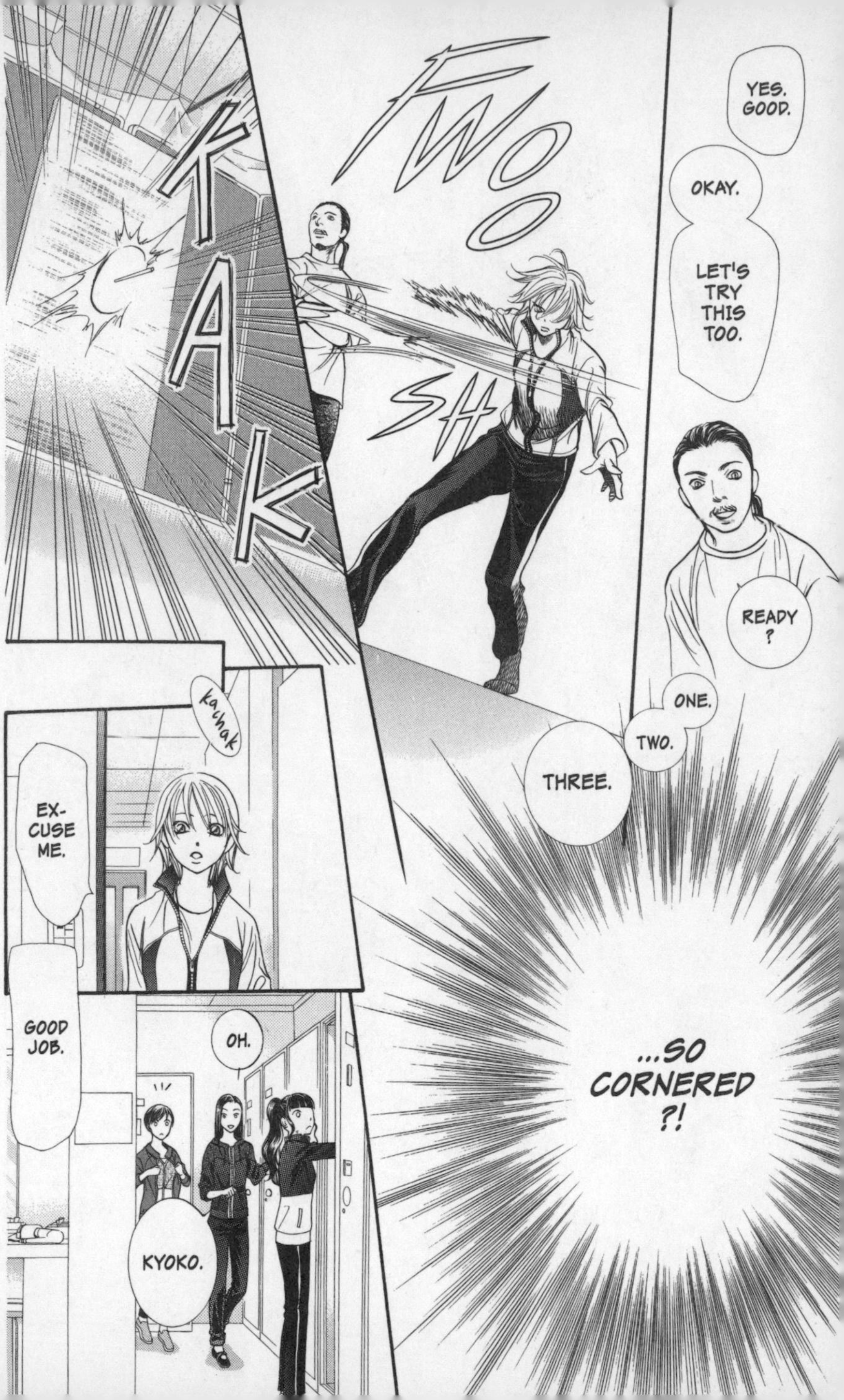
YES. GOOD.
OKAY.
LET'S TRY THIS TOO.
READY?
ONE.
TWO.
THREE.
FWOO
SHH
KAK
...SO CORNERED?!
kachak
EX-CUSE ME.
GOOD JOB.
OH.
KYOKO.

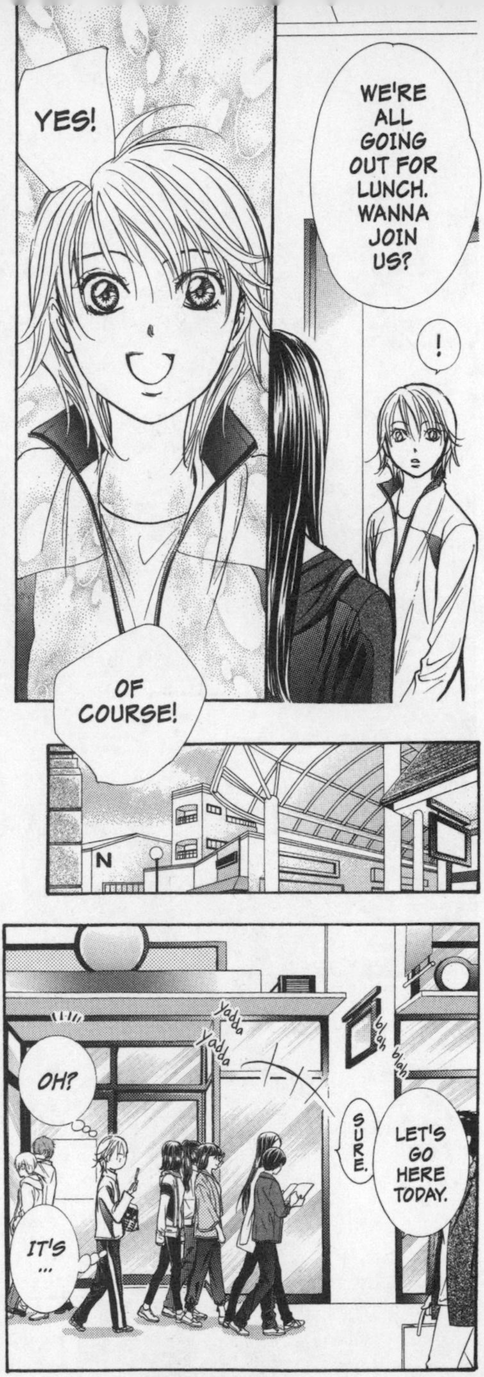
WE'RE ALL GOING OUT FOR LUNCH. WANNA JOIN US?
!
YES!
OF COURSE!
LET'S GO HERE TODAY.
SURE.
blah blah
yadda yadda
OH?
IT'S ...

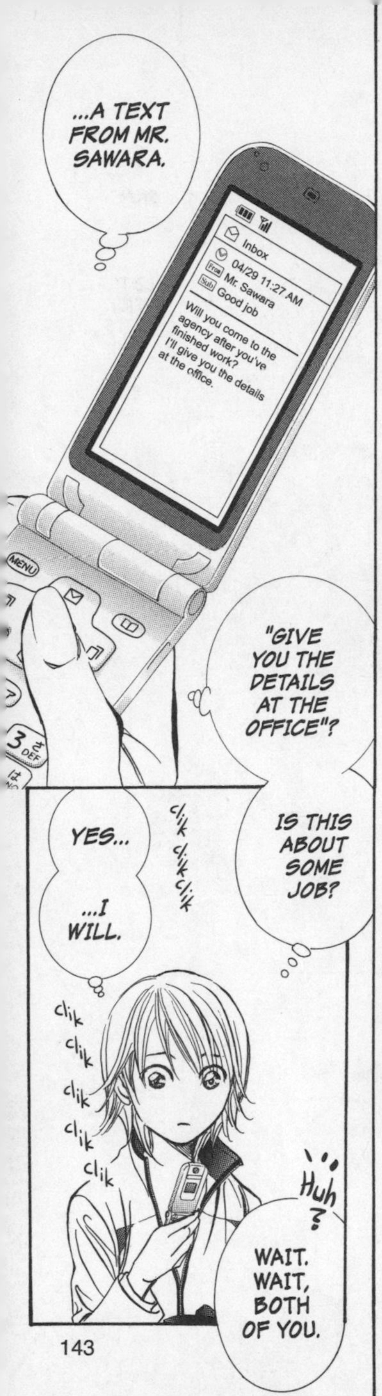
...A TEXT FROM MR. SAWARA.
Inbox
04/29 11:27 AM
From Mr. Sawara
Sub Good job
Will you come to the agency after you've finished work? I'll give you the details at the office.
MENU
3 DEF
"GIVE YOU THE DETAILS AT THE OFFICE"?
IS THIS ABOUT SOME JOB?
clik clik clik clik
YES...
...I WILL.
clik
clik
clik
clik
clik
Huh?
WAIT. WAIT, BOTH OF YOU.

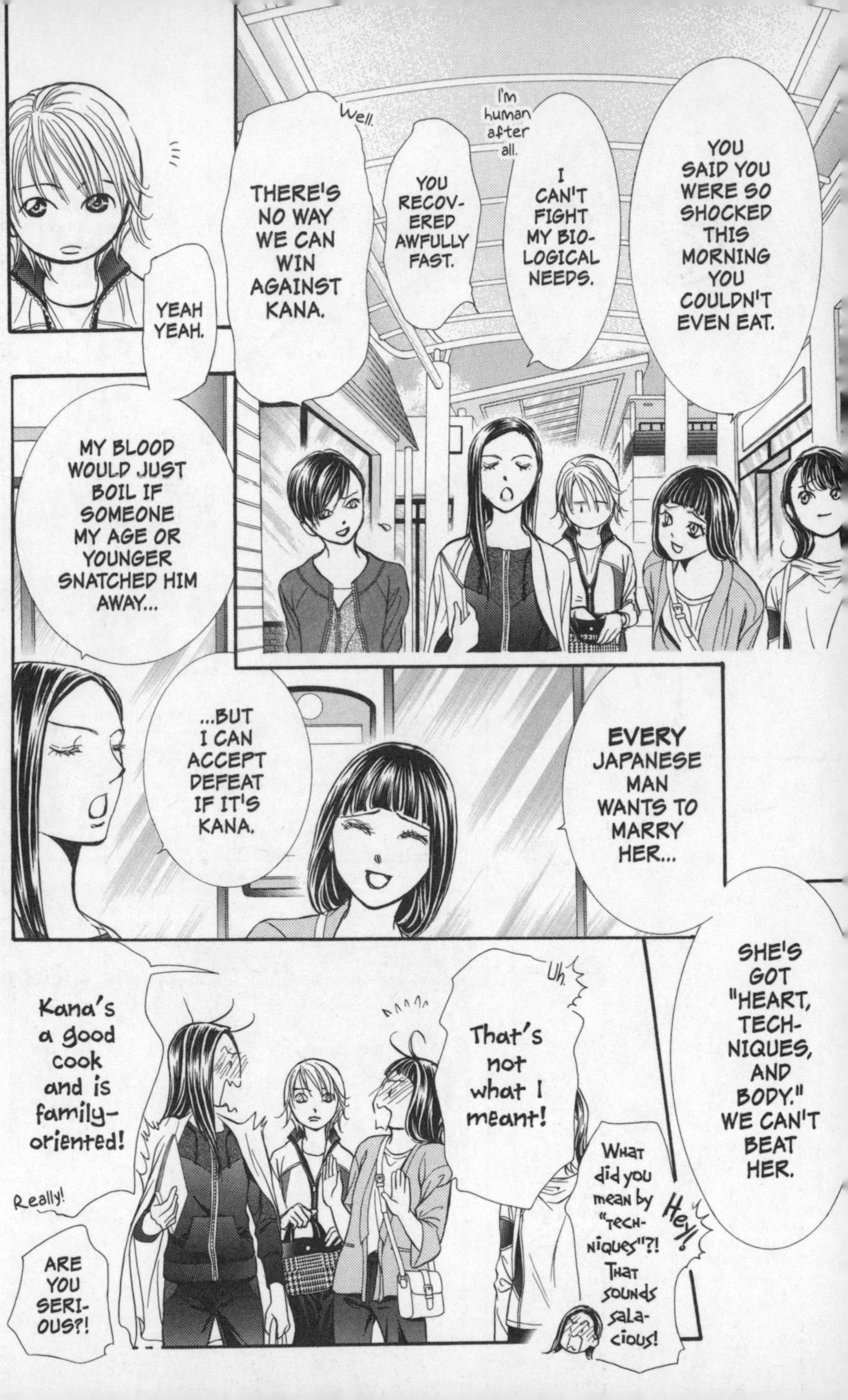
YOU SAID YOU WERE SO SHOCKED THIS MORNING YOU COULDN'T EVEN EAT.
I'm human after all.
I CAN'T FIGHT MY BIO-LOGICAL NEEDS.
YOU RECOV-ERED AWFULLY FAST.
Well.
THERE'S NO WAY WE CAN WIN AGAINST KANA.
YEAH YEAH.
MY BLOOD WOULD JUST BOIL IF SOMEONE MY AGE OR YOUNGER SNATCHED HIM AWAY...
EVERY JAPANESE MAN WANTS TO MARRY HER...
...BUT I CAN ACCEPT DEFEAT IF IT'S KANA.
SHE'S GOT "HEART, TECH-NIQUES, AND BODY." WE CAN'T BEAT HER.
Hey!
What did you mean by "tech-niques"?! That sounds sala-cious!
Uh.
That's not what I meant!
Kana's a good cook and is family-oriented!
Really!
ARE YOU SERI-OUS?!

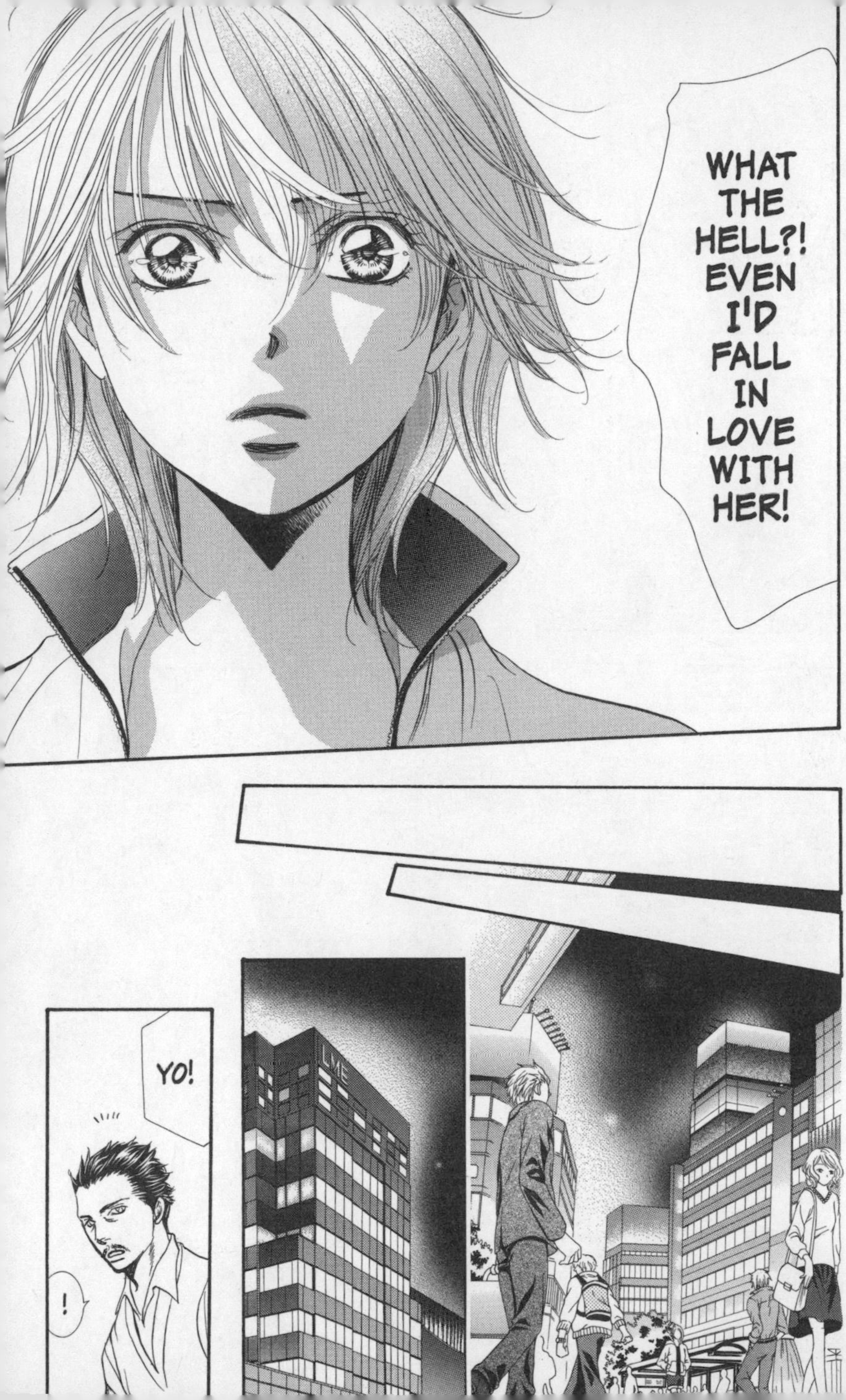
WHAT THE HELL?! EVEN I'D FALL IN LOVE WITH HER!
YO!
!

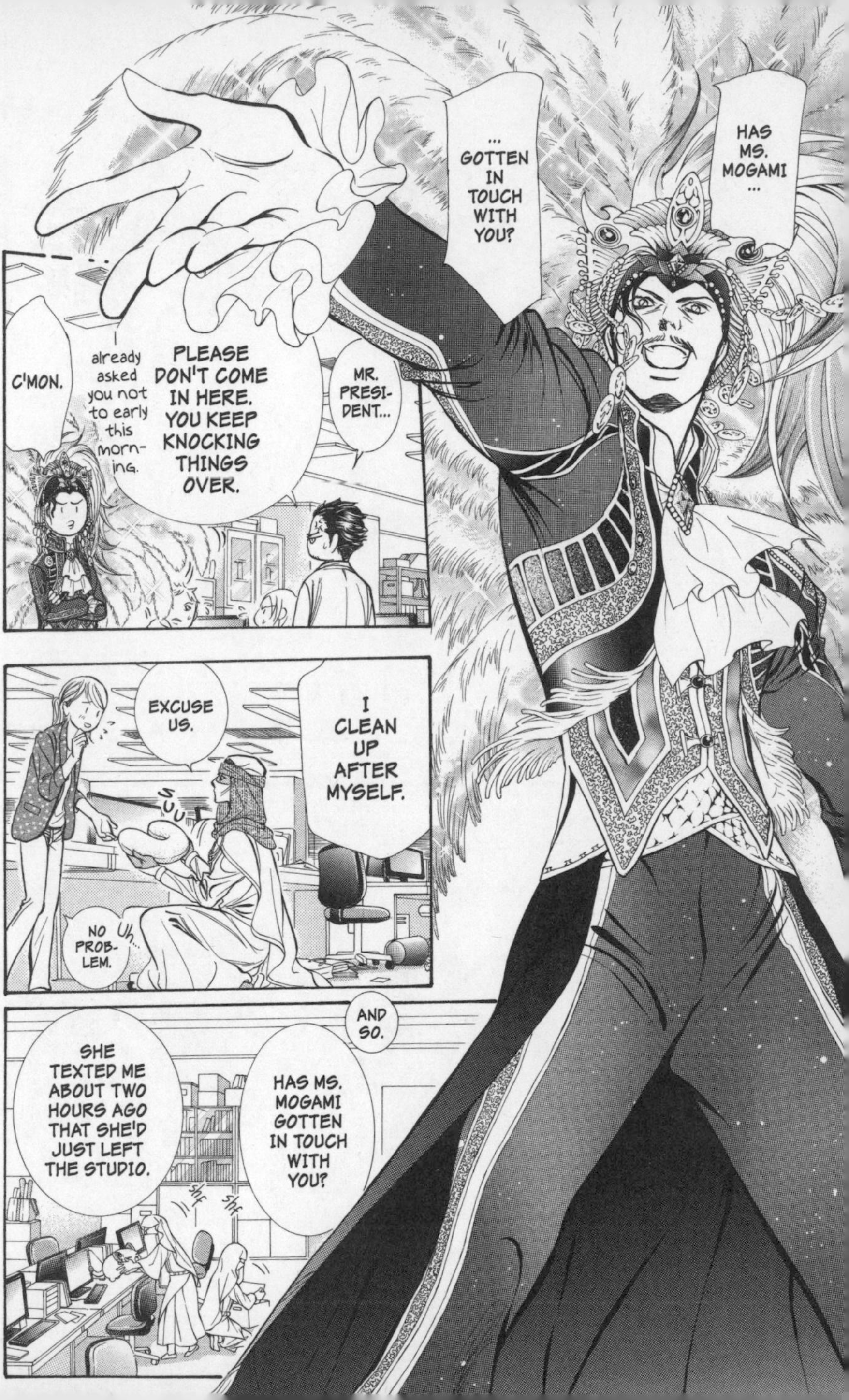
HAS MS. MOGAMI ...
... GOTTEN IN TOUCH WITH YOU?
MR. PRESIDENT...
PLEASE DON'T COME IN HERE. YOU KEEP KNOCKING THINGS OVER.
I already asked you not to early this morning.
C'MON.
I CLEAN UP AFTER MYSELF.
EXCUSE US.
SUU
Uh...
NO PROBLEM.
AND SO.
HAS MS. MOGAMI GOTTEN IN TOUCH WITH YOU?
SHE TEXTED ME ABOUT TWO HOURS AGO THAT SHE'D JUST LEFT THE STUDIO.
shf
shf

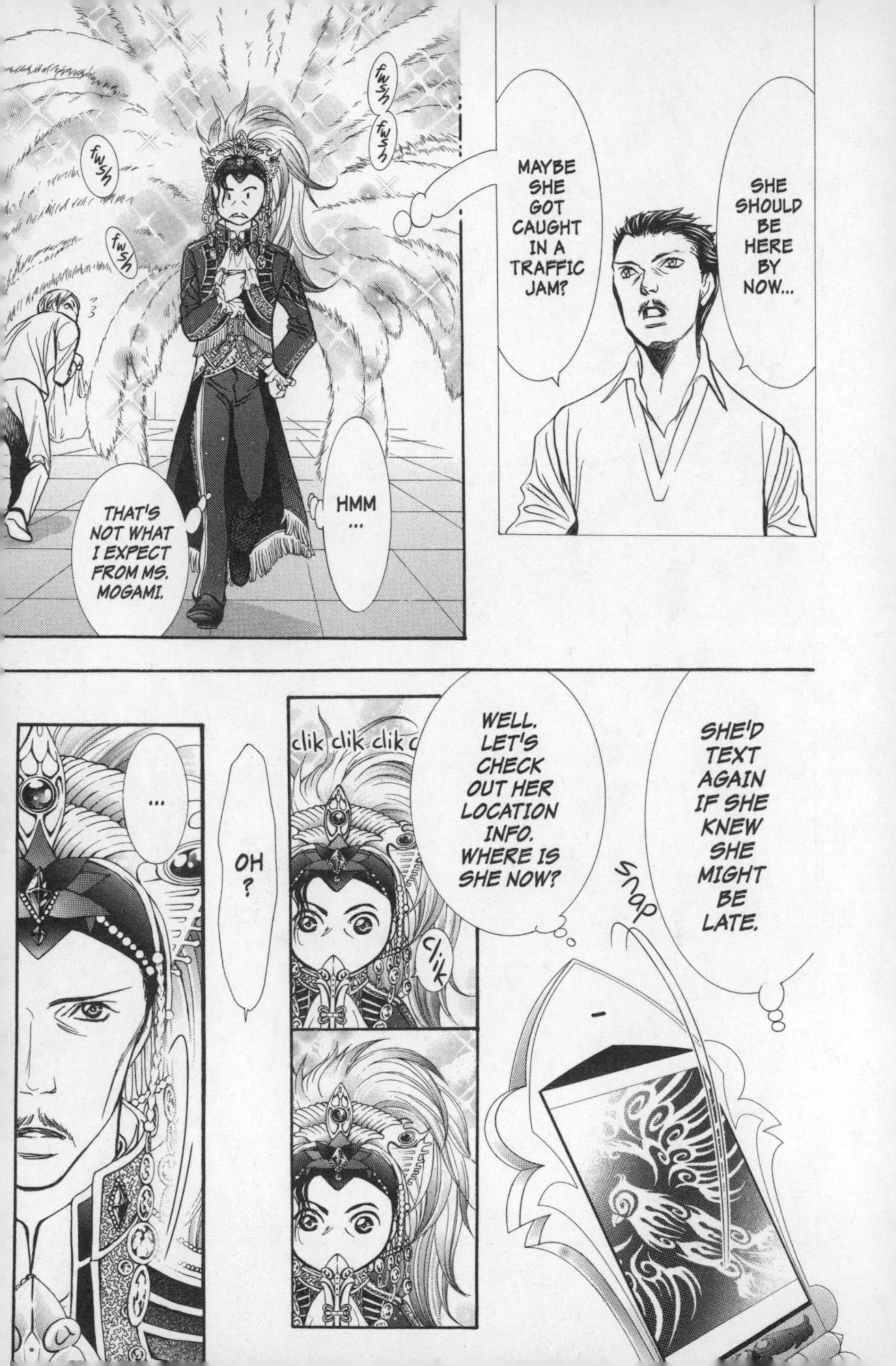
SHE SHOULD BE HERE BY NOW...
MAYBE SHE GOT CAUGHT IN A TRAFFIC JAM?
fwsh
fwsh
fwsh
fwsh
HMM ...
THAT'S NOT WHAT I EXPECT FROM MS. MOGAMI.
SHE'D TEXT AGAIN IF SHE KNEW SHE MIGHT BE LATE.
snap
WELL. LET'S CHECK OUT HER LOCATION INFO. WHERE IS SHE NOW?
clik clik clik c
clik
OH ?
...

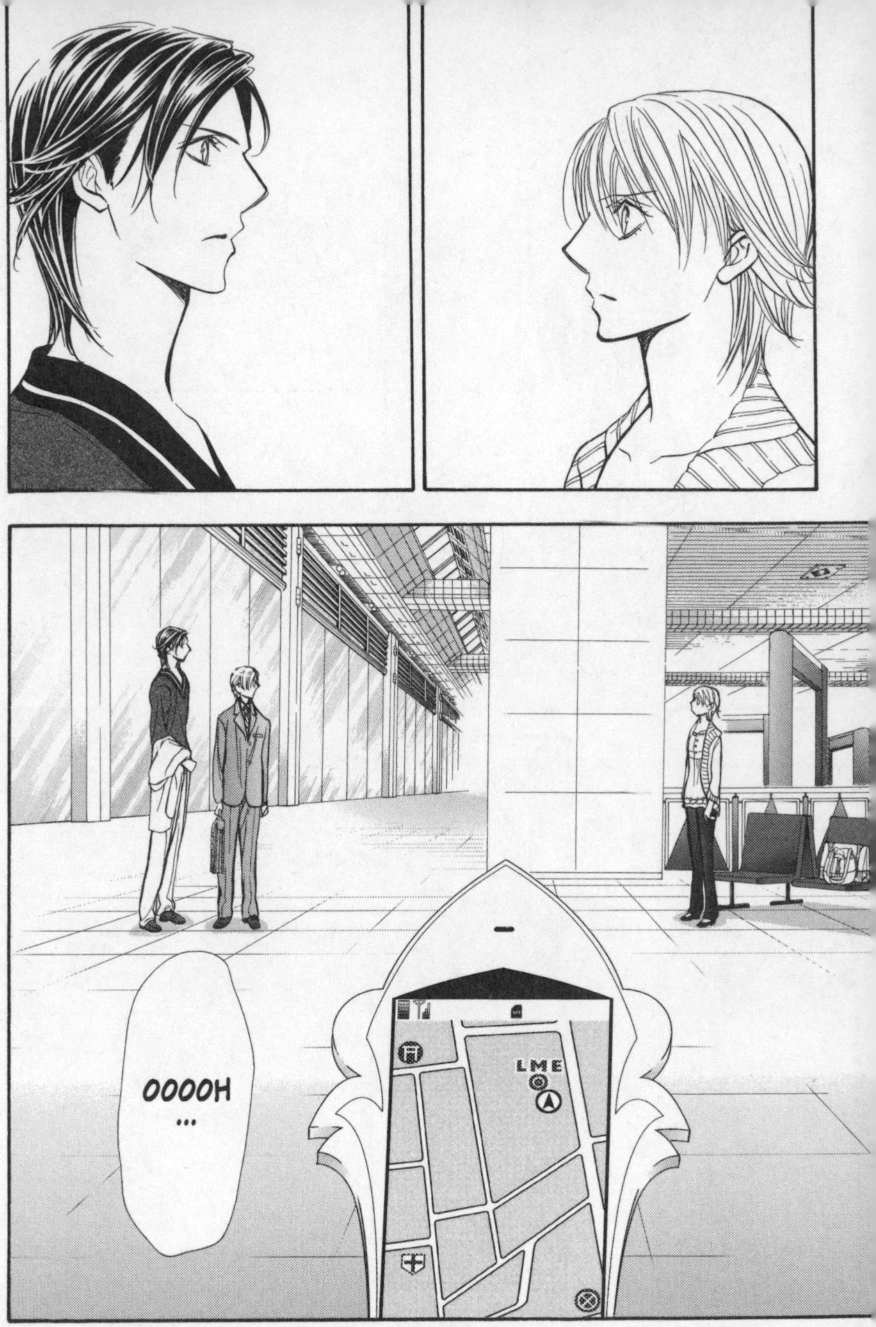
OOOOH
...
LME

End of Act 270

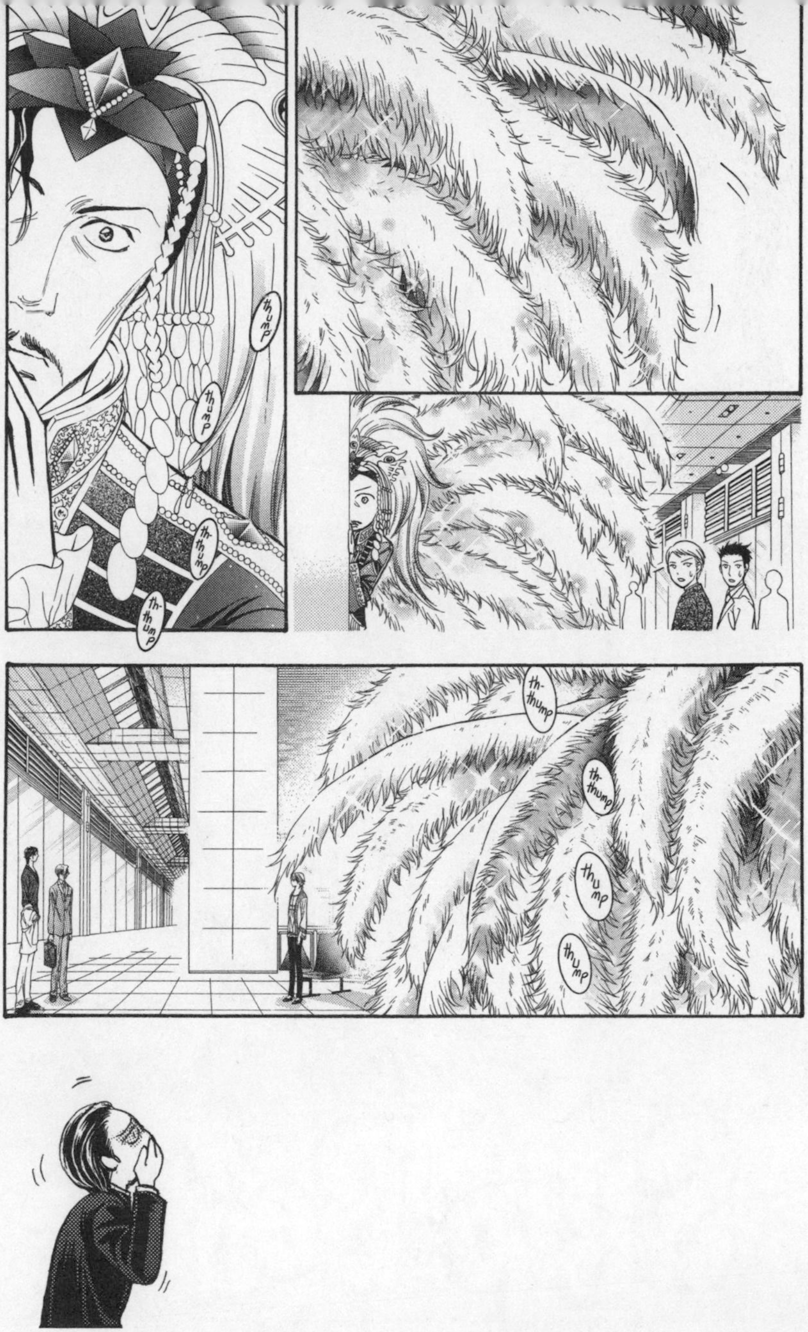
thump
thump
th-thump
th-thump
th-thump
th-thump
thump
thump

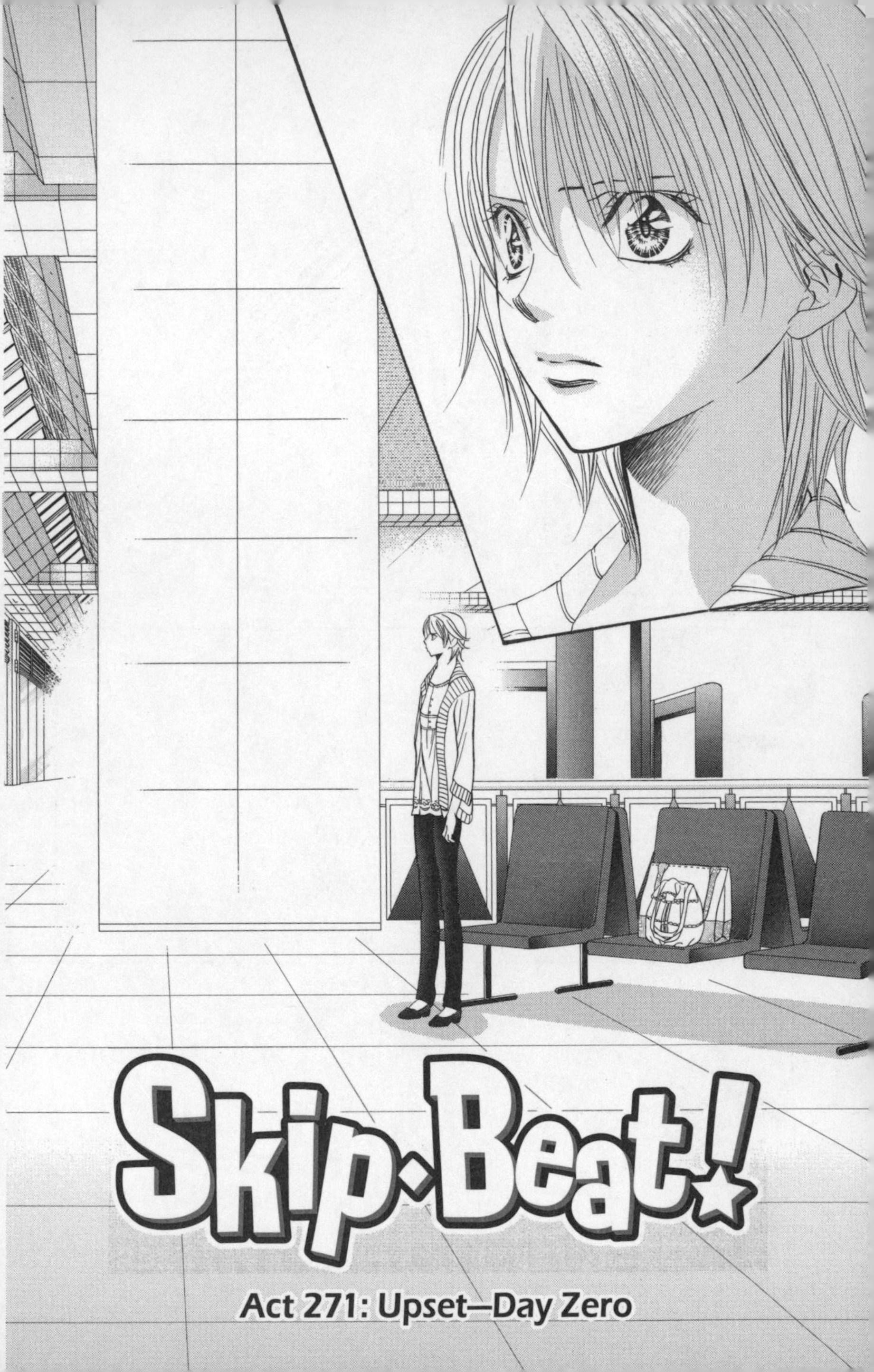
Skip·Beat!
Act 271: Upset—Day Zero

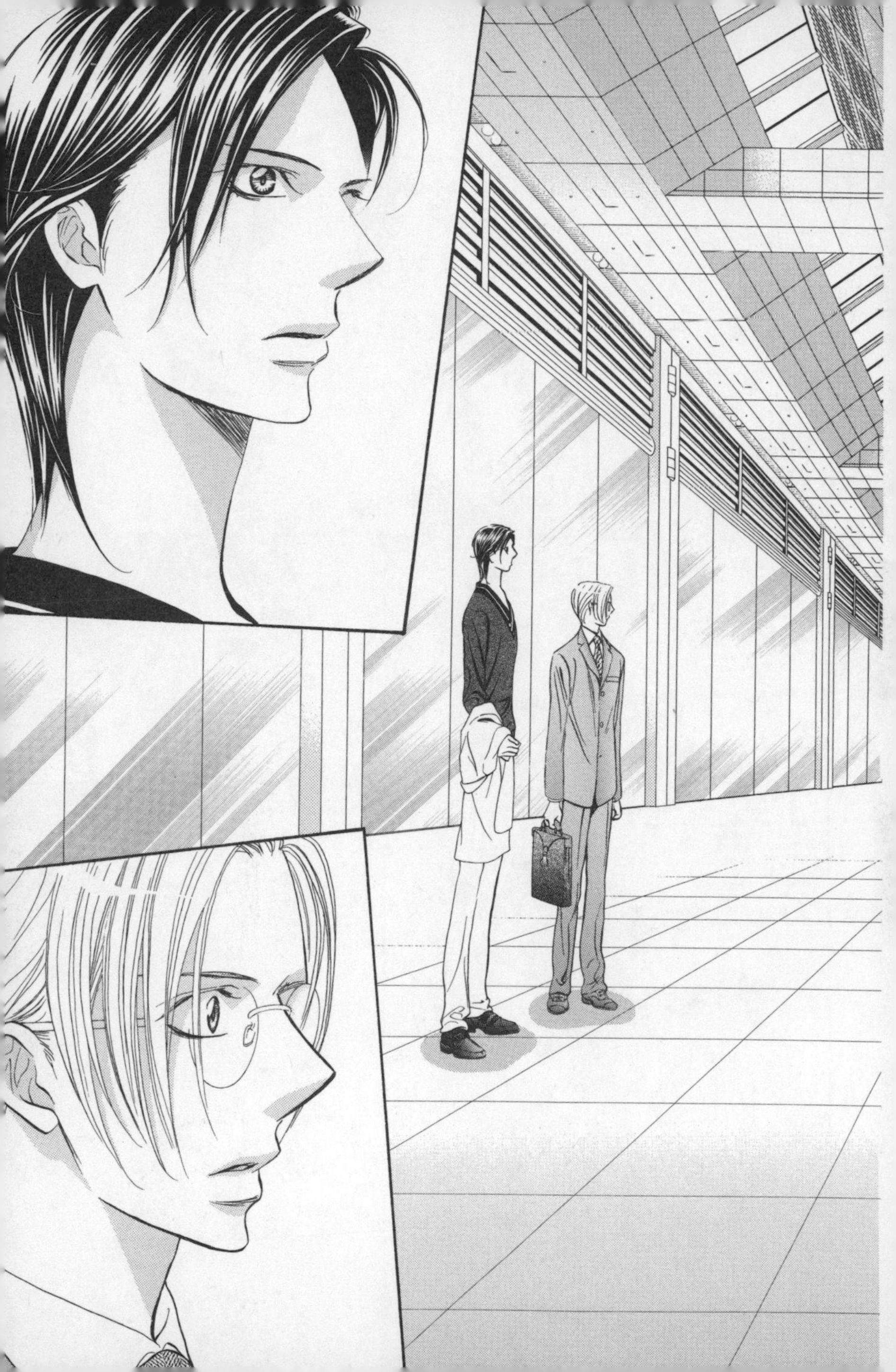

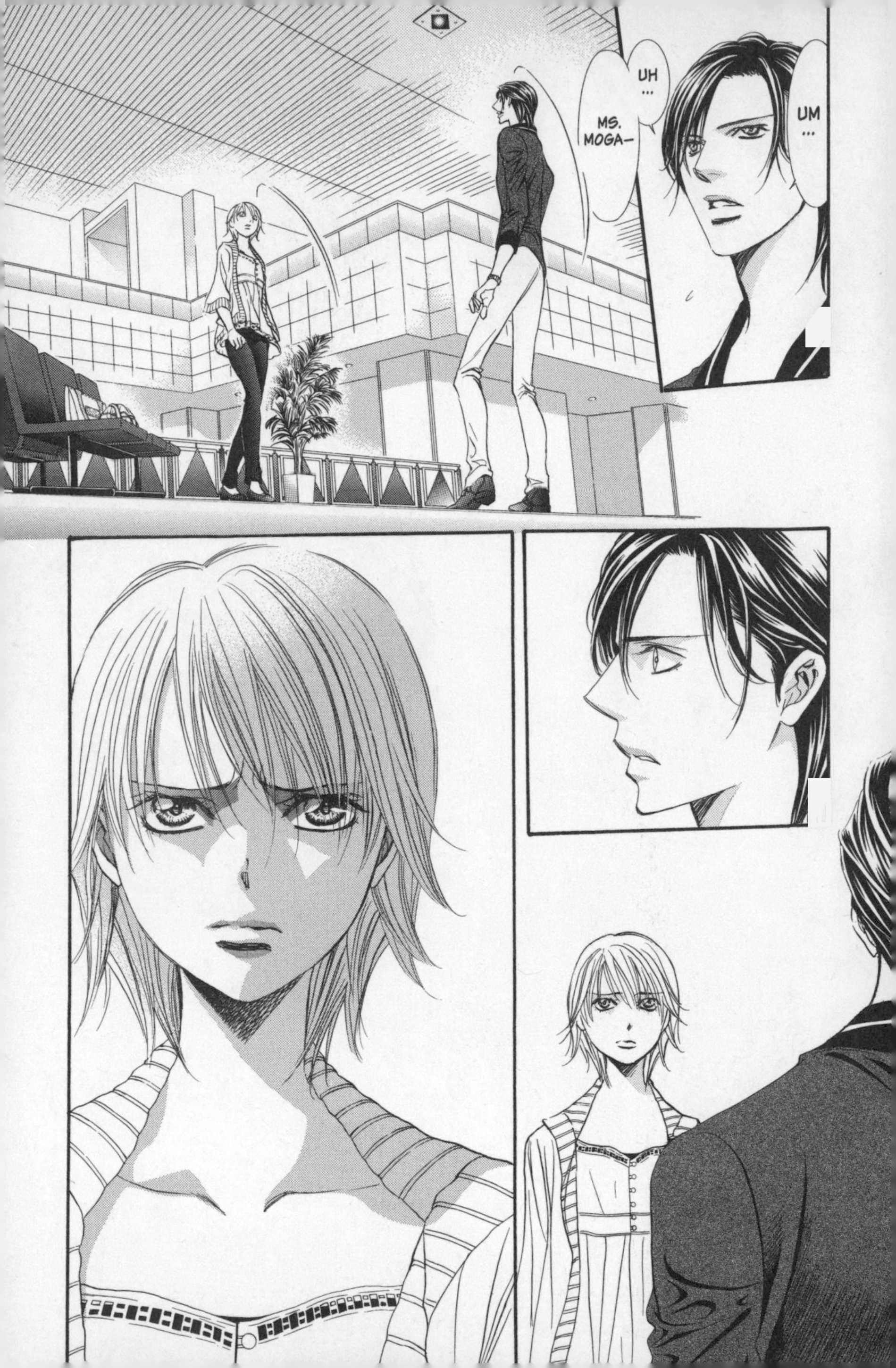
UM ...
UH ...
MS. MOGA—

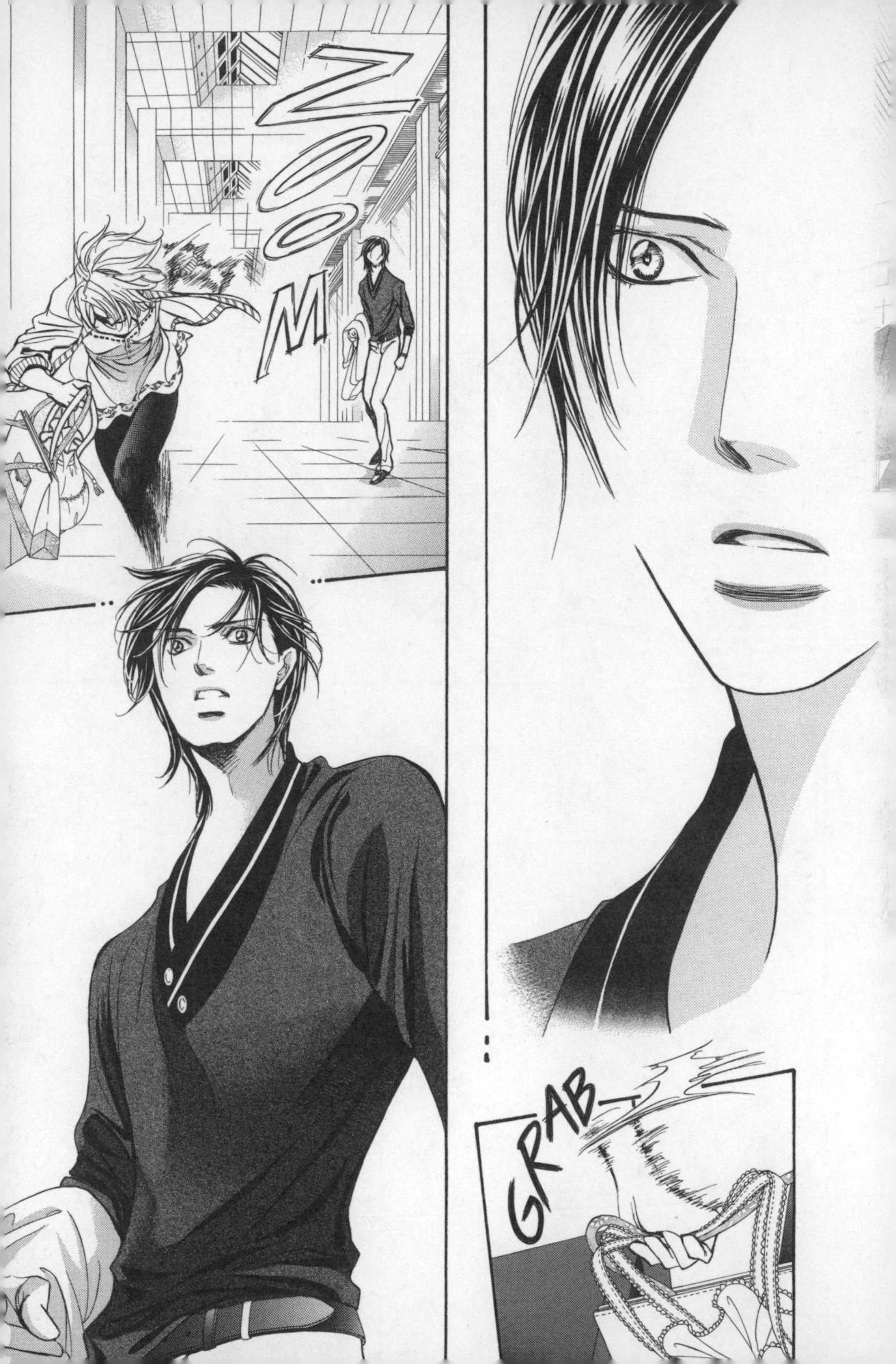
GRAB
ZOOM

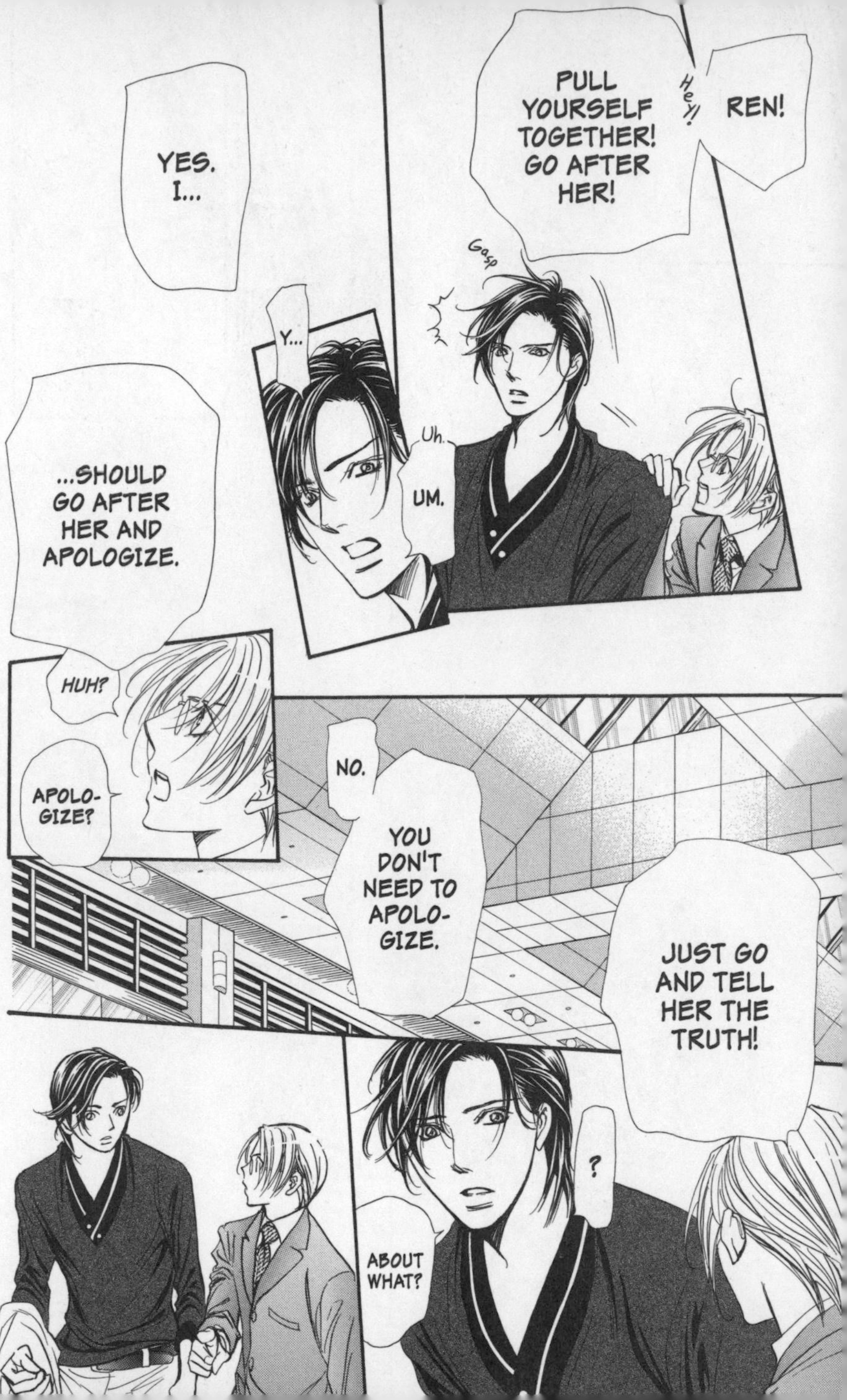
REN!
Hey!!
PULL YOURSELF TOGETHER! GO AFTER HER!
Gasp
Y...
Uh.
UM.
YES. I...
...SHOULD GO AFTER HER AND APOLOGIZE.
HUH?
APOLO-GIZE?
NO.
YOU DON'T NEED TO APOLO-GIZE.
JUST GO AND TELL HER THE TRUTH!
?
ABOUT WHAT?

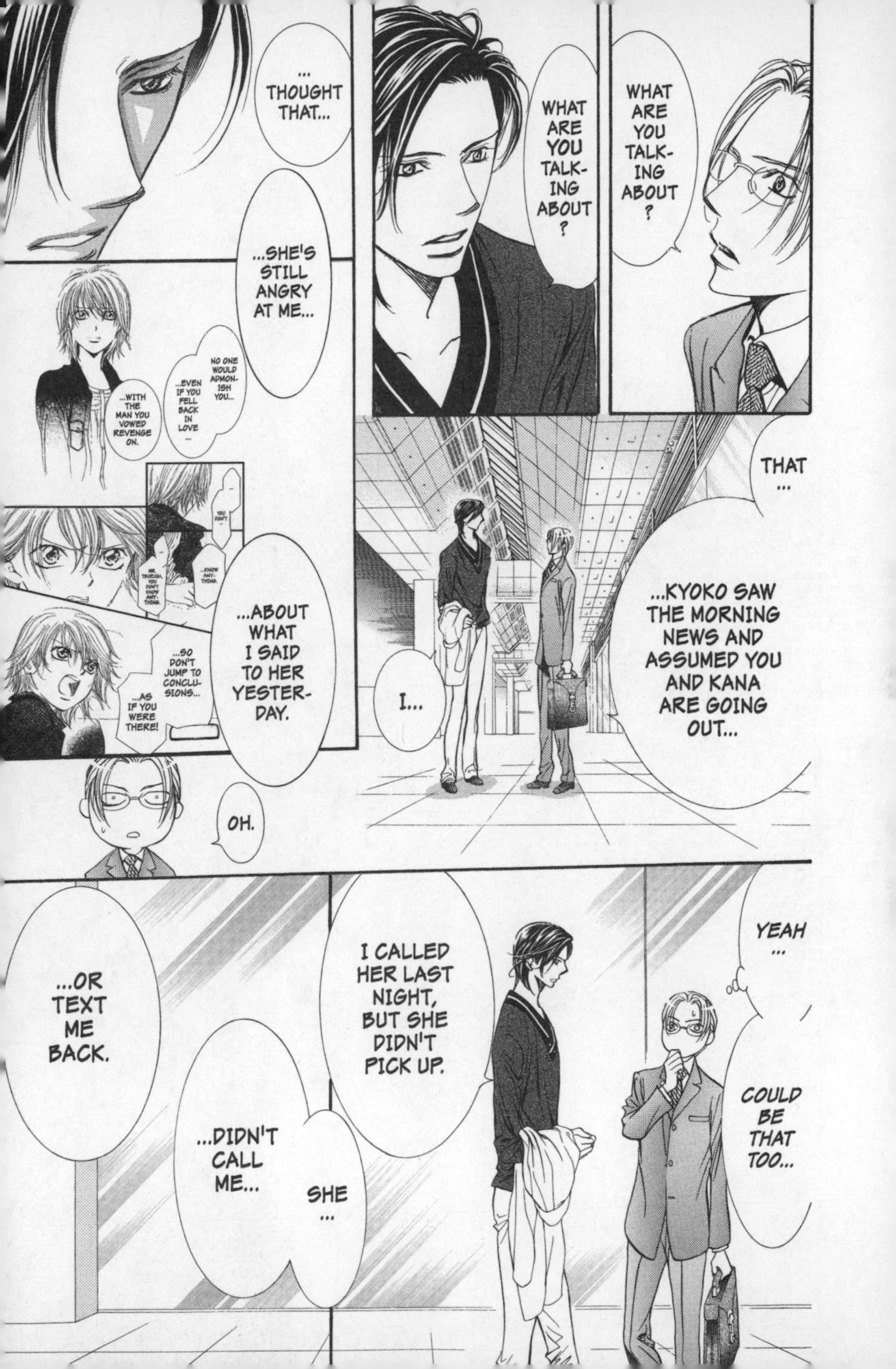
WHAT ARE YOU TALK-ING ABOUT?
WHAT ARE YOU TALK-ING ABOUT?
THAT...
...KYOKO SAW THE MORNING NEWS AND ASSUMED YOU AND KANA ARE GOING OUT...
I...
...THOUGHT THAT...
...SHE'S STILL ANGRY AT ME...
NO ONE WOULD ADMON-ISH YOU...
...EVEN IF YOU FELL BACK IN LOVE...
...WITH THE MAN YOU VOWED REVENGE ON.
...
YOU DON'T...
...KNOW ANY-THING.
...
MR. TSURUGA, YOU DON'T KNOW ANY-THING.
...SO DON'T JUMP TO CONCLU-SIONS...
...AS IF YOU WERE THERE!
...ABOUT WHAT I SAID TO HER YESTER-DAY.
OH.
YEAH...
COULD BE THAT TOO...
I CALLED HER LAST NIGHT, BUT SHE DIDN'T PICK UP.
SHE...
...DIDN'T CALL ME...
...OR TEXT ME BACK.

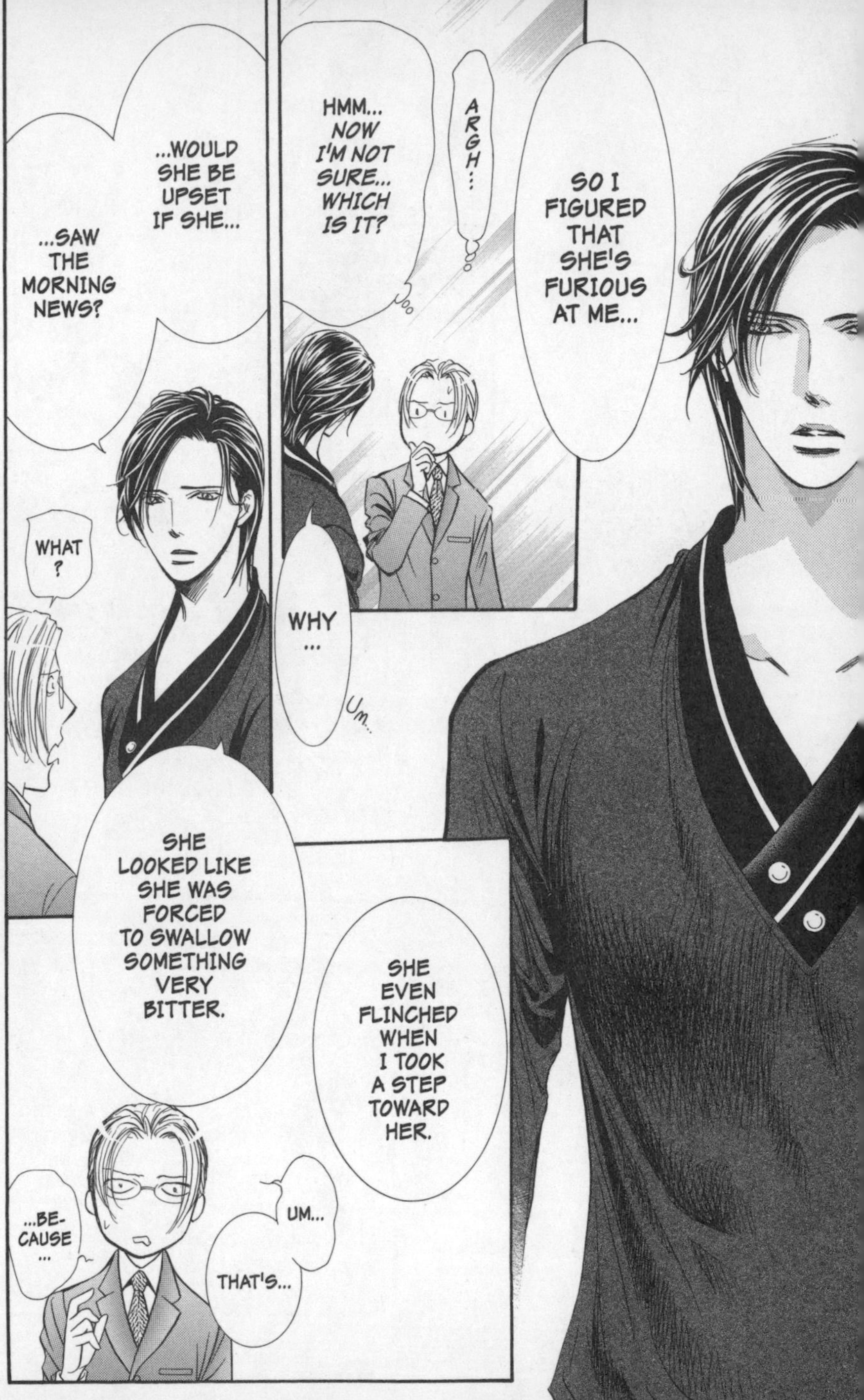
SO I FIGURED THAT SHE'S FURIOUS AT ME...
ARGH...
HMM... NOW I'M NOT SURE... WHICH IS IT?
...WOULD SHE BE UPSET IF SHE...
...SAW THE MORNING NEWS?
WHAT?
WHY...
Um...
SHE LOOKED LIKE SHE WAS FORCED TO SWALLOW SOMETHING VERY BITTER.
SHE EVEN FLINCHED WHEN I TOOK A STEP TOWARD HER.
UM...
THAT'S...
...BE-CAUSE...

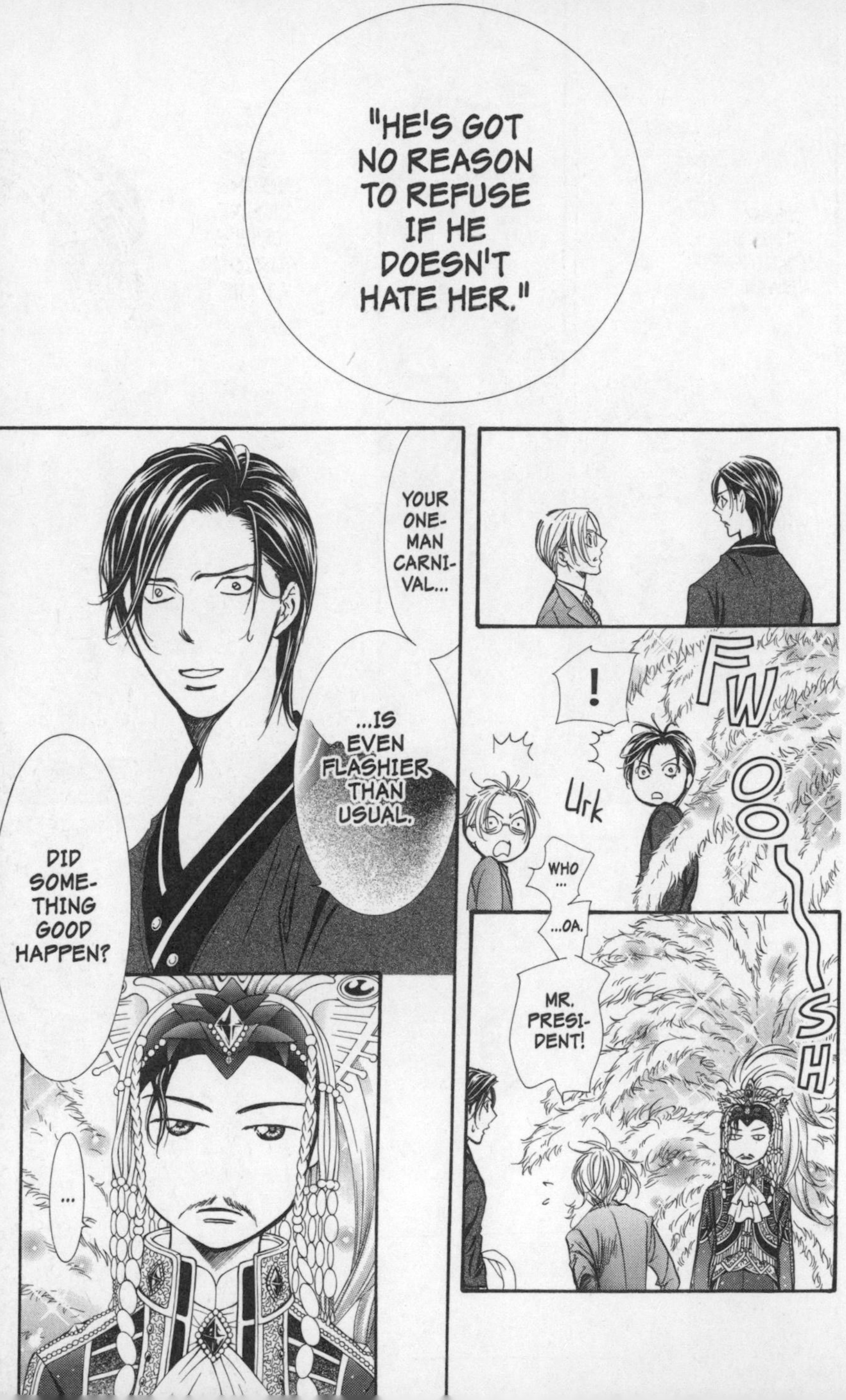
"HE'S GOT NO REASON TO REFUSE IF HE DOESN'T HATE HER."
!
FWOOOSH
Urk
WHO...
...OA.
MR. PRESIDENT!
YOUR ONE-MAN CARNIVAL...
...IS EVEN FLASHIER THAN USUAL.
DID SOMETHING GOOD HAPPEN?
...

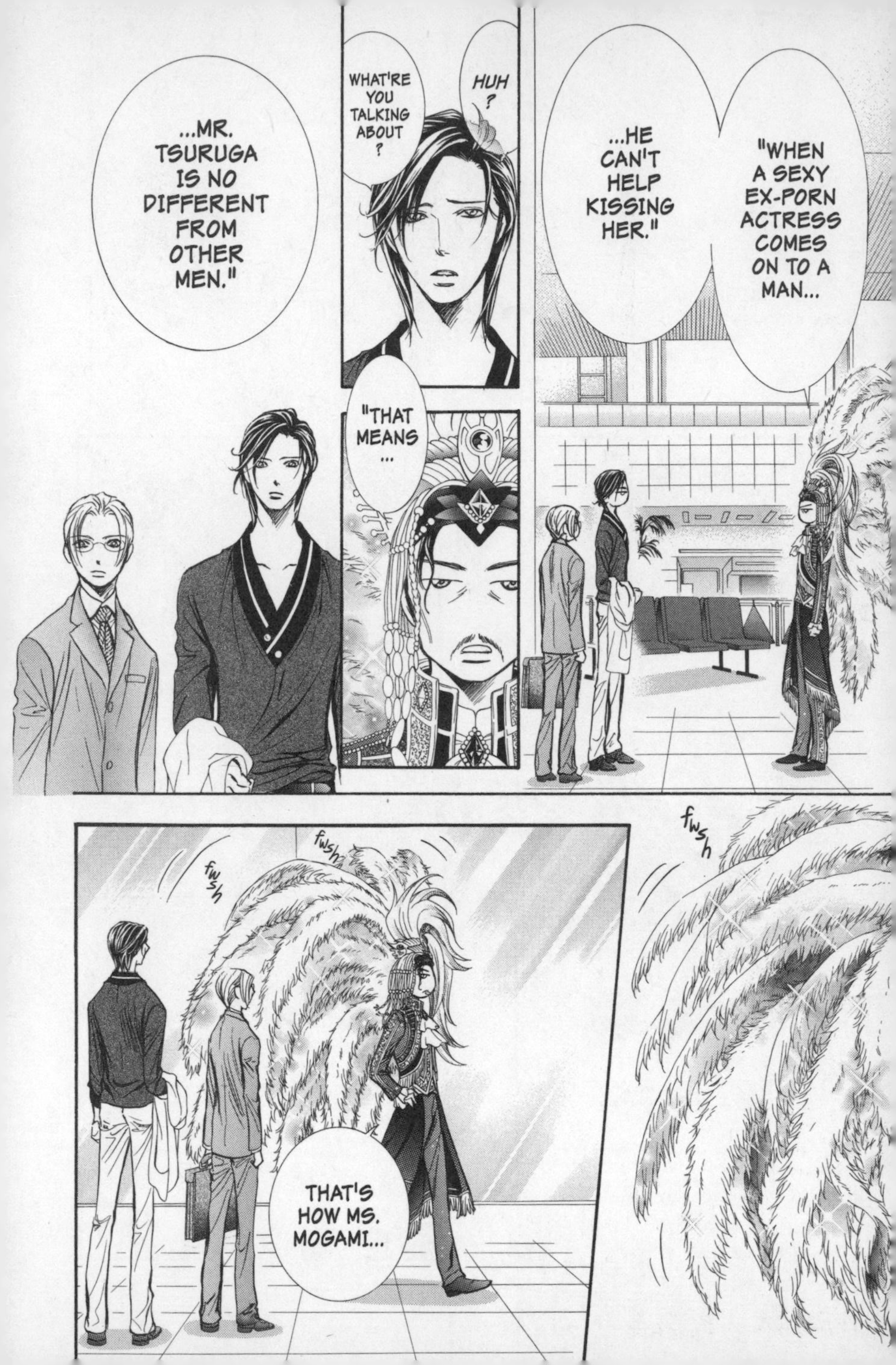
"WHEN A SEXY EX-PORN ACTRESS COMES ON TO A MAN...
...HE CAN'T HELP KISSING HER."
HUH?
WHAT'RE YOU TALKING ABOUT?
"THAT MEANS...
...MR. TSURUGA IS NO DIFFERENT FROM OTHER MEN."
fwsh
fwsh
fwsh
THAT'S HOW MS. MOGAMI...

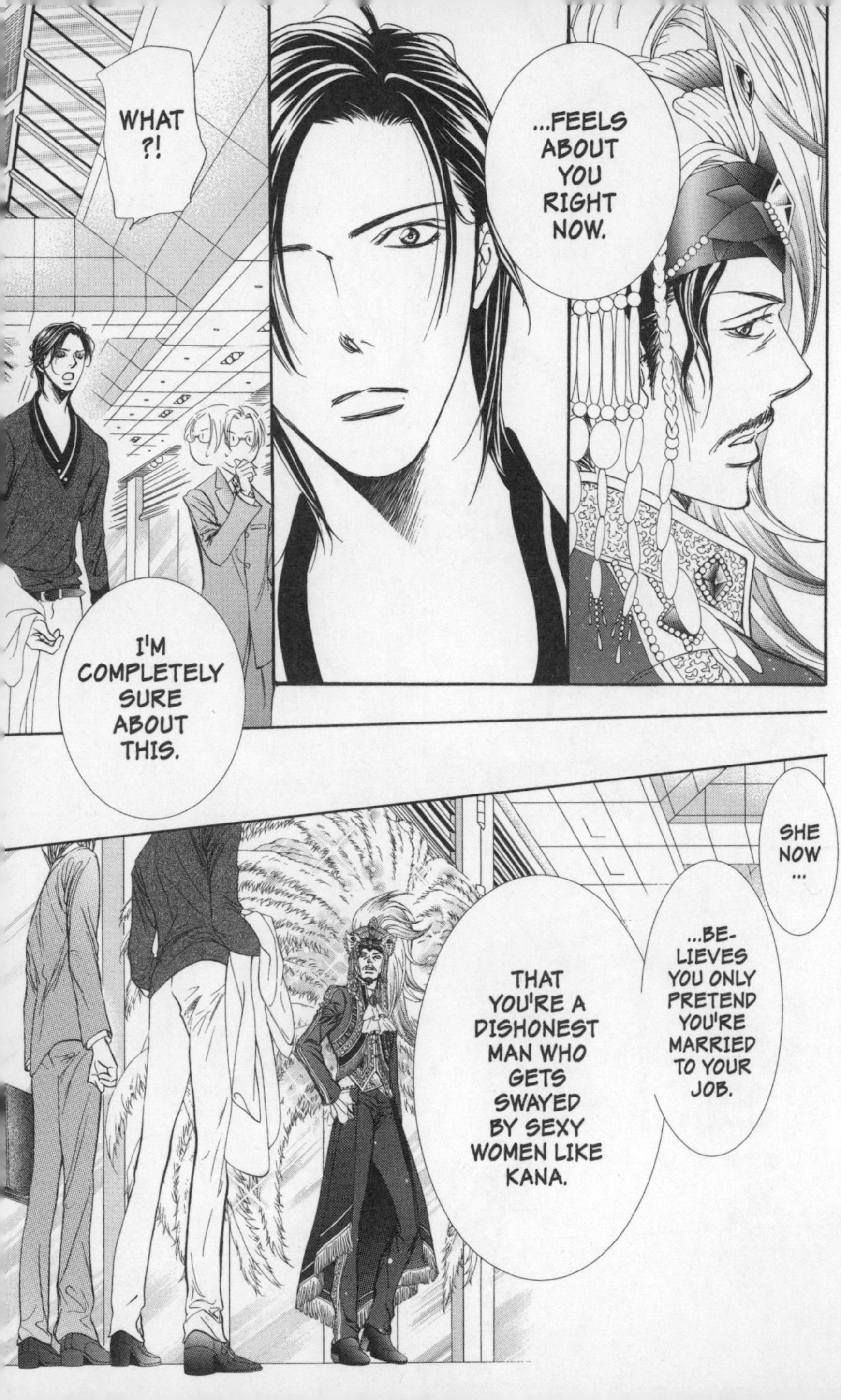
...FEELS ABOUT YOU RIGHT NOW.
WHAT ?!
I'M COMPLETELY SURE ABOUT THIS.
SHE NOW ...
...BE-LIEVES YOU ONLY PRETEND YOU'RE MARRIED TO YOUR JOB.
THAT YOU'RE A DISHONEST MAN WHO GETS SWAYED BY SEXY WOMEN LIKE KANA.

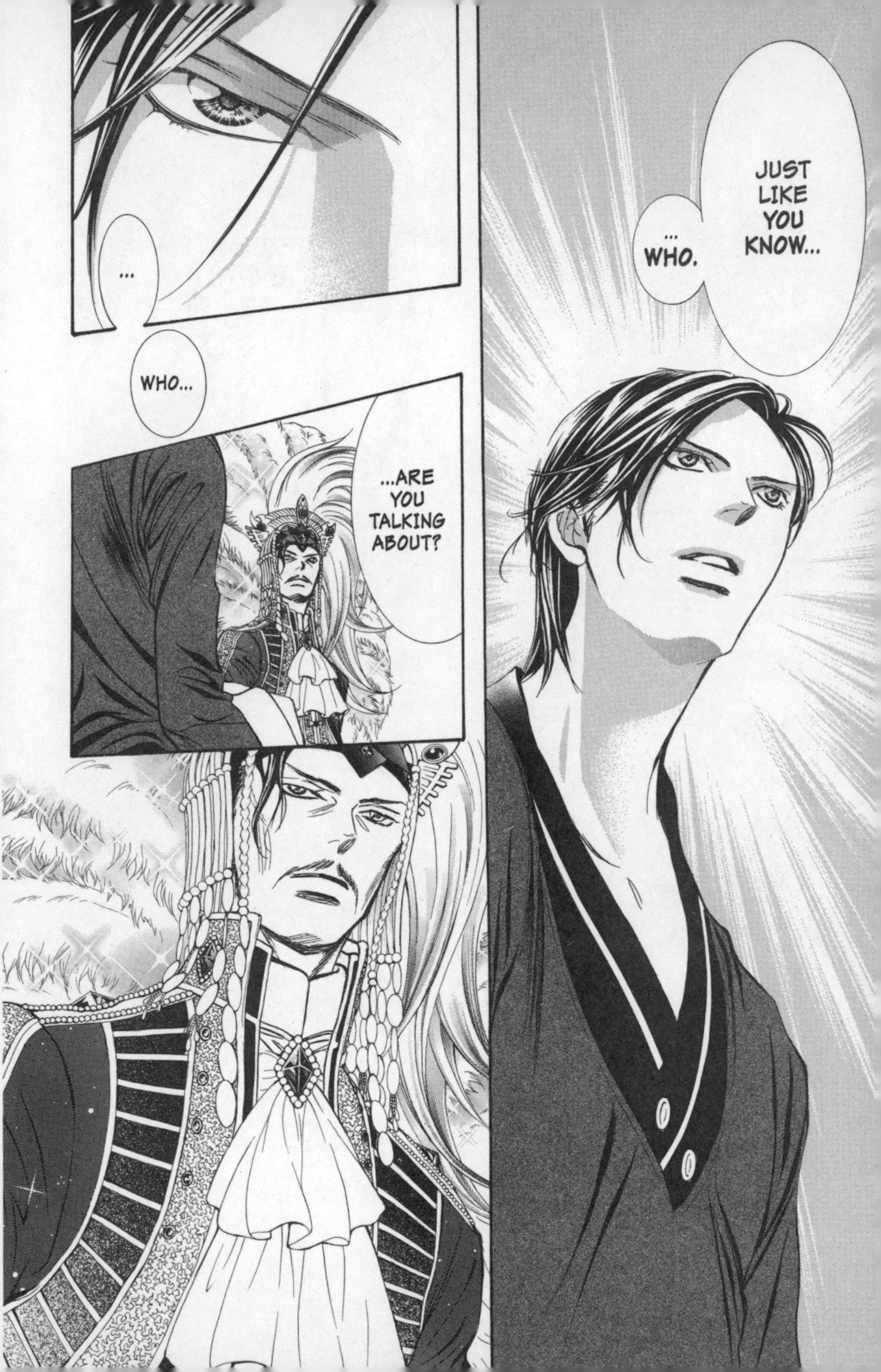
JUST LIKE YOU KNOW...
... WHO.
...
WHO...
...ARE YOU TALKING ABOUT?

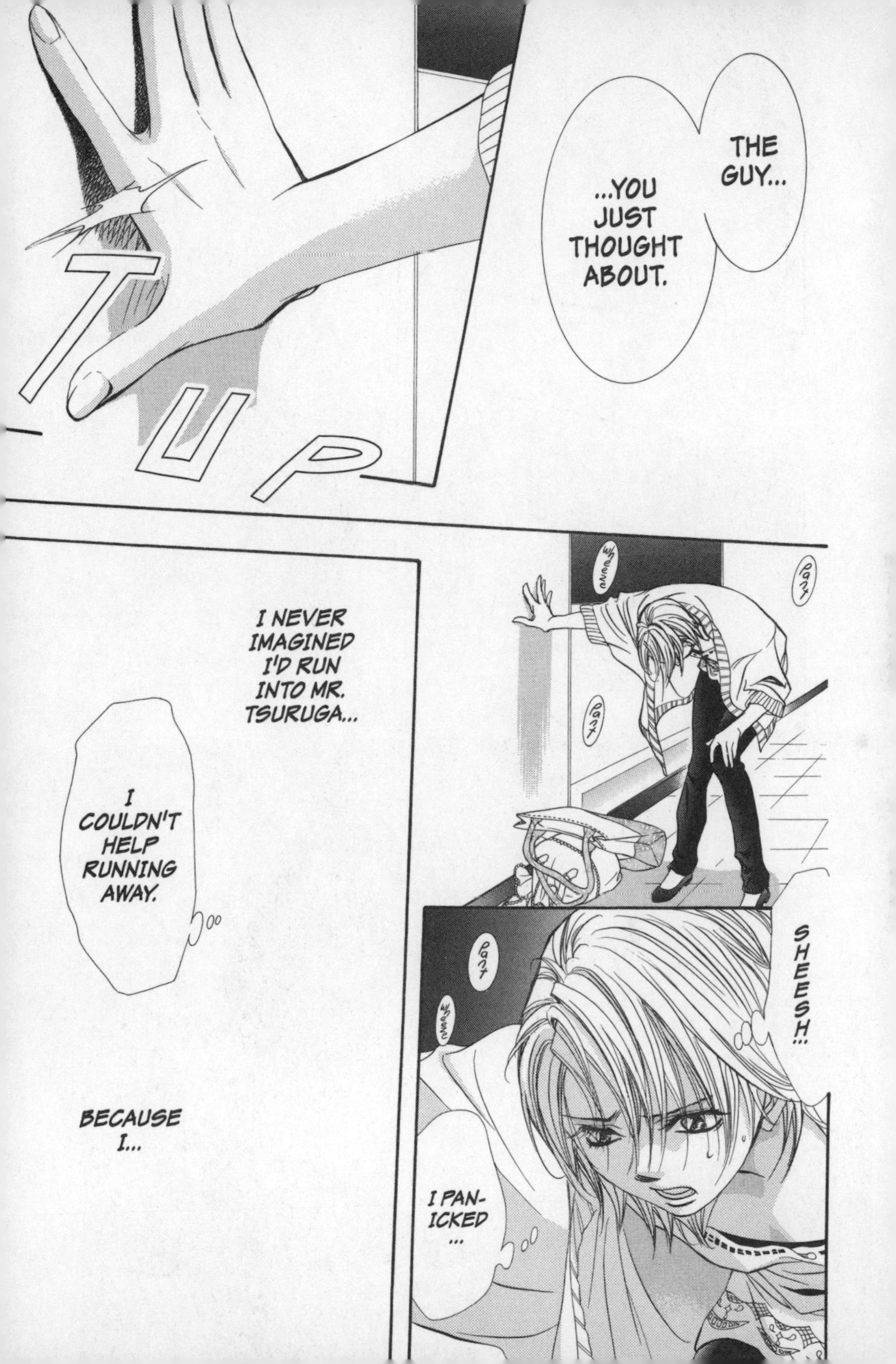
THE GUY...
...YOU JUST THOUGHT ABOUT.
TUP
pant
wheeze
pant
SHEESH...
pant
wheeze
I PAN-ICKED...
I NEVER IMAGINED I'D RUN INTO MR. TSURUGA...
I COULDN'T HELP RUNNING AWAY.
BECAUSE I...

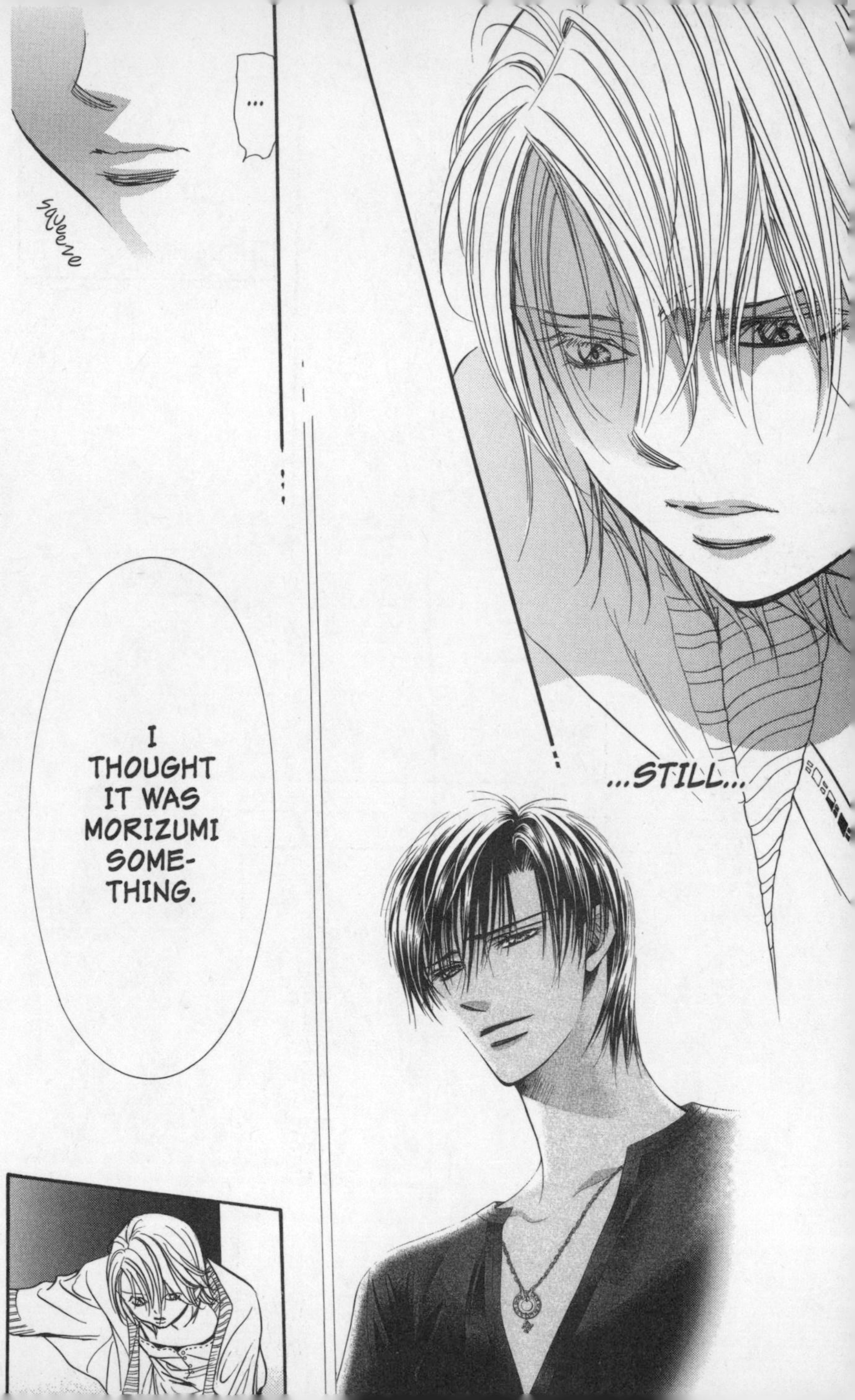
...STILL...
...
squeeze
I THOUGHT IT WAS MORIZUMI SOME-THING.

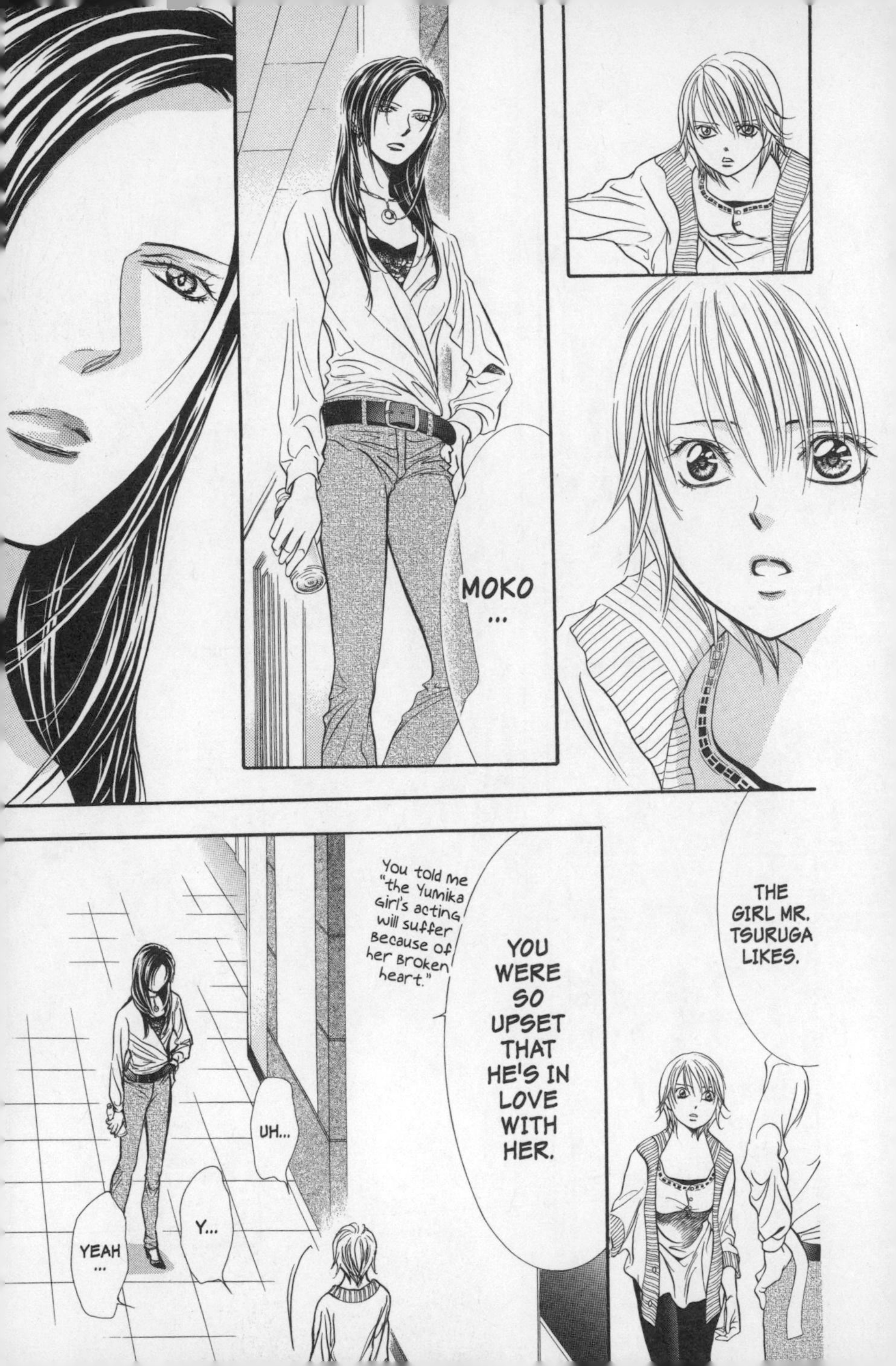

MOKO ...
THE GIRL MR. TSURUGA LIKES.
YOU WERE SO UPSET THAT HE'S IN LOVE WITH HER.
You told me "the Yumika Girl's acting will suffer because of her broken heart."
UH...
Y...
YEAH ...

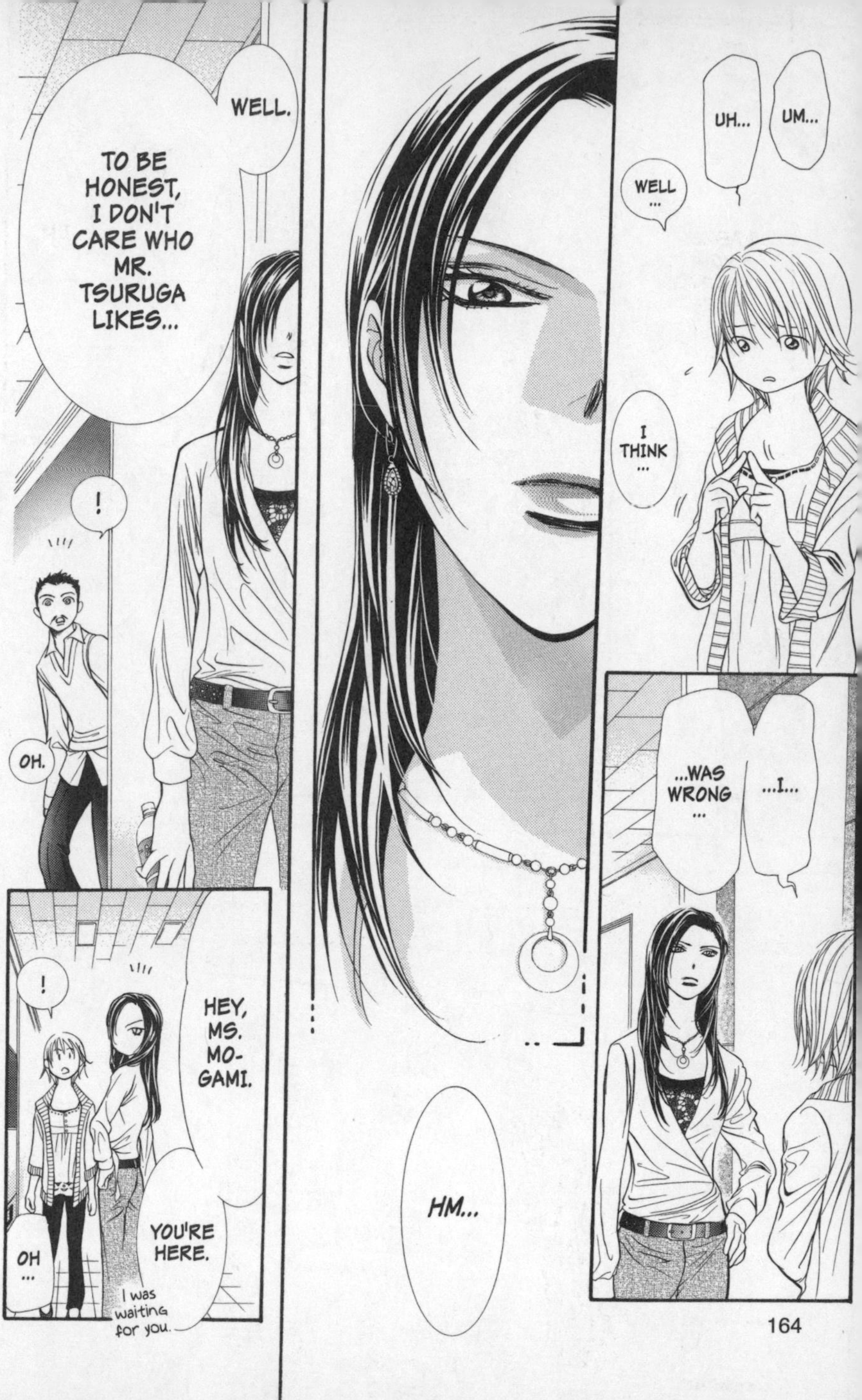
UM...
UH...
WELL ...
I THINK ...
...I...
...WAS WRONG ...
HM...
WELL.
TO BE HONEST, I DON'T CARE WHO MR. TSURUGA LIKES...
!
OH.
HEY, MS. MO-GAMI.
!
YOU'RE HERE.
I was waiting for you.
OH ...

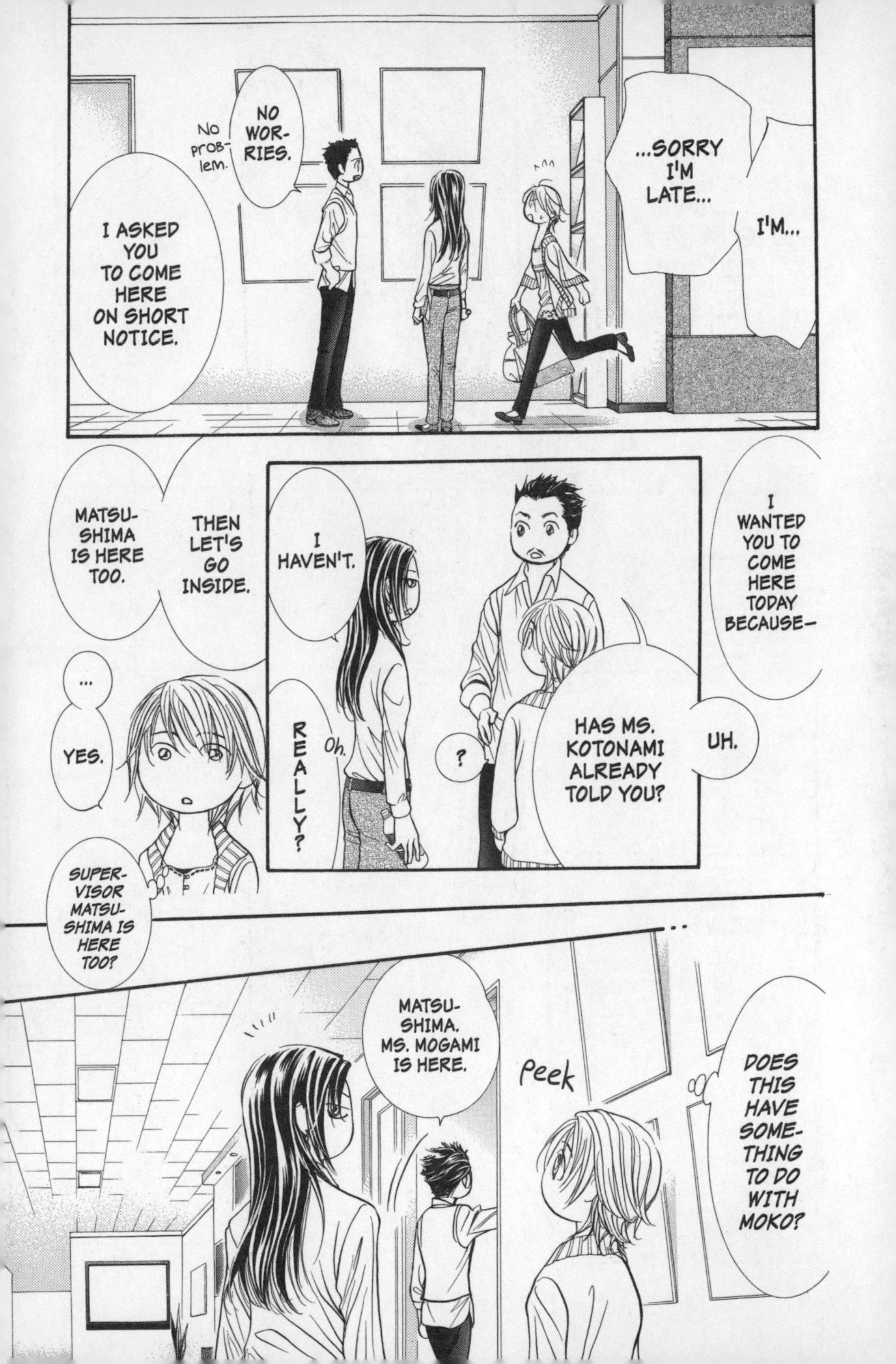
I'M...
...SORRY I'M LATE...
NO WORRIES.
No problem.
I ASKED YOU TO COME HERE ON SHORT NOTICE.
I WANTED YOU TO COME HERE TODAY BECAUSE—
UH.
HAS MS. KOTONAMI ALREADY TOLD YOU?
I HAVEN'T.
?
Oh.
REALLY?
THEN LET'S GO INSIDE.
MATSUSHIMA IS HERE TOO.
...
YES.
SUPERVISOR MATSUSHIMA IS HERE TOO?
DOES THIS HAVE SOMETHING TO DO WITH MOKO?
Peek
MATSUSHIMA. MS. MOGAMI IS HERE.

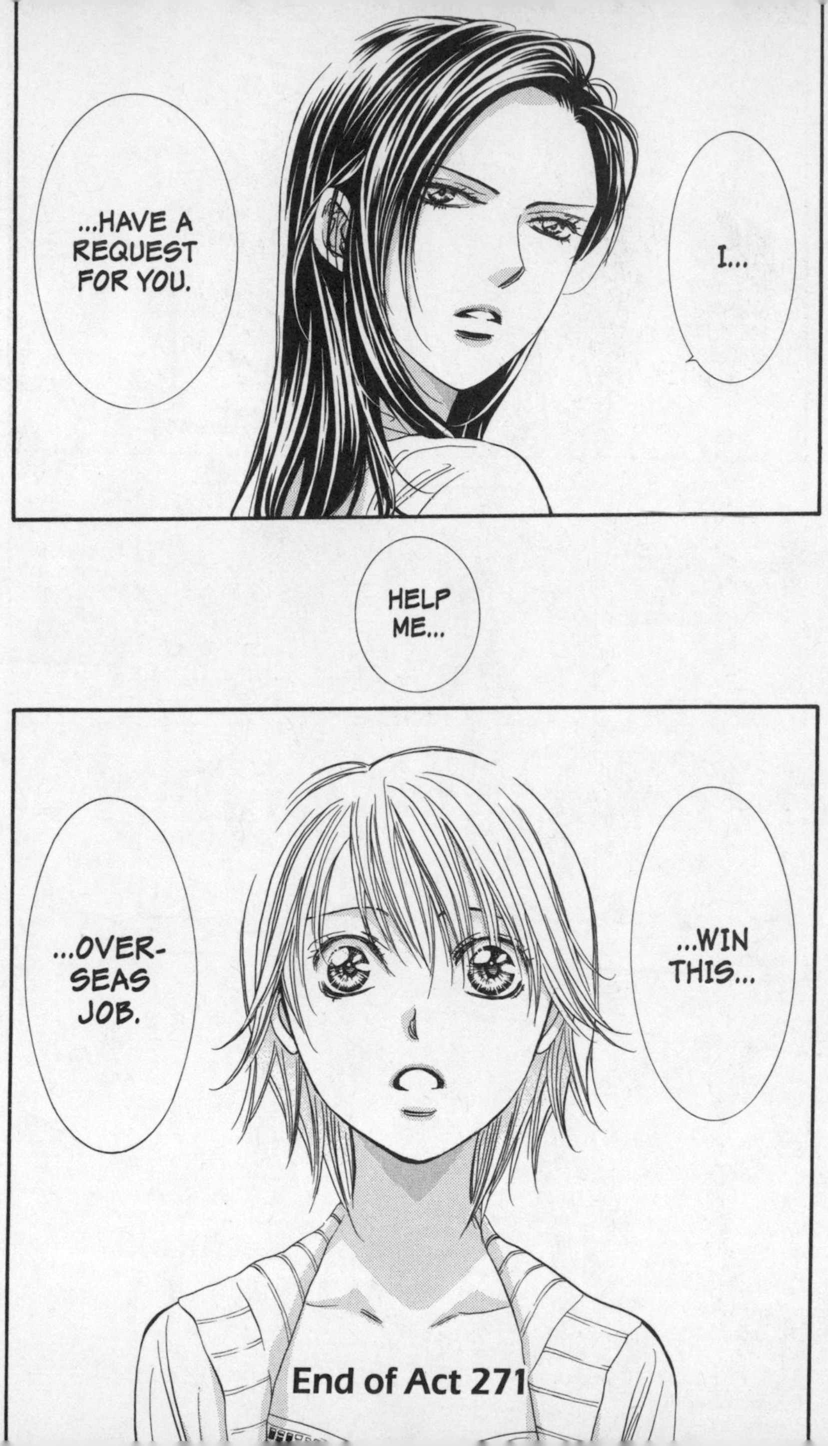
I...
...HAVE A REQUEST FOR YOU.
HELP ME...
...WIN THIS...
...OVER-SEAS JOB.
End of Act 271

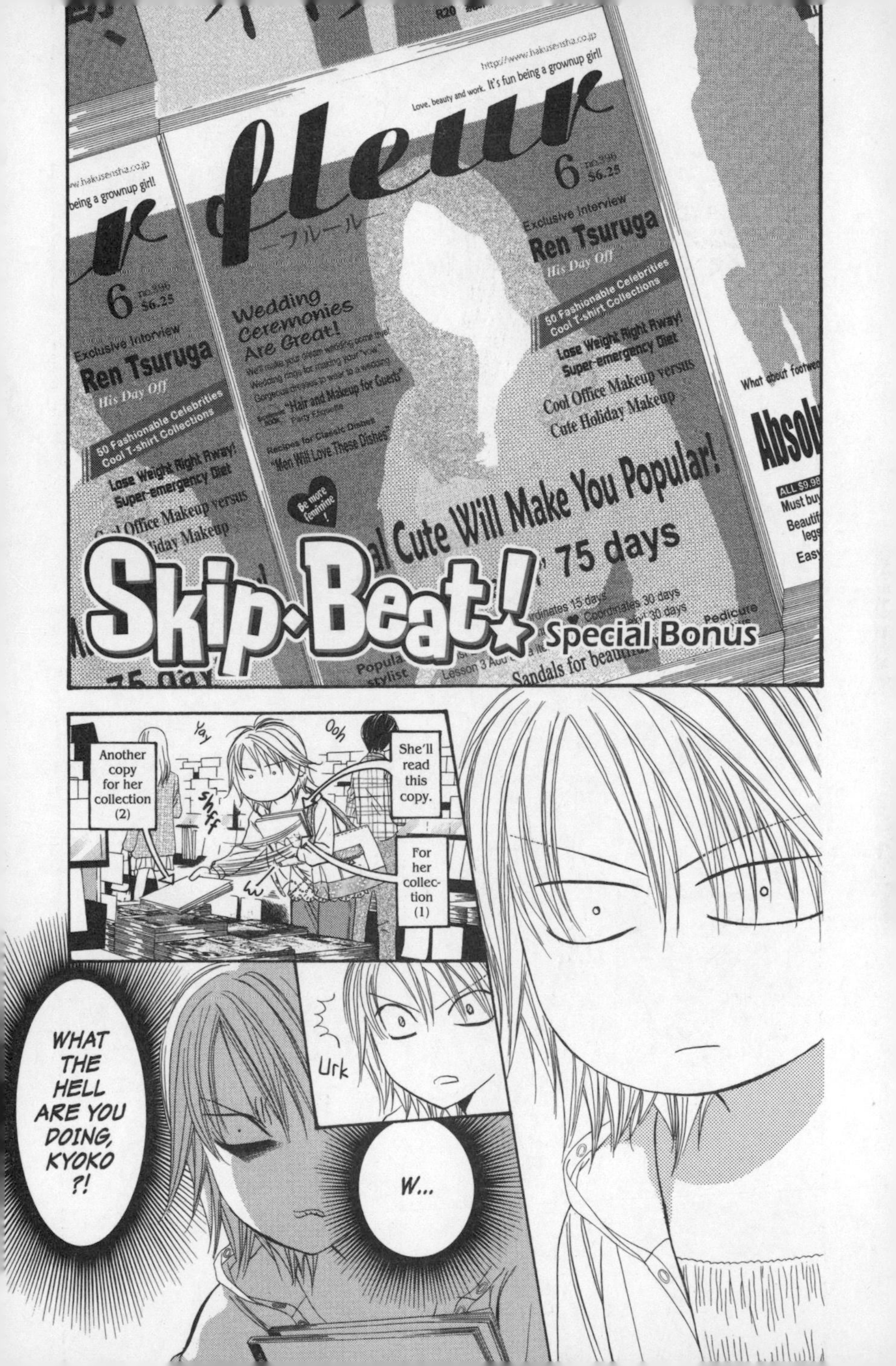

http://www.hakusensha.co.jp
Love, beauty and work. It's fun being a grownup girl!
fleur
フルール
6 no.396 $6.25
Exclusive Interview
Ren Tsuruga
His Day Off
Wedding Ceremonies Are Great!
50 Fashionable Celebrities
Cool T-shirt Collections
Lose Weight Right Away!
Super-emergency Diet
Cool Office Makeup versus
Cute Holiday Makeup
Recipes for Classic Dishes
"Men Will Love These Dishes"
Be more feminine!
al Cute Will Make You Popular!
75 days
What about footwe
Absolu
ALL $9.98
Skip·Beat!
Special Bonus
Ooh
She'll read this copy.
Yay
Another copy for her collection (2)
shff
For her collection (1)
Urk
W...
WHAT THE HELL ARE YOU DOING, KYOKO?!

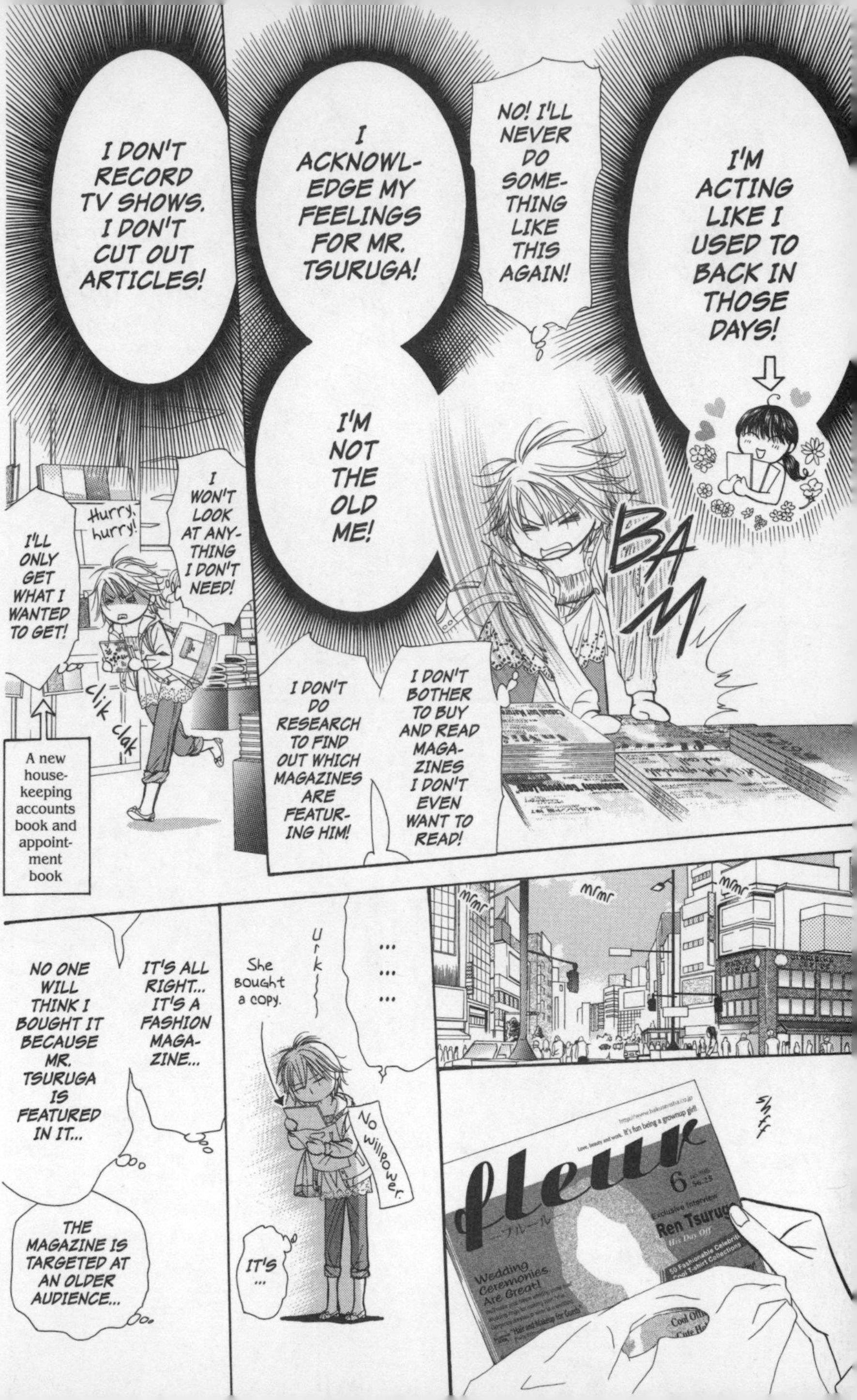
I'M ACTING LIKE I USED TO BACK IN THOSE DAYS!
NO! I'LL NEVER DO SOMETHING LIKE THIS AGAIN!
I ACKNOWLEDGE MY FEELINGS FOR MR. TSURUGA!
I'M NOT THE OLD ME!
BAM
I DON'T BOTHER TO BUY AND READ MAGAZINES I DON'T EVEN WANT TO READ!
I DON'T DO RESEARCH TO FIND OUT WHICH MAGAZINES ARE FEATURING HIM!
I DON'T RECORD TV SHOWS. I DON'T CUT OUT ARTICLES!
I WON'T LOOK AT ANYTHING I DON'T NEED!
Hurry, hurry!
I'LL ONLY GET WHAT I WANTED TO GET!
clik clak
A new housekeeping accounts book and appointment book
mrmr
mrmr
mrmr
shff
Love, beauty and work. It's fun being a grownup girl!
fleur
6
Exclusive Interview
His Day Off
Wedding Ceremonies Are Great!
...
...
...
Urk
She bought a copy.
No willpower.
IT'S ...
IT'S ALL RIGHT... IT'S A FASHION MAGAZINE...
NO ONE WILL THINK I BOUGHT IT BECAUSE MR. TSURUGA IS FEATURED IN IT...
THE MAGAZINE IS TARGETED AT AN OLDER AUDIENCE...

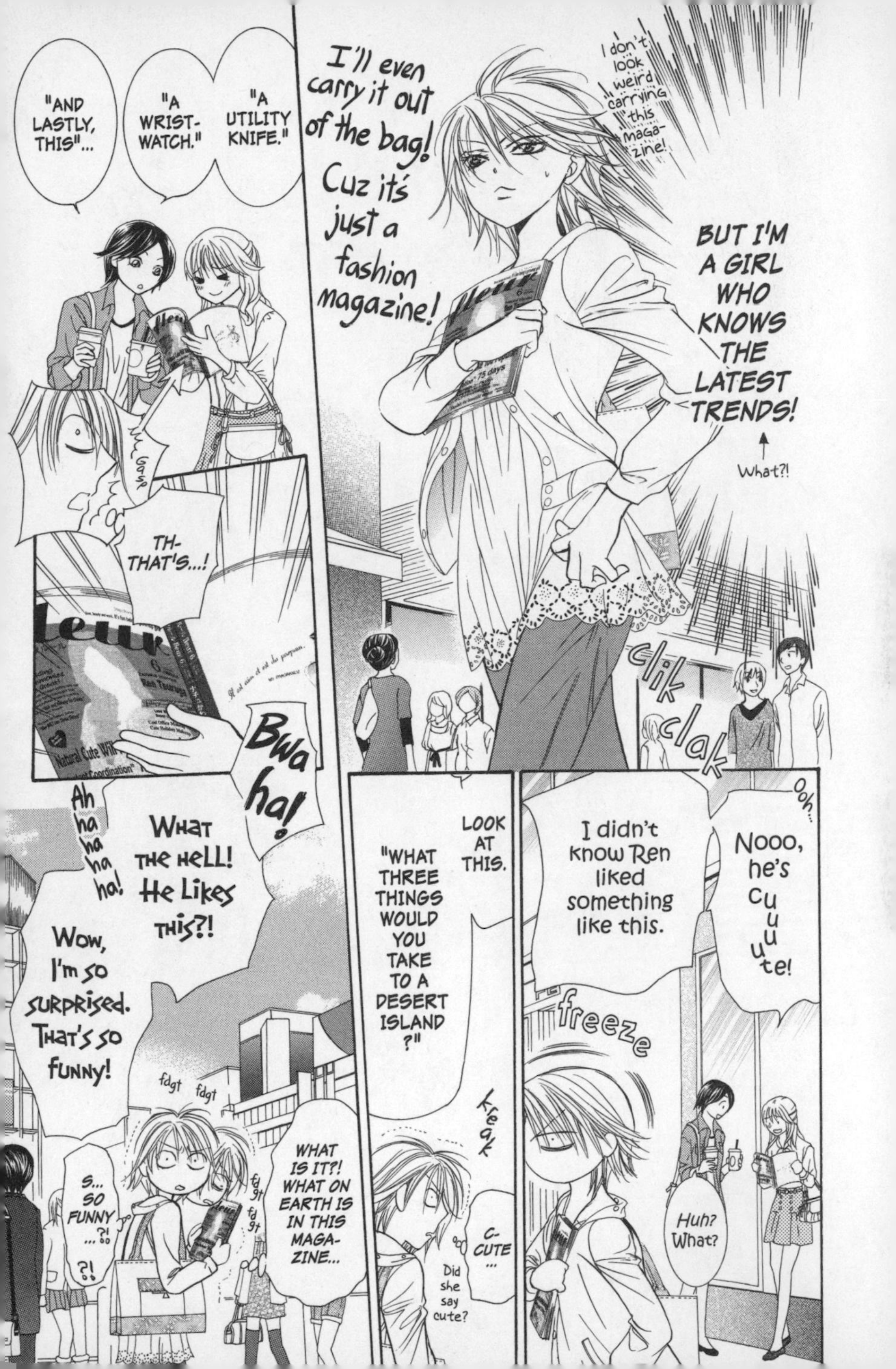

I don't look weird carrying this maga-zine!
I'll even carry it out of the bag! Cuz it's just a fashion magazine!
BUT I'M A GIRL WHO KNOWS THE LATEST TRENDS!
What?!
clik clak
"A UTILITY KNIFE."
"A WRIST-WATCH."
"AND LASTLY, THIS"...
Gasp
TH-THAT'S...!
Bwa ha ha!
Ooh...
Nooo, he's cuuuute!
I didn't know Ren liked something like this.
freeze
Huh? What?
LOOK AT THIS.
"WHAT THREE THINGS WOULD YOU TAKE TO A DESERT ISLAND?"
kreak
C-CUTE...
Did she say cute?
WHAT IS IT?! WHAT ON EARTH IS IN THIS MAGA-ZINE...
Ah ha ha ha ha!
WHAT THE HELL! HE LIKES THIS?!
Wow, I'm so surprised. That's so funny!
fdgt fdgt
fdgt fdgt
S... SO FUNNY...?! ...?!
?!

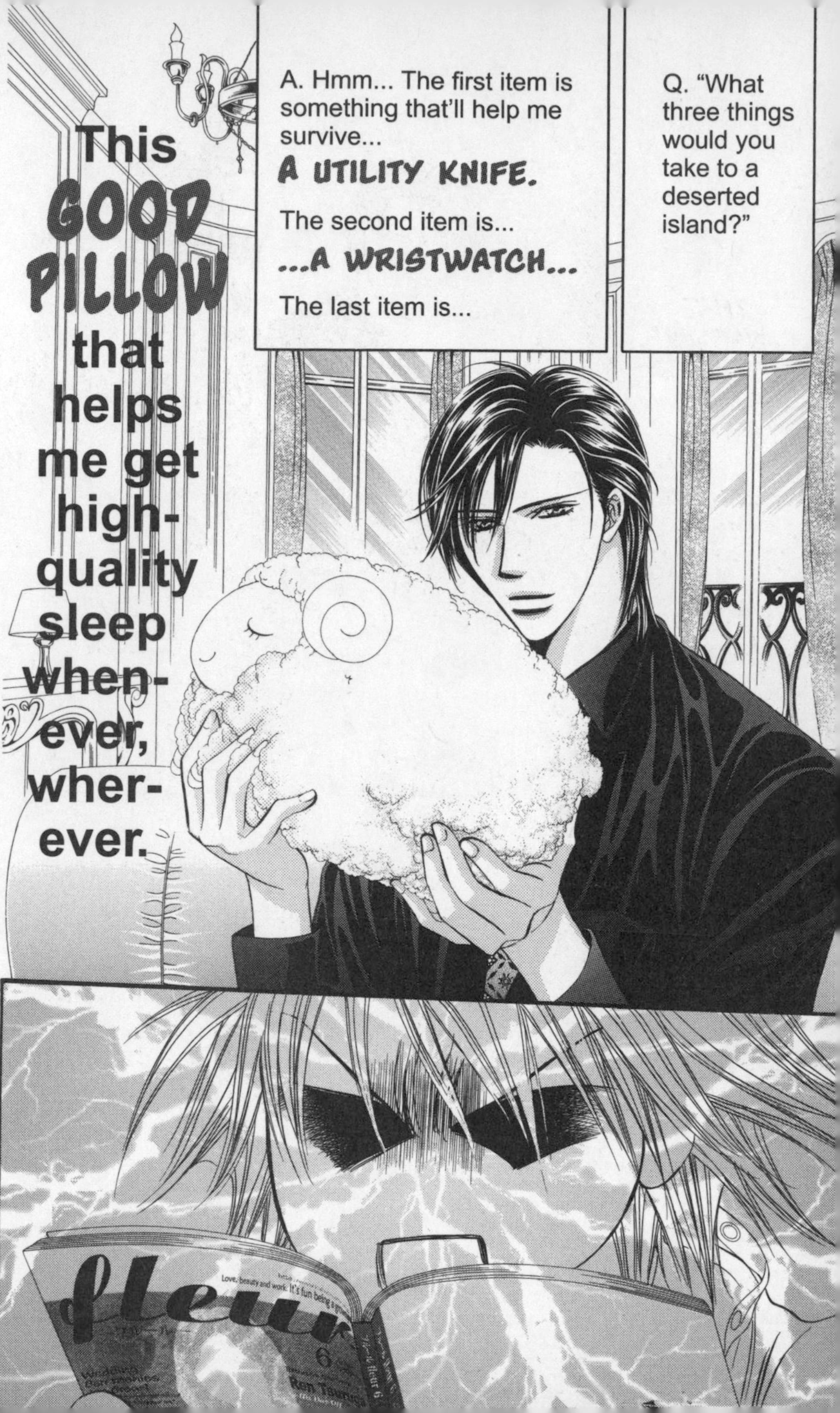
Q. "What three things would you take to a deserted island?"
A. Hmm... The first item is something that'll help me survive...
A UTILITY KNIFE.
The second item is...
...A WRISTWATCH...
The last item is...
This GOOD PILLOW that helps me get high-quality sleep when-ever, wher-ever.
fleur

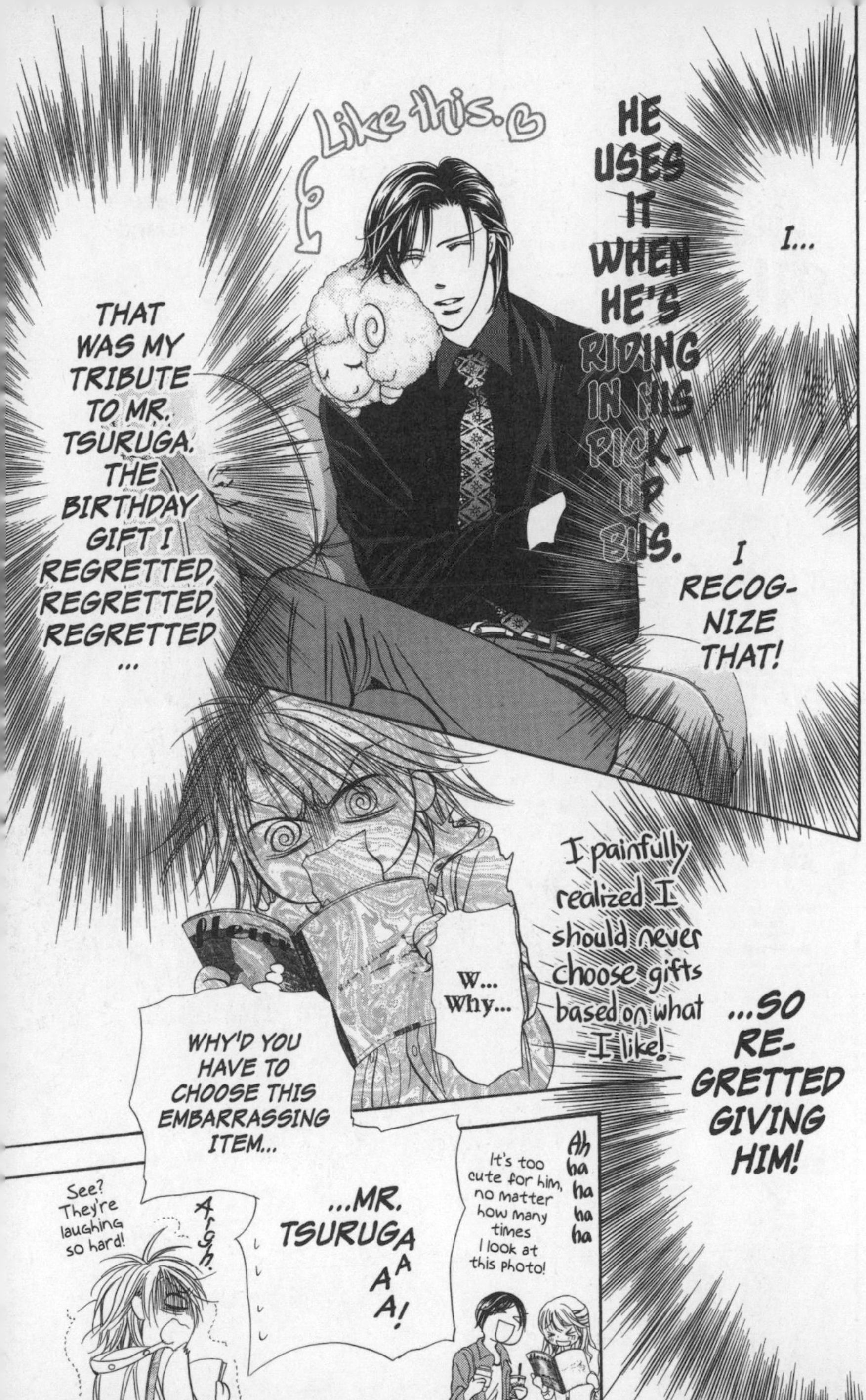
I...
I RECOGNIZE THAT!
HE USES IT WHEN HE'S RIDING IN HIS PICK-UP BUS.
Like this.
THAT WAS MY TRIBUTE TO MR. TSURUGA. THE BIRTHDAY GIFT I REGRETTED, REGRETTED, REGRETTED...
...SO REGRETTED GIVING HIM!
I painfully realized I should never choose gifts based on what I like!
W... Why...
WHY'D YOU HAVE TO CHOOSE THIS EMBARRASSING ITEM...
...MR. TSURUGAAAA!
Ah ha ha ha ha
It's too cute for him, no matter how many times I look at this photo!
Argh.
See? They're laughing so hard!

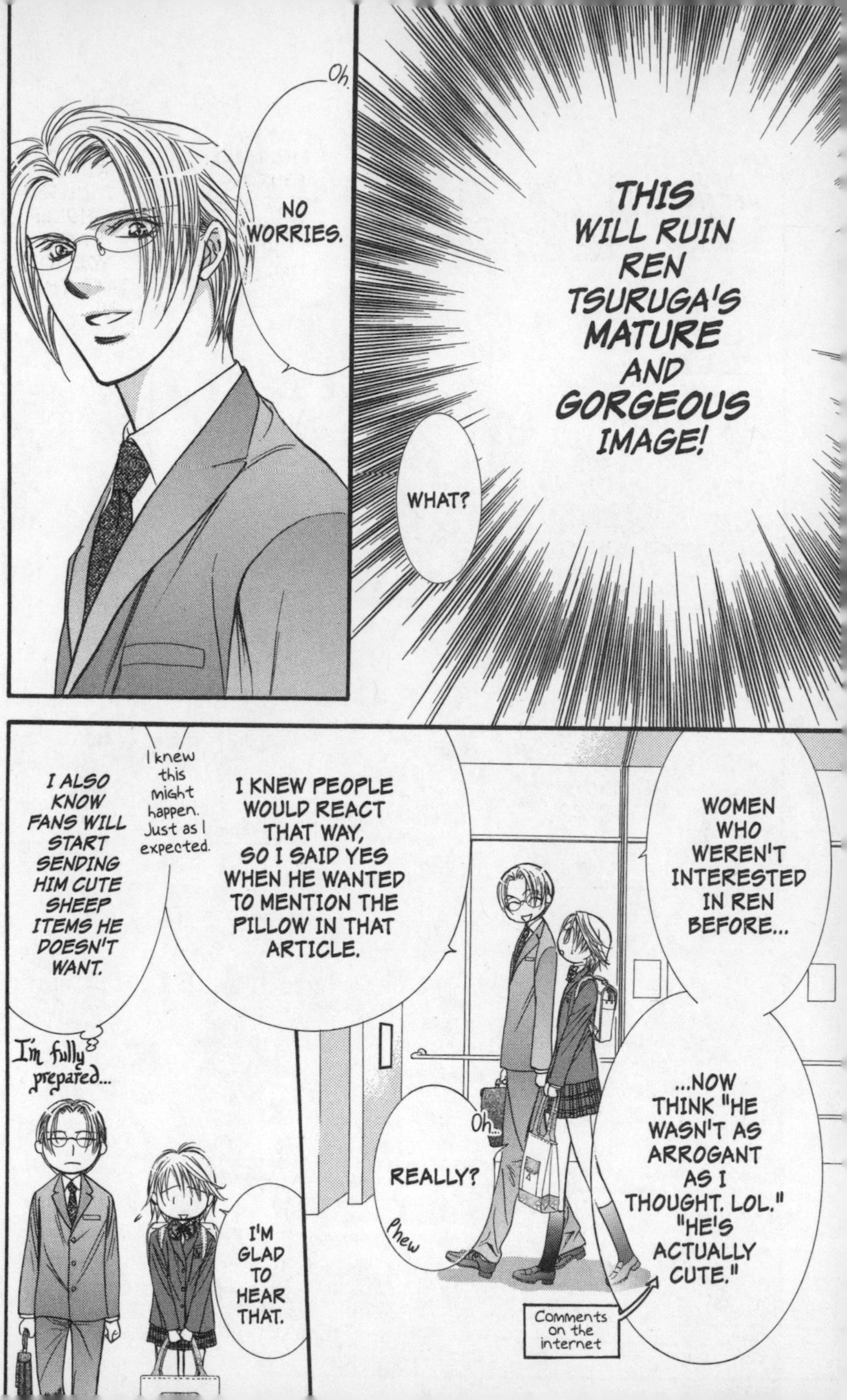
THIS WILL RUIN REN TSURUGA'S MATURE AND GORGEOUS IMAGE!
WHAT?
Oh.
NO WORRIES.
WOMEN WHO WEREN'T INTERESTED IN REN BEFORE...
...NOW THINK "HE WASN'T AS ARROGANT AS I THOUGHT. LOL." "HE'S ACTUALLY CUTE."
Comments on the internet
Oh...
REALLY?
Phew
I KNEW PEOPLE WOULD REACT THAT WAY, SO I SAID YES WHEN HE WANTED TO MENTION THE PILLOW IN THAT ARTICLE.
I knew this might happen. Just as I expected.
I ALSO KNOW FANS WILL START SENDING HIM CUTE SHEEP ITEMS HE DOESN'T WANT.
I'm fully prepared...
I'M GLAD TO HEAR THAT.

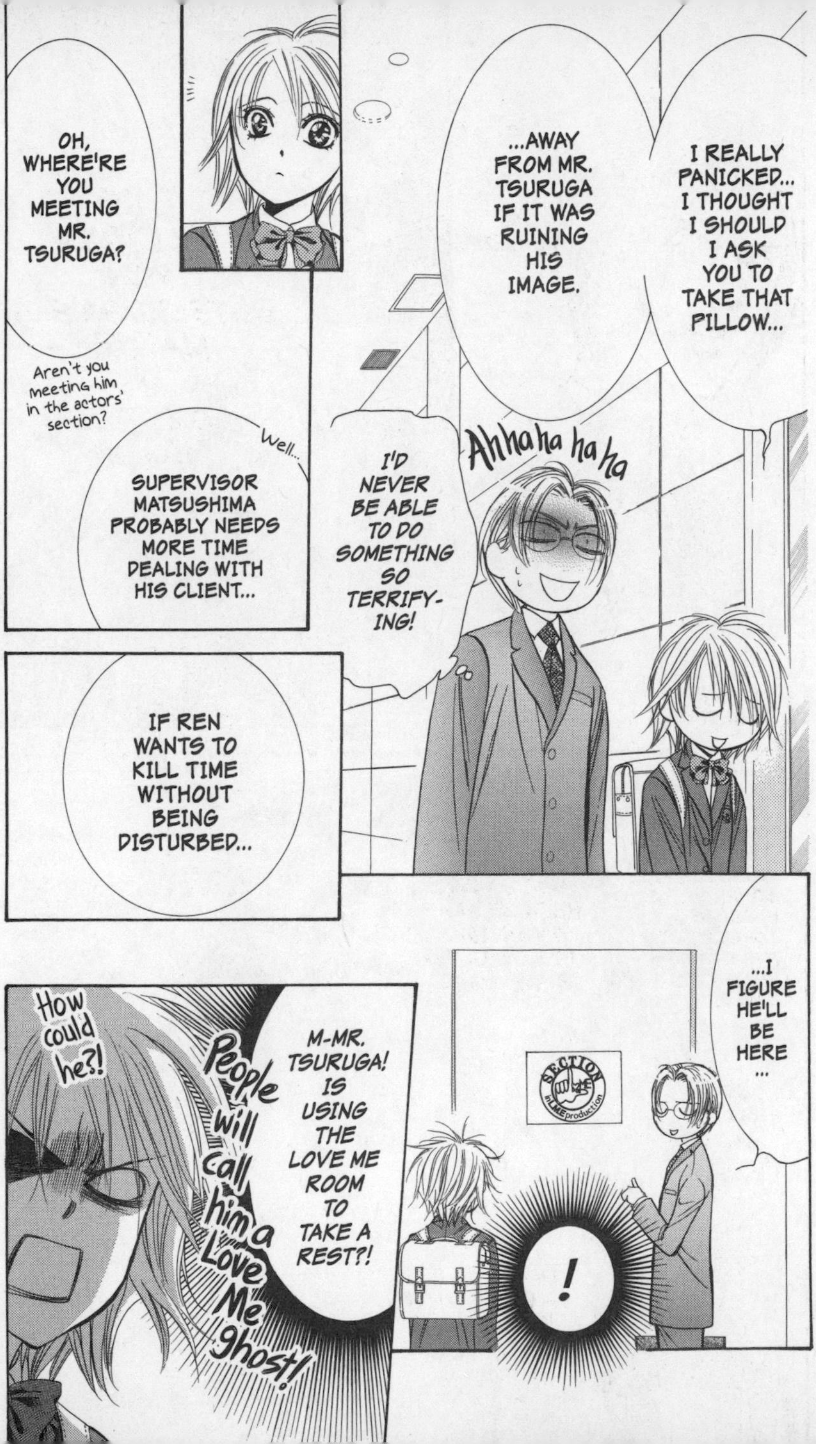
I REALLY PANICKED... I THOUGHT I SHOULD I ASK YOU TO TAKE THAT PILLOW...
...AWAY FROM MR. TSURUGA IF IT WAS RUINING HIS IMAGE.
Ahhahahahaha
I'D NEVER BE ABLE TO DO SOMETHING SO TERRIFY-ING!
OH, WHERE'RE YOU MEETING MR. TSURUGA?
Aren't you meeting him in the actors' section?
Well...
SUPERVISOR MATSUSHIMA PROBABLY NEEDS MORE TIME DEALING WITH HIS CLIENT...
IF REN WANTS TO KILL TIME WITHOUT BEING DISTURBED...
...I FIGURE HE'LL BE HERE...
SECTION
!
M-MR. TSURUGA! IS USING THE LOVE ME ROOM TO TAKE A REST?!
How could he?!
People will call him a Love Me ghost!

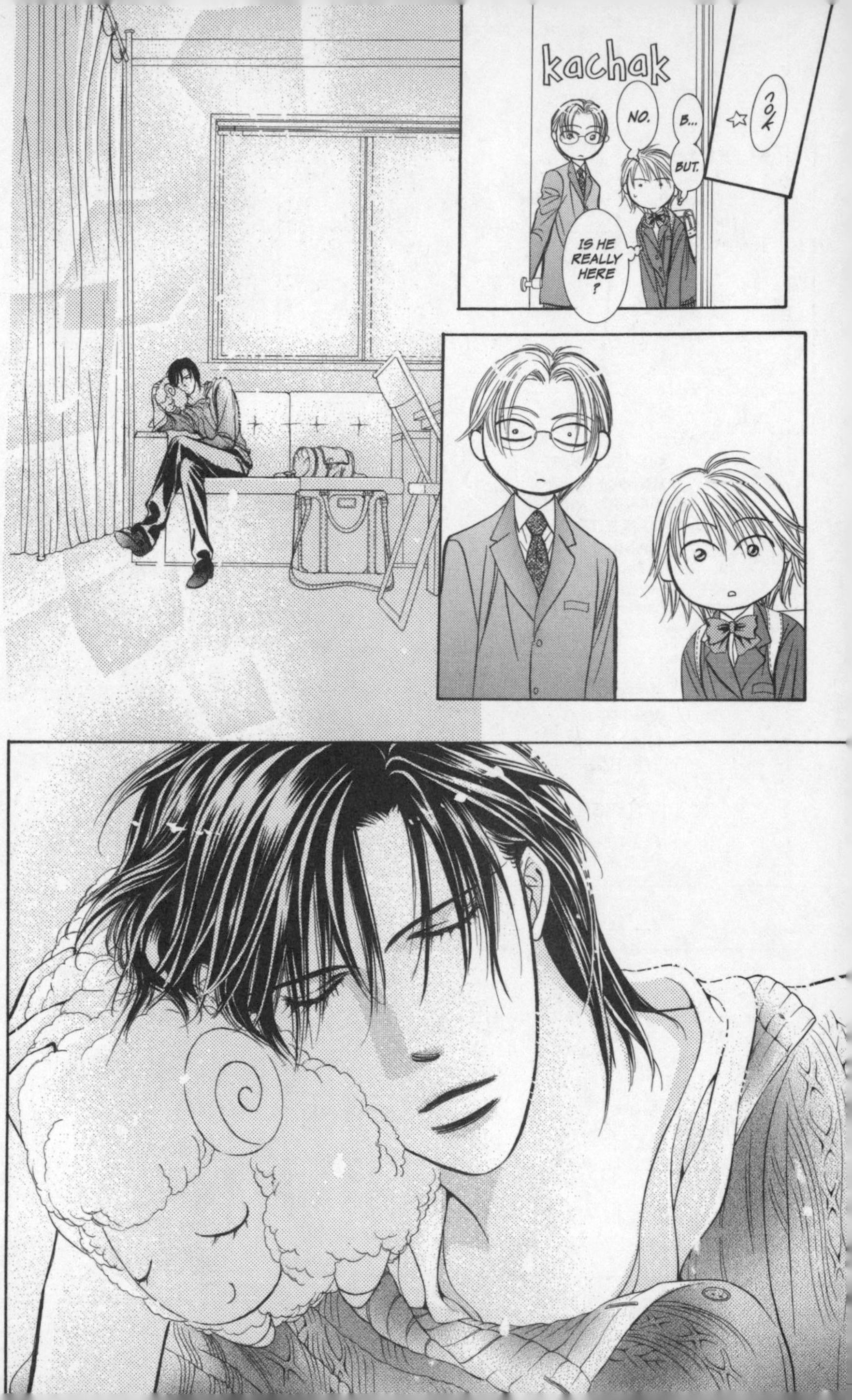
kachak
B... BUT.
NO.
IS HE REALLY HERE?

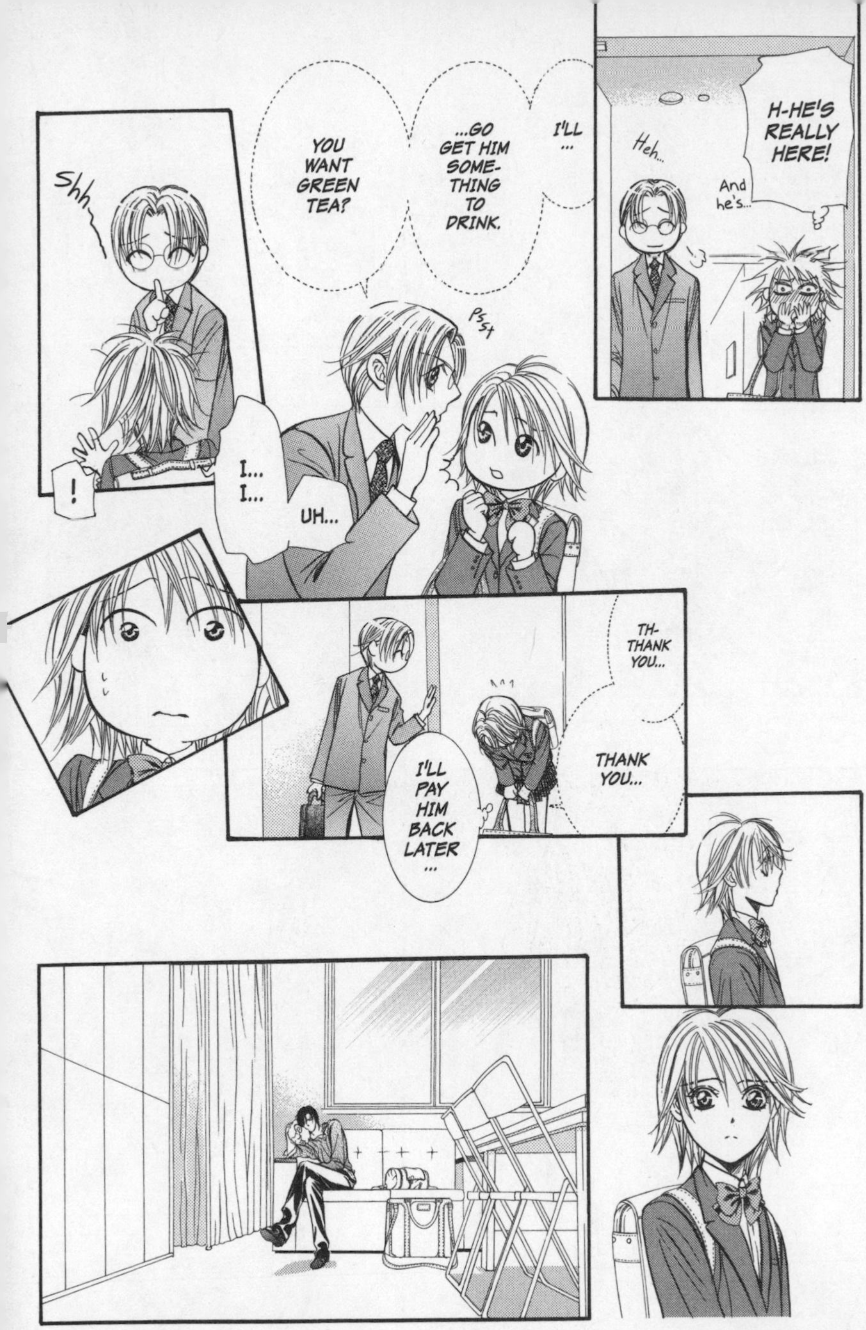
H-HE'S REALLY HERE!
And he's...
Heh...
I'LL ...
...GO GET HIM SOME-THING TO DRINK.
YOU WANT GREEN TEA?
Psst
I... I...
UH...
Shh
!
TH-THANK YOU...
THANK YOU...
I'LL PAY HIM BACK LATER ...

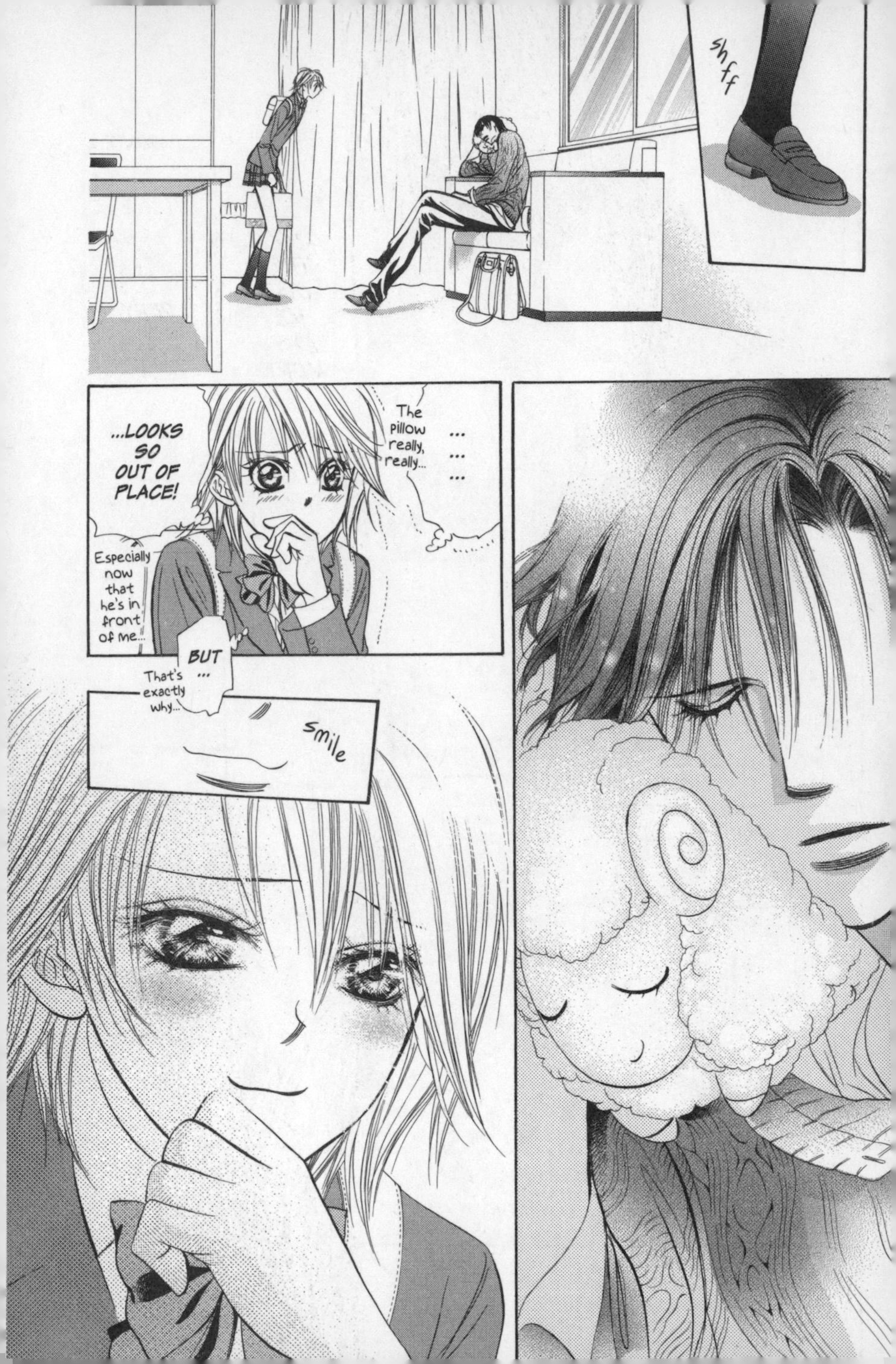
shff
The pillow really, really...
... ...
...LOOKS SO OUT OF PLACE!
Especially now that he's in front of me...
BUT ...
That's exactly why...
smile

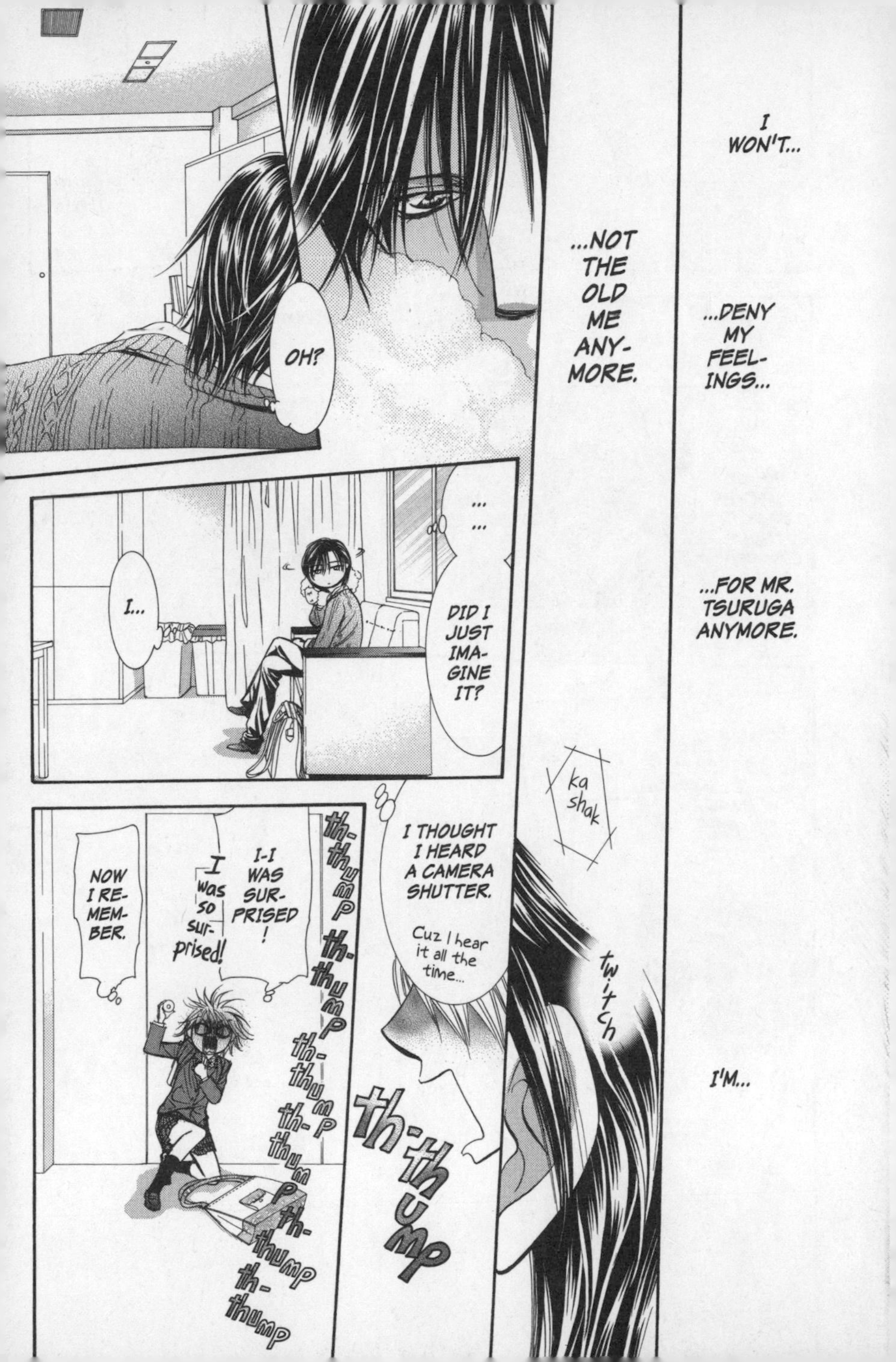
I WON'T...
...DENY MY FEELINGS...
...FOR MR. TSURUGA ANYMORE.
I'M...
...NOT THE OLD ME ANYMORE.
ka shak
twitch
th-thump
OH?
... ...
DID I JUST IMAGINE IT?
I...
I THOUGHT I HEARD A CAMERA SHUTTER.
Cuz I hear it all the time...
th-thump th-thump th-thump th-thump th-thump th-thump
I-I WAS SURPRISED!
I was so surprised!
NOW I REMEMBER.

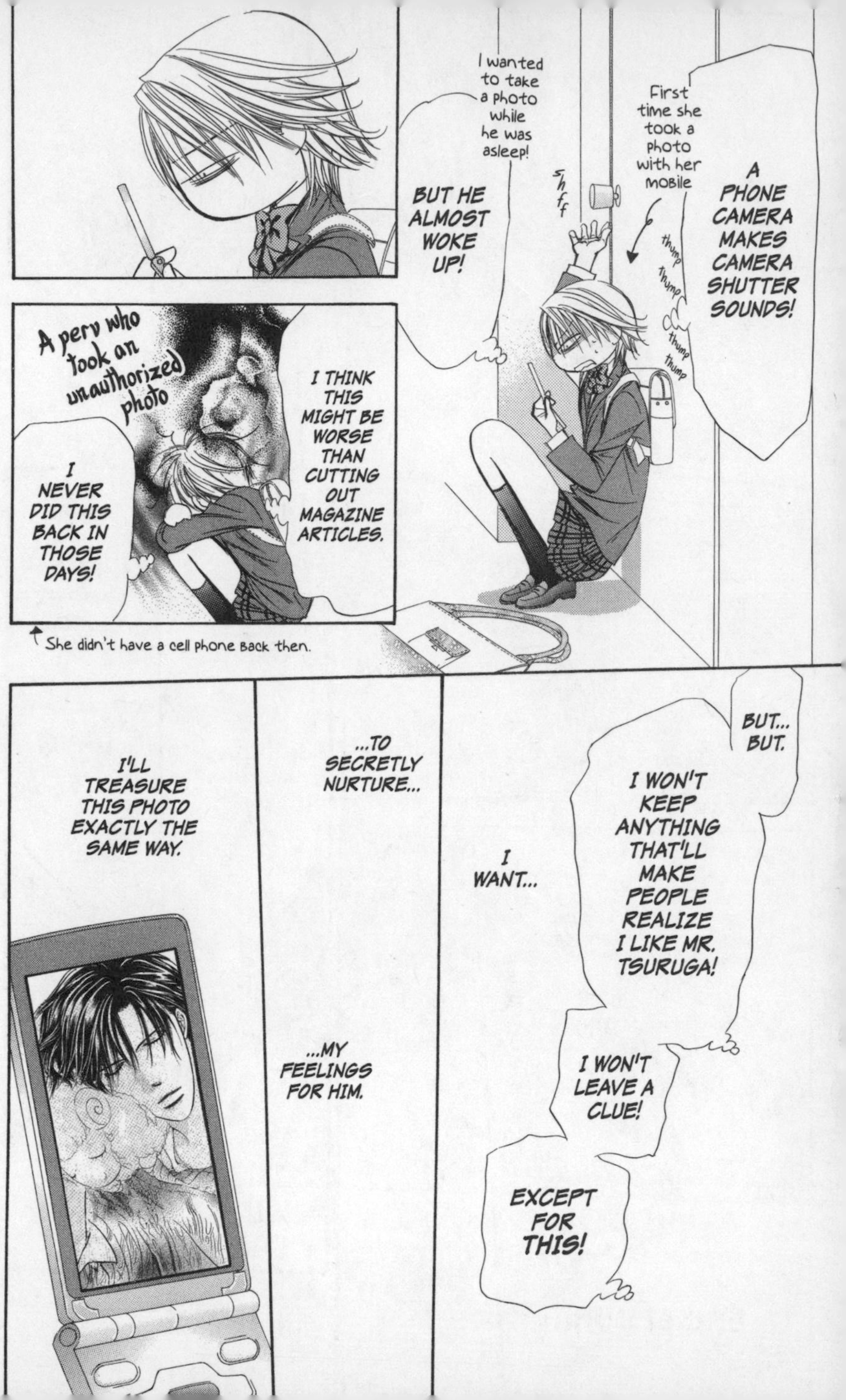
A PHONE CAMERA MAKES CAMERA SHUTTER SOUNDS!
First time she took a photo with her mobile
thump thump thump thump
shff
I wanted to take a photo while he was asleep!
BUT HE ALMOST WOKE UP!
I THINK THIS MIGHT BE WORSE THAN CUTTING OUT MAGAZINE ARTICLES.
A perv who took an unauthorized photo
I NEVER DID THIS BACK IN THOSE DAYS!
She didn't have a cell phone back then.
BUT... BUT.
I WON'T KEEP ANYTHING THAT'LL MAKE PEOPLE REALIZE I LIKE MR. TSURUGA!
I WON'T LEAVE A CLUE!
EXCEPT FOR THIS!
I WANT...
...TO SECRETLY NURTURE...
...MY FEELINGS FOR HIM.
I'LL TREASURE THIS PHOTO EXACTLY THE SAME WAY.

SURPRISE!

You may be reading the wrong way!

It's true: In keeping with the original Japanese comic format, this book reads from right to left—so action, sound effects, and word balloons are completely reversed. This preserves the orientation of the original artwork—plus, it's fun! Check out the diagram shown here to get the hang of things, and then turn to the other side of the book to get started!

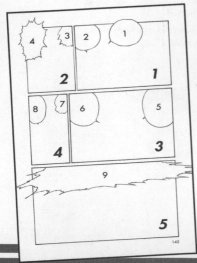

SKIP·BEAT!
Vol. 44
Shojo Beat Edition

STORY AND ART BY YOSHIKI NAKAMURA

English Translation & Adaptation/Tomo Kimura
Touch-up Art & Lettering/Sabrina Heep
Design/J. Shikuma
Editor/Pancha Diaz

Printed in Canada

Published by VIZ Media, LLC
P.O. Box 77010
San Francisco, CA 94107

10 9 8 7 6 5 4 3 2 1
First printing, September 2020

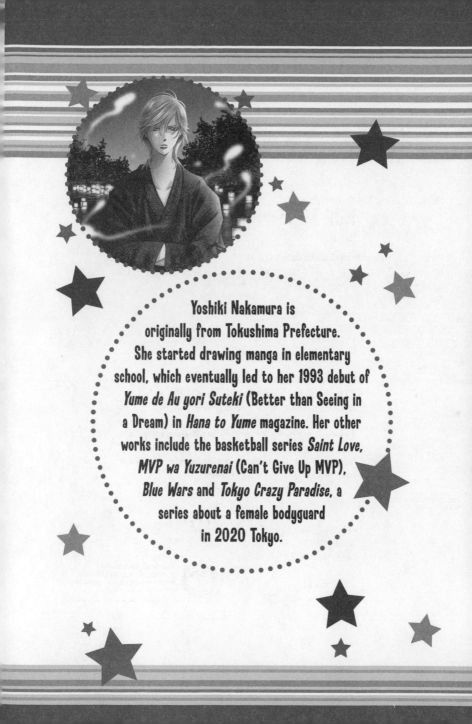

Yoshiki Nakamura is
originally from Tokushima Prefecture.
She started drawing manga in elementary
school, which eventually led to her 1993 debut of
Yume de Au yori Suteki (Better than Seeing in
a Dream) in *Hana to Yume* magazine. Her other
works include the basketball series *Saint Love*,
MVP wa Yuzurenai (Can't Give Up MVP),
Blue Wars and *Tokyo Crazy Paradise*, a
series about a female bodyguard
in 2020 Tokyo.

Skip·Beat! End Notes
Everyone knows how to be a fan, but sometimes cool things from other cultures need a little help crossing the language barrier.

Page 31, panel 3: Goldfish poop
A term for people who are close followers, trailing after their leader like a string of fish poop.

Page 111, panel 5: Rekindled chestnuts
"Rekindled romance" and "roasted chestnuts" sound similar in Japanese.